khwxqmxwmk
xwkxkwwxgöxk

the medicene
he govt
d off
t paid off
d
gain
ing for new friend

got ten

f black soot
the bed but
ys that many say
rom the d.a.
did
bows/xx better stay away from those

the plain clothers
which way the wind blows

clothes
 do not chew gen

Treasures from the

BOB DYLAN CENTER   TULSA, OK

BOB DYLAN

MIXING UP THE MEDICINE

WRITTEN AND EDITED BY

MARK DAVIDSON AND PARKER FISHEL

WITH EDITORIAL ASSISTANCE BY AUSTIN SHORT

ADDITIONAL ESSAYS SELECTED BY MICHAEL CHAIKEN AND ROBERT POLITO

CALLAWAY

NEW YORK   2023

CONTENTS

CONTRIBUTORS

WRITERS

Douglas Brinkley
Peter Carey
Anne Margaret Daniel
John Doe
Raymond Foye
Terry Gans
Jeff Gold
Joy Harjo
Richard Hell
Clinton Heylin
Marvin Karlins
Alan Licht
Greil Marcus
Allison Moorer
Barry Ollman
Griffin Ondaatje
Michael Ondaatje
Gregory Pardlo
Amanda Petrusich
Tom Piazza
Lee Ranaldo
Alex Ross
Robert M. Rubin
Ed Ruscha
Lucy Sante
Jeff Slate
Larry Sloman
Greg Tate
Sean Wilentz

PHOTOGRAPHERS

Howard Alk
Joe Alper
Richard Avedon
Ralph Baxter
Ruth Bernal
Joel Bernstein
Jeff Bridges
Larry Busacca
Camouflage Photo
Peter J. Carni
William Claxton
Al Clayton
Danny Clinch
John Cohen
John Byrne Cooke
Dick Cooper
Frank Dandridge
Henry Diltz
Kevork Djansezian
Deborah Feingold
Barry Feinstein
Robert Frank
Carol Friedman
David Gahr
Stephen Goldblatt
Edward Grazda
Herb Greene
Deanna Harris
  Hoffman
Don Hunstein
Sharon Johnson
Steve Kagan
Hirosuke Katsuyama
David Michael Kennedy
Michael Kovac
Daniel Kramer

Elliott Landy
Björn H. Larsson Ask
Annie Leibovitz
Ben Martin
Darryl Matthews
Kevin Mazur
Richard McCaffrey
Fred W. McDarrah
Frank Micelotta
Reid Miles
Marcelo Montealegre
Mandel Ngan
Petra Niemeier
John Orris
Hank Parker
Gilles Peress
Abe Perlstein
Neal Preston
Suzie Q
Ken Regan
Morgan Renard
Ebet Roberts
Arthur Rosato
Merlyn Rosenberg
Ted Russell
William E. Sauro
Bill Savran
Jerry Schatzberg
Rowland Scherman
Harry Scott
Lorey Sebastian
Mark Seliger
Stephen Shames
John Shearer
Brian Shuel
Len Siegler
Hedi Slimane

Dale Smith
W. Eugene Smith
Ettore Sottsass
Gloria Stavers
Marcia Stehr
Randee St. Nicholas
Paul Till
John Vachon
Ana María Vélez Wood
Dick Waterman
Vinnie Zuffante

ARTISTS

Marcel Duchamp
Milton Glaser
Duncan Hannah
Jaime Hernandez
Catherine Kanner
Ed Ruscha
Eric von Schmidt
William Stetz
Tony Wright

FILMMAKERS

Gillian Armstrong
Charlie Chaplin
Nash Edgerton
Alma Har'el
Julius Kuney
Jennifer Lebeau
Murray Lerner
Albert and David
  Maysles
D. A. Pennebaker
TVTV
Kinka Usher

PAGE 6: Bob Dylan, "Jokerman" music video shoot, 1984.
Photographer unknown

Bob Dylan
1962

The Freewheelin' Bob Dylan
1963

The Times They Are A-Changin'
1964

Another Side of Bob Dylan
1964

Bringing It All Back Home
1965

Self Portrait
1970

New Morning
1970

Bob Dylan's Greatest Hits Volume II 1971

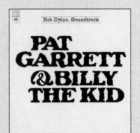

Pat Garrett & Billy the Kid
1973

Dylan
1973

Hard Rain
1976

Street-Legal
1978

Bob Dylan at Budokan
1978

Slow Train Coming
1979

Saved
1980

Down in the Groove
1988

Dylan & the Dead
1989

Oh Mercy
1989

Under the Red Sky
1990

Good as I Been to You
1992

Modern Times
2006

Together Through Life
2009

Christmas in the Heart
2009

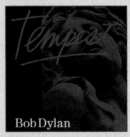

Tempest
2012

Shadows in the Night
2015

BOB DYLAN

Highway 61 Revisited
1965

Blonde on Blonde
1966

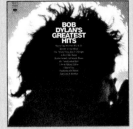

Bob Dylan's Greatest Hits
1967

John Wesley Harding
1968

Nashville Skyline
1969

Planet Waves
1974

Before the Flood
1974

Blood on the Tracks
1975

The Basement Tapes
1975

Desire
1976

Shot of Love
1981

Infidels
1983

Real Live
1984

Empire Burlesque
1985

Knocked Out Loaded
1986

**The 30th Anniversary
Concert Celebration 1993**

World Gone Wrong
1993

MTV Unplugged
1995

Time Out of Mind
1997

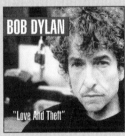

"Love and Theft"
2001

Fallen Angels
2016

Triplicate
2017

Rough and Rowdy Ways
2020

Shadow Kingdom
2023

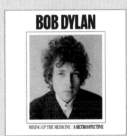

Mixing Up the Medicine
2023

The Albums 1962–2023

The Perpetual Motion of Illusion

Mark Davidson and Parker Fishel

Everybody knows by now that there's a gazillion books on me either out or coming out in the near future. So I'm encouraging anybody who's ever met me, heard me or even seen me, to get in on the action and scribble their own book. You never know, somebody might have a great book in them.
—Bob Dylan, 2011

For six decades and counting, the world has been reckoning with Bob Dylan and his musical journey. His artistic achievements mark him as one of history's important cultural figures. Emerging from the crucible of postwar America, Dylan fused an expansive set of musical, literary, and other influences into a peerless body of song that demonstrates "new poetic expressions within the great American song tradition," as was acknowledged by his 2016 Nobel Prize in Literature. From the 1962 album *Bob Dylan* to the 2023 release of *Shadow Kingdom*, and most vividly in his live performances, Dylan's oeuvre has proved itself to be dynamic and evolving, his restless creativity in search of the heart of a song. And as he has continually set trends only to break them, Dylan himself has also become a subject of endless fascination. Often made out to be a cipher for his music, Dylan has pushed against that interpretation—or any other, for that matter—making an art of reinvention while consistently taking risks and defying expectations. As an artist, Bob Dylan remains beholden only to his muse, his sights kept firmly fixed on the horizon line.

Yet, for an artist so reluctant to dwell on the past, what's remarkable is that so much of it has survived. In fact, the existence of the audio, papers, and other records that constitute the Bob Dylan Archive was not general knowledge until March 2, 2016, when *The New York Times* broke the news that a philanthropic organization and a small private university in Oklahoma had acquired it. The news sparked a lot of curiosity, not only about the collection's contents, but also about the decision to place his archive in Tulsa. However, there was logic and precedent.

In 2013, the George Kaiser Family Foundation, the Tulsa-based nonprofit, acquired the archive of the archetypal American folksinger Woody Guthrie, one of Dylan's early idols, establishing the Woody Guthrie Center as part of a citywide cultural revitalization project. Meanwhile the University of Tulsa had just completed a brand-new research facility at Gilcrease Museum to facilitate access to their important holdings, which include hundreds of thousands of artifacts from Indigenous peoples from across the Americas, a copy of the Declaration of Independence, a copy of the Emancipation Proclamation signed by Abraham Lincoln, and an unrivaled collection of artwork dedicated to the American West. Bob Dylan noted his place in this continuum of American history when the acquisition was announced:

I'm glad that my archives, which have been collected all these years, have finally found a home and are to be included with the works of Woody Guthrie and especially alongside all the valuable artifacts from the Native American Nations. To me it makes a lot of sense and it's a great honor.

Bob Dylan, NYC, 1963. Photograph by Ralph Baxter

From even the most cursory glance, it was clear that the Bob Dylan Archive was an enormous and unparalleled collection representing one of the largest, most important, and most valuable archives devoted to a single artist. Spanning Dylan's entire musical career, from his first recordings to his most recent performances, the still-growing Archive contains thousands of manuscript drafts, hundreds of notebooks and notepads, tens of thousands of photographs, hundreds of hours of video and film footage, and countless hours of studio, rehearsal, and live recordings.

Archives, however, are by their very nature incomplete—and Dylan's is no exception. In the early years of his burgeoning career, Dylan was seemingly always on the move. It fell to publishers and record companies—who had been historically unsentimental about archiving works—to begin collecting his writings and recordings. Thus, the trail of lyric manuscripts begins with "Chimes of Freedom" from *Another Side of Bob Dylan* (1964), and ends with songs from *Tempest* (2012), Dylan's last album of original material before the collection was acquired. Yet taken as a whole, the Archive offers new revelations about a story that the world (thinks it) knows so well, while also providing essential insights about the creative process of one of the greatest songwriters in the history of popular music.

In May 2022, the Bob Dylan Archive moved to its current home in the newly opened Bob Dylan Center, taking its place as part of the vibrant arts district emerging in downtown Tulsa. As the Archive's public face, the Center showcases a set of stories from the Archive designed to illuminate different dimensions of Dylan's long and ever-shifting career, whether they be the writing and development of particular songs, his relationship to the recording studio, or his many professed influences. With contributions from musician Elvis Costello, Poet Laureate Joy Harjo, filmmaker Jen Lebeau, writer Tom Piazza, actress Kimber Elayne Sprawl, and historian Sean Wilentz, the Center employs a multiplicity of voices to tell the story of an artist who himself has been reluctant to analyze or speak on behalf of his own work. The Center is a visceral, dynamic, and progressive vision of Dylan's artistry, a space for anyone with even a passing interest in the man or his music to find inspiration in the twists and turns of his ongoing creative odyssey.

Bob Dylan: Mixing Up the Medicine expands upon the Center's inaugural exhibitions, taking a similar curatorial approach in presenting archival material—whether complementary, divergent, or conflicting—alongside a panoply of voices. Wherever possible, items from the Archive itself have been selected to illustrate vignettes, and when necessary supplementing that foundational material with fascinating items subsequently acquired by the Archive, including the massive fan collections of Bill Pagel and Mitch Blank, as well as from Dylan's friends and peers like Cynthia Gooding, Mell and Lillian Bailey, and Bruce Langhorne. In some cases, special and unique materials from supporters of the Archive have also been integrated into the visual narrative to help set particular episodes against the longer arc of Dylan's life story.

MARK DAVIDSON AND PARKER FISHEL

Punctuating the book are essays by a number of artistic and scholarly luminaries, who came to Tulsa at the behest of Michael Chaiken, then curator of the Bob Dylan Archive, and poet and scholar Robert Polito, to experience the Archive firsthand. In Chaiken and Polito's initial conception of the book, "Each of these distinguished writers, artists, and musicians was asked to choose a single item from the Bob Dylan Archive—a draft lyric, a photographic image, a notebook, an outtake, a bit of ephemera—something that enticed, beguiled, stirred, perplexed, or galvanized them, and write a short essay about it." Many of the essays in the present volume come from these early visits to Tulsa in the first three and a half years of the Archive's existence.

While invoking Dylan's creative spirit, these essays contribute to the unusual mix of interpretive text that helps *Bob Dylan: Mixing Up the Medicine* explore the dusty corners of Dylan's past to understand their relation to his present and still-evolving body of work. In addition, expansive descriptive texts contextualize items, casting familiar episodes in a new light while developing an ever-surprising network of themes and connections drawn from Dylan's expansive universe. Throughout the book, Dylan's peers and collaborators are given voice, through extensive interviews conducted by the Bob Dylan Center or drawn from the never-before-heard full interviews conducted for the 2005 Martin Scorsese documentary *No Direction Home: Bob Dylan*. The resulting book is a kind of inside-out biography, one that lets the Archive drive Dylan's story. As such, it establishes numerous ways of looking at Bob Dylan, his music, and his place in the world's cultural imagination. The constant throughout—whether in the known body of work or in the unpublished material contained within this volume—is Dylan's artistry and genius, defined not only by a singular intellect but also a thoughtful dedication to craft.

Yet as befits an artist who once said, "Art is the perpetual motion of illusion," the Bob Dylan of his archive, like the Bob Dylan of real life, can seem just out of reach. While this may stymie those looking for easy answers, the rich and vast holdings of the Bob Dylan Archive provide an unprecedented opportunity to finally ask the right questions of Dylan and his music. Hopefully this book poses a few good ones.

Bob Dylan, Rolling Thunder Revue, 1975.
Photograph by Ken Regan

Endless Highway

Life isn't about finding yourself, or finding anything.
Life is about creating yourself and creating things.

—BOB DYLAN, 2019

Although Bob Dylan speaks to eternal matters—and although he has made an art out of collapsing the past and present—he has worked at a particular time and in particular places. Yet his career has also unfolded very differently than is generally depicted. Supposedly sudden shifts that have become iconic—like his "going electric" in 1965, or his turn to gospel in 1979—seem a lot less sudden when viewed in terms of his creativity's uneven arc. Topics that may seem to have been covered and dispensed with during one phase of Dylan's story—political engagement, for example, or religious devotion—reappear in new ways in later phases. Casual hints and signals that one may not notice the first time pop up on a second look. Think again.

A cliché about Dylan—one, I confess, I have used myself—is that his work has proceeded through sharply definable periods, marking one style off from another. Although valid enough, this view overlooks the continuities in Dylan's work, embedded in the artistic template he has built and rebuilt over six decades and more. Informed by Dylan's gargantuan curiosity about history, literature, and the visual arts, that template has always been fundamentally musical. ("The songs are my lexicon," he once told an interviewer.) Although Beethoven's compositions or, a more exact modern comparison, Louis Armstrong's compositions and performances repeatedly defined new boundaries, at every turn their work was (and is) instantly recognizable as their own. No matter how you look at it, sustained creativity always requires displacement and renewal, but it can seldom afford renunciation. So it has been with Bob Dylan.

The story begins in Minneapolis in 1959 and 1960. Robert Zimmerman, a restive teenager, has honed a fixation on rhythm and blues, country and western, doo-wop, and rock 'n' roll to the point where he is just good enough to perform as a brief temporary fill-in on the piano in Bobby Vee's touring band, playing under the name Elston Gunn. He has otherwise had a conventional small-town middle-class upbringing in remote Hibbing, remarkable mainly because it is in a Jewish family milieu on the gentile Minnesota Iron Range. Arriving in the Twin Cities for his freshman year at the state university, he falls in with the local bohemian crowd and picks up a rapid but substantial introduction to Beat poetry and traditional folk music, the latter initially through recordings by Odetta. Abjuring his studies as well as rock 'n' roll, Zimmerman begins to sing solo with guitar, or with a friend or two, in a local pizza parlor and at coffeehouses. It is in one of the latter, the 10 O'Clock Scholar, that he first calls himself Bob Dylan. The story of his self-creation through art, and of creating art through a created self, has begun.

Dylan's metamorphosis becomes noticeable in several ways. After a summer's stint in Colorado during the summer of 1960, he seems changed to his friends, acting more self-assured, affecting a cowboyish accent they can't quite place, and touting a newfound absorption with the harmonica

13

to go along with his acoustic guitar. When a friend hands him Woody Guthrie's autobiographical *Bound for Glory*, Dylan discovers an epic persona as well as a musical model to serve his growing, self-absorbed ambition. He departs Minneapolis at the end of the year and winds up in New York in January, resembling, he would later remark, "a Woody Guthrie jukebox." But as some recently unearthed tape recordings affirm, he has also mastered techniques that would propel his artistic advance over the next three years.

Dylan stood out quickly among the young folksingers in Greenwich Village, in part because of the intensity and stagecraft in his performances, in part because of the curiosity of his (mostly fabricated) personal history, a string of exploits that some thought unlikely but others took at face value. Dylan also managed to befriend and win the singular approval of the circle of elders surrounding his now-stricken hero Guthrie, the remnants of the Popular Front folk movement of the 1930s and 1940s. Bridging two generations, it did not take long for Dylan to turn himself into someone special, or who at least seemed special.

What he lacked was artistic distinction, in every sense of the word, and he knew it. For all of his admiration of those, he would later write, who "lived / in the hungry thirties / an' blew in like Woody / t' New York City," the times had changed, and the "forces of yesteryear" in the union halls and workingmen's bars were spent. Dylan could not sing to them, let alone of them, and still be real: "The very last thing that I'd want to do /," he sang in one of his earliest compositions, "Song to Woody," "Is to say I've been hittin' some hard travelin' too." Dylan also sensed the limits of a purist strain common to many of the younger folkies, who worked out an idiom of authenticity as an alternative to counterfeit postwar suburban materialism, fashioned from old recordings like those collected on Harry Smith's influential *Anthology of American Folk Music*. Dylan immersed himself in that older music, revered it, but he would seek an idiom and a grammar as well as a spirit of his own, impressed less with projected authenticity than with the music's mysteries and myths.

New York in the early 1960s offered endless inspiration and source material in its cabarets and libraries, theaters and galleries, bars and bookshops, and in its communities of avant-garde artists of every conceivable genre. It extended eros along with enlightenment. It also offered unique opportunities for a kind of commercial success that most folkies, old and young, either thought unattainable or outwardly rejected. Dylan—turned away initially by the small folk labels and happy enough just making a living playing music—did not spurn the chance when, after just over nine months in New York, the most prestigious music talent scout in the business, John Hammond, offered him a contract with the nation's most prestigious recording label, Columbia Records.

Moving rapidly beyond his first album for Columbia, which consisted mostly of traditional folk songs and blues, Dylan spent 1962 and most of 1963 building an enduring foundation. His girlfriend at the time, Suze Rotolo, played an important part in his development, as lover and muse but also as a guide, introducing him to the likes of Bertolt Brecht and Paul Gauguin as well as organized civil rights politics. Dylan's melodic base remained the traditional one he had started singing since Minneapolis, augmented, after a sojourn to England in late 1962, by a spurt of old British balladry. His writing, however, revised the received forms, turning a song of wistful romance into a modern farewell ("Don't Think Twice, It's All Right"), or an ancient tale of a poisoned lover into a journey through apocalypse ("A Hard Rain's A-Gonna Fall").

With his third album, *The Times They Are A-Changin'*, Dylan's image sharpened into that of the unmatched contemporary protest singer, an image he has not completely shed even now in the public imagination—the modern Woody Guthrie for the civil rights and peace movements. Yet here, too, even as Dylan wrote stirring righteous anthems, his best work broke with the norms, rebuffing grand social themes in favor of small, concrete but morally complex stories of injustice ("The Lonesome Death of Hattie Carroll"), challenging self-ratifying moralism by unmasking a system of subjugation that cut across the color line ("Only a Pawn in Their Game"). Think again—and think harder.

Late in 1963, Dylan hit a creative crisis. Aside from his ally and sometime girlfriend Joan Baez, he had outstripped all of his folksong rivals, critically and commercially, and his career had reached a new peak with a triumphant concert in Carnegie Hall in late October. Yet he had also gone as far as he could with his folksong template, and he was fed up with the presumptions imposed by some of the left-wing elders. He began writing experiments in streams of prose, free verse, and dramatic dialogue, thinking he might even drop songwriting altogether. (The new writing would eventually produce the manuscript that became *Tarantula* as well as some powerful song lyrics.) In December, following the shock of President John F. Kennedy's assassination and a nervous, inciting

Bob Dylan, Columbia Records photo shoot, NYC, 1963. Photograph by Don Hunstein

speaking appearance at an old-line leftist awards dinner, Dylan met Allen Ginsberg, who rekindled his love of Beat poetry and prose. He also took on the French symbolists, above all Arthur Rimbaud, to whom Suze Rotolo had introduced him and who had helped inspire the Beats.

Out of this crisis came the shift that would reshape Dylan's art for the next two years and more. *Another Side of Bob Dylan*, musically quite simple, asserted individuality with a contempt for conformist egalitarianism ("To Ramona," "I Shall Be Free No. 10") and announced a break from leftist pieties ("My Back Pages"). The album's finest song, "Chimes of Freedom," ventured into a symbolic style, filled with strong metaphor and alliteration and, in Ginsberg's words, "chains of flashing images," to describe a moment of perception that embraced all of humanity's confused and abused. Other songs included hip phrases and popular culture allusions previously unheard of in contemporary folk music, tied to absurd, satirical, and hilarious mini-dramas. Yet if the album—including one song held off for a later re-recording, "Mr. Tambourine Man"—marked the initial turn to what Dylan would soon call "vision music," it also bore Dylan's hatred of injustice and insistence on honest personal reckonings. With all of its inwardness, "Chimes of Freedom" might be the most capacious protest song ever written.

At the point in 1965 that D. A. Pennebaker partly captured in his documentary *Dont Look Back*, Dylan had opened the way for explorations that produced some of the most powerful songs he would ever compose, among them "It's Alright, Ma (I'm Only Bleeding)," "Maggie's Farm," "Highway 61 Revisited," and "Desolation Row." Inside of eighteen months, inscribed on three albums, the exploring culminated in the Rimbaud-inspired rational dissociation of the senses of *Blonde on Blonde*.

This period is normally linked to Dylan's decision to "go electric," on vinyl and at the Newport Folk Festival, as if he'd made a decision, less artistic than ideological—or, to some cynics, commercial—to break with the hallowed folk forms. Dylan's forays into rock and electric rhythm and blues certainly marked his crossover into pop stardom. The music of The Beatles and The Rolling Stones (and, in a

Bob Dylan, Columbia Records Studio A, NYC, 1965. Photograph by Don Hunstein

different way, The Beach Boys) opened new possibilities by revivifying American sounds that had either gone stale or been overlooked. But Dylan's songwriting in 1965 and 1966, while evoking a downtown demimonde, also marked a retrieval of music he'd loved and played since he was a teenager along with Muddy Waters's Chicago blues (and those of Lightnin' Hopkins), while it helped him deepen themes and motifs already present in his work, of love, loss, and American jitters.

Almost overlooked amid the tempest over Dylan's "going electric," meanwhile, were the mutations of his most salient instrument, his own voice. Known as a sweet singer as a boy, Dylan now used Guthriesque inflections that imparted a blunt, contracted simplicity to many of his early songs. Yet even on his first three albums, and in his early landmark performances, that was not Dylan's only voice; and in the mid-1960s, he sang in several others, from the accusatory hipster voice on "Like a Rolling Stone," to the hushed three-in-the-morning voice on "Visions of Johanna," to the alternately hallucinatory and defiant voices in his fraught concert shows with The Hawks in 1966.

The 1966 concerts also showed Dylan spinning at the edge, at times on the verge of collapse. Surviving a freak motorcycle accident in July gave him the space to quit touring and stay put in Woodstock, New York (where he had been spending much of his spare time since 1964), recover his health, and build a different kind of family life with his newly wed wife, Sara. Yet the withdrawal, contrary to conventional accounts, hardly halted his creativity. Sequestered with The Hawks, now calling themselves The Band, inside protective Woodstock, he reconnected with the folk elements of his template and produced new experiments in vision music, albeit stripped down and more connected to biblical cadences and imagery. Within eighteen months, he both produced the informal recordings that would become *The Basement Tapes* and released one of his most enduring albums, *John Wesley Harding*.

The very end of the 1960s into the mid-1970s brought truly severe setbacks, artistic and personal. Serene Woodstock, increasingly trampled by curiosity seekers, provided only so much imaginative stimulation. Recovering an older voice and returning to an early inspiration, country and western music—as well as to Nashville, recording home of *Blonde on Blonde* and *John Wesley Harding*—produced the commercially successful and brilliantly performed but artistically straitened *Nashville Skyline*, followed by the mostly forgettable (though, as a sampler of Dylan's interests, archivally interesting) *Self Portrait*. Dylan's business affairs ran into major difficulties (and brought a temporary defection from Columbia); an attempt to resettle his family in Greenwich Village brought more unwanted attention in a scene gone to seed; his marriage began hitting serious rocks. The period was not barren of strong compositions, many of them on the comeback New York album *New Morning*, released in 1970, as well as two lasting songs, "Knockin' on Heaven's Door" and "Forever Young." Yet a return to live touring in 1974 with The Band, now a major act in their own right, led to astounding ticket sales but a sense of creative exhaustion, projecting power void of feeling. Dylan confessed to suffering from an "amnesia" for writing songs as he once had written them.

Before too long, though, he would remark that he had learned "to do consciously what I had unconsciously felt." During the summer of 1974, on a tip from friends, he attended classes in midtown Manhattan offered by a strong-minded painting teacher and philosopher/guru, Norman Raeben, who pushed him to reconfigure time and space. A few years later, Dylan would in passing credit Raeben's teaching, although he would subsequently deny it, as ever guarding the secrecy of his songwriting approach. Whatever the case, Dylan was back in the studio in September recording a breakthrough, *Blood on the Tracks*, best rendered in the original spare recorded version replaced at the last minute by the less edgy do-over released by Columbia. Themes and moods familiar from his work of ten years earlier reappeared but with a new assurance and economy, as in the truth-telling anti-romance "Idiot Wind." Dylan's always-elusive persona wafted through one song after another, emerging most clearly as the wandering troubadour, on the road in fact and in metaphor.

The following summer, after a journey through France that led him to the King of the Gypsies, Dylan returned to New York, where Greenwich Village was springing back to life thanks partly to the punk scene headquartered at CBGB on the Bowery. Calling on an assortment of old friends and sometimes random new ones, he pulled together a kind of troupe he had long had in mind and called it the Rolling Thunder Revue, which mostly played small New England theaters during the fall before the launching of America's bicentennial celebrations—a concert tour unlike any other ever attempted before or since. Dylan also recorded a batch of new, decidedly theatrical songs (released, theatrically enough, as an album named *Desire*, as in the streetcar), all of which matched the theatrics of his stage performances in whiteface. Behind the scenes, Dylan was also filming a movie, at once formless and minutely contrived, while he generated a mini-political movement (and recording a remarkable cinematic narrative) on behalf of the boxer, Rubin "Hurricane" Carter, imprisoned on dubious evidence for a murder he said he didn't commit.

The Rolling Thunder adventure at once assembled aesthetic avatars and revised them, embodied in a traveling community that was part *commedia dell'arte* and part all-American carnival. A summary of where Dylan had been and was now, replete with poetry and politics, it defied post-Vietnam, post-Watergate disillusionment. It also dramatized more clearly than ever the complications of Dylan's continued self-creation. At a New York concert on Halloween night in 1964, Dylan had joked with the audience that, befitting the occasion, he had his "Bob Dylan mask on." He was performing in a guise, as every artist does—although Dylan took the blurring of image and reality more seriously than others, while confounding anyone who would try to peek inside. Ten years later, in Rolling Thunder, the white-faced Pierrot was his latest artifice, who was not the same as the person behind it, or the person behind that person.

The force of that artifice, though, did not last. A second leg of the Revue in 1976, stretching from Florida to Colorado, although full of fiery performances, had a different feel, more hit or miss, and lacked the special atmosphere and intensity of the first leg. Dylan's film, *Renaldo and Clara*, the editing of which took up much of his time and energy in 1977, bombed in the United States. His marriage finally collapsed into messy divorce and child custody proceedings. The sudden death of a hero, Elvis Presley, in 1977 left him morose. A new album in 1978, *Street-Legal*, and extensive touring with a large band and back-up singers, although well received abroad, were widely panned at home.

Bob Dylan, Tour 1974. Photograph by Barry Feinstein

SEAN WILENTZ

Toward the end of the draining 1978 tour, at a show in San Diego, Dylan spied a small crucifix someone had thrown onstage and pocketed it; two days later, in a hotel room in Tucson, he experienced a literal visitation from Jesus Christ. Born again and soon connected with the hellfire premillennialist Vineyard Fellowship in California, Dylan shifted once more, writing and performing original gospel songs, backed by a mighty complement of Black female singers and a hard-driving rock ensemble, in live shows punctuated by Dylan's sermonizing. Regarded by an influential segment of critics and fans as Dylan's latest sellout—his turn coincided with the rise of the right-wing Moral Majority in support of Ronald Reagan—Dylan's Christian writing would produce one of his best-selling albums, *Slow Train Coming*. (It also built, as few at the time remarked, on a fascination with gospel themes long part of Dylan's foundation, from his recording of "Gospel Plow" on his first album to an early lyric of his own, "Gospel News.") Thereafter, a pair of gospel tours converted even some skeptical listeners to Dylan's newfound art if not to his doomsday doctrine, although it only received full appreciation forty years later with the release of *The Bootleg Series Vol. 13: Trouble No More 1979–1981*.

The three studio albums grouped as his Christian gospel period form a progression, from damnation to grateful redemption to redemption mixed with reflection, the last of these inscribed in one of Dylan's most moving recordings, of the Blakean/biblical song "Every Grain of Sand" on the severely underrated *Shot of Love*. The albums expanded on elements of Dylan's ever-evolving template, from the apocalyptic themes in early songs like "When the Ship Comes In" to the parables on *John Wesley Harding* like "All Along the Watchtower." They also marked a plunge into the American South—not country-and-western Tennessee, as before, but the deeper African American South of Alabama (where two of the albums were recorded), recreated in staged performances that, instead of the Rolling Thunder carnival shows, resembled tent-show revivals.

By 1983, when he shifted yet again on *Infidels*, Dylan had rethought his specifically Christian devotion without abandoning biblical references and images of apocalypse. He seemed to round off his reflections with a contemplation of human corruption and a world teetering on doom rendered as a passage through Southern history, from slavery days on—a progress founded on Dylan's reworking of the melody of the venerable "St. James Infirmary." The song's touchstone was a 1930s bluesman-songster who had himself reworked "St. James Infirmary" decades earlier into a song about a dying crapshooter, the sightless witness whose name became the song's title, "Blind Willie McTell."

For reasons best known to himself, Dylan decided to shelve "Blind Willie McTell"—it would only appear eight years later, on the first of his official "bootleg" releases—which weakened *Infidels*, an album widely if not always wisely hailed as Dylan's latest return to form. The rest of the 1980s brought frenzy but less songwriting success. In 1988, Dylan admitted that he could not get to the requisite frame of mind for composing as quickly as he once had, which was "real quick." Looking back twenty years later, in his memoir *Chronicles: Volume One*, he described himself as "an empty burned-out wreck . . . in the bottomless pit of cultural oblivion." Although he recorded albums of new material, they yielded only a very few remarkable songs, above all a long movie-based saga co-written with Sam Shepard, "Brownsville Girl," and another collaboration, the hard rocker "Silvio," co-written with Robert Hunter. Bad decisions led him to appear in doomed projects like the scatterbrained film *Hearts of Fire* (which even his personal charisma could not rescue) and an ill-planned ramshackle tour with the Grateful Dead, the closest he would ever get to becoming an oldies act.

What force was missing in his new songs Dylan seemed to plow into his best live performances on his own tours, backed by a changing cast of superb musicians, notably Tom Petty and his band the Heartbreakers. Out of those efforts came the start of what fans dubbed the Never Ending Tour (a title Dylan detested and disowned), an unrelenting succession of concert dates, sometimes more than one hundred a year, which has continued to this day. At the very end of the decade, he teamed in New Orleans with the producer-musician Daniel Lanois and a group of local musicians to record a spurt of strong writing on *Oh Mercy*. At around the same time, what began as a jape with George Harrison turned into a relaxed team enterprise of writing and recording with Harrison, Petty, Roy Orbison, and Jeff Lynne as The Traveling Wilburys. Indeed, most of Dylan's most interesting work after 1983 and for the rest of the decade came in partnerships and not in the willful isolation on which he said he had once relied.

Bob Dylan, Rolling Thunder Revue, 1975. Photograph by Ken Regan

Suddenly, in 1991, Columbia released as a set the first three volumes of what would become Dylan's Bootleg Series, consisting of rare and previously uncollected recordings. Although heavy on material from Dylan's early years, the compilation included a few unissued, revelatory works like "Blind Willie McTell." Then, a year later, Dylan released *Good as I Been to You*, his first album consisting entirely of solo acoustic performances since *Another Side* but now devoted to traditional folk and blues numbers. Although it looked backward, the new album proved a harbinger of things to come, much as *Another Side* had prefigured the vision music of the mid-1960s.

For several years, Dylan's live shows had included an acoustic segment performing songs like "Rank Strangers to Me" and "The Lakes of Pontchartrain" (a rewrite of "Lily of the West," popularized by the Irishman Paul Brady). Listening to a long personal compilation recording of older songs—a kind of extended personal update of Smith's *Anthology*—then helped him reconnect with the fundamentals of his lexicon. On *Good as I Been to You*, as on an even stronger follow-up album, *World Gone Wrong*, released in 1993, Dylan performed with a renewed ragged intensity and originality, making songs he'd long known inside out fully his own. Then, in a powerful appearance on the *MTV Unplugged* series in 1995—decked out in his circa 1965 Ray-Ban shades and polka dot shirt, and backed by his latest superb band, anchored by bassist Tony Garnier—he brought that same intensity to fresh takes of his own compositions, dating back to the early 1960s. A mysterious heart ailment nearly killed him in 1997, but he recovered in time to be back on the road when Columbia released his first album of original songs in seven years, *Time Out of Mind*.

From its opening staccato organ notes of its first track, "Love Sick," the new album sounded different from all of Dylan's previous recorded work, the performances encased in a swampy echo effect added by Daniel Lanois, with whom Dylan had reunited. The effect muffles the music, but the musicianship shines through, as do Dylan's songs of time running short, of being caught or trapped or tightly bound, of a singer traversing a landscape blasted by private human folly. ("I'm walking / through streets that are dead," the first track begins, the walker sickened by a love that he cannot quit.) Then, gradually, it becomes clear that Dylan has borrowed snatches of lyric and melody from an assortment of writers and artists ranging from Charley Patton to Robert Burns, and transformed them for his own purposes.

SEAN WILENTZ

Bob Dylan, *Tempest* sessions, 2012. Photograph by John Shearer

There was, it needs noting, nothing new about this kind of appropriation in Dylan's work, even (or perhaps especially) in his most startling lyrics from the mid-1960s. A close reading of "Desolation Row," for example, turns up images evidently borrowed from Jack Kerouac's novel *Desolation Angels*, published a few months before Dylan recorded the song and put by Dylan to different uses. But on *Time Out of Mind*, the technique seemed more obvious and resolute. "Well my heart's in the highlands," the long final track, "Highlands," begins, an undisguised borrowing from Burns, but the lyric goes on to merge the Scottish Highlands with the highlands of the American heartland where Robert Zimmerman grew up.

Take away the special effects—after *Time Out of Mind*, Dylan began producing his studio work exclusively, under the name Jack Frost—and similar combinations of theme and technique would dominate two masterful albums to come, *"Love and Theft"* and *Modern Times*. Both contain songs that confront and defy aging, songs about still being in fighting trim, but that also say the effort is partly—and maybe entirely—self-deluded: "I got my hammer ringin', pretty baby, but the nails ain't goin' down," Dylan sings on "Summer Days." There are songs that, if not exactly post-apocalyptic, are post-catastrophic, whether the catastrophe be flood ("High Water [For Charley Patton]"), or some unmentioned personal misdeed ("Mississippi"), or the destruction of an entire way of life ("Workingman's Blues #2"). Through the mayhem and mortality, a devotion to kin, friends, lovers, and other loved ones seems the strongest earthly counterforce (as in "When the Deal Goes Down" on *Modern Times*).

Dylan also expanded upon and refined his technique of lifting phrases and melodies and reassembling them, not simply as a pastiche but as a reclamation of the past in discouraging, fragmented modern times. Some of the more obvious borrowings were from the kinds of sources out of which Dylan forged his original template forty years earlier and never relinquished, from the 1920s country banjo player Charlie Poole to bluesmen like Robert Johnson and Hambone Willie Newbern. But Dylan drew on all sorts of sources, setting entire phrases from Ovid and Virgil and the Japanese gangster writer Junichi Saga to melodies composed by the likes of Guy Lombardo's brother Carmen and recorded by, above all others, Bing Crosby.

Once again, Dylan's latest creative shift raised a storm, as critics charged his new songs were outrageous plagiarisms, appropriations without acknowledgment of other people's work. Quite apart from the intricacies of fair use and copyright law, the accusers completely missed the point, approaching the songs with a censorious rectitude that prevented them from listening to the play of Dylan's imagination. In 1964, when certain guardians of folk virtue began objecting to the artistic redirections on *Another Side of Bob Dylan*, Johnny Cash bid them, in an open letter, to "SHUT UP and let him sing." Dylan, though stung by the attacks, sang regardless and soon enough the furor subsided. So it would be with the objections to Dylan's minstrel-like theft in his later work. *Modern Times*, in particular, enjoyed more rapid commercial success than any of Dylan's previous recordings. By the second decade of the new millennium, the critical consensus held that the trio of albums beginning with *Time Out of Mind* ranked alongside the other peak clusters in Dylan's career.

Dylan turned 65, the traditional age of retirement, the year that *Modern Times* appeared, but his output actually increased, only now along a broad range of endeavors. The publication of a memoir that few knew was in the works, *Chronicles: Volume One*, came in 2004. Lucid and evocative, the book contained some of the elements of his latest songwriting style, disjointed in structure, drawing silently on many sources, and suffused with gratitude toward people he'd met along the way—not necessarily what most critics and readers expected of the author of "Like a Rolling Stone" and "Positively 4th Street." The book would help earn Dylan a special Pulitzer Prize citation and contribute, eight years later, to his winning the Nobel Prize in Literature. Then, the release of *Modern Times* coincided with the commencement of a new project, a weekly radio show in which Dylan, playing DJ, archivist, and deadpan wisecracker, introduced a wide variety of music devoted to a particular topic, again in the spirit of his latest songwriting. Blending the seemingly archaic with the latest satellite radio technology, *Theme Time Radio Hour* would run for two years in one hundred installments.

Dylan picked up the experiments in filmmaking that had seemingly ended with *Renaldo and Clara*, collaborating with Larry Charles in 2003 on *Masked and Anonymous*, a story of hustlers and circus performers in a blasted land, focused on one Jack Fate, the latest semi-cloaked, refracted Dylan character. He also participated in two acclaimed films directed by Martin Scorsese, a biographical documentary, *No Direction Home*, and a more fanciful rendition of the 1975 tour, *Rolling Thunder Revue*.

Dylan's work as a sketcher and painter had begun long before his encounter with Norman Raeben. (In 1973, he decided to add some drafts and cartoons to a book of his song lyrics to produce *Writings and Drawings*.) He kept it up, originally as a diversion during his concert tours, then more seriously as a painter. From the *Drawn Blank* series, consisting of filled-in sketches, his work advanced to *The Asia Series* and then to *The Beaten Path*, a large series of landscapes that captured anew Dylan's attachments to an archaic America that lies off the superhighway exit ramps. When not painting, Dylan also picked up metal welding, fashioning large artistic gates and other creations out of found objects.

Throughout, Dylan sustained his unremitting international tour schedule, with bassist Garnier a stalwart presence. A major collection of new songs, *Tempest*, released in 2012—its title song a retelling of the sinking of the *Titanic*—followed an album of work originally composed for a French film and an album of Christmas tunes that also amounted to an homage to Bing Crosby. As early as the mid-1980s, Dylan had talked about recording a sampler of American standards; beginning in 2015, he followed through with a spate of five records, three of them collected in one release, consisting of reinterpretations of material mostly associated with Frank Sinatra.

The COVID-19 pandemic halted Dylan's touring early in 2020, but then, in late March, approaching age 80, he dropped on the internet the longest recorded song of his career. Songs about presidential assassinations ("Charles Guiteau," "Mr. Garfield," "White House Blues") are as much a part of American folklore as ballads about the *Titanic*; and Phil Ochs wrote what some consider his greatest song, "Crucifixion," about the assassination of John F. Kennedy. Dylan's incantatory, sixteen-minute-plus piece about JFK, "Murder Most Foul," describes the gruesome act more exactly—intimately, graphically—than any earlier assassination song, yet it is also more historical, depicting a trauma at once global and deeply personal (for Dylan like everyone else) as the moment when the fall of America began. History likewise pervaded the album that soon followed, *Rough and Rowdy Ways*, including the death of President William McKinley that commences "Key West (Philosopher Pirate)," a dreamlike song about a divine paradise down at the end of the line.

SEAN WILENTZ

The story has continued, leading up to the present day, with a major art retrospective (*Retrospectrum*, 2019), a long-form video (*Shadow Kingdom*, 2021), and the 2022 release of a new book, *The Philosophy of Modern Song*, his first since *Chronicles*. The controversies have also persisted. Does a songwriter really deserve to receive the Nobel Prize in Literature? Some defenders point to Homer and Sappho and Robert Burns, lyricists all. Who can say they wouldn't have been deserving? Other defenders say, so what? On the subject of what's literature and what is not: think again.

But what about all of those unacknowledged borrowings, now discovered in his paintings and writings as well as his songs? Whatever happened to transparency and originality (as if art is supposed to be transparent and origins are everything)?

For the sake of argument, let me propose an experiment. Go to a computer and type the epigram that begins this essay into a Google search. You will come up with (as of when I'm writing this) 339 results referring to Bob Dylan. Then type in just the first part of the epigram, "Life isn't about finding yourself," and you'll come up with 358 *million* results ascribing the quotation to George Bernard Shaw, coupled with the observation that life is about creating yourself. Did Dylan just lift those lines from Shaw? Has he duped me yet again—and, evidently, at least 339 others? Does it matter?

It doesn't matter at all—and it matters less than zero once you try to discover where Shaw wrote those arresting sentences and find no reference, no text, either on the internet or in any Shaw concordance. We may never know the details, but we do know that Shaw evidently never wrote those words whereas Dylan certainly spoke them. We also know that, even if Dylan somewhere picked up the lines about self-creation, he added his own lines about creating things, which make all the difference to the remark. It gets to be a mug's game, lost in the same Möbius strip of illusion and reality that has been one of Bob Dylan's trademarks since the moment he called himself Bob Dylan.

U.S. 285, New Mexico, 1955, from *The Americans.* Photograph by Robert Frank

There is no end to this story and there never will be. But for now, let three images convey the continued inspiration of an artist coming into his ninth decade and still very much on the road.

The first image, Dylan's large canvas *Endless Highway*, from *The Beaten Path* series, depicts that road. It is an image of some place he has been (or maybe not) but also of where he could be moving at right this very minute. It traces, though, only the top layer of Dylan's imagination.

Deeper down, the second image is very much in the spirit of that painting, and might very well have inspired it. But it also sprang from a milieu that molded Dylan's work and life early on: Robert Frank's photograph, *U.S. 285, New Mexico,* 1955, from his once-misapprehended and now-classic collection, *The Americans.*

Beneath that photograph, envisage an excerpt from the opening of Jack Kerouac's introduction to Frank's collection:

THAT CRAZY FEELING IN AMERICA when the sun is hot on the streets and music comes out of the jukebox or from a nearby funeral. . . . The humor, the sadness, the EVERY-THING-ness and American-ness of these pictures!

Endless Highway, from *The Beaten Path*, 2016. Painting by Bob Dylan

Finally, deepest down, a still from the end of Charlie Chaplin's *Modern Times* from 1936. In his very early performances, before he had truly found his voice, Dylan snared his audiences with little stage moves that people called Chaplinesque; and, although he had long since given up tramp-like trappings, he signaled an abiding link to Chaplin decades later when he entitled one of his albums *Modern Times*. The still shows Chaplin's oft-beleaguered character and a woman (it is Paulette Goddard), down on their luck, their backs to us, on a road remarkably like the one in Dylan's painting and the one in Frank's photograph. (Look closely at Dylan's picture, and his road might be a combination of the other two.) Chaplin and Goddard walk that road at dawn, lit by the rising sun, with just enough hope that their fortunes will change.

Beneath that picture, envisage as an envoi an excerpt from a famous press conference in San Francisco in 1965:

Film still from *Modern Times*, 1936. Directed by Charlie Chaplin

REPORTER: Is there anything in addition to your songs that you want to say to people?
BOB DYLAN: Good luck.
REPORTER: You don't say that in your songs.
DYLAN: Oh yes I do, every song tails off with "Good luck—I hope you make it."

An Accident of Geography

1941–1960

It was just an accident of geography. Like if I was born and raised in New York or Kansas City, I'm sure everything would have turned out different.

—Bob Dylan, March 1966, Nat Hentoff interview, *Playboy*

Bob Dylan, 1957 yearbook photo. Photographer unknown

ROBERT ZIMMERMAN

On May 24, 1941, Abe and Beatty welcomed their first child, Robert Allen Zimmerman. Bob Dylan spent the first six years of his life in Duluth. In 1946, his father Abe contracted polio, and the following year Dylan's family left Duluth for the North Country town of Hibbing, where Beatty's family lived.

Abe and Beatty Zimmerman, Niagara Falls, NY, May 1939. Photographer unknown

ABE AND BEATTY ZIMMERMAN

Bob Dylan's parents Abram "Abe" Zimmerman and Beatrice "Beatty" Stone were first-generation immigrants and part of a tight-knit Jewish community in Duluth, Minnesota. Hailing from Odessa in what was then the Russian Empire (now Ukraine), the Zimmermans emigrated following the devastating 1905 anti-Jewish pogrom in the city. The Stones made their way from Lithuania to the United States in 1902. Married in 1934, Abe and Beatty were photographed during a May 1939 trip that took them to New York City and Niagara Falls.

Zimmerman home, Hibbing, MN. Photographer unknown

ZIMMERMAN RESIDENCE, HIBBING

The Zimmerman home in Hibbing at 2425 7th Avenue East. Dylan lived there with his family from 1947 until 1959 when he left to attend the University of Minnesota.

Larry Kegan, Jerry Waldman, Bob Dylan, Louie Kemp, Dave Unowsky, Herzl Camp, Webster, WI, summer 1957. Photographer unknown

When I was about 10, I started playing the guitar.
I found a guitar in the house that my father bought, actually.
I found something else in there that had these kinds of mystical
overtones. There was a great big mahogany radio that had a 78
turntable when you opened up the top. I opened it up one day and
there was a record on there, a country record—a song called
"Drifting Too Far from the Shore." The sound of the record
made me feel like I was somebody else, that I was maybe
not even born to the right parents or something.

—Bob Dylan, 2005, interview, *No Direction Home: Bob Dylan*

Hibbing postcard, circa 1950s

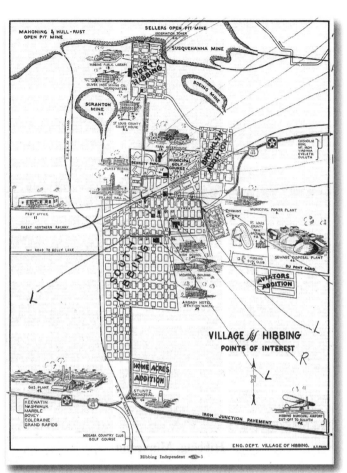

Village of Hibbing map, early 1950s

HIBBING

In 1893, after discovering evidence of iron ore in the area, the German miner Frank Hibbing founded the town that would bear his name. Hibbing, in its original location, was situated atop the Mesabi Iron Range, one of the world's largest deposits of iron ore. As the mines around Hibbing fueled America's industrial growth at the turn of the century, they began to surround a town that was also booming. Eventually the pressures of expansion led the mining companies to negotiate with the city leaders of Hibbing to move its location. Starting in 1919, nearly 180 homes and twenty businesses were placed on steel wheels and logs and moved nearly two miles from "North Hibbing" to "South Hibbing."

DOWNTOWN HIBBING

In 1963 Dylan wrote, "You can stand at one end of Hibbing on the main drag an' see clear past the city limits on the other end." The main drag he was referring to was Howard Street, the main commercial thoroughfare known as downtown Hibbing. Much of the excitement for a teenager in Hibbing was situated in this vicinity, and Dylan knew the area well.

Dylan frequented the L&B Café, which boasted a jukebox featuring the latest hit songs, sometimes in the company of his girlfriend Echo Helstrom. Nearby was the Lybba Theater, owned by an uncle, where Bobby first saw films like *Rebel Without a Cause*, spurring on a lifelong love for cinema. As Dylan's budding interest in music grew, he stocked up on records, instruments, and sheet music at Crippa Music. He bought his second electric guitar—a striking, Deco-styled Supro Ozark—at Hautala Music Store on 1st Avenue, with his friend John Bucklen in tow.

Hull–Rust–Mahoning Open Pit Iron Mine, Hibbing, circa 1942. Photograph by John Vachon

HIBBING OPEN PIT IRON MINE

Located on the Mesabi Iron Range, Hibbing is home to the Hull-Rust-Mahoning Open Pit Iron Mine. At the time this Farm Security Administration photo was taken in the early 1940s, the pit measured two and a half miles long, three-quarters of a mile wide, and four hundred feet deep. Miner John Palumbo Jr. stands atop the mine for scale. At its peak between WWI and WWII, the mine was producing as much as one-quarter of the United States' supply of iron ore. The Mine was later deemed a National Historic Landmark and added to the National Register of Historic Places.

BLACK BUFFALO IRONWORKS

In 2013, on the occasion of his first exhibition of ironworks sculptures, Dylan alluded to the possible influence of the North Country mines on his exploration of the visual arts: "I've been around iron all my life ever since I was a kid. I was born and raised in iron ore country—where you could breathe it and smell it every day. And I've always worked with it in one form or another."

Although Dylan began experimenting with metalwork in the late 1980s as a hobby, the process has become a more formal part of his artistic practice as his career in the visual arts has developed and expanded in the past decade. Dylan is shown here at his welding studio, Black Buffalo Ironworks, in 2013. From that studio, Dylan has created gates, decorative wall hangings, tables, railings, and, most recently, a rail car now permanently exhibited at Château La Coste in Provence. To commemorate the opening of the Bob Dylan Center in 2022, he created a unique sixteen-foot gate for the entry foyer.

PAGE 31: Bob Dylan in his ironworks studio, 2013. Photograph by John Shearer

FIFTH-GRADE CLASS PORTRAIT

Dylan (seated right, holding drum) in grade school during a class music lesson.

TEEN-AGE BOWLING CHAMPS—Winning the 1955-56 Teen-age Bowling League competition were the Gutter Boys. Members of the team are l-r, Ron DeSellier, Bob Zimmerman, Jerry Erickson, Pat Toomey, Den Keller and Dave Westurn.

The Gutter Boys bowling team, newspaper clipping, 1956

Latin Club

Students Promote Study of Roman Culture and Life

Initiation of new members and a tea in November began the year's activities of the Latin Club. During the year the group published a newspaper, containing articles written by many of the Latin students.

This club's main purpose is to further interest in the Latin language and promote study of Roman life and customs. Membership consists of students taking Latin and students with two years of Latin. Miss Irene Walker is the group's adviser and Mary Ann Peterson and Joe Perpich are the consuls.

ROW 1: John Milinovich, Mike Minelli, Bob Zimmerman, Frank Sherman. ROW 2: Pat Lamprecht, Carole Del Grande, Marsha Banen, Verlene Carpenter, Bonnie Schoenig, Sally Jolowsky, Carol Tappero, Mary Jane Svigel. ROW 3: Pierina Maracchini, Helen Taylor, Colleen Schulz, Barbara Rostvold, Barbara Satovich, Darlene Solinger, Jean Wright, Donna Urbia, Pat Baumgardner.

Hibbing High Latin Club, yearbook clipping, 1957

EXTRACURRICULARS

Dylan's extracurricular activities during his high school years were not limited to playing in musical groups—he also was a member of his high school Latin club and The Gutter Boys bowling team. Dylan also first became enamored with motorcycles while in high school, and he and his friends all had bikes. They would often ride around Hibbing in the evenings and take trips as far as Duluth to see musical acts.

Bob Dylan on motorcycle with classmate Dale Boutang, circa 1956. Photographer unknown

Bob Dylan and Larry Kegan, 1957. Photographer unknown

BOB DYLAN AND LARRY KEGAN, 1957

A teenage Dylan first met Kegan (right) at Herzl Camp, and the pair remained close friends until Kegan's death in 2001. Dylan listed Kegan as "Champion of All Causes" in the credits to his 1978 album *Street-Legal*.

Hibbing High School exterior. Photographer unknown

HIBBING HIGH SCHOOL

In 1924, Hibbing High School opened its doors to its inaugural class of students. Funded by the mining companies as part of their agreement in resettling the village, the magnificent Jacobean-style edifice, replete with greenhouse and medical facility, took many years and nearly $4 million to complete. Dylan attended Hibbing High from second grade through his high school graduation in spring of 1959.

The crowning architectural feature of the school is its 1,800-seat auditorium, which was modeled after the Capitol Theatre in New York City. With four resplendent Belgian-style chandeliers with glass crystals fashioned in Czechoslovakia, and a grand balcony, the auditorium featured a massive Barton pipe organ and a 1922 Steinway grand piano, which was made famous by a young Bob Dylan. On February 6, 1958, Dylan and his band The Golden Chords, featuring classmates Monte Edwardson on guitar and Le-Roy Hoikkala on drums, performed their own brand of rock 'n' roll in front of the entire assembled class body at the school's "Jacket Jamboree." B. J. Rolfzen, Dylan's high school English teacher, recalled the infamous performance in a 2004 interview for the Martin Scorsese documentary *No Direction Home: Bob Dylan*:

> I saw Robert stand there at the piano and my guess is that he was trying to destroy it because he pounded on it . . . it was a most unusual thing to observe. . . . When it was all over, he came up to my classroom and he looked at me as if to say "Mr. Rolfzen, you never would have guessed it, would you?" I'll always remember that.
>
> I heard later that Mr. [Kenneth] Pederson, the principal, pulled the curtain on him. [Many years later I visited] Mr. Pederson in the nursing home . . . and I said, "Mr. Pederson, do you remember the concert with Robert Zimmerman?" "Oh, yes," he says, "I remember that. You know, I pulled the curtain on him because I didn't think *that* music was suitable for the audience."

Hibbing High School auditorium. Photographer unknown

YEARBOOK PORTRAITS

Bob Dylan and a few of his high school friends, as taken from the Hibbing High School 1958 yearbook.

Robert Zimmerman

John Bucklen

Bucklen and Dylan made a series of home recordings in 1958, performing skits, cover songs, and a few originals.

Monte Edwardson

Monte Edwardson, the naturally talented guitarist in The Golden Chords, taught Bob Dylan some of his first chords on the instrument.

Larry Fabbro

Guitarist Larry Fabbro performed with Dylan in a series of bands, including The Shadow Blasters, playing two Little Richard cover songs at Hibbing High School's "Jacket Jamboree" on April 5, 1957.

Lawrence Furlong

Larry, his brother Pat, and Dylan were neighborhood friends since childhood.

Echo Helstrom

Echo Helstrom dated Dylan in 1957–58 when they were both 16 years old. The pair bonded over a shared taste in music. She is often considered one of the in-spirations for Dylan's classic early song, "Girl from the North Country."

LeRoy Hoikkala

LeRoy Hoikkala played drums in The Golden Chords.

HIGH SCHOOL GRADUATION, 1959

Dylan graduated from Hibbing High School in June 1959, walking across the same auditorium stage where he'd caused musical controversy the year before. Although he had plans to attend the University of Minnesota in Minneapolis that fall, his yearbook aspiration "to join 'Little Richard'" makes clear that Dylan's real passion was music.

Bob Dylan, 1959 yearbook photo. Photographer unknown

Robert Zimmerman: to join "Little Richard"— Latin Club 2; Social Studies Club 4.

Original painting by Duncan Hannah of The Jokers acetate recorded at Terlinde Music, December 24, 1956

I Just Wanna See It

Lee Ranaldo

I *just wanna see it.* That's all I kept saying, to anyone who'd listen: I wanted to see the actual object, to confirm its existence. A simple photo would do; that flat, black disc with grooves cut like a zillion others, yet nobody'd seen this one, and it was *Dylan's first record.* That means something, doesn't it? A singular object it was, at that, an edition of one! By some counts the beginning of everything. I'm not saying the teenage Robert Zimmerman was already Bob Dylan on that December afternoon in St. Paul, Minnesota, but something was forming, I told myself. There must be a spark within those grooves, even if just a chronological time-peg marker, right?

And yet, the last time I heard it, it was plain as day: I need to throw out my whole romantic theory about this acetate right now. It's juvenilia, plain and simple. There's no kid going by the name "Dylan" in evidence here. There's only Robert Allen Zimmerman, a son of the great Midwest, in his first recording studio. But in spite of that I still believe that the young Dylan was in the room that day.

It was Christmas Eve, 1956, and young Robert was down from Hibbing visiting his Herzl Camp buddies Larry Kegan and Howie Rutman, and the three of them ducked out of the twenty-degree cold and into the Terlinde Music Shop, where for five bucks they preserved themselves singing their own versions of early rock 'n' roll and doo-wop classics, two four-minute 78 rpm sides, ranging across the hit parade. Bob banged out the chords on the shop's piano and sang lead; Larry and Howard harmonized along. Singing together was just something they did, gathered around the old piano at camp. They were all of 15, and music-obsessed. By the mid-fifties the rumblings of early rock 'n' roll were taking shape and could be dialed in on their late-night radios, Little Richard, Buddy Holly, Elvis, Johnny Ray, The Platters—*everyone*—drifting in on the airwaves. It was new and exciting, and they'd caught the drift. They'd studied these songs much more than their maths! They even had a name for themselves: The Jokers. *This was the juvenile Jokerman's first strike!*

Finally, after tugging repeatedly on a few sleeves, I did get to see images of the actual disc. Generic printed labels stated "SOUNDCRAFT" in white letters on a blue ring, and "AUDITION RECORDING DISC" in red on a white field. One side was rubber stamped *Recorded by Terlinde Music, 184 W 7th*, phone number *CA 2-4574*.

I managed to hear it a bunch of times as well, across many weeks, hanging on every scratchy moment. One side has bits of six songs, just a verse or two of each and on to the next. Once it was rolling they couldn't stop, back up, or do over, it was *go cat go!* They had to squeeze in what they could on the disc's four-minute length. Bob would hit the first chord and the others would jump in almost immediately, starting with Shirley and Lee's "Let the Good Times Roll." A couple verses, a quick ending and bang, new first chord—another one. They rolled into an offhand take of Carl Perkins's "Boppin' the Blues"; a passable rendition of Frankie Lymon's "I Want You to Be My Girl"; nearly falling apart on Lloyd Price's classic "Lawdy Miss Clawdy"—none of them really knew the words, and the key was all wrong for their young voices, but you can tell they sensed that this song *swung* like the devil! Little Richard's "Ready Teddy" and Sonny Knight's "Confidential" closed it out. Rock 'n' roll tunes, mostly, a mere thirty or forty seconds of each.

There must've been a momentary breather while old man Terlinde flipped the acetate disc, a brief moment before he called *"Okay, ready boys, here we go again"* and bang they were back into it. The other side is devoted to two doo-wop hits. The Five Satins' "In the Still of the Nite" takes up a generous two and a half minutes, followed by The Penguins' hit "Earth Angel" for a minute-ten.

Bob knew the songs, if not always the actual lyrics. He already had that familiar blocky chordal playing style. The other two were throwing in what they could—sometimes harmonies, sometimes off-key bombs, sometimes simply joining in with Bob on the lead. You can hear Dylan's boyish voice leading them forward. I wanted to believe that young Bob and his friends had prepared mightily for this monumental day, that they had their harmonies all worked out, but, no, that's not how it was. Hearing it in close up, it's all quite impromptu. Raggedy harmonies. *Juvenilia*. It was a casual lark for three Jewish boys on Christmas Eve, and for five bucks (about $50 in today's coin) old man Terlinde was recording them doing it!

It was a *bona fide* recording studio, however, not the Voice-O-Graph booth I'd long pictured it to be. The second floor of Terlinde Music held a modest performance room and a small control booth, where local singers and small combos would come and make proper recordings. As a sideline to the serious studio work, anybody could walk in and cut a live-to-lathe disc on the spot—a letter home, a testimonial, a song or two—for five bucks a pop.

Ed Terlinde, the shop owner, was the engineer. He had some patents to his name, microphone systems for accordions (his shop specialty) and harmonicas. He'd have been in his mid-fifties when these three teenagers wandered in—on a whim, it seems. I tried to picture the scene, dwelling on the future-historical import of that moment. Were visions of a life in music already in young Bob's sights? *"To join 'Little Richard,'"* he'd state in his high school yearbook just a couple years later. So it was ironic to learn "through channels" in 2020 that Bob claims to have no recollection of this teenage milestone, no memory at all of the shop or of cutting a record with his friends. It threw me somehow to think that he'd not recall such an event—it shattered my notion of the significance of the moment—but then I recalled, when a similar teenage record I'd cut with my cousins in Brooklyn some forty-odd years ago came to me in the mail recently, I had no memory of its existence either. So perhaps this isn't Bob pulling the wool over our eyes, but just another event in the mad rush of youth.

No matter, indulge me while I imagine that moment: It probably took a minute or two for Mr. Terlinde to bring the pressed platter out to them. He might have sat up on a high stool behind the counter, pushing his glasses up on his nose as he penned "12/24/56" and "Larry Kegan, Bob Zimmerman, Howard Rutman" onto the label, to make no mistake of what had transpired.

And then. . .

And then. . .

And then he handed it to them, and they held that 10-inch plate by their fingertips, like a most delicate jewel. It had four holes in it—one in the center as normal, and three others punched through the label, for the cutting machine to grip it tight. And this one was *their* record. They had dog-gone gone and done it. *The Jokers had waxed it up*!

Did they back off the counter a bit, to be alone with it, winter sunlight streaming in through the shop's big hoarfrost-covered panes? I'd like to imagine that, for one of them at least, the world shifted just a bit on that afternoon. That the fuzzy outline of a future so brilliant, so incredible as to be incomprehensible, might've briefly flickered into view. Or perhaps, for *that* boy, at *that* moment, maybe it already seemed somehow matter-of-fact, preordained, with such clarity and certainty as if it was already written down in the books. Just a shrug, nothing special. Life and life only. Maybe not. But. . . *maybe*.

Would they have played it right there in the shop, to make sure it came out all right? With Terlinde standing over them, arms folded, sly grin on his face, breaking up at the sight of these three boys, urgently listening, legs twitching, practically rolling on the floor with excitement. Each trying to pick out his own voice: *"Hey that's me, hear it?" "Yep, we're all in there!"*

Or perhaps they bundled themselves out into the street and took it back to Howard's living room record console before they could play it. How many times did they flip it over? *"Play it again! That's us! It's a record of our veryownvoices, aint that amazin'? We made a record today!"* They stared at the label with its hand-scrawled date and their names written after. Played it over and over again until those soft plastic grooves quickly grew scratchy and full of static. Maybe they kinda fried the speaker on the console by turnin' it up too loud. Anyway it sounded great! Maybe they ran from house to house on the block screaming *"Listen to this!"* while jumping over themselves, laughing at the fantastic reality of it all, turning it up louder and louder still, until the adults cried out "We can't hear ourselves think!" and drove them back out into the street. For them it couldn't be loud enough. Now they'd study their own record as they'd studied the great sides of Chuck Berry, Buddy Holly, Little Richard, Elvis Presley, and the rest.

It may have been an ordinary day, a happenstance circumstance, but I'd like to imagine that Bob had a confirmation of his future self on that day, the bountiful onrushing stream of it all. There was so much to come—he couldn't have imagined it, but perhaps that black disc whispered of liberation, of power and, yes, even portents of the revolution that was to come. He was discovering within himself a song and dance man, if not a prophet—a poet-troubadour. That acetate bestowed an acknowledgment of who he was; pushed him closer to his future, away from teachers and parents, after-school clubs and dreary normality, and into history. He was en route to becoming *Bob Dylan*, even if he didn't know it yet. The future—his future—and *our* future—inched closer in that moment.

I wanted this disc to be something it's not. I wanted it to be not just the first record Bob ever cut but *the first appearance of Bob Dylan on record*. But it's not. It's three teenagers with a shared musical bug having some fun. But everybody starts somewhere, right? Everyone learns the classics, gathering the forms, before heading off to twist, shout, and rip it up. This acetate documents the apprentice stage. It wasn't yet exactly Bob Dylan, there in front of the microphone. It's a kid and his buddies, out larkin', not the ground-shaking reveal of our illustrious hero. That would come a few years later as the 1950s were turning over and Bob was preparing to head east, to find Woody, and the world, waiting for him.

So where did it go? I heard Larry Kegan had it for a while, maybe in a cheap brown paper sleeve in a box with other 78s or eventually placed away in some dusty attic hideaway. It's said he left it with Louie Kemp, who kept it for decades in a safe deposit box, before passing it back to Larry sometime before he died. There'd been talk of it, rumors of its existence, and for a brief moment it was on the auction block before disappearing again. But finally I did see it, or at least a photo of it, and to me that was important. My life has revolved around these magic black discs since forever, and none more so than Bob's. So many of our lives have. The object is important.

Bob Dylan with Sears Silvertone electric guitar, September 1958. Photographer unknown

LEE RANALDO

SUN
RECORD COMPANY

Hi-Lo Music
U-194 BMI   Vocal

BOPPIN' THE BLUES
(Perkins-Griffin)

CARL PERKINS

243

MEMPHIS, TENNESSEE

Dot
REG. U. S. PAT. OFFICE
DOT RECORDS, INC.   HOLLYWOOD 28, CALIF.

Prestige Pub. Co.   15507
ASCAP
Time 1:55   MB-9344

CONFIDENTIAL
(Dorinda Morgan)

SONNY KNIGHT
With
Jack Collier Orchestra

"ULTRA HIGH FIDELITY"
9-56

ember
RECORDS

(E-2105)   Vocal Group
Angel Music (BMI)   Time: 2,30

IN THE STILL OF THE NITE
(F. Parris)

THE FIVE SATINS

E-1005

Manufactured by
Herald Records

EMBER RECORDS, INC. NEW YORK, NEW YORK

Specialty

Publisher
Venice Music, Inc.
BMI - 2:20

Chinaman

LAWDY MISS CLAWDY
(L. Price)

LLOYD PRICE
And His Orchestra

SP 428 A

DooTone

RECORDS   9514 S. CENTRAL AVE.
LOS ANGELES 2, CALIF.

348-B   DOOTSIE WILLIAMS
Blues & Rhythm   PUBLICATIONS - BMI
Vocal Group

EARTH ANGEL

(WILL YOU BE MINE)
(Curtis Williams)

THE PENGUINS

GEE

GG-1012   Jump
Kahl Music   Jimmy Wright
(BMI) 2:30   & his Orch.

I WANT YOU TO BE MY GIRL

(Goldner-Barett)
THE TEENAGERS
FEATURING
FRANKIE LYMON
(RR-3090)

Aladdin

REG. U.S. PAT OFF

HOLLYWOOD   CALIFORNIA

NO-268B   Vocal - 2:30
X   BMI
Aladdin Music Publ.

LET THE GOOD TIMES ROLL

(Leonard Lee)

SHIRLEY & LEE
3325

NOT LICENSED FOR RADIO BROADCAST

Specialty

Pub: Venice-BMI
Time: 2:05

READY TEDDY

(Blackwell-Marascalco)

LITTLE RICHARD
And His Band

SP-579

78 rpm record labels of songs recorded by The Jokers

Buddy Holly, Duluth Armory, 1959. Photograph by Sharon Johnson

Winter Dance Party with Buddy Holly
advertisement, Duluth Armory, 1959

BUDDY HOLLY AT THE DULUTH ARMORY, 1959

Dylan has offered numerous reflections on seeing one of Buddy Holly's last performances on January 31, 1959, at the Duluth Armory. In 2017, he elaborated on the electrifying experience as part of his Nobel Lecture:

> *If I was to go back to the dawning of it all, I guess I'd have to start with Buddy Holly. Buddy died when I was about eighteen and he was twenty-two. From the moment I first heard him, I felt akin. I felt related, like he was an older brother. I even thought I resembled him. Buddy played the music that I loved—the music I grew up on: country western, rock 'n' roll, and rhythm and blues. Three separate strands of music that he intertwined and infused into one genre. One brand. And Buddy wrote songs—songs that had beautiful melodies and imaginative verses. And he sang great—sang in more than a few voices. He was the archetype. Everything I wasn't and wanted to be. I saw him only but once, and that was a few days before he was gone. I had to travel a hundred miles to get to see him play, and I wasn't disappointed.*
>
> *He was powerful and electrifying and had a commanding presence. I was only six feet away. He was mesmerizing. I watched his face, his hands, the way he tapped his foot, his big black glasses, the eyes behind the glasses, the way he held his guitar, the way he stood, his neat suit. Everything about him. He looked older than twenty-two. Something about him seemed permanent, and he filled me with conviction. Then, out of the blue, the most uncanny thing happened. He looked me right straight dead in the eye, and he transmitted something. Something I didn't know what. And it gave me the chills.*

The Golden
Chords at the
Winter Frolic
Talent Contest,
Little Theater
of the Memorial
Building, Hibbing
Community
College, February
14, 1958.
Photographer
unknown

Rock & Roll
HOP
FOR TEEN-AGERS
WITH YOUR FAVORITE
100 TOP RECORDS
plus
Intermission Entertainment
by Hibbing's Own
GOLDEN CHORDS
FEATURING:
Monte Edwardson
Leroy Hoikkala
Bobby Zimmerman

SAT., MARCH 1st
9 to 12 P.M.

NATIONAL GUARD
ARMORY — HIBBING
—ADMISSION 50c—

THE GOLDEN CHORDS

The Golden Chords were composed of Dylan singing and playing piano or guitar depending on the gig, Monte Edwardson
on the guitar, and LeRoy Hoikkala on the drums. The group
played a mixture of originals and cover songs, and by most
accounts, they were *very* loud.

45

Newspaper advertisement, 1958

REFLECTIONS FROM LEROY HOIKKALA

LeRoy Hoikkala, drummer in Dylan's high school band The Golden Chords, interviewed 2019 at the Little Theater in the Hibbing Memorial Building, where The Golden Chords performed in 1958.

INTERVIEWER:

You all went to high school together at Hibbing High, you, Monte [Edwardson], and Bob? And you were all the same age? When did you start playing together?

LeRoy Hoikkala:

Pretty close to the same age, yeah. I was the oldest. Bob's a couple years younger and then Monte was maybe three, four years younger. Our parents knew each other. I went out to Monte's house and we were playing two pieces—tough for guitar and drums—but I just played quiet and Monte could pick up a guitar. He single-picked at the time. And then Bob said one day walking from school, he says, "I hear you guys been jamming, you and Monte, two pieces kind of hard." He says, "What if I come and play some songs for you?" I said, "Great." So that's when we started playing together, just practicing. Pretty soon we got the name Golden Chords from my golden Ludwig drums. We started just jamming. And a lot of songs we played that were known songs, but Bob liked to basically play something brand new, never to play it again. It sounds impossible but he did.

INTERVIEWER:

I remember you saying last time that you and Bob would go to a magazine shop and that you both were obsessed with James Dean and Marlon Brando.

LeRoy Hoikkala:

That was part of our "mission." We'd go down and we'd stop at Stevens' Grocery, and as soon as you walked in, they had all kinds of magazines, comic books and everything. And I remember we read about James Dean and how he grew up on his uncle's farm. James Dean told his uncle, "I definitely want to act, and there is a place in California where I can try out, and it doesn't cost anything to try." So his uncle finally said, "Okay, I'll take you there." When James Dean went there, they loved him and he got a job almost right away. Bob looked at me and said, "Believe in yourself and you'll figure it out."

INTERVIEWER:

When did you start playing shows, and what kind of reaction did you get?

LeRoy Hoikkala:

Well, in high school Val Peterson was our music teacher. They had pep rallies and Val said, "We need some music for a little intermission. Would you guys play?" We said, "Sure." So that's what we did. Didn't get paid for it or nothing.

When we started playing, people liked us, and then Bob, he got a little loud. The teachers didn't care for that. Well the thing is, Bob really liked Little Richard and he liked to play, I call it "loud music." But in a way, as I said, Bob had a lot of feeling for music. He got a feeling when he played that kind of music at that particular time in his life, he liked the "loud music," y'know.

INTERVIEWER:

What was it like when you played at the Duluth Armory, where Buddy Holly played?

LeRoy Hoikkala:

Monte said one day, "Duluth has been having rock hops." And we said, "What's a rock hop?" He said, "Well a rock hop is where you play 45s or whatever you have, maybe for 15, 20 minutes, half hour, then a band would play for a half hour. It alternates." And we said, "Hey, we could do that."

So Monte found out when the Armory was open, found out about the police—you had to have a policeman there, when he could be there, you give him a few bucks—and you have to have a clean-up person. You had to hire these people. And then we had to have a PA system, so we went to Jay's and Chisholm on Main Street and it was a TV shop, but he had these amplifiers with a turntable on top.

So we'd go there and I would just bring a snare drum and sock cymbals and Bob would bring his guitar and an amplifier and Monte would bring his amp. And we would set up as you first walk in, we'd set up right there and start playing. We'd just jam for a while. Had the doors open and pretty soon a few kids would show up, because everybody walked downtown on a Sunday. Well, they could hear the music because we were half a block away. Pretty soon kids were all over the place. We really enjoyed that—to us it was like a captive audience, kind of.

INTERVIEWER:

How long did your band last? Did everyone go their separate ways after high school?

LeRoy Hoikkala:

Right after high school I went to work, and Bob said he was going to go to the Minn U and go to school. Well, school didn't last too long because he's too restless, seriously. I mean he was restless and it's nothing bad, that's just the kind of person he was.

After he decided to leave university he said to me, "I'm going to see Woody [Guthrie]. He's sick and I want to go and play him a couple of songs out east." And I said, "Great, Monte and I are going to California. We got jobs there." Before long, his dad played me a Harry Belafonte record that Bob had played harmonica on. It was unbelievable. He said, "Listen, *that's Bob*." His dad was very proud of him.

LeRoy Hoikkala, 1956. Photographer unknown

LeRoy Hoikkala, 2019. Video still by Elvis Ripley and Jeremy Lamberton

Every Wednesday at 2 P.M.

MARVIN KARLINS

I t was 1959–60, a pivotal moment in America, a time of transition from the innocence of the '50s to the disillusionment of the '60s. I was in my first year of undergraduate study at the University of Minnesota and an avid folk guitarist, dividing my time between my academic assignments and my passion for folksinging. As part of my musical contribution, I gave free folksinging and guitar lessons to students at the Hillel Foundation, a religious organization on campus. Anyone could attend the sessions, which included both group and individual instruction.

One particular session stands out in my mind. I was in the room reserved for my group lessons, strumming a song on my guitar, when a young man appeared in the open doorway. I had never seen him before. I nodded "hello" and invited him in.

"I heard the guitar," he said, walking in and stopping a few feet from where I sat with a group of my students. "I play, too. Would you like to see?"

"Sure," I said, and handed him my guitar. He fingered a few basic chords and sang part of a "Top 40" song. I could tell he didn't know much about the guitar or singing, but he did seem interested in what he was doing. For an instructor, interest is what makes teaching worthwhile.

The young man handed me back my guitar. "What kind of music was that you were playing?" he asked.

"Folk guitar," I answered. "If you're interested, I give lessons for free."

"Really?" That seemed to catch my visitor's interest. "When?"

"Every Wednesday at 2 P.M. Stop by if you'd like."

"OK—I think I'll do that."

"Fine." I wondered silently whether he would actually return. "By the way my name's Marv," I said, extending my hand.

"I'm Bob," he replied, and we shook hands.

As it happened, Bob did return. He became one of my "regulars."

I always looked forward to the guitar lessons because they allowed me to pursue the two activities I loved most: teaching and folksinging. And that's exactly what made things so difficult when, trying to balance my school obligations with my folksinging interests, I realized I couldn't pursue both activities and do justice to either. I reluctantly came to the conclusion I would have to choose between training for a career in folksinging or one in academics.

I choose academics.

A few days after I made my decision, I met with my folksinging group and announced that it would be the last class I would be teaching. At the end of the session, I was approached by Bob. He wanted to know where he could continue to develop his folksinging skills now that I would no longer be available as his teacher.

I thought about his request. In the short time he had been my student it had become obvious to me that Bob didn't have a gifted voice or a great command of the guitar; yet if he was motivated enough to want to pursue folk guitar, who was I to object? "Try the 10 O'Clock Scholar," I suggested. "It's a coffeehouse a few blocks from the campus, and there are always a few folksingers hanging out there."

He thanked me for the suggestion and went on his way. It was the last time I ever saw Bob in person. It wasn't the last time I heard about him, however.

In a few short years, the freshman undergraduate from Hibbing, Minnesota, who had attended my folk guitar lessons as Bob Zimmerman had transformed himself into Bob Dylan, musical legend for the ages.

I am humbled when I think of my good fortune to have known this cultural icon at the outset of his career. I only wish, in retrospect, that I had recognized his musical genius and been there when he composed the songs that would capture the spirit and soul of an entire generation of Americans.

Bob Dylan with Marvin Karlins (seated, with guitar), University of Minnesota, September 1959. Photographer unknown

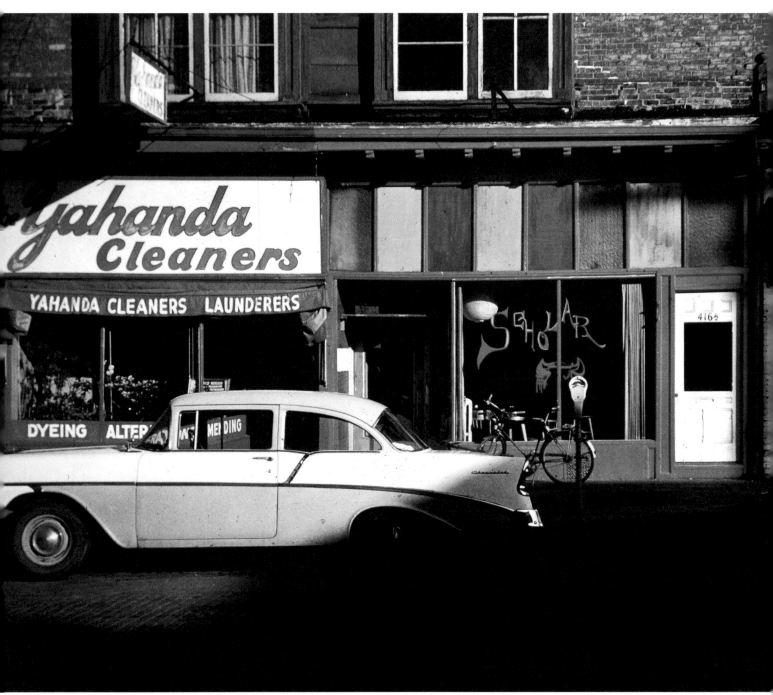

10 O'Clock Scholar exterior, April 1961. Photographer unknown

10 O'CLOCK SCHOLAR

Just a stone's throw from campus, in the hip, student-oriented neighborhood known as Dinkytown, the 10 O'Clock Scholar coffeehouse was a gathering place for the young folkies and bohemians who attended the University of Minnesota. It was onstage at the Scholar where Bobby Zimmerman first introduced himself as Bob Dylan.

10 O'Clock Scholar matchbook, circa 1960s

10 O'Clock Scholar interior, 1958. Photograph by Bill Savran

The Madison party tape, late 1960

Madison, WI / Fall–Winter 1960 / Bob Dylan, Danny Kalb, Jeff Chase

GREIL MARCUS

When Bob Dylan left Minneapolis in the late fall of 1960, seeking New York City as if he didn't exactly know where it was, he landed in Madison, Wisconsin, in the bohemian milieu around the university. He has spoken often over the years of a kind of secret society of folk-music people—if you knew where to go, who to call, where to wait, within hours you could find yourself within the confines of what he called "like-minded people," sharing songs, sharing food, sharing tiny apartments, even if you slept on the floor—there wasn't room for a couch. For Madison, Dylan had a number for Ron Radosh. Born in New York, he was from a Communist Party background; Pete Seeger was his guitar teacher. Now he was a folkie and a graduate student: "I was a 5-string banjo picker and guitarist and wanted to be a professional folksinger," he wrote to me in 2021, "and gave that up when I realized my limitations." (As a scholar, notable among his books is, with Joyce Milton, from 1983, *The Rosenberg File*, a convincing case for the guilt of Julius and Ethel Rosenberg. Radosh must have flinched when he heard the bootlegged "Julius and Ethel," from the same year, perhaps as musically bad and intellectually clueless as anything Bob Dylan has ever written or recorded; it was never released.) Radosh didn't have room to put Dylan up, but he had those secret society connections: he sent Dylan to Danny Kalb, then an 18-year-old freshman and guitar player. Within hours Dylan was meeting people, staying at different apartments, part of whatever was happening. He was playing at parties; at one Socialist Club night, people complained that he wouldn't stop singing his Woody Guthrie songs when there were serious politics that needed talking about.

The tape that survives from one of those nights, from November or December, at the house of the guitarist Jeff Chase, with Chase and Kalb sometimes in the background, has a different tone from party tapes made in Minneapolis both before and after, and after Dylan reached New York. You don't hear mastery, a scholastic command of folk song, authority, an original style, or for that matter humor. You hear someone finding his way into an attitude, where songs can take shape not as icons to be treated with respect, but mere occasions to put one foot in front of the other, trying to find out just what it is you're looking for. The Memphis Jug Band recorded "K. C. Moan" in 1929; they were chasing a death-bound train, three voices chiming in over a story that they've been told too many times without ever finding an ending they can live with. It was a masterpiece then; today it sounds unearthly, the last kind words of people before they vanish from the earth and memory. Quickening the pace, Dylan, Kalb, and Chase have fun with it. The pace Dylan finds is jaunty. The rhythm pops. "Hey, hey, ho, ho," Dylan lets out from the start of the night to the end: this is the one time where it feels part of the song, because it lands square on the beat. It's an early catch of the uncanny timing Dylan would mine for the rest of his career (I think of the first "all *right*" in "Sitting on a Barbed-Wire Fence"): proof, as the late Ralph J. Gleason put it, that "Bob Dylan can *swing*."

When Dylan returned to Minneapolis from New York in the spring of 1961, people were shocked at the change. In Martin Scorsese's *No Direction Home*, Tony Glover recounts how it was like "Tommy Johnson, Robert Johnson"—"like he'd gone to the crossroads," made his deal with the devil, came back better than anyone in town ever thought of being. That night in Madison, it's clear that wherever the crossroads might be—somewhere down in Greenwich Village, maybe where West 4th Street crosses West 12th?—he hasn't been there yet. Such timeless songs as "Danville Girl" and "East Virginia Blues" don't begin to come off. You don't believe the singer was ever on a platform smoking a big cigar—the "big cigar" of the 1944 Woody Guthrie version, making you think that even if the character telling the story is waiting for a freight to hop, any cigar has to be a big cigar, like the plutocrats in their tuxedos resting their feet on the necks of honest workers in cartoons in *The Masses* always had it, rather than the "cheap cigar" the song originally carried, as Dock Boggs sang "Danville Girl" in 1927, with countless people in the background before him: an image that actually tells you something, that from the bitter tone the word demands lets you picture the singer. And yet the songs are there, something to investigate, something to test yourself against, blues chords curling around a melody: thirty-seven years later, when the singer on *Time Out of Mind*, in "Standing in the Doorway," tells you he's smoking a cheap cigar, not only do you believe him, you can see the same man doing the same thing for twenty years, over and over, getting nowhere every time.

It's interesting that a 19-year-old Bob Dylan is more convincing on Jimmie Rodgers's "Let Me Be Your Sidetrack" than on Guthrie's "Hard Travelin'." By the end of 1960 he was doing Woody Guthrie in his sleep, when he sat down to eat, drank coffee, had a beer, shook hands. A few steps away from that little constructed Guthrie world, he had to look for the song, to find out where he was in relation to it, and homage wouldn't do, because he didn't yet know the song well enough to imitate it. He had to reach for the song, as if it were a testament and a joke at the same time, and so it is: "Let Me Be Your Sidetrack" is closer to rock 'n' roll than anything that was passing for folk music. That's the attitude: songs are a way to get from one place to another, in the course of the night, across a life, and who knows what they're really about? "Ramblin' Railroader," a song so folk it seems to have been composed by the genre as an advertisement for itself, comes up; hidden inside of it are a few lines from Elvis Presley's "Mystery Train." He wasn't at the crossroads, but you can sense him looking for it on a map.

The Madison recordings of Bob Dylan, Danny Kalb,
and Jeff Chase, late 1960

WOODY GUTHRIE JUKEBOX

Woody Guthrie's life and music has been a lasting inspiration throughout Dylan's long career. In a 1991 interview, Dylan explained, "There are so many reasons why [Guthrie] was different, you could fill a book. He had a sound. . . . And he had something that needed to be said. And that was highly unusual to my ears. . . . You could listen to his songs and actually learn how to live, or how to feel. He was like a guide." Dylan later joked, "I was like a Woody Guthrie jukebox."

    In this early period, while Dylan was immersing himself in folk-music records, he was also reinventing himself according to the model of Guthrie's hard-travelin' persona, as this professional portrait clearly shows. Taken in St. Paul, Minnesota, sometime in 1960, the photo captures the budding musician in a pivotal moment between becoming Bob Dylan and striking out east to New York to find Guthrie.

Woody Guthrie, 1945.
Photographer unknown

Bob Dylan, professional portrait, St. Paul, MN, 1960. Photograph by Deanna Harris Hoffman

A Way of Life

1961–1964

The people I knew—the people who were like-minded as myself—were trying to be folk musicians. That's all they wanted to be, that's all the aspirations they had. . . . There was no money in folk music. It was a way of life.

—Bob Dylan, September 2001, Mikal Gilmore interview, *Rolling Stone*

Bob Dylan, Columbia Records photo shoot, NYC, October 1964.
Photograph by Hank Parker

Bob Dylan, NYC, 1962. Photograph by John Cohen

ARRIVAL IN NEW YORK CITY

In January 1961, Bob Dylan arrived in New York City. Within weeks, Dylan trekked out to Greystone Park Psychiatric Hospital in Morris Plains, New Jersey, to visit Woody Guthrie, who was now suffering from Huntington's disease, a progressive, degenerative brain disorder. Despite Guthrie's debilitating illness, he was able to receive visitors, such as Ramblin' Jack Elliott, Pete Seeger, Sonny Terry, and a young Bob Dylan, who would play songs for him.

Dylan later remembered the promise of those early days in his 2004 memoir *Chronicles: Volume One*:

> *I was there to find singers, the ones I'd heard on record—Dave Van Ronk, Peggy Seeger, Ed McCurdy, Brownie McGhee and Sonny Terry, Josh White, The New Lost City Ramblers, Reverend Gary Davis and a bunch of others—most of all to find Woody Guthrie. New York City, the city that would come to shape my destiny.*

Dylan made his way to the epicenter of New York City's cultural scene: Greenwich Village. There Dylan quickly made his name known in the folk community, taking the stage as often as he could at the many basket-houses like the Café Wha?, Gerdes Folk City, or the Gaslight Cafe, where young performers could cut their teeth, earning whatever was in the hat when it was passed around after each set. Dylan soon befriended folksingers such as Dave Van Ronk, John Cohen, and Peter Yarrow, who later founded Peter, Paul and Mary. Yarrow recalled his early impressions of the new arrival's talents in a 2005 interview for the documentary *No Direction Home*:

I remember meeting Bobby when we were in Greenwich Village, and he was singing, I think, at Gerdes Folk City. We sang some songs together. I don't remember the exact moment, but there was a time when we were on stage, singing, "I asked my love to take a walk / We'd only walk just a little ways." This is a Southern mountain murder ballad called "The Banks of the Ohio." It was apparent Bobby could sing as sweetly as one wanted, although he was developing another way of delivering his music. Just as Dave Van Ronk didn't have to sing in this gruff voice, but it became his best way to say, "That's who I am when I sing," it wasn't adopting a style. It was adopting an internal rightness of place.

MacDougal Street between West 3rd and
Bleecker Street, Greenwich Village, April 1961.
Photograph by John Orris

62

L–R: Bob Dylan, Peter Yarrow, Dave Van Ronk, Gerdes Folk City, early 1961. Photographer unknown

Bob Dylan, Gerdes Folk City, early 1961.
Photographer unknown

FIRST BREAK

Dylan got his first big break on April 11, 1961, when he began a two-week stint opening for bluesman John Lee Hooker at Gerdes Folk City. The gig marked the start of a rapidly ascending career that would see Dylan signed to one of the world's largest record labels within the year.

Folksinger Mark Spoelstra reminisced about that moment during a 2000 interview for *No Direction Home*:

> You walked into the door [at Gerdes] and there was a long bar—you could sit forty, fifty people maybe. There were mirrors behind the bar and a wooden separation that you could lean on to look into the dining room and the stage area. The dining room had candles on the tables and checkered tablecloths. There would always be in the window, and on the sidewalk outside, "No Charge, No Minimum" and then, written in black marker, who was performing and how long they would be performing, a week or maybe two weeks. You had to be a union musician to play there, and it was good money.
>
> You made it if you played Gerdes. If you got actually hired to play there, you were on the verge of making it. When Bob Dylan got his gig there, he got it with John Lee Hooker.
>
> I remember going up to John Lee Hooker's hotel room, which was nearby, and Bob was so excited. He wanted things to be just right. Gone was the mischievous Bob. We both were kind of mischievous. We liked to have fun. But this was serious stuff, you know? He was worried about what he was going to wear, so he was trying on my corduroy jacket, John Lee Hooker's pants, which didn't quite fit him. So we had to get a belt, and the belt didn't fit. The belt hung down about that far, but there was something about that he liked.
>
> So he was wearing partly my clothes and partly John Lee Hooker's clothes for his first big-time gig at Gerdes Folk City.

Bob Dylan, 1962. Photograph by John Cohen

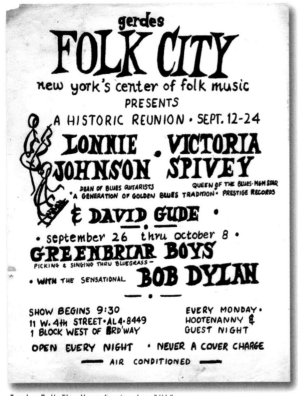

Gerdes Folk City flyer, September 1961

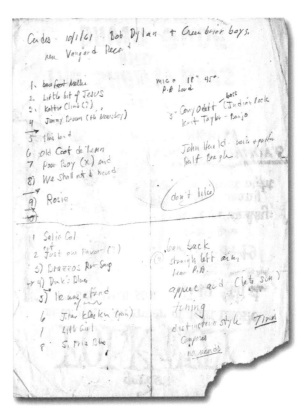

CYNTHIA GOODING

A supporter of Bob Dylan from his earliest days in the city, Cynthia Gooding was a pioneering woman in folk and world music as performer, documentarian, and radio host. In 1953, after years of travel and learning songs in the field, she began a four-year association with Elektra Records, using the opportunity to record folk songs from Turkey, Spain, England, Italy, and Mexico. Gooding expanded her efforts into radio broadcasting around 1960 and began hosting the WBAI-FM radio program out of New York City that became *Folksinger's Choice*. Some broadcasts were hour-long master classes on specific topics like Turkish folk music or bluegrass, often involving outside experts such as musician Mike Seeger or folklorist Douglas Kennedy. Other broadcasts took advantage of live recordings of artists who performed at the folk clubs and coffeehouses of Greenwich Village, including The Clancy Brothers, John Lee Hooker (in the run-up to Bob Dylan opening for him), and Jean Ritchie.

Gooding also made a number of recordings of a young Bob Dylan, including performances at Izzy Young's Folklore Center and a party at her own apartment in the Village. Her recording of Dylan at Gerdes Folk City, during his time sharing the bill with The Greenbriar Boys, represents some of the earliest audio documentation of Dylan performing in the Village. As her engineer ran audiotape, Gooding jotted down a running commentary on the performance in which she homed in on Dylan's "distinctive style." Although it is unknown whether parts of these audio recordings were subsequently broadcast on *Folksinger's Choice*, airchecks from 1962 suggest that Gooding was likely the first to play Dylan's debut album on radio, and she was likely the first broadcaster to conduct a major interview with the budding folksinger. Gooding sent a reel-to-reel copy of that interview to Columbia Records publicist Billy James, which was rediscovered in contents of the Bob Dylan Archive.

Bob Dylan, Gerdes Folk City, fall 1961. Photograph by Ted Russell

GREENWICH VILLAGE

Greenwich Village in the 1950s and early '60s was a magnet for droves of young creative and talented people who came to the city to live, work, and attend school, including Marcia Stehr, a resident of the Village since 1950. She saw Woody Guthrie perform on two occasions, and was captured in Arthur Dubinsky's famous 1954 photo of Guthrie and Ramblin' Jack Elliott performing at Washington Square Park. In the early '60s she attended art school at Cooper Union and worked as a waitress at Gerdes Folk City, providing her a front-row seat to all that was happening in the Village. Every afternoon she would head to the Café Wha? to catch Fred Neil's set, which is where she first saw Dylan perform. She married musician Mark Spoelstra in 1962, and Dylan and his girlfriend Suze Rotolo attended the wedding, as did Ramblin' Jack Elliott.

A budding photographer, Stehr captured Dylan onstage in 1961 when he was still an unknown. In a photo taken at Café Wha?, she snapped Dylan playing harmonica with Fred Neil and Mark Spoelstra. She also photographed Dylan at Gerdes accompanying his friend, the flamenco guitarist Jonathan Talbot, who performed under the stage name Juan Moreno.

Dylan later memorialized his short-lived days as a basket-house performer, and his friend Moreno, in *Chronicles*:

> *I left the Folklore Center and went back into the ice-chopping weather. Towards evening, I was over at the Mills Tavern on Bleecker Street where the basket-house singers would bunch up, chitchat and make the scene. My flamenco guitar-playing friend, Juan Moreno, told me about a new coffeehouse that had just opened on 3rd Street, called the Outré, but I was barely listening. Juan's lips were moving, but they were moving almost without sound. I'd never play in the Outré, didn't have to. I'd soon be hired to play at the Gaslight and never see the basket houses again.*

PAGE 69, TOP: L–R: Bob Dylan and Juan Moreno (Jonathan Talbot), Gerdes Folk City, early 1961

PAGE 69, BOTTOM: L–R: Fred Neil, Bob Dylan, [unidentified], Mark Spoelstra, Café Wha?, early 1961

Photographs by Marcia Stehr

Izzy Young, Folklore Center, October 1963. Photograph by David Gahr

IZZY YOUNG AND THE FOLKLORE CENTER

Born in 1928 in the Lower East Side of New York City, Izzy Young was not quite 30 years old when he opened the Folklore Center in 1957. Located at 110 MacDougal Street in Greenwich Village, the Folklore Center quickly became, in the words of Dave Van Ronk, a "clubhouse for the folk scene." In addition to selling books, records, instruments, and all manner of accessories and ephemera related to folk music, Young cultivated an environment that was warm and inviting, hosting informal get-togethers and backroom jam sessions.

In *Chronicles*, Dylan recounted the importance of Izzy Young and the Folklore Center, which Dylan called "the citadel of Americana folk music." After arriving in New York City, Dylan quickly found the Center and became a frequent visitor, so much so that Young convinced him to write a song about this Village institution. On March 19, 1962, Dylan authored "Talkin' Blues, written for the Folklore Center," also known as "Talking Folklore Center." Although Dylan apparently never performed the song live, it remains a fascinating piece of his

Bob Dylan, Folklore Center, March 1965. Photograph by David Gahr

Bob Dylan, Folklore Center, May 1962. Photograph by David Gahr

own folkloric mythology, as he signed the draft "Bob Dylan '62 of Gallup, Phillipsburg, Navasota Springs, Sioux Falls & Duluth." Young had the song printed up as a broadside bearing the Folklore Center's logo, which he sold for twenty-five cents. The Folklore Center remained an important landmark in Dylan's New York even as his music developed in the early 1960s.

In 1973, Young moved to Stockholm, Sweden, and established his Folklore Centrum. He lived there with his family until his death at age 90 on February 4, 2019. Young's papers went to the Library of Congress, and his library came to the Bob Dylan Center.

Photographer David Gahr first photographed Dylan in front of the store in May 1962, a time when Dylan was still looking and playing the part of the archetypal folksinger. In a moment of fortuitous timing, Gahr happened to be on hand once again when a leather-jacket-clad Dylan and his pal Bobby Neuwirth dropped in for a visit in March 1965, around the time of the release of Dylan's acoustic-electric hybrid album *Bringing It All Back Home*. Dylan perused the February 17, 1965, issue of *The Broadside of Boston* magazine featuring The Clara Ward Singers on the cover.

"Talking Folklore Center" sheet music, published 1962

71

BOB DYLAN

L–R: Bruce Langhorne, Carolyn Hester, Bob Dylan, Bill Lee, September 29, 1961. Photograph by Don Hunstein

Bob Dylan, Columbia Records Studio A, NYC, November 1961. Photograph by Don Hunstein

COLUMBIA RECORDS RECORDING ARTIST

On September 29, 1961, Bob Dylan arrived at Studio A of Columbia Recording Studios, not for his own session, but rather to contribute harmonica to the music of Texas folksinger Carolyn Hester. Producing the session was legendary talent scout John Hammond Sr., who, having met Dylan fifteen days earlier at a rehearsal at Hester's apartment, was already impressed with the young man's charisma and burgeoning talent.

By his own account, Hammond had been primed to sign Dylan from that initial meeting, with John Hammond Jr. and Liam Clancy (of The Clancy Brothers) roundly supporting Hammond's first impressions of Dylan. And it certainly didn't hurt that on the morning of the Hester session, *The New York Times* ran Robert Shelton's glowing review of Dylan's recent performances supporting The Greenbriar Boys at Gerdes Folk City. Shelton wrote, "But if not for every taste, his music-making has the mark of originality and inspiration, all the more noteworthy for his youth. Mr. Dylan is vague about his antecedents and birthplace, but it matters less where he has been than where he is going, and that would seem to be straight up."

Immediately after the session, Hammond, having already had the young folksinger audition for Columbia A&R head Mitch Miller, brought Dylan up to his office to sign Columbia's standard five-year contract.

John Hammond's decision to sign Dylan caused controversy, as his rough-edged sound cut against the polished brand that Columbia had established for itself with artists such as Frankie Laine, Rosemary Clooney, Johnny Mathis, and Doris Day. Yet the man who helped launch the careers of Billie Holiday, Benny Goodman, and Aretha Franklin (and later Bruce Springsteen and Stevie Ray Vaughan) remained steadfast in his belief in Dylan's talents.

Recorded on November 20 and 22, 1961, the resulting self-titled debut album did little to dispel Dylan's reputation as "Hammond's Folly." Upon its release on March 19, 1962, *Bob Dylan* received little critical notice or commercial sales. Yet it was a start. Dylan was now recording for one of the largest and most important record companies in the world. And amid the traditional folk, blues, and gospel songs that populated Dylan's first album, there was a hint of what was to come: two self-penned originals, "Talkin' New York" and "Song to Woody."

Bob Dylan, Columbia Records Studio A, NYC,
November 1961. Photograph by Don Hunstein

Victoria Spivey business card,
given to Bob Dylan

TEL. (212). UL 7-7003
7736839
VICTORIA SPIVEY
ORIGINAL SPIVEY RECORD PRODUCTIONS
COMPOSER - VOCALIST - PIANIST - ORGANIST - UKE

BLUES IS MY BUSINESS

65 GRAND AVENUE
BROOKLYN, N. Y. 11205

Bob Dylan holding Big Joe Williams's guitar with Victoria Spivey, Cue Recording Studios, NYC, March 2, 1962. Photographer unknown

EARLY SESSIONS

Many of Dylan's earliest recording sessions found him fulfilling a musical role that he'd expertly learned in the coffeehouses of Greenwich Village (and anticipating one that he'd reprise in future guest appearances): adding his distinctive harmonica to others' music.

Singer Victoria Spivey earned her title of blues queen in the 1920s and 1930s, writing songs like "Black Snake Moan," "T. B. Blues," and "You Done Lost Your Good Thing Now" and performing and recording with the likes of Blind Lemon Jefferson, King Oliver, Louis Armstrong, Memphis Minnie, Tampa Red, and Bessie Smith. Spivey continued to perform throughout the Great Depression, becoming a successful film and stage actress, and was featured in the historic all-Black film *Hallelujah!* in 1929. Although her career ebbed in the 1940s, she began to perform again in the 1950s, setting the stage for a second act in the 1960s.

In 1962 she co-founded Spivey Records, and that March, "Queen Victoria" (as she was nicknamed) hired Bob Dylan to play harmonica and sing back-up vocals for her album *Three Kings and the Queen*—the "three kings" being Big Joe Williams, Lonnie Johnson, and Roosevelt Sykes. Dylan never forgot that session, and for the back cover of his 1970 *New Morning* album, Dylan chose a photo that had been taken during the session of himself standing next to the queen. "I knew that this photo would be on the cover even before I recorded the songs," he later wrote in *Chronicles*.

Just a month earlier in February 1962, Dylan had performed on folksinger, movie star, and progressive activist Harry Belafonte's arrangement of the folk song "Midnight Special." Even though Dylan had recorded previously as a sideman with Carolyn Hester, and the sessions for his own first album had been completed the previous November, the release of "Midnight Special," on an album of the same name, was the first time the world would hear any music featuring Bob Dylan. As Dylan recalled in *Chronicles*,

> *Strangely enough this was the only one memorable recording date that would stand out in my mind for years to come.... With Belafonte I felt like I'd become anointed in some kind of way.*

University of Michigan Folk Festival poster, April 1962

UNIVERSITY OF MICHIGAN FOLK FESTIVAL, 1962

In the first years of his career, Dylan traveled the folk circuit as he made a name for himself—or at least tried to, as this poster from the 1962 University of Michigan Folk Festival reveals. An ad in the *Michigan Daily* student newspaper made a similar mistake. However, after he played the Union Ballroom on April 22, Dylan had made enough of an impression that the paper issued a correction, noting, "The *Michigan Daily* would like to point out that the folk singer who played at the Michigan Union on April 22 bears the surname of a well-known poet [Dylan Thomas], not that of a well-known marshal [Matt Dillon of the TV show *Gunsmoke*]. The *Daily* wishes to apologize for this unfortunate error."

Collecting and Connecting Woody and Bob

BARRY OLLMAN

My collecting life began when my dad wound up in an elevator with all five of The Rolling Stones. It was June of 1964, and I was at school, fourth grade I believe, and I desperately wanted to be with him as he photographed their Milwaukee press conference for *Billboard Magazine*. After the event he got all five of their autographs on a single page to give to me as a consolation for making me spend the day in school, missing my chance to meet one of the hottest bands in the world. I was about to turn 11 and I was not happy.

That signed page, along with some great photographs and 4×5-inch negatives, became the cornerstone of my original collection, along with signatures of The Smothers Brothers, Carlos Montoya, various Milwaukee Braves players, and separately, in its own little plastic case, a few hairs from the head of Ringo Starr. It was all in a small box in my bedroom along with a modest but evocative coin collection. Fifteen years later, my folks sold the house that my brothers and I grew up in, and I had moved to Colorado. On my first visit home to their new condo, that box was conspicuously missing, and it haunted me.

Jumping ahead a few years, I made a life-changing discovery: there were people who actually bought and sold this sort of stuff for a living. A little light went on in my head, and everything changed.

I had a bit of money, enough to buy an autograph book signed by The Beatles and a number of other British Invasion bands, $400 I recall, about what I was paying for the mortgage payment on my first house. My thinking, then as now, was that my $400 is the same as your $400, but you don't have anything even remotely similar to this autograph book I just bought! Over time I learned to focus on those handwritten items that sparked a certain passion in me. Lincoln, Steinbeck, Einstein, Jimi Hendrix, and, yes, those same Rolling Stones, part of my futile attempt to fill that unfillable hole.

Seven years later I had a chance to buy a very charming self-portrait drawn by the great Woody Guthrie. I called the issuer of the catalog I saw it in, but it had just been sold! I nearly begged the dealer to ask the new owner-to-be if he'd consider reselling it for a reasonable profit, and following no less than two years of negotiations with an eccentric collector in Chicago, it was mine.

Woody Guthrie! I knew a few of his songs, "This Land Is Your Land," "Riding in My Car," but he somehow seemed to be more of a mythological character. Think Johnny Appleseed who, as it turns out, was a real person as well. By that time, Bob Dylan loomed large in my mind, right up there with The Beatles, but didn't he have a Woody Guthrie connection? This was pre-internet, so I dragged out Anthony Scaduto's Dylan biography and found a paperback of Joe Klein's *Woody Guthrie: A Life*. There it was, plain as day. Their stories were riveting, and I knew what I wanted to do. I would collect all things Guthrie, including his close circle, which to me meant Lead Belly, Pete Seeger, and The Weavers, and, of course, Bob Dylan. But where to begin?

I started by tearing through Klein's book and making note of people who had known Woody personally. Any reference to where they lived was gold. I dialed "Information" in Los Angeles, New York, Nevada, Tennessee, Texas, Oklahoma, and more. Slowly, Woody's world began to open to me. I went to used bookstores, told them I was collecting autograph material, and asked if they had anything related to Woody Guthrie. Fortunately, most of those people looked at me like I was sort of goofy, and all with the same sly grin, offered to sell me their own autograph. That's actually how I knew I was on to something! They didn't get it. It was 1987, and markets for such "pop culture" items were inefficient and not well established. I felt strongly that I had a window of time before the world would certainly catch up to me. Woody was pretty much at the root of the tree that fed into all the music I loved. I knew it, and it seemed to me that others didn't. How was this possible? To me, it didn't really matter, and I got to work. This felt like a creative and challenging pursuit, and I let my mind wander.

"Song to Woody" draft manuscript

Some things came easy, and others took months and more money than I could put my hands on. The inscribed first edition of *Bound for Glory* that I found in a Denver bookstore for $250 helped balance out the one I paid $3,000 for in Manhattan. The colorful 1936 oil painting, signed W. Guthrie, looked nearly black and white from years of cigarette smoke exposure until I had it professionally cleaned. The result was stunning. You can see it on the cover of Woody's novel, *House of Earth*, first published by HarperCollins in the 100th anniversary year of Woody's birth, 2012.

One thing I've learned along the way: if someone had received a letter from Woody, they may well have received five or even ten! I've gone through a number of those wonderful shoeboxes over the years. His old friends, who I loved meeting, knew those letters were special enough to set aside and keep, but ultimately, they didn't really know what to do with them. Many expressed being happy that I showed up, with seriousness of purpose and a checkbook. I listened well and soaked up their stories. Some of them introduced me to their friends who had also known Woody.

For instance, in 1987, I ran a classified ad seeking Guthrie memorabilia in the local newspaper in Pampa, Texas. Woody had lived there after leaving his hometown of Okemah, Oklahoma, and the ad yielded exactly one reply. The call came from a gentleman named Matt Jennings, the brother of Woody's first wife, Mary. We spoke for more than an hour, and he was delightful. I think he sensed my sincerity as he gave me the contact information for the daughter of Cluster and Jewel Baker. In the 1930s, Cluster had been the third member of The Corncob Trio, along with Woody and Matt. The group played for weddings, dances, and anyone willing to listen. A small press clipping from the time said that they played harmonica, Jew's harp, banjo, and guitar and that they would be playing on the radio the next afternoon, followed by a wrestling match in Amarillo. It went on to say that they "will probably play *during* the match"!

BARRY OLLMAN

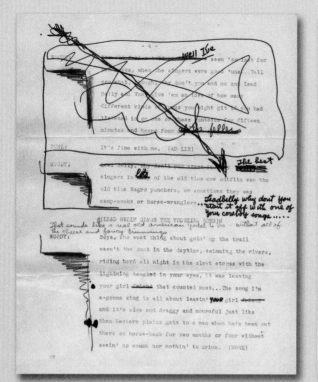

Radio script for Alan Lomax and Nicholas Ray's 1940–41 radio show, *Back Where I Come From*, annotated by Woody Guthrie

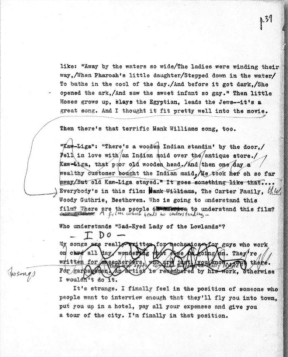

Transcription of December 18, 1977, *Rolling Stone* interview with Jonathan Cott, annotated by Bob Dylan

Fortunately for me, their daughter lived nearby in Colorado at that time, and after a year and many conversations, she brought her mother's small but wonderful collection up from Santa Fe to see if I would be interested. This included the aforementioned painting, one that they had held onto since Woody had originally given it to them in the late 1930s. There was more, but Woody's Santa Fe painting, *In El Rancho Grande*, stands out as being unique in Woody's artistic output. After I acquired these items, Jewel unexpectedly introduced me to Mary Guthrie, Woody's first wife, who also had a box of Woody's things with nowhere to go. Mary wrote a letter to Jewel, also in my collection, asking her to let me contact her. We spoke, and I flew to Los Angeles, returning with another important archive, including the earliest items in my Guthrie collection.

Interestingly, a number of close-in Woody people had originally thought of Dylan as a young upstart, one of many wannabes along the way. Whether or not they had met Bob, he was clearly next generation and therefore somewhat suspect. Slowly, I began to be offered interesting Dylan material, and while my Dylan collection is relatively small compared to Guthrie, everything in it is, to me, quite incredible.

One of the first Dylan items I bought was a lengthy, typed interview transcript from the late '70s on which Bob made notes, and there's a particular paragraph around which he drew a rectangle with a distinctive arrow through the middle. I couldn't help but notice that it looks strikingly similar to a 1940 typed CBS radio transcript, eleven pages, that I found in an old trunk in Tennessee, where Woody himself had drawn a box around a paragraph with a very similar arrow through it. A coincidence, of course, nearly forty years apart and never seen by Bob, but I've learned to spot such occurrences and pay attention.

Another Bob moment . . .

One day Harold Leventhal, by then a great friend and an important connection between Woody and Bob, called me and said that Sotheby's wanted to auction his hand-painted poster that had sat in the glass case outside New York's Town Hall for Dylan's first major concert, produced by Harold himself on April 12, 1963. Was I interested? Why, yes, as a matter of fact I was! We made a deal on the phone and as soon as I hung up, I suddenly wondered if there may have actually been two glass cases at a place the size of Town Hall. I called him back and asked if there might be two of these posters? He said, "Are you kidding? It's hand-painted. I couldn't afford this one!"

Other wonderful things happened. One evening in Tulsa at an art opening, I bumped into Phil Buehler, who had recently written and published one of the most fascinating, as well as one of my favorite, books on Guthrie, *Wardy Forty*. He told me that in the course of his research, he had met the son of Bob Gleason, who had inherited, among other powerful items, Dylan's handwritten manuscript for "Song to Woody." Bob and Sid Gleason were the couple who famously picked Woody up at the hospital every Sunday and brought him to their home in East Orange, New Jersey, to give him a break from the madness and a weekly afternoon of musical nourishment with whichever of his friends could make it over; Pete Seeger, Ramblin' Jack Elliott, Cisco Houston, John Cohen, and many others, as well as a young and new to the East Coast Bob Dylan, were regulars. I contacted the gentleman and a couple of visits later, one in Denver and one in Los Angeles, and that wonderful piece of connective tissue between Bob and Woody had found a new home.

Now that their massive paper trails have landed in the same block in Woody's home state of Oklahoma, I've had a chance to expand my own understanding of their collective force. The threads and connections are everywhere. These two people are wildly different individuals, fiercely independent and to me, nearly otherworldly. Certainly, of a different age and era. Like my own father, neither spent a lot of their creative time far from a typewriter, pen, or pencil. Both visual artists as well, painting from their experience and inner visions. Each one, relentless and self-motivated. The fact that they met and became friends at the end of Woody's journey and the beginning of Bob's fascinates me in much the same way that the origin story of The Beatles does. How did these things happen?

Having had the chance to handle and live with the papers and artworks of these two artists over many years has given me a combination of respect and near disbelief for their rigor and focus.

In 1946, for instance, Woody Guthrie did not seem to sleep. An unusual concentration of items in my own Guthrie collection, which for the most part spans 1935 to 1960, as well as watercolors and writings in the Smithsonian Folklife Collections, comes from that year. Lengthy correspondences, diaries, essays, and artworks seemingly created at any time of the day or night are shocking in their beauty, originality, humor, and clarity. In 1940, at the age of 34, with only another ten, or at most fifteen, creative years ahead, he wrote "This Land," a little more than a year before Dylan's birth. He had already written hundreds of songs. And one can easily make the case that Dylan, then in his early 20s, barely slept from 1961 to 1966. Blessed with apparent good health and stamina, unlike his friend and early mentor, Dylan has an output that has come in waves, very large and powerful waves. Now in his 80s, he continues to produce hundreds of paintings and elaborate metalworks, as well as writing, recording, and touring with new music that holds up beautifully within his singular catalog.

The painting by Woody that I bought all those years ago has been on loan to Tulsa's Woody Guthrie Center since it opened in 2013, and I'm told that a few years back when Mr. Dylan walked through the Center, he paused for a long moment in front of that painting and said something to the effect of "Woody painted that?"

As I said, the threads and connections are everywhere, plain to see.

Bob Dylan at the Singers Club Christmas party in London, during his first visit to the UK, December 22, 1962. Photograph by Brian Shuel

THE FREEWHEELIN' BOB DYLAN

The Freewheelin' Bob Dylan promotional LP, with early, alternate track listing, 1963

Unknown to even the most hardcore Dylan collectors prior to the Bob Dylan Archive's announcement of their acquisition, the Milton ("Mell") and Lillian Bailey Collection includes more than a half-dozen open-reel audiotapes of Dylan performing in various settings throughout 1961 and 1962. Mell and Lillian Bailey, noted folk-music and calypso enthusiasts, were friends of Dylan's and early champions of his music. Their apartment at 185 3rd Street served as a sort of salon for Greenwich Village's vibrant folk-music scene. Their intimate, private parties attracted the likes of Paul Clayton, Ramblin' Jack Elliott, Cynthia Gooding, Ian & Sylvia, Bruce Langhorne, Tom Paxton, Dave Van Ronk, and Dylan himself.

Oftentimes, the Baileys would record the informal proceedings on their Wollensak tape recorder, providing a glimpse into Dylan's social milieu and his development as a songwriter. One tape made at the Baileys' apartment in 1962 includes the first-known recordings of "Oxford Town" and "Don't Think Twice, It's All Right," which would soon be featured on Dylan's breakthrough album, *The Freewheelin' Bob Dylan*. In addition, the Baileys recorded Dylan's first major headlining performance at Carnegie Chapter Hall on November 4, 1961, as well as pivotal folk-music broadcasts off the radio from New York City stations WBAI and WRVR. One of those is an aircheck of the July 29, 1961, "Saturday of Folk Music" hootenanny at Harlem's Riverside Church, where Dylan first met his future girlfriend Suze Rotolo, who would later appear alongside him on the cover of *The Freewheelin' Bob Dylan*.

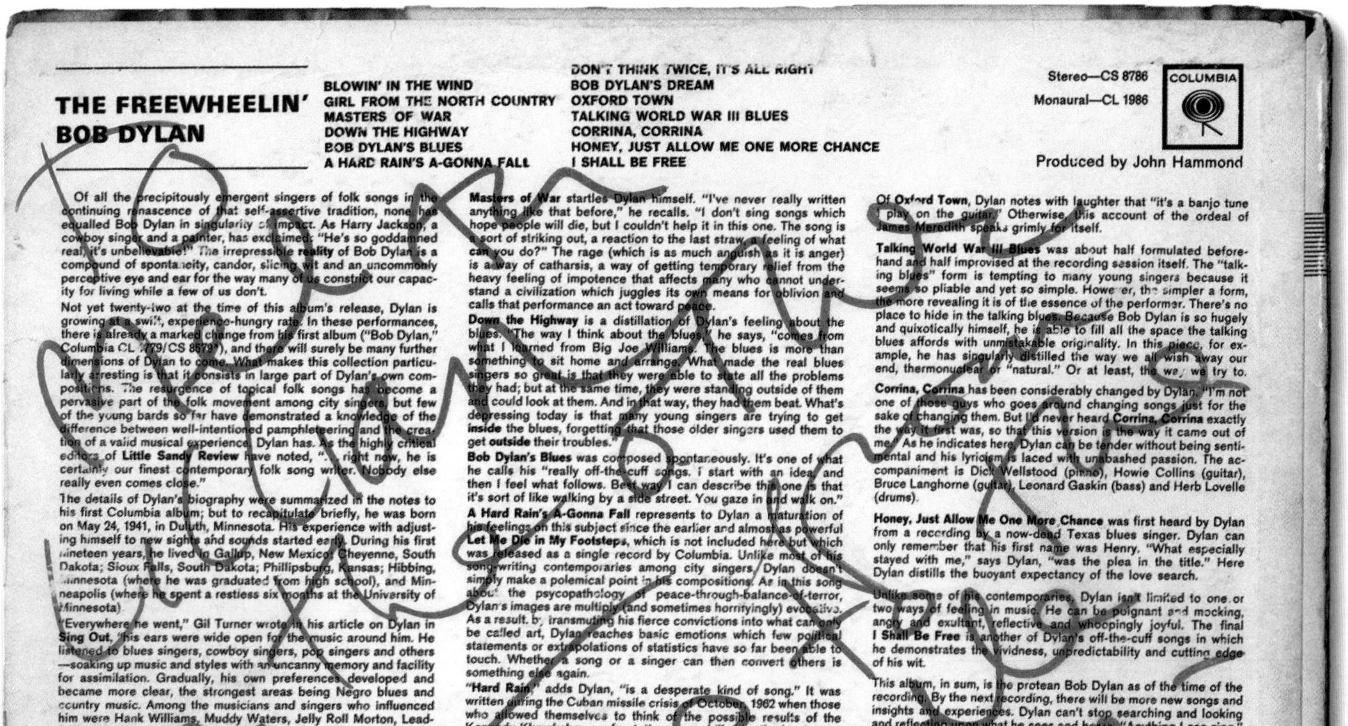

THE FREEWHEELIN' BOB DYLAN

BLOWIN' IN THE WIND
GIRL FROM THE NORTH COUNTRY
MASTERS OF WAR
DOWN THE HIGHWAY
BOB DYLAN'S BLUES
A HARD RAIN'S A-GONNA FALL

DON'T THINK TWICE, IT'S ALL RIGHT
BOB DYLAN'S DREAM
OXFORD TOWN
TALKING WORLD WAR III BLUES
CORRINA, CORRINA
HONEY, JUST ALLOW ME ONE MORE CHANCE
I SHALL BE FREE

Stereo—CS 8786
Monaural—CL 1986

COLUMBIA

Produced by John Hammond

Of all the precipitously emergent singers of folk songs in the continuing renascence of that self-assertive tradition, none has equalled Bob Dylan in singularity of impact. As Harry Jackson, a cowboy singer and a painter, has exclaimed: "He's so goddamned real, it's unbelievable!" The irrepressible reality of Bob Dylan is a compound of spontaneity, candor, slicing wit and an uncommonly perceptive eye and ear for the way many of us constrict our capacity for living while a few of us don't.

Not yet twenty-two at the time of this album's release, Dylan is growing at a swift, experience-hungry rate. In these performances, there is already a marked change from his first album ("Bob Dylan," Columbia CL 1779/CS 8579), and there will surely be many further dimensions of Dylan to come. What makes this collection particularly arresting is that it consists in large part of Dylan's own compositions. The resurgence of topical folk songs has become a pervasive part of the folk movement among city singers, but few of the young bards so far have demonstrated a knowledge of the difference between well-intentioned pamphleteering and the creation of a valid musical experience. Dylan has. As the highly critical editors of Little Sandy Review have noted, "... right now, he is certainly our finest contemporary folk song writer. Nobody else really even comes close."

The details of Dylan's biography were summarized in the notes to his first Columbia album; but to recapitulate briefly, he was born on May 24, 1941, in Duluth, Minnesota. His experience with adjusting himself to new sights and sounds started early. During his first nineteen years, he lived in Gallup, New Mexico; Cheyenne, South Dakota; Sioux Falls, South Dakota; Phillipsburg, Kansas; Hibbing, Minnesota (where he was graduated from high school), and Minneapolis (where he spent a restless six months at the University of Minnesota)

"Everywhere he went," Gil Turner wrote in his article on Dylan in Sing Out, "his ears were wide open for the music around him. He listened to blues singers, cowboy singers, pop singers and others —soaking up music and styles with an uncanny memory and facility for assimilation. Gradually, his own preferences developed and became more clear, the strongest areas being Negro blues and country music. Among the musicians and singers who influenced him were Hank Williams, Muddy Waters, Jelly Roll Morton, Leadbelly, Mance Lipscomb and Big Joe Williams." And, above all others, Woody Guthrie. At ten, he was playing guitar, and by the age of fifteen, Dylan had taught himself piano, harmonica and autoharp.

In February, 1961 Dylan came East, primarily to visit Woody Guthrie at the Greystone Hospital in New Jersey. The visits have continued, and Guthrie has expressed approval of Dylan's first album, being particularly fond of the "Song to Woody" in it. By September of 1961, Dylan's singing in Greenwich Village, especially at Gerdes Folk City, had ignited a nucleus of singers and a few critics (notably Bob Shelton of the New York Times) into exuberant appreciation of his work. Since then, Dylan has inexorably increased the scope of his American audiences while also performing briefly in London and Rome.

The first of Dylan's songs in this set is Blowin' in the Wind. In 1962, Dylan said of the song's background: "I still say that some of the biggest criminals are those that turn their heads away when they see wrong and know it's wrong. I'm only 21 years old and I know that there's been too many wars ... You people over 21 should know better." All he prefers to add by way of commentary now is: "The first way to answer these questions in the song is by asking them. But lots of people have to first find the wind." On this track, and except when otherwise noted, Dylan is heard alone—accompanying himself on guitar and harmonica.

Girl from the North Country was first conceived by Bob Dylan about three years before he finally wrote it down in December, 1962. "That often happens," he explains. "I carry a song in my head for a long time and then it comes bursting out." The song—and Dylan's performance—reflect his particular kind of lyricism. The mood is a fusion of yearning, poignancy and simple appreciation of a beautiful girl. Dylan illuminates all these corners of his vision, but simultaneously retains his bristling sense of self. He's not about to go begging anything from this girl up north.

Masters of War startles Dylan himself. "I've never really written anything like that before," he recalls. "I don't sing songs which hope people will die, but I couldn't help it in this one. The song is sort of striking out, a reaction to the last straw, a feeling of what can you do?" The rage (which is as much anguish as it is anger) is a way of catharsis, a way of getting temporary relief from the heavy feeling of impotence that affects many who cannot understand a civilization which juggles its own means for oblivion and calls that performance an act toward peace.

Down the Highway is a distillation of Dylan's feeling about the blues. "The way I think about the blues," he says, "comes from what I learned from Big Joe Williams. The blues is more than something to sit home and arrange. What made the real blues singers so great is that they were able to state all the problems they had; but at the same time, they were standing outside of them and could look at them. And in that way, they had them beat. What's depressing today is that many young singers are trying to get inside the blues, forgetting that those older singers used them to get outside their troubles."

Bob Dylan's Blues was composed spontaneously. It's one of what he calls his "really off-the-cuff songs. I start with an idea, and then I feel what follows. Best way I can describe this one is that it's sort of like walking by a side street. You gaze in and walk on."

A Hard Rain's A-Gonna Fall represents in Dylan a maturation of his feelings on this subject since the earlier and almost as powerful Let Me Die in My Footsteps, which is not included here but which was released as a single record by Columbia. Unlike most of his songwriting contemporaries among city singers, Dylan doesn't simply make a polemical point in his compositions. As in this song about the psycopathology of peace-through-balance-of-terror, Dylan's images are multiple (and sometimes horrifyingly) evocative. As a result, by transmuting his fierce convictions into what can only be called art, Dylan reaches basic emotions which few political statements or extrapolations of statistics have so far been able to touch. Whether a song or a singer can then convert others is something else again.

"Hard Rain" adds Dylan, "is a desperate kind of song." It was written during the Cuban missile crisis of October, 1962 when those who allowed themselves to think of the possible results of the Kennedy-Khrushchev confrontation were chilled by the imminence of oblivion. "Every line in it," says Dylan, "is actually the start of a whole song. But when I wrote it, I thought I wouldn't have enough time alive to write all those songs so I put all I could into this one." Dylan treats Don't Think Twice, It's All Right differently from most city singers. "A lot of people," he says, "make it sort of a love song —slow and easy-going. But it isn't a love song. It's a statement that maybe you can say to make yourself feel better. It's as if you were talking to yourself. It's a hard song to sing. I can sing it sometimes, but I ain't that good yet. I don't carry myself yet the way that Big Joe Williams, Woody Guthrie, Leadbelly and Lightnin' Hopkins have carried themselves. I hope to be able to someday, but they're older people. I sometimes am able to do it, but it happens, when it happens, unconsciously. You see, in time, with those older singers, music was a tool—a way to live more, a way to make themselves feel better at certain points. As for me, I can make myself feel better some times, but at other times, it's still hard to go to sleep at night." Dylan's accompaniment on this track includes Bruce Langhorne (guitar), George Barnes (bass guitar), Dick Wellstood (piano), Gene Ramey (bass), and Herb Lovelle (drums).

Bob Dylan's Dream is another of his songs which was transported for a time in his mind before being written down. It was initially set off after an all-night conversation between Dylan and Oscar Brown, Jr. in Greenwich Village. "Oscar," says Dylan, "is a groovy guy and the idea of this came from what we were talking about." The song slumbered, however, until Dylan went to England in the winter of 1962. There he heard a singer (whose name he recalls as Martin Carthy) perform Lord Franklin, and that old melody found a new adapted home in Bob Dylan's Dream. The song is a fond looking back at the easy camaraderie and idealism of the young when they are young. There is also in the Dream a wry but sad requiem for the friendships that have evaporated—specific routes, geographical or otherwise, are taken.

Of Oxford Town, Dylan notes with laughter that "it's a banjo tune —play on the guitar." Otherwise, this account of the ordeal of James Meredith speaks grimly for itself.

Talking World War III Blues was about half formulated beforehand and half improvised at the recording session itself. The "talking blues" form is tempting to many young singers because it seems so pliable and yet so simple. However, the simpler a form, the more revealing it is of the essence of the performer. There's no place to hide in the talking blues. Because Bob Dylan is so hugely and quixotically himself, he is able to fill all the space the talking blues affords with unmistakable originality. In this piece, for example, he has singularly distilled the way we all wish away our end, thermonuclear or "natural." Or at least, the way we try to.

Corrina, Corrina has been considerably changed by Dylan. "I'm not one of those guys who goes around changing songs just for the sake of changing them. But I'd never heard Corrina, Corrina exactly the way it first was, so that this version is the way it came out of me." As he indicates here, Dylan can be tender without being sentimental and his lyricism is laced with unabashed passion. The accompaniment is Dick Wellstood (piano), Howie Collins (guitar), Bruce Langhorne (guitar), Leonard Gaskin (bass) and Herb Lovelle (drums).

Honey, Just Allow Me One More Chance was first heard by Dylan from a recording by a now-dead Texas blues singer. Dylan can only remember that his first name was Henry. "What especially stayed with me," says Dylan, "was the plea in the title." Here Dylan distills the buoyant expectancy of the love search.

Unlike some of his contemporaries, Dylan isn't limited to one or two ways of feeling in music. He can be poignant and mocking, angry and exultant, reflective and whoopingly joyful. The final I Shall Be Free is another of Dylan's off-the-cuff songs in which he demonstrates the vividness, unpredictability and cutting edge of his wit.

This album, in sum, is the protean Bob Dylan as of the time of the recording. By the next recording, there will be more new songs and insights and experiences. Dylan can't stop searching and looking and reflecting upon what he sees and hears. "Anything I can sing," he observes, "I call a song. Anything I can't sing, I call a poem. Anything I can't sing or anything that's too long to be a poem, I call a novel. But my novels don't have the usual story-lines. They're about my feelings at a certain place at a certain time."

In addition to his singing and song writing, Dylan is working on three "novels." One is about the week before he first came to New York and his initial week in that city. Another is about South Dakota people he knew. And the third is about New York and a trip from New York to New Orleans.

Throughout everything he writes and sings, there is the surge of a young man looking into as many diverse scenes and people as he can find ("Every once in a while I got to ramble around") and of a man looking into himself. "The most important thing I know I learned from Woody Guthrie," says Dylan. "I'm my own person. I've got basic common sense—whether I'm here in this country or any other place. I'll never finish saying everything I feel, but I'll be doing my part to make some sense out of the way we're living, and not living, now. All I'm doing is saying what's on my mind the best way I know how. And whatever else you say about me, everything I do and sing and write comes out of me."

It is this continuing explosion of a total individual, a young man growing free rather than absurd, that makes Bob Dylan so powerful and so personal and so important a singer. As you can hear in these performances.

NAT HENTOFF

Mr. Hentoff is a frequent contributor to such periodicals as "The Reporter," "The New Yorker," "Playboy," "Commonweal" and "The Village Voice," and is a Contributing Editor to Stereo Review."

COVER PHOTO: DON HUNSTEIN   © "COLUMBIA" [MARCAS] REG. PRINTED IN U.S.A. © COLUMBIA RECORDS 1963/ALL RIGHTS RESERVED

DEMONSTRATION NOT FOR SALE

Back side of *The Freewheelin' Bob Dylan* promotional LP, with Dylan's inscription to Mell and Lillian Bailey

"Blowin' in the Wind" sheet music, 1963

A WAY OF LIFE

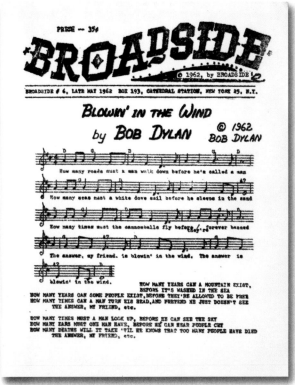

Broadside magazine, May 1962

"BLOWIN' IN THE WIND"

Upon its release on May 27, 1963, *The Freewheelin' Bob Dylan* demonstrated the budding songwriter's distinctive talents with songs like "Girl from the North Country," "Masters of War," and "A Hard Rain's A-Gonna Fall," which remain timeless classics forming the bedrock of Dylan's reputation. However, the song that cemented Dylan's place in the pantheon of political folksingers stretching back to Woody Guthrie was the album's leadoff track, "Blowin' in the Wind."

Dylan's masterpiece had a life before and after the release of *Freewheelin'*, however. In May 1962, he performed the song on Izzy Young's radio program *The Broadside Show* on WBAI-FM. Agnes "Sis" Cunningham—who, along with her husband Gordon Friesen, founded the small-run, mimeographed *Broadside Magazine* that year—transcribed the lyrics from that broadcast and published them on the cover of their May issue, the first of many Dylan songs they published.

Meanwhile in June 1963, just weeks after the release of Dylan's own version of "Blowin' in the Wind," Peter, Paul and Mary released a cover version of the song that became a massive success. It became the centerpiece of their third album, *In the Wind*, released in October of that year. The album featured two other Dylan songs, "Don't Think Twice, It's All Right," and "Quit Your Low Down Ways," and Dylan himself wrote the album's liner notes, using the occasion to recall the halcyon days of a rapidly changing Greenwich Village folk scene.

Dylan never forgot the importance of this moment to his career, recalling it in his 2015 MusiCares acceptance speech:

> *I also have to mention some of the early artists who recorded my songs very, very early, without having to be asked. Just something they felt about them that was right for them. I've got to say thank you to Peter, Paul and Mary, who I knew all separately before they ever became a group. I didn't even think of myself as writing songs for others to sing but it was starting to happen and it couldn't have happened to, or with, a better group.*
>
> *They took a song of mine that had been recorded before that was buried on one of my records and turned it into a hit song. Not the way I would have done it—they straightened it out. But since then hundreds of people have recorded it and I don't think that would have happened if it wasn't for them. They definitely started something for me.*

Bob Dylan, Gramercy Park, NYC, 1963. Photograph by Ralph Baxter

DYLAN'S NEW YORK

In 1963, Bob Dylan was photographed with girlfriend Suze Rotolo around Gramercy Park. As a New York City native, Rotolo was one of Dylan's early guides to the city's vibrant cultural scene. In 2004, Rotolo was interviewed for the documentary *No Direction Home* and offered a typical night for the pair:

> First, you'd wander around from place to place. You could start at Gerdes Folk City, then go to the Gaslight and see who was playing there. And then at the Village Gate, there was jazz. We'd go there. At the Bitter End, there was maybe somebody doing stand-up. Then you could even go over to the Five Spot, which is an old jazz club that had already moved, and then it was on St. Marks Place. But you'd make this round. It wasn't just folk music. It was music, and poetry readings, and stand-up comedy, and offbeat stuff that later became performance art, you know. It was all boiling; there was all this going on.
>
> So we'd go to all these different places, and hook up with other people and then you'd end up at Sam Wo's in Chinatown and eat. Then everybody would go back to [folksinger Dave] Van Ronk's house. And he lived on Waverly Place, and he'd put a stack of LPs on his turntable because he was the commander of what music you'd listen to. Then we would play poker. We'd sit around this big table, under a haze of smoke, and whatever it was we were drinking and nod our brows over debts and poker bets and nickels and dimes. All night.

PAGE 86: Bob Dylan and Suze Rotolo, Gramercy Park, NYC, 1963. Photograph by Ralph Baxter

On Mojo

I t all started fifty years ago, when I traded a grocery bag full of baseball cards for a friend's copy of *Smash Hits* by The Jimi Hendrix Experience. Pretty quickly, record collecting became my all-consuming passion. Since that fateful day, I've spent tens of thousands of hours (and a *lot* of money) tracking down rare records and music memorabilia, trying to capture just a tiny bit of the mojo of my favorite artists.

And mojo is exactly why I collect records that were owned by my musical heroes.

Owning the actual vinyl records that my favorite artists listened to and obsessed over, the albums that inspired some of the greatest musicians—and music—of all time, feels like the closest I'll ever get to these mythic beings. I have records from the collections of Jimi Hendrix, members of The Beatles, Rolling Stones, Velvet Underground, and happily, Bob Dylan.

Among my most treasured possessions are two blues albums Dylan owned in the early '60s, *Blues Fell This Morning: Rare Recordings of Southern Blues Singers*, and *Country Blues: Blind Boy Fuller 1935–1940*. As you might imagine, finding and authenticating this kind of thing can be near impossible. These albums, however, came with extraordinary provenance: they were sold at auction by Dylan's girlfriend in the early '60s, Suze Rotolo (that's her walking alongside Bob on the cover of *The Freewheelin' Bob Dylan*). And even better, Dylan added his own handwritten inscriptions to both album covers.

What might we learn about this notoriously private artist from two albums he owned nearly sixty years ago? More than you might think.

First, though, a caveat. While appraising the Bob Dylan Archive, I examined over five thousand items Dylan had written, from jottings on the back of business cards to manuscripts for some of his most famous songs. Dylan seems to have always been writing, sometimes lyrics, but often making lists, or notes to himself, as if he were processing things he'd read or was thinking about. His writings were sometimes oblique, but the constant editing and revising left me with the distinct impression that he knew exactly what he was after. My main takeaway: despite the never-ending stream of books about Dylan, it's a fool's errand for anyone to think they know what's going on in this man's extraordinary mind.

Let's start with some facts.

Dylan the folksinger arrived in New York in January 1961; once there, his exposure to—and interest in—the blues increased significantly. His New York circle included blues enthusiasts Dave Van Ronk and Mark Spoelstra, and before long, he was opening for blues giant John Lee Hooker and sharing stages with blues singers Brother John Sellers, Big Joe Williams, Lonnie Johnson, and Victoria Spivey.

Sometime in late 1961, the legendary record producer John Hammond, who had signed Dylan to Columbia Records, gave Dylan an acetate of the not-yet-released Robert Johnson compilation *King of the Delta Blues Singers*. Dylan had never heard of Johnson, and wrote at length in his memoir *Chronicles* about the huge impact Johnson's 1930s recordings had on him: "From the first note, the vibrations on the loudspeaker made my hair stand up. . . . I fixated on every song and wondered how Johnson did it. Songwriting for him was some sophisticated business."

ON MOJO 1961–1964   **88**

Bob Dylan's annotated Blind Boy Fuller
LP, circa 1963

Dylan recorded his debut album in November 1961; the songs were mostly standards, some of which were originally performed by artists on the two blues albums from his collection. *Blues Fell This Morning* and *Country Blues: Blind Boy Fuller* are both collections of 78s recorded between 1927 and 1940. Both are British pressings, compiled and annotated by English blues historian Paul Oliver, and issued in 1960 and 1962 respectively.

Dylan listened to these records a lot—we know this from the scuffed-up surfaces. He owned them during the time he lived with Rotolo, from 1962 to 1964, and left them with her after their breakup. He was clearly affected by both the music and the liner notes on these albums, making notations on the back covers of each. (Rotolo told me Dylan wrote these notes as one might make notes to oneself in the margins of a book.)

Blues Fell This Morning features a number of Dylan-related artists and songs, including "When the Levee Breaks" by Kansas Joe and Memphis Minnie, the jumping-off point for Dylan's "The Levee's Gonna Break" from his 2006 album *Modern Times*. The duo also recorded "Can I Do It for You," a song that evolved (with help from Blind Boy Fuller, also represented here) into "Baby, Let Me Follow You Down," which Dylan recorded for his debut album. Also represented is Bukka White, whose "Fixin' to Die" also appears on Dylan's first album. There's a track by Peg Leg Howell, whose "Rocks and Gravel Blues" Dylan recorded during the sessions for his second album, *The Freewheelin' Bob Dylan*. Finally, there's a song by Texas Alexander with guitar by Lonnie Johnson—decades later, Johnson gave Dylan guitar tips when they played together in Greenwich Village.

Now let's do some speculating.

In mid-December 1962, Dylan traveled to London for the first time, having landed a role as a folksinger in a BBC teleplay, *Madhouse on Castle Street*. During his month there, in addition to acting, Dylan played at various folk clubs, meeting English folk musicians including Martin Carthy.

Perhaps most relevant to the issue at hand, on January 15, 1963, Dylan participated in a recording session in the basement studio of Dobell's Jazz Shop, playing harmonica and singing background vocals on tracks by his friends Richard Fariña and Eric Von Schmidt (later released by Dobell's Folklore label; as Dylan was signed to Columbia Records, he was credited as "Blind Boy Grunt").

The British Record Shop Archive website describes Dobell's as "the place where musicians used to hang out, smoke and where you find certain records nowhere else." This is likely an important clue. Dylan's two blues albums are very obscure records—these were special-order items few retailers in London—or anywhere else—would have stocked. But they are *exactly* the sort of records that Dobell's, a collector's shop of the first order, specialized in. We know Dylan was in the store at least once for a protracted period of time, during the recording session, and that he owned these records between 1962 and 1964. So, it's not much of a leap of faith to imagine he acquired them there. Perhaps they were given to him as payment for the session by the low-budget label. It's quite likely—but impossible to know for sure.

On the back cover of *Blues Fell This Morning*, Dylan wrote, "Made for and about Bob Dylan," while below Oliver's liner notes he added, "Hand read by Bob Dylan." From the notes:

> One of the richest folk music forms to develop in the Western world during the present century, the blues of the Negroes of the Southern United States, has been a major influence on both jazz and popular music . . . the countless coloured troubadours who sang their vigorous improvised songs to the music of battered guitars and home-made instruments are lost in an obscure and remote history. Only the rare and neglected recordings made between the wars remain to bear witness to the artistry of these folk blues singers, of which these are import-

BLUES FELL THIS MORNING

Rare Recordings of Southern Blues Singers

Bob Dylan's annotated blues compilation LP, circa 1963

PHILIPS B 07586 L   *Made for and about Bob Dylan*   BBL 7369

Blues Fell This Morning — RARE RECORDINGS OF SOUTHERN BLUES SINGERS

GRAVEL CAMP BLUES by LEWIS BLACK (vocal, guitar) (145566-3). Recorded in Dallas 10/12/27 (CO 14291).
STARVATION FARM BLUES by BOB CAMPBELL (vocal, guitar) (15503-2). Recorded 1934 (Vo 02798).
CHOCOLATE TO THE BONE by BARBECUE BOB (vocal, guitar) (146054-1). Recorded in Atlanta 13/4/28 (CO 14331).
COURT STREET BLUES by STOVEPIPE No. 1 (stovepipe, vocal) and DAVID CROCKETT (guitar) (80749-1). Recorded in Atlanta -/3/27 (OK 8514).
WHEN YOU GET TO THINKING by "TEXAS" ALEXANDER (vocal) acc. Lonnie Johnson (guitar) (403359-1). Recorded in Chicago 27/11/29 (OK 8764).
TALLAHASSEE BLUES by TALLAHASSEE TIGHT (vocal, guitar) (14637-1). Recorded 18/1/34 (Mlt-M-13073).
SKIN GAME BLUES by PEG LEG HOWELL (vocal, guitar) (145185-2). Recorded in Atlanta 9/11/27 (CO 14473).
ELM STREET BLUES by TEXAS BILL DAY (vocal, guitar) and BILLIKEN JOHNSON (vocal) acc. piano (149538-2). Recorded in Dallas (3/12/29) (CO 14514).
BAD BOY by BAREFOOT BILL (vocal, guitar) (150306-1). Recorded in Atlanta 20/4/30 (CO14526).
WHEN THE LEVEE BREAKS by KANSAS JOE (vocal, guitar) and MEMPHIS MINNIE (guitar) (148711). Recorded 18/6/29 (CO 14439).
WHEN YOU ARE GONE by BLIND BOY FULLER (vocal, guitar) (WC 3144). Recorded in Chicago 19/6/40 (OK 05756).
STRANGE PLACE BLUES by BUKKA WHITE (vocal, guitar) acc. washboard. (WC2978A). Recorded in Chicago -/6/40 (OK 05526).
LONESOME BLUES by HENRY WILLIAMS (vocal, guitar) and EDDIE ANTHONY (vocal, violin) (146149-2). Recorded in Atlanta 20/4/28 (CO 14328).
WAKING BLUES by OTIS HARRIS (vocal, guitar) (147608-1). Recorded in Dallas 8/12/28 (CO 14428).

[Liner notes by PAUL OLIVER]

A PRODUCT OF PHILIPS

Hand read by Bob Dylan

Bob Dylan 1963

Your Weekend Sunday

The Madhouse on Castle Street

Left to right: David Warner, Bob Dylan, Maureen Pryor, James Mellor, Ursula Howells and Reg Lye

9.0

'I HAVE decided to retire from the world. I shall leave your name with Mrs. Griggs, my landlady, who will notify you when I die. Please arrange for my burial, as I do not wish to trouble the occupants of the house more than is necessary.' The ominous letter from the brother whom she has not seen for fourteen years brings Martha Tompkins to his boarding-house in Castle Street — only to find that Walter has locked himself in his room and is slowly starving to death. But why? Has he committed some crime? His fellow boarders, Bernard the truck driver, Lennie the student, and Bobby the guitar-playing hobo, together with Martha and two strange visitors, try to unravel Walter's secret—and in so doing find themselves revealing the secrets of their own past

The Madhouse on Castle Street is the third play for BBC-tv by **Evan Jones**, following *The Widows of Jaffa* and *In a Backward Country*. His film scripts include *The Damned*, which has yet to be released, and *Eve*, which stars the outstanding French actress Jeanne Moreau in her first English-speaking part.

In **Philip Saville's** production, Martha Tompkins is played by **Ursula Howells**, while **Maureen Pryor** is cast as Mrs. Griggs the landlady and **James Mellor** as Bernard.

Appearing as Bobby the hobo is **Bob Dylan**, brought over from America especially to play the part. Only twenty-one, he is already a major new figure in folk-music, with a reputation as one of the most compelling blues singers ever recorded. The song for which he is best known is 'Talkin' New York,' about his first visit to the city in 1961. A skilled guitarist, his special kind of haunting music forms an integral part of tonight's strange play.

The Madhouse on Castle Street newspaper review, January 1963

ant examples . . . [recordings] such as these were generally made on location by traveling units who literally gathered their singers from the fields and sidewalks . . .

It's easy to imagine how Dylan, a committed disciple of Woody Guthrie and fan of his fictionalized autobiography *Bound for Glory*, would be moved by both Oliver's words and the music within.

In the last paragraph of the notes, Oliver writes about "unknown" singer Otis Harris, concluding: "On him the blues fell, and though *times and conditions are changing* today, the blues still fell this morning" (my italics).

Hold on a minute. "Times and conditions are changing," as the concluding thought on an album that belonged to Bob Dylan, almost certainly in 1963, on which he wrote "Made for and about Bob Dylan" and "Hand read by Bob Dylan"? Could this be a Rosetta stone? The genesis of "The Times They Are A-Changin'," one of Dylan's best-known lyrics, written in September or October of 1963? Dylan is well known for picking out a phrase from another source and using it in a song.

It's tantalizingly within the realm of possibilities.

On the back of the second album, *Country Blues: Blind Boy Fuller 1935–1940,* Dylan has written, "Drinked up and let out by Bob Dylan" and below the liner notes, "Read thoroughly and with full throttle by Bob Dylan."

On this single-artist album, Oliver's notes include more biographical details about Fuller:

> Blind Boy Fuller was the name by which a small, compact negro guitarist, Fulton Allen, was known to farmers and mill-hands, tobacco-cultivators and hog keepers—and to countess thousands of Negroes who bought his records in the thirties. . . . His recordings, of which these are sixteen of the best, are as fresh today as when he made them more than a score of years ago and are a permanent tribute to the unique talents of one of the greatest folk blues singers.

As noted, Fuller's Dylan connection includes his key role in the complex history of "Baby, Let Me Follow You Down," which Dylan included on his debut album. (Dylan learned it from Eric von Schmidt, who adapted it from Fuller's "Mama, Let Me Lay It on You.") And *Country Blues* features Fuller's version of the standard "Step It Up and Go," recorded by Dylan for his 1992 album of folk and blues covers, *Good as I Been to You.*

Finally, consider this: In mid-1959, after graduating high school, 18-year-old Bobby Zimmerman left Hibbing, Minnesota, for Minneapolis. Near the end of that year, he began using the name Bob Dylan when playing folk songs in local coffeehouses. Traveling to New York in January 1961, Dylan continued his reinvention, claiming that he'd lived in New Mexico, Iowa, North and South Dakota, and Kansas, and had played with various well-known musicians.

Though Dylan's first album was released in March 1962, it took him until August of that year to legally change his name. Could his writing of these four inscriptions, about how "Bob Dylan" had absorbed this music and carefully read these liner notes, be a way for the now 21-year-old to further affirm his new name and identity? It's certainly possible.

Ultimately, I see Dylan's inscriptions on these albums as a trail of breadcrumbs, clues he left behind about the deep meaning these records had for him during a formative time in his career. It's clear the blues deeply influenced the music Bob Dylan made and continues to make. As he's well known for his encyclopedic knowledge of music, it's a good bet all of these songs still live inside him.

And that's good enough for me.

FOLK SONGS AND
MORE FOLK SONGS

On March 3, 1963, Bob Dylan taped an appearance on the Westinghouse TV program *Folk Songs and More Folk Songs*. Hosted by John Henry Faulk, a radio and TV personality with an interest in folklore and storytelling who'd been blacklisted during the "Red Scare" years of the early 1950s, the program also featured familiar faces like Carolyn Hester and Barbara Dane (accompanied by bassist Bill Lee, filmmaker Spike Lee's father, who played on *The Freewheelin' Bob Dylan*). The show also put the spotlight on some of Dylan's childhood heroes, The Staple Singers including Mavis and Pops Staples.

The Brothers Four rounded out the program, and their banjo player, Michael Kirkland, accompanied Dylan on the "Ballad of Hollis Brown." Dylan also performed "Blowin' in the Wind" and his arrangement of "Man of Constant Sorrow" on the show, which was ultimately broadcast that May.

PAGE 94: *Clockwise from top left: The Staple Singers, The Brothers Four, Carolyn Hester, Barbara Dane with Bill Lee, Bob Dylan, John Henry Faulk. Video stills from* Folk Songs and More Folk Songs, *Westinghouse Studios, NYC, March 1963. Directed by Julius Kuney*

HAROLD LEVENTHAL
presents
BOB DYLAN
AT TOWN HALL
FRI. EVE. APRIL 12th
AT 8:30 P.M.
Tickets $3.00 $2.75 $2.00 on Sale at Box Office

Hand-painted sign for Bob Dylan's Town Hall concert, NYC

TOWN HALL

This original hand-painted sign for Bob Dylan's concert at Town Hall in New York City on April 12, 1963, was commissioned and owned by the concert's producer, Harold Leventhal. A legend in the music world, Leventhal started as a song plugger for Irving Berlin and Benny Goodman before transitioning to music management. He would go on to steer the careers of The Weavers (with Pete Seeger), Woody Guthrie, Joan Baez, Ravi Shankar, Jacques Brel, Odetta, and many others. Leventhal and Dylan would work together once again in 1968 as part of the tribute concerts to Woody Guthrie held at Carnegie Hall to mark the singer's passing.

"LAST THOUGHTS ON WOODY GUTHRIE"

At the conclusion of the Town Hall performance, Dylan read an original piece of prose poetry—something that he never did publicly again. In his introduction to the piece, titled "Last Thoughts on Woody Guthrie," he explained the circumstances surrounding its genesis and his decision to share it with the audience:

> *There's this book coming out and they asked me to write something about Woody. Sorta like "What does Woody Guthrie mean to you" in twenty-five words. And I couldn't do it. I wrote out five pages and . . . I have it here, I have it here by accident, actually. But I'd like to say this out loud. So, if you could sorta roll along with this thing here, this is called "Last Thoughts on Woody Guthrie."*

Columbia Records recorded the Town Hall concert for a possible live album, and accordingly, a staff photographer was on hand to document the proceedings, capturing Dylan walking off the stage with the pages of "Last Thoughts" in hand. A four-page typescript with handwritten edits comes from the files maintained by publishing companies and likely relates to the subsequent registration of the piece in 1973 rather than its original composition.

Page 1 — Last Thoughts on Woody Guthrie

When yer head gets twisted and yer mind grows numb
And you think you're too old to young too smart or too dumb
In a slow motion crawl or life's busy race
No matter what yer doing if you start givin up
If the wine don't come to the top of yer cup
If the wind's got you sideways with one hand holdin on
And the other starts slipping and the feeling is gone
And yer train engine fire needs a new spark to catch it
And the wood's easy findin but yer lazy to fetch it
And yer sidewalk starts curlin and the street gets to long
And you start walkin backwards tho you know that it's wrong
And lonesome comes up and down goes the day
And tomorrow's mornin seems so far away
And you feel the reins from yer pony are slippin'
And yer rope is a slidin' cause yer hands are a drippin'
And yer sun decked desert and evergreen valleys
Turn to broken down slums and trash can alleys
And yer sky cries water and yer drain pipe's a pourin'
And the lightnin's a flashing and the thunder's a crashin'
And the windows are a rattlin add the breakin and the roof tops
a bangin' shakin'
And yer whole world's a shaking slammin' and bangin'
And yer minutes of sun turn to hours of storm
And to yourself you sometimes say
I never knew it was gonna be this way
Why didn't they tell me the day I was born
And you start gettin' chills and yer jumping from sweat
And you're lookin' for somethin you ain't quite found yet
And yer knee deep in dark water with yer hands in the air
And the whole world's a watchin with a window peek stare
And yer good gal leaves and she's long gone a-flying
And yer heart feels sick like fish when they're fryin
And yer jackhammer falls from your hands to yer feet
And you need it badly but it lays on the street
And yer bell's bangin loudly but you can't hear it's heat
And you think that yer ears might a been hurt
Or yer eyes've turned filthy from the sight blindin dirt-
And you figured you failed in yesterday's rush
When you were faked out an' fooled while facing a four flush
And all the time you were holdin' three queens
And it's makin you mad, it's makin you mean
You feel like in the middle of Life Magazine
And yer bouncing around in a pinball machine
And there's something on yer mind that you wanna be saying
That somebody some place oughta be hearing
But it's trapped on yer tongue and sealed in yer head
And it bothers you badly when you're layin in bed
And no matter how you try you just can't say it
And yer scared to yer soul that you just might forget it
And yer eyes get swimmy from the tears in yer head
And yer pillows of feathers turn to blankets of lead
And the lion's mouth opens and yer staring at his teeth
And his jaws start closin with you underneath
And yer flat on yer belly with yer hands tied behind
And you wish you'd never taken that last detour sign--

Page 2

And you say to yerself just what am I doing
On this road I'm a walkin on this trail I'm a turning
On this curve that I'm hanging
On this pathway I'm strolling in the space that I'm taking
In this air I'm inhaling--
Am I mixed up too much - Am I mixed up too hard--
Why am I walking where am I running
What am I saying - what am I knowing
On this guitar I'm playing on this banjo I'm frailin
On this mandolin that I'm strummin in the song that I'm singin
In the tune that I'm hummin in the words that I'm writin
In the words that I'm thinkin
In this ocean of hours I'm all the time drinkin
Who am I helping what am I breaking
What am I giving what am I taking--
But you try with yer whole soul best
Never to think these things and never to let
them kind of thoughts gain ground
Or make yer heart round
But then again you know when they're around
Just waiting for a chance to slip and drop down
And sometime you hear him in the nite time come creeping
And you fear that they might catch you a sleeping
And you jump from yer bed from yer last chapter of dreamin
And you can't remember for the best of yer thinking
If that was you in the dream that was screaming
And you know that it's somethin special you're needin
And you know that there's no drug that'll do for the healin
And no liquor in the land to stop yer brain from bleeding
And you need something special
Yeah you need something special alright
You need a fast flyin train on a tornado track
To shoot you someplace and shoot you back
You need a cyclone wind on a steam engine howler
That's been banging and booming and blowing for ever
That knows yer troubles a hundred times over
You need a greyhound bus that don's bar no race
That won'd laugh at yer looks
Your voice or your face--
And by any number of bets in the book
Will be rollin long after the bubblegum craze
You need something to open up a new door
To show you something you seen before
But overlooked a hundred times or more
You need something to open yer eyes
You need something to make it known
That it's you and no one else that owns
That spot that yer standing that space that you're taking (sitting)
That the world ain't got you beat
That it ain't got you licked
It can't get you crazy no matter how many
Times you might get kicked

"Last Thoughts on Woody Guthrie" draft typescript

Bob Dylan with "Last Thoughts on Woody Guthrie" manuscript, Town Hall,
NYC, April 12, 1963. Photograph by Don Hunstein

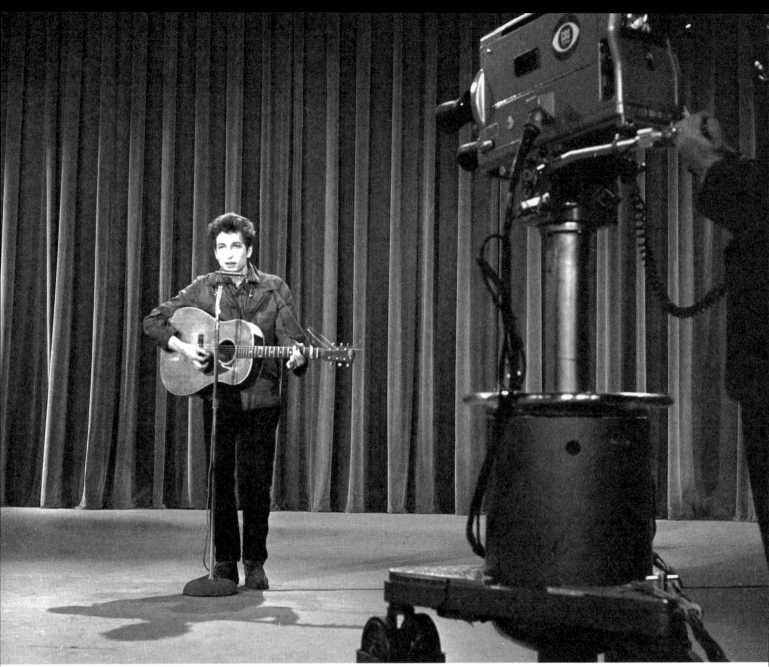

Bob Dylan during rehearsals for *The Ed Sullivan Show*, May 12, 1963. Photographer unknown

THE ED SULLIVAN SHOW

Bob Dylan was slated to perform on the May 12, 1963, episode of the wildly popular *Ed Sullivan Show*, which had catapulted Dylan's hero Elvis to international fame in 1956 and would do the same for The Beatles in February 1964. For Dylan, it was to be his first appearance in front of a nationwide TV audience. Dylan had chosen to perform a song from his upcoming album, *The Freewheelin' Bob Dylan*, which was to be released just weeks later, on May 27. The song, "Talkin' John Birch Paranoid Blues" (or "Talkin' John Birch Blues," as it was listed on the album's track listing), utilized the style of Woody Guthrie's talking songs to deliver a scathing, yet hilarious, indictment of the right-wing paranoia and red-baiting that the John Birch Society fomented. Despite getting the approval to perform the song, during rehearsal the censors at CBS decided that the song might invite defamation lawsuits. Rebuffing a request to perform a different song, Dylan walked off the show. In the aftermath, the song was left off the album, and perhaps two dozen copies of the LP with the inclusion of the song are known to exist.

Monterey Folk Festival program, May 1963

MONTEREY FOLK FESTIVAL, 1963

Less than a week after the Ed Sullivan incident, on May 18, 1963, Bob Dylan made his first-ever West Coast appearance. The setting was the first annual Monterey Folk Festival, held that year at the fairgrounds in Monterey, California. He performed four songs: "Masters of War," "A Hard Rain's A-Gonna Fall," a talking blues (presumably "Talkin' John Birch Paranoid Blues"), and "With God on Our Side," with Joan Baez singing harmonies.

Dylan was in good company at the festival, sharing the bill with folk stalwarts and legends like Roscoe Holcomb, Mance Lipscomb, Bessie Jones and the Georgia Sea Island Singers, Peter, Paul and Mary, The Weavers, and The New Lost City Ramblers. A young Jerry Garcia also performed at the festival as part of The Wildwood Boys, which included future Grateful Dead lyricist and Dylan collaborator Robert Hunter, as well as David Nelson and Ken Frankel.

Dylan's bio for the program, reflecting the playfulness with which he obscured his upbringing during these early years, was taken from Columbia's publicity sheet for the artist:

Bob Dylan, Gallup, NM. When you tour with the carnival at age fourteen playing piano and guitar, you're bound to learn a lot of life, land and of music. In the course of this learning process, Bob heard Woody Guthrie's "Dust Bowl Ballads" and headed east to meet the great Woody. Arriving in New York, he found that the city people referred to much of the music he had been playing and writing as folk music. To Bob this didn't matter. He's continued to write, sing and dress in a highly individual fashion. This has landed him an envitable [sic] record contract with Columbia and publication by Leeds Music of a collection of his works. The songs he writes (often topical paradies [sic] or talkin' blues) and sings relate to what he's heard and seen in America. The closest he comes to international material is the parody of an Israeli song, "H'ava Ngilla" [sic]. Play jazzy blues piano, guitar and harmonica (often both at once).

As Dylan told Nat Hentoff in a 1964 profile for *The New Yorker*,

"My background's not all that important. . . . It's what I am now that counts."

NEWPORT FOLK FESTIVAL, 1963

As Dylan was establishing himself as a leading new songwriter,
the Newport Folk Festival was one in a series of high-profile 1963
appearances that added to his growing reputation as a dynamic
performer in his own right. Although all these appearances were
important for the development of Dylan's rising public profile, his
standout performances at Newport in late July held particular
resonance, as the festival was *the* event for folk music.

The annual Newport Folk Festival was a unique space for folk
musicians, folklorists, and fans to participate in concerts, workshops, and informal jam sessions that served as a way for the
tradition to be passed along to the next generation. For young
performers like Dylan, it presented the opportunity to learn from
those who'd been living these songs for decades, including coal
miner, activist, and folksinger Jim Garland (pictured backstage
with Dylan), or with musicians whose names might only be familiar
from records, such as blues singer Mississippi John Hurt.

Alongside powerful solo sets, Dylan also shared the stage with Pete
Seeger and Joan Baez in performances that served as an endorsement
of Dylan's talents and helped to introduce him and his music to a wider
audience. When the festival's first evening closed with Baez, Seeger,
Theo Bikel, The Freedom Singers, and Peter, Paul and Mary joining
Dylan for stirring versions of "Blowin' in the Wind" and the traditional
"We Shall Overcome," it was evident that Dylan had arrived.

100

MARCH ON WASHINGTON

The March on Washington for Jobs and Freedom was a galvanizing moment in US history that contributed to the passage of the Civil Rights Act of 1964, which outlawed discrimination based on race, color, religion, sex, and national origin. Organized by activists A. Philip Randolph and Bayard Rustin, the landmark event mobilized between two hundred and three hundred thousand people who converged on August 28, 1963, in the nation's capital to advocate for the civil and economic rights of African Americans. From the steps of the Lincoln Memorial, representatives of the sponsoring organizations (including the Student Nonviolent Coordinating Committee's chair, future congressional representative John Lewis), three religious denominations, and the United Auto Workers and the American Federation of Labor and Congress of Industrial Organizations delivered impassioned remarks, culminating in Martin Luther King Jr.'s iconic "I Have a Dream" speech in which he called for an end to racism and discrimination in America.

As an essential component of the civil rights movement, music was also an important part of the event. Performers included the multifaceted singer Marian Anderson, gospel queen Mahalia Jackson, and folksingers Joan Baez, Odetta, and Peter, Paul and Mary (who included "Blowin' in the Wind" in their program). Accompanied by Baez, the 22-year-old Bob Dylan also sang "When the Ship Comes In" and "Only a Pawn in Their Game" from the podium, performances that would have been heard across the nation as part of the radio and television coverage of the march.

Bob Dylan with Joan Baez at the Lincoln Memorial during the March on Washington, August 23, 1963. Photograph by Fred W. McDarrah

THE FOLKLORE CENTER

Presents

BOB DYLAN

IN HIS FIRST NEW YORK CONCERT

ᨆᨆᨆᨆᨆᨆᨆᨆᨆᨆᨆᨆᨆᨆ

SAT. NOV. 4, 1961   8:40pm

CARNEGIE CHAPTER HALL

154 WEST 57th STREET • NEW YORK CITY

All seats $2.00

Tickets available at: The Folklore Center
                             110 MacDougal Street
GR 7 - 5987   New York City 12, New York

                             or at door

HAROLD LEVENTHAL PRESENTS

BOB DYLAN
at
CARNEGIE HALL

SAT. EVE. OCTOBER 26, 1963 at 8:40 P.M.

COLUMBIA RECORDS

Order Tickets ────────────────────────────

Mail & checks payable: Carnegie Hall, W. 57th St. & 7th Ave., New York

Enclosed check for $.......... Please send .... tickets for
BOB DYLAN Sat. Eve. Oct. 26, 1963

Parq.....@ $3.50   1st Tier....@ $3.50   2nd Tier....@ $3.00

Dress Circle....@ $2.50   Balcony....@ $2.00

Send to

Name_____ Address _____

City _____ Zone_____ State _____

PLEASE ENCLOSE STAMPED, SELF-ADDRESSED ENVELOPE FOR RETURN OF TICKETS

Carnegie Hall ticket order form, October 1963

CARNEGIE HALL

On November 11, 1961, Folklore Center proprietor Izzy Young rented out the smaller Carnegie Chapter Hall to host Dylan's largest concert to date. Just eleven months after his arrival in the city, Dylan performed a set of folk songs, covers, and handful of originals for an estimated fifty to seventy-five people, two of whom made recordings of the concert that are now part of the Archive's holdings.

Less than two years later, Dylan was back on October 26, 1963, performing to a sold-out crowd of more than thirty-five hundred people in Carnegie Hall's main auditorium. Dylan was now a Columbia recording artist, and the label was trying to gather material for a potential live album, having previously recorded an April show at New York City's Town Hall. A sold-out show at the world-famous Carnegie Hall was too precious an opportunity to miss, so Columbia recording engineers were onsite again to document the concert. Acetates and even a front cover were prepared before *In Concert* was indefinitely shelved. Columbia Records eventually included songs from the concert on *The Bootleg Series Volumes 1–3 (Rare & Unreleased) 1961–1991* and *The Bootleg Series Vol. 7: No Direction Home: The Soundtrack* before releasing a six-song EP titled *Live at Carnegie Hall 1963* in 2005.

Photograph by Richard Avedon

BOB DYLAN, 132ND STREET AND FDR DRIVE, HARLEM, NOVEMBER 4, 1963

Just days after the final recording session for his next album, *The Times They Are A-Changin'*, Dylan posed for photographer Richard Avedon on November 4, 1963. Page 107 features the image Avedon selected for publication, and page 106 is a never-before-published outtake.

Photograph by Richard Avedon

THE TIMES THEY ARE A-CHANGIN'

Dylan's third album, *The Times They Are A-Changin'*, was released in January 1964 and contained perhaps his most overtly political songs to date, like "The Lonesome Death of Hattie Carroll," "When the Ship Comes In," and the titular track, tackling difficult issues of discrimination, inequality, and social change. Yet the album also had space for more introspective songs such as "Boots of Spanish Leather" and "One Too Many Mornings," while the Dylan-penned liner notes for the album hinted at a new direction. Titled "11 Outlined Epitaphs," the work straddles the plain-talking patter of Woody Guthrie that dominated some of his earlier prose and poetry with the notes of Symbolist and Beat influence that would imbue his next cycle of songs. Thirty-six lines from the piece were reprinted as part of "The Angry Young Folksinger" profile published in the April 10, 1964, issue of *Life* magazine.

```
Yes, I am a thief of thoughts

not, I pray, a stealer of souls

I have built an rebuilt

on what has been opened

before my time

a word, a tune, a story, a line

keys in the wind t unlock my mind

an t grant my closet thoughts back yard air

it is not of me t sit an ponder

wonderin an wastin time

thinkin of thoughts that haven't been thunk

thinkin of dreams that haven't been dreamt

an new ideas that haven't been wrote

an new words t fit into rhyme

(if it rhymes, it rhymes

if it don't, it don't

if it comes, it comes

if it wont, it wont)

no I must react an spit fast

with weapons of words

wrapped in tunes

that
```

"11 Outlined Epitaphs" typescript liner notes from *The Times They Are A-Changin'*

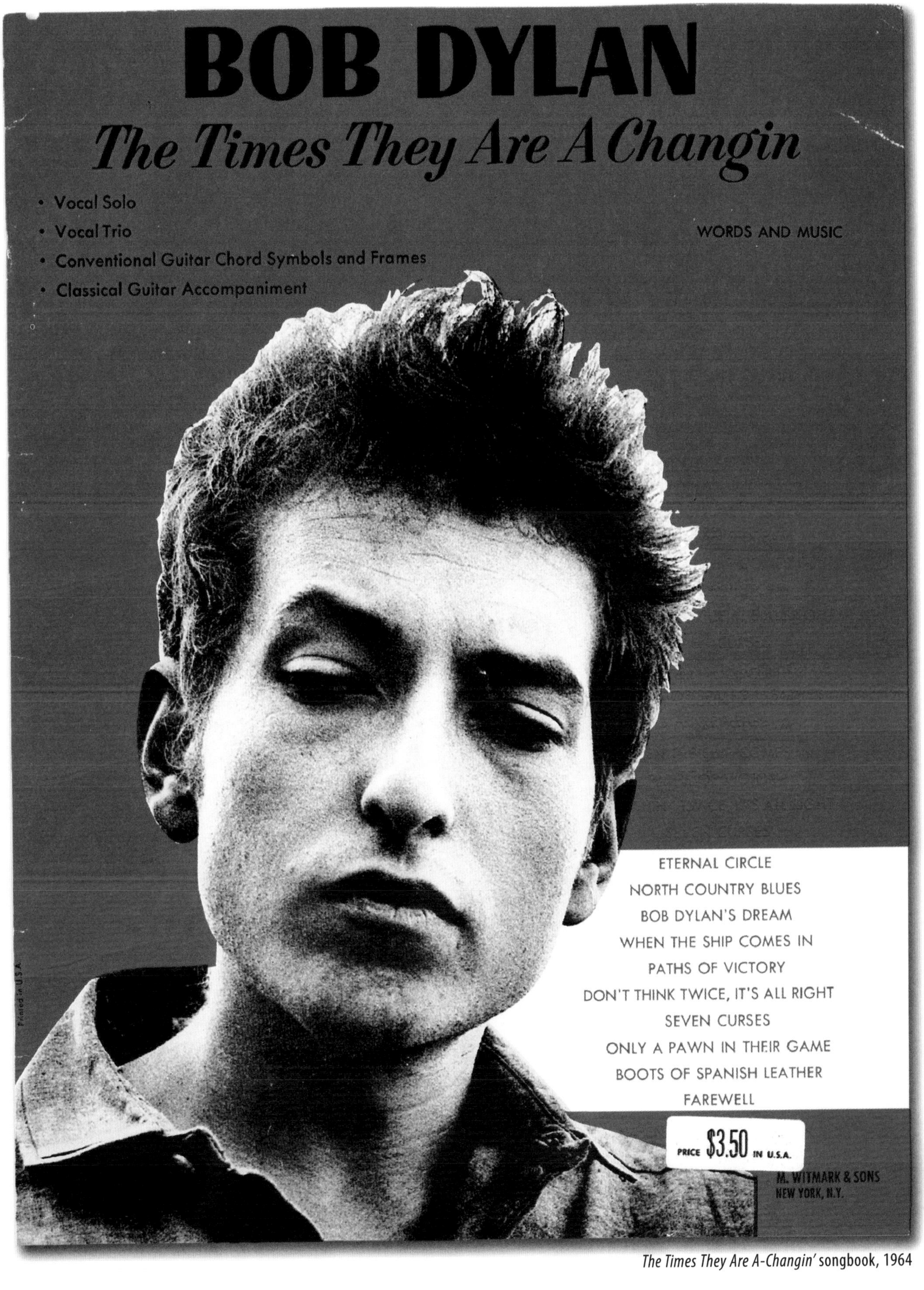

The Times They Are A-Changin' songbook, 1964

ANOTHER SIDE OF BOB DYLAN

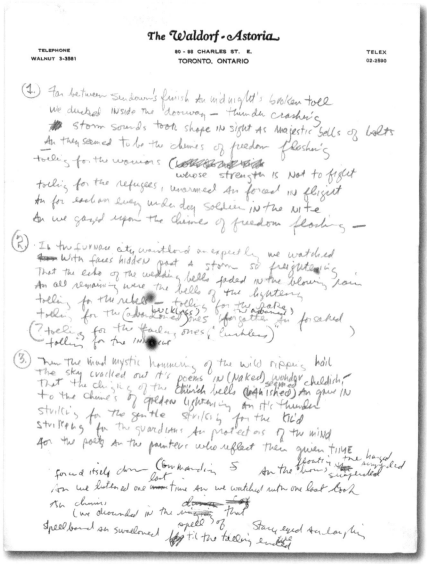

"Chimes of Freedom" draft manuscript

"CHIMES OF FREEDOM"

On February 1, 1964, Dylan was in Toronto to tape a television appearance, for the CBC-TV program *Quest* (the episode aired March 10). While there, Dylan stayed at the Waldorf-Astoria, where he used the hotel stationery to write "Chimes of Freedom."

Upon returning to the States from Canada, Dylan set about on a three-week, cross-country road trip with fellow musician Paul Clayton, tour manager Victor Maymudes, and journalist Pete Karman, which took them from New York City to California, with a few detours along the way: Flat Rock, North Carolina, where they dropped in on an unsuspecting Carl Sandburg; New Orleans for Mardi Gras; and Denver for Dylan's only concert before arriving in the Golden State.

As Dylan traveled across America, he worked on the new song titled "Chimes of Freedom," which had been inspired in part by a traditional song he'd learned from Dave Van Ronk, "The Chimes of Trinity."

A WAY OF LIFE

"Chimes of Freedom" draft manuscript, back

Although he didn't record the song until June 9, during the one-night session for his fourth record, *Another Side of Bob Dylan*, Ralph Gleason's concert review of Dylan's February 22 concert at the Berkeley Community Theater, where he mentions the song by name, indicates that Dylan started performing the song almost immediately after writing it.

The first major manuscript in the Bob Dylan Archive, "Chimes" represents a kind of turning point for Dylan lyrically, with the songwriter expanding his style into symbolic and at times fragmented imagery, reflecting his growing literary appetite and his immersion in French symbolist poets and the Beats, some of whom Dylan had just met, such as Allen Ginsberg.

```
6.

for francois hardy

at the seine's edge
a giant shadow
of notre dame
seeks t grab my foot
sorbonne students
whirl by on thin bycicles
swirlin lifelike colors of leather  spun
                                       the breeze yawns food
far from the bellies
of ehhard meetin johnson
piles of lovers
fishing
kissing
lay themselves on their books. bouts.
   old men
clothed in curly mushaches
float on the benches
blankets of tourests
in bright red nylon shirts
with straw hats of ambassadors
(cannot hear nixon's
dawg barkin now)
will sail away
as the sun goes down
the doors of the river are open
i must remember that
i too play the guitar
it's easy t stand here
more lovers pass
on motorcycles
roped together
from the wall of the water then
i look across t what they call
the right bank
an envy
your
trumpet
player
```

Françoise Hardy and Bob Dylan, Paris, May 1966. Film still from 1966 European Tour footage, by D. A. Pennebaker

"For Françoise Hardy" from "Some Other Kinds of Songs . . . ," *Another Side of Bob Dylan* liner notes, draft typescript

FRANÇOISE HARDY

Dylan also provided the liner notes for *Another Side*, drafting a set of poems that he playfully titled, "Some Other Kinds of Songs . . . " One of those, "For Françoise Hardy," was dedicated to the glamorous French pop star. A singer-songwriter like Dylan, Hardy combined American and British pop and rock with the emerging musical and cultural phenomenon known as "yé-yé" music, which was popular with French teens and critics alike. Capable of singing in French, English, German, and Italian, Hardy soon found international acclaim.

Nearly two years after writing the poem, Dylan had the opportunity to meet Hardy backstage at his May 24, 1966, show at the Olympia Hall in Paris.

A WAY OF LIFE

Bob Dylan and Françoise Hardy,
Olympia Hall, Paris, May 1966.
Photograph by Barry Feinstein

HOME MOVIES, 1964

A set of film stills taken from silent Super 8mm footage dating to late summer 1964 captures Dylan in and around Woodstock, New York, as well as his social circle, including manager Albert Grossman, folksingers Joan Baez and Mimi Fariña, author Mason Hoffenberg, publicist Al Aronowitz, and poet Allen Ginsberg. Filmmaker unknown

NEWPORT FOLK FESTIVAL, 1964

THURSDAY EVENING —7:30 P.M.

MAIN PARK (Freebody Park)

Concert of Traditional Music

Cajun Band
Elizabeth Cotten
Jimmie Driftwood
Seamus Ennis
Jesse Fuller
Elgia Hickok
Hindman Settlement School Dancers
Clayton McMichen
Mississippi John Hurt
Bessie Jones &
The Georgia Sea Island Singers
Fred & Annie Mae McDowell
Moving Star Hall Singers

Glenn Ohrlin
Chet Parker
Joe Patterson
Phipps Family
Doc Reese
Almeda Riddle
Sacred Harp Singers
Dewey Shepherd
Hobart Smith
Stanley Brothers
Bill Thatcher
Muddy Waters
Watson Family
with Doc Watson
Rev. Robert Wilkins
Robert Pete Williams

FRIDAY MORNING —10:00 A.M.

ST. MICHAEL'S SCHOOL

Singing Styles
Ronnie Gilbert & Ralph Rinzler, Hosts

Joan Baez
Cajun Band
John Davis
Seamus Ennis
Ollie Gilbert
Fred & Annie Mae McDowell

Glenn Ohrlin
Almeda Riddle
Sacred Harp Group
Dewey Shepherd
Ralph Stanley
Mary Travers
Rev. Robert Wilkins

Autoharp and Dulcimer
Mike Seeger & Jean Ritchie, Hosts

Ken & Neriah Benfield
Elgia Hickock
Chet Parker
Phipps Family
Frank Proffitt
Doc Watson

FRIDAY AFTERNOON —1:30 P.M.

ST. MICHAEL'S SCHOOL

Broadsides (Topical Songs)
Pete Seeger, Host

Johnny Cash
Len Chandler
Jimmie Driftwood
Bob Dylan
Seamus Ennis
Sarah Gunning

Phil Ochs
Chad Mitchell Trio
Tom Paxton
Frank Proffitt
Malvina Reynolds
Rodriguez Brothers
Bill Thatcher
Hedy West

Guitar
Doc Watson & Ralph Rinzler, Hosts

Elizabeth Cotten
Willie Doss
Noelani Mahoe
Phipps Family

Hobart Smith
Muddy Waters
Clarence White
Rev. Robert Wilki...
Robert Pete Willia...

Films
Paul Nelson, Host
Shown in the theater

FRIDAY AFTERNOON —3:30 P.M.

ST. MICHAEL'S SCHOOL

Freedom Songs
Guy Carawan, Host
Guy Carawan, Freedom Group and Dock Reese
(in addition to those on topical song workshop)

Banjo:
Bill Keith & Mike Seeger, Hosts
Bluegrass:
Billy Ray Lathum
Ralph Stanley
Don Stover
Doc Watson

Old Time:
Gaither Carlton
Elizabeth Cotten
Ollie Gilbert
Frank Proffitt
Hobart Smith
Ralph Stanley
Doc Watson
Arnold Watson

FRIDAY EVENING —8:00 P.M.

MAIN PARK (Freebody Park)

Concert
Joan Baez
Johnny Cash
Cajun Band
Sleepy John Estes with
Hammie Nixon & Yank Rachel
Greenbriar Boys
Fred & Annie Mae McDowell
Clayton McMichen
Chad Mitchell Trio
Moving Star Hall Singers
Phil Ochs
The Watson Family with Doc Watson
Kaupena Wong & Noelani Mahoe

(PROGRAM IS...

Bob Dylan, Newport Folk Festival, July 24, 1964. Photograph by Edward Grazda

Program

NEWPORT FOLK FESTIVAL
JULY 23 TO 26, 1964

ALL PROGRAM WORKSHOPS FRIDAY AND SATURDAY IN
ST. MICHAEL'S SCHOOL, MEMORIAL BLVD. & RHODE ISLAND AVE.

PHOTO BY ROBERT YELLIN

Country Music
D. K. Wilgus, Host
Jimmie Driftwood
Clayton McMichen
Carter Stanley
Doc Watson

SATURDAY MORNING —10:00 A.M.

ST. MICHAEL'S SCHOOL
String Bands
Ralph Rinzler & Mike Seeger, Hosts
Sleepy John Estes with Hammie Nixon
& Yank Rachel
Greenbriar Boys
Clayton McMichen
Osborne Brothers
Phipps Family
Hobart Smith
Stanley Brothers
Watson Family

International Songs
Theo Bikel, Host
Joan Baez
Cajun Band
Clancy Brothers with
Tommy Makem
Ron Eliran
Hamsa El Din
Seamus Ennis
Kaupena Wong & Noelani Mahoe
Rodriguez Brothers

Negro Group Singing & Rhythmic Patterns
Alan Lomax, Willis James
& Pete Seeger, Hosts

Jesse Fuller
Mississippi John Hurt
Bessie Jones &
The Georgia Sea Island Singers
Fred & Annie Mae McDowell
Dock Reese
Moving Star Hall Singers

SATURDAY AFTERNOON —1:30 P.M.

ST. MICHAEL'S SCHOOL
Blues
Willis James & Sam Charters, Hosts
Willy Doss
Koerner, Ray & Glover
Son House
Fred & Annie Mae McDowell
Judy Roderick
Hobart Smith
Dave Van Ronk
Robert Pete Williams

Play Party & Children's Songs
Jean Ritchie, Host
Joan Baez
Blue Ridge Mountain Dancers
Seamus Ennis
Hindman School Dancers
Bessie Jones
Almeda Riddle
Pete Seeger
Hedy West

Fiddle
Jimmie Driftwood, Host
Gaither Carlton
Louis Vinis LeJeune
Clayton McMichen
Dewey Shepherd
Hobart Smith

SATURDAY AFTERNOON —3:30 P.M.

ST. MICHAEL'S SCHOOL
Traditional Dance
Jean Ritchie, Host
Blue Ridge Mountain Dancers
Hindman School Dancers

(...T TO CHANGE)

SATURDAY EVENING —8:00 P.M.

MAIN PARK (Freebody Park)
Concert
Theo Bikel
Blue Ridge Mountain Dancers
Judy Collins
Seamus Ennis
Jesse Fuller
Osborne Brothers
Peter, Paul, and Mary
Phipps Family
Frank Proffitt
Rodriguez Brothers
Swan Silvertones
Robert Pete Williams

SUNDAY MORNING —10:00 A.M.

MAIN PARK (Freebody Park)
Concert of Religious Music
D. K. Wilgus, Host
Kentucky Colonels
Jimmie Driftwood
Moving Star Hall Singers
Phipps Family
Bessie Jones & The Georgia Sea
Island Singers
Sarah Gunning
Ollie Gilbert
Dock Reese
Almeda Riddle
Jean Ritchie
Rodriguez Brothers
Sacred Harp Group
Dewey Shepherd
Swan Silvertones
Hobart Smith
Stanley Brothers
Staple Singers
Watson Family
Rev. Robert Wilkins

SUNDAY AFTERNOON —1:30 P.M.

Academic Workshop
ST. MICHAEL'S SCHOOL
(No Admission Charge)
Herbert Halpert
Willis James
Alan Lomax
Tristram P. Coffin
D. K. Wilgus

SUNDAY AFTERNOON —2:30 P.M.

MAIN PARK (Freebody Park)
Afternoon Concert
Peter Yarrow, Host
Len Chandler
Hamsa El Din
Ron Eliran
José Feliciano
Koerner, Ray
Son House
Jim Kweskin
Tom Paxton
Judy Roderick
Buffy Sainte-M...

SUNDAY EVENING —8:00 P.M.

MAIN PARK (Freebody Park)
Concert
Clancy Brothers and Tommy Makem
Bob Dylan
Freedom Group with Guy Carawan
Mississippi John Hurt
Kentucky Colonels

Newport Folk Festival program, 1964

Newport Folk Festival advertisement, 1964

NEWPORT FOLK FESTIVAL

THURS. • FRI. • SAT. • SUN.
JULY 23-24-25-26
Freebody Park • NEWPORT, R.I.

Tickets: $3, $4, $5
On Mail Orders, add 25 cents
*Evening concerts will be
augmented by morning and
afternoon panels and workshops.*

Special group rates can be
arranged in advance now.
For Tickets and Program Information:
Newport Folk Festival, Newport, R.I.

DIRECTORS
Theodore Bikel
Clarence Cooper
Ronnie Gilbert
Alan Lomax
Jean Ritchie
Mike Seeger
Peter Yarrow

George Wein
Chairman

BOB DYLAN AND JOHNNY CASH

I originally called this, "To Bob D. and other Poets & Dreamers"

Also, do you know if "Broadside" magazine published the poem I sent them about a month ago? It was of you.

In Nashville, as always, I stayed at the home of Maybelle and "Pop" Carter. I took your new album out and you completely warped the head of "Pop" Carter. He is a rare jewel. He's a great writer.....and reader. He says you're the greatest poet of the century. I said, "huh?"

Mother Maybelle woke me up every morning playing "Lonesome Farewell." She digs you deeply.

Letter from Johnny Cash to Bob Dylan, March 1964

L–R: Frank Wakefield, Johnny Cash, Bob Dylan, Newport Folk Festival, July 25, 1964. Photograph by David Gahr

FIRST MEETING, 1964

I wrote Bob a letter telling him how much of a fan I was. He wrote back almost immediately, saying he'd been following my music since "I Walk the Line," and so we began a correspondence.

—JOHNNY CASH, *Cash: The Autobiography* (1996)

Of course, I knew of him before he ever heard of me. In '55 or '56, "I Walk the Line" played all summer on the radio, and it was different than anything else you had ever heard. The record sounded like a voice from the middle of the earth.

—BOB DYLAN, "Thoughts on Johnny Cash" (2003)

It wasn't a long correspondence. We quit after we actually met each other, when I went to play the Newport Folk Festival in July of 1964. I don't have many memories of that event, but I do remember June [Carter] and me and Bob [Dylan] and Joan Baez in my hotel room, so happy to meet each other that we were jumping on the bed like kids.

—JOHNNY CASH, *Cash: The Autobiography*

What survives of the correspondence from Johnny Cash to Bob Dylan is a fascinating glimpse at the start of a friendship that would last nearly fifty years. One letter, started March 10, 1964, in Indianapolis, Indiana, but not finished until March 14 in Duluth, Minnesota (with a stop in Green Bay, Wisconsin), sets the tone. Mailed in a North Central Airlines airsickness bag, the letter reveals Cash's thoughts moving a mile a minute. He riffs on Dylan lyrics, talks about a trip to New York City including an appearance on *The Tonight Show* with Johnny Carson and a performance at the Gaslight in Greenwich Village, recounts meeting Peter La Farge and recording the "Ballad of Ira Hayes," asks Dylan for new songs to perform, and shares his own poetry. But perhaps the best moment involves a visit to Nashville where Cash stays at the home of Mother Maybelle Carter of The Carter Family, an early country group who long had a profound influence on Dylan's work. "Mother Maybelle woke me up every morning playing 'Lonesome [*sic*] Farewell.' She digs you deeply." (The song Cash references is titled "Restless Farewell.")

Dylan and Cash finally met in person for the first time backstage at the 1964 Newport Folk Festival. That evening Cash performed "Don't Think Twice, It's All Right" during his twenty-minute set. Back at the hotel, Cash gave Dylan his Martin guitar, an old country tradition that signified a passing of the torch.

CROSSING PATHS, 1966

In May 1966, Dylan and Cash crossed paths in London while on separate concert tours of the UK. That year, Cash moved back from California to the Nashville area and took up residence at the Fontaine Royale Apartments with Waylon Jennings.

JOHNNY CASH N.Y.C.
April 8 1999

Hi Bob
It was 1955 and I was in the dressing room at Louisiana Hayride with Sam Phillips, Elvis and Luther. Sam asked me if I had written anything new. I sang the first two verses of "Train of Love." He said, "Finish it and lets record it." — Memories — you brought them all back. — Nice memories.
Thank you Bob, for doing my song. You looked great and sounded great.
And thank you for the kind words.
With much love and respect.
your Friend, Johny Cash

Fax letter from Johnny Cash to Bob Dylan, April 8, 1999

Bob Dylan and Johnny Cash at the May Fair Hotel, London, May 9, 1966. Film stills from 1966 European Tour footage, by D. A. Pennebaker

Bob Dylan and Johnny Cash during rehearsals for *The Johnny Cash Show*, Nashville, May 1, 1969. Photograph by Al Clayton

THE JOHNNY CASH SHOW, 1969

The Johnny Cash Show was an ABC-TV musical variety show that ran for fifty-eight episodes between June 1969 and March 1971. Hosted by Cash himself, the show was filmed at the historic Ryman Auditorium in Nashville. Dylan appeared on the first-ever show, performing three songs including a reprise of the "Girl from the North Country" duet with Cash, which had been featured on the recently released *Nashville Skyline* album.

"TRAIN OF LOVE," 1999

While rehearsing for an upcoming tour, Dylan taped a performance of Johnny Cash's "Train of Love" to be played as part of a tribute concert at Hammerstein Ballroom in New York City on April 6, 1999. Dylan introduced the song with a short personal message to his longtime friend, closing with an allusion to the March 1964 letter Cash had penned to *Sing Out!* in Dylan's defense:

> *Hey Johnny, I wanna say, "Hi" and "I'm sorry we can't be there, but that's just the way it is." I want to sing you one of your songs about trains. I used to sing this song before I ever wrote a song and I also want to thank you for standing up for me way back when.*

Johnny Cash's handwritten address, circa May 1966

A Daily Reminder of Important Matters

LUCY SANTE

STANDARD TIME
DIFFERENCES AT 12:00 NOON
WASHINGTON, D. C.
Authority: U. S. Navy Hydrographic Office.

Athens...... 7:00 P. M.	Melbourne next
Auckland next day	day....... 3:00 A. M.
.... 5:00 A. M.	Milwaukee..11:00 A. M.
Berlin....... 6:00 P. M.	Minneapolis.11:00 A. M.
Bombay....10:30 P. M.	Montreal....12:00 noon
Boston......12:00 noon	Natal....... 2:00 P. M.
Buffalo......12:00 noon	New Orleans 11:00 A. M.
Cape Town.. 7:00 P. M.	New York...12:00 noon
Chicago.....11:00 A. M.	Omaha......11:00 A. M.
Cincinnati..12:00 noon	Ottawa.....12:00 noon
Cleveland...12:00 noon	Panama.....12:00 noon
Denver.....10:00 A. M.	Paris....... 6:00 P. M.
Detroit.....12:00 noon	Philad'p'a...12:00 noon
Galveston...11:00 A. M.	Pittsburgh...12:00 noon
Halifax..... 1:00 P. M.	Portland,Ore 9:00 A. M.
Hamburg.... 6:00 P. M.	Quebec......12:00 noon
Havana......12:00 noon	Rio de J'n'ro 2:00 P. M.
Hong Kong next	Rome....... 6:00 P. M.
day...... 1:00 A. M.	Salt L. City.10:00 A. M.
Honolulu... 7:00 A. M.	SanFrancisco 9:00 A. M.
Istanbul.... 7:00 P. M.	St. Louis....11:00 A. M.
Jerusalem... 7:00 P. M.	Seattle..... 9:00 A. M.
Kans. City..11:00 A. M.	Suez....... 7:00 P. M.
Lisbon..... 5:00 P. M.	Toledo......12:00 noon
Liverpool... 5:00 P. M.	Vancouver... 9:00 A. M.
London..... 5:00 P. M.	Vienna...... 6:00 P. M.
Madrid..... 6:00 P. M.	Winnipeg....11:00 A. M.
Manila next day	Yokohama next
.... 1:00 A. M.	day...... 2:00 A. M.

Notebook, circa 1964

I
t's a small black imitation-leather dime-store notebook, about the size of a cell phone, like an address book or a day planner or a diary, but a bit more vague. "A Daily Reminder of Important Matters," it says on the title page, and the inner pages are ruled. The calendar up front is for 1963, although the book seems to have been used in 1964. Its spine has been repaired, crookedly, with packing tape. Clusters of addresses and references suggest its owner might have been in Mississippi, New Orleans, Texas, Los Angeles, Paris, London, and San Francisco during the term of its use. It is about three-quarters filled, with spurts and sequences of writing appearing in various sizes and permutations of the owner's script, inscribed with different implements and with varying

observance of the ruling and the page orientation. It was written on the move, in short bursts, on trains and airplanes and in hotel rooms and the backs of cars.

I was drawn to the book because I'm more inclined to be a detective than a literary scholar. I liked the fact that it was a three-dimensional object that got carried around in a pocket and collected all kinds of stray marginal items in addition to bits of songs caught on the fly. And I liked it, too, because of its place in the chronology. It documents the time when Dylan was turning away from the expectations of the folk-protest crowd. He was writing pop songs, although he was employing the free-associative methods and collage use of the folk-lyric that had marked his work since the beginning. (He was writing pop songs back then, too, although "Baby, I'm in the Mood for You" and "Tomorrow Is a Long Time," for example, waited decades before being officially released.) Dylan was reinventing himself yet again, as his circumstances changed and the Western world experienced a wildcat surge of creativity and release from social constraints. Dylan was becoming a star in an arena that stretched far beyond the world of coffeehouses and folklore centers. At the very same time, The Beatles appeared out of nowhere on television, launching a thousand ships. Muhammad Ali knocked out Sonny Liston; the New York World's Fair was on; Pop Art dominated the art world. It was the year of *Dr. Strangelove* and *Band of Outsiders*, of *Goldfinger* and *The Naked Kiss*. It was the moment of a brash new contract between high and low.

The 1964 notebook begins with a verse:

> *On the banks*
> *of leaf river on*
> *route 11*
> *from Meridian*
> *high roads*

According to Clinton Heylin's dogged *Bob Dylan: A Life in Stolen Moments* (1996), the author was indeed in Meridian, Mississippi, on February 9, 1964, and he traveled on by way of New Orleans, Dallas, and Denver to San Francisco and Los Angeles. In May he was off to London, Paris, and Berlin for a month. On these trips he met people, and their phone numbers and such accrue here and there along the course of the notebook. There's Lenny Bruce ("OL7 4384 / 8825 Hollywood Boulevard"); Nico, then a model, two years before The Velvet Underground ("TRO 7746 / 69 rue de la Pompe"); Mason Hoffenberg, hangout artist and co-author of *Candy*; Al Aronowitz, the journalist who introduced Dylan to The Beatles that summer (when Dylan introduced The Beatles to cannabis); the English folksinger Martin Carthy; the San Francisco music critic Ralph J. Gleason; and City Lights Books, which had Dylan signed up to write a chapbook for their Pocket Poets series—a book that, many years and several publishers later, appeared as *Tarantula*.

The first thing in the notebook to catch my eye seemed to be a sort of Top Ten list:

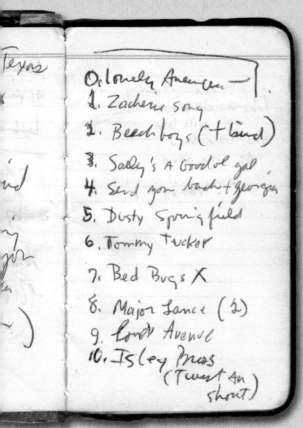

Notebook, circa 1964

0. lonely American
1. Zacherie song
2. Beach Boys (T bird)
3. Sally's a Good ol gal
4. Send you back t Georgia
5. Dusty Springfield
6. Tommy Tucker
7. Bed Bugs X
8. Major Lance (2)
9. Lonely Avenue
10. Isley Bros (Twist an Shout)

And it does turn out to be a playlist, of mostly then current pop, country, and R&B. "Zacherie sing" might refer to the Draculaesque New York television host John Zacherle, who put out an array of 45s around then, such as "Eighty-Two Tombstones" and "I Was a Teenage Caveman"; "Bed Bugs X" might be his jab at The Beatles (Don Adams, later the star of *Get Smart*, appeared then in a television skit as manager of the singing group The Bedbugs, perhaps on *The Jimmy Dean Show*). The others are, in order: The Beach Boys' "Fun Fun Fun" (1964); Hank Cochran's "Sally Was a Good Old Girl" (1962); Timmy Shaw's "Gonna Send You Back to Georgia" (1962); most likely Dusty Springfield's "I Only Want to Be with You" (1963); Tommy Tucker's "Hi-Heel Sneakers" (1964); most likely Major Lance's "The Monkey Time" (1963, written by Curtis Mayfield) and "Um, Um, Um, Um, Um, Um" (1964); Ray Charles's "Lonely Avenue" (1956, written by Doc Pomus); and The Isley Brothers' "Twist and Shout" (1963). At first glance the genres are all over the map, from The Beach Boys' apple-cheeked blend of Chuck Berry and The Four Preps to Timmy Shaw's uncompromisingly specific gutbucket R&B, and from Dusty Springfield's Mod London wall-of-sound anthem of joy to Ray Charles's noir-tinged call-and-response shuffle. But that was the very time when Black and white pop musics were just beginning to sound more like each other, and Dylan was clearly setting out to explore that field of intersection. All of the songs are absolutely sincere; all of them are tough; all of them pack bright hooks in their choruses; you could do the Frug to pretty much every one; you could imagine Dylan covering all of them (except maybe "I Only Want to Be with You"), maybe at Big Pink with The Hawks.

And then the songs begin to emerge. Lines and riffs accrue and intersect and combine, take solid form, wait for words and phrases to fall into the empty slots. Sometimes a song will arrive as an airmail delivery—if not exactly whole then at least balanced on three legs and unlikely to tip over. Thus when three lines appear, "Maybe it's the color of the sun cut flat / An floatin / perhaps it's the weather or something like that," you hear the song immediately. Dylan is within striking distance of

> *Perhaps it's the color of the sun cut flat*
> *An' cov'rin' the crossroads I'm standing at*
> *Or maybe it's the weather or something like that*
> *But mama, you been on my mind*

And then he spends a few pages worrying at the rest of the verses. "When you wake up in the mornin', baby, look inside your mirror," from the fifth verse, is given three varied initial stabs, and "you just been on my mind" appears in a cloud of attempts: "You aint been on my breath / nor thought"; "you're in my dreams [that word crossed out] but then again [that phrase crossed out] you're not." He presumably worked out the rest on a typewriter, but in any case "Mama, You Been on My Mind" was recorded on June 9 and first performed in public on August 8 at Forest Hills Stadium in New York. And then he inexplicably omitted it from *Another Side of Bob Dylan*.

Within a page of the foregoing, three words sit by themselves: "go away from." Once again that is the only prompt the inner jukebox requires. If you are aged and scholarly you might possibly hear John Jacob Niles's keening "Go 'Way from My Window," but more likely you will at once be treated to the entirety of "It Ain't Me, Babe." Those words are followed by "A crimson skyline / climbs it's throne," which might be a first go at "My Back Pages" ("Crimson flames tied through my ears"), but it isn't developed. A dozen pages later, though, he picks up the original scent:

> *You say you are looking*
> *for someone strong*
> *it aint*
> *Please go away from my window baby*
> *   you'll only in time turn around*
> *without using vulgar words*
> *   Please go from my doorway*
> *You'll only be let down*
> *You say you are looking*
> *for someone who stands strong*
> *t protect you or defend you*
> *Constantly thru right or wrong*

Which requires only minor tweaking before it can become

> *Go 'way from my window*
> *Leave at your own chosen speed*
> *I'm not the one you want, babe*
> *I'm not the one you need*
> *You say you're looking for someone*
> *Never weak but always strong*
> *To protect you an' defend you*
> *Whether you are right or wrong*

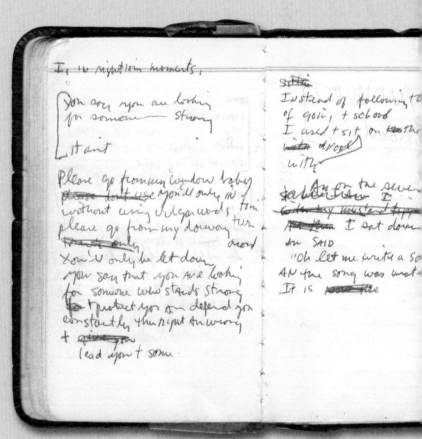

"It Ain't Me, Babe" draft lyrics, circa 1964

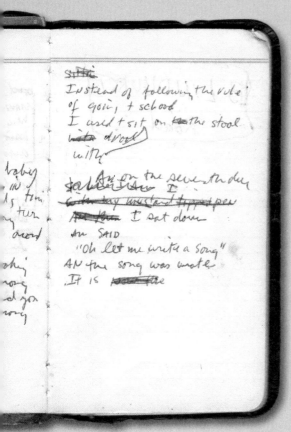

Notebook, circa 1964

He knows he has hit a jackpot (one of many, to be sure), and he celebrates the occasion by following the draft verse above with a bit of doggerel:

> *Instead of following the rule*
> *of going to school*
> *I used to sit on the stool*
> *with drool*
> *An on the seventh day*
> *I sat down*
> *an said*
> *"oh let me write a song"*
> *An the song was wrote*
> *It is*

He first performed "It Ain't Me, Babe" on July 24 at the Newport Folk Festival.

A second, similar notebook from about a year later in 1965 collects all kinds of stray bits of verse and a single diaryish item: "I once said to the German press that i called the music tractor music and one of them said 'oh you mean working class music.'" It is impossible to read that or the verse fragments without hearing them in Dylan's voice, from "cigarette ashes they cover the grass / the street it smells of broken glass" to "20 zebras with riders each wearing" to "Bodyguard is on the floor his head is in the pail." Now and then a song will seem like it's lurking right around the corner:

> *An death doesn't exist*
> *not owning but moaning*
> *not moaning but mourning*
> *not morning but evening*
> *not evening but ?*

What might be an early glimmer of "Like a Rolling Stone" (or "She's Your Lover Now") puts in an appearance:

> *She's been raised in the castle yet her*
> *mind's in the gutter, she borrows*
> *people's heads promising tomorrow*
> *she's convinced every body except herself*

But then the songs do start coming. All by itself appears "She aint no woman / she's a man," which will eventually become the chorus of the fragmentary "Jet Pilot." (Also on this page is reference to Bob Kaufman, San Francisco poet and the first African American member of the Beat crowd.) A few pages later a quatrain ends with the line "death will not come, it's not poison" and then a three-line sequence goes "see themselves in the funnel swallow their pride / life is hard / they do not die, it's not poison." Two lines further: "worthless knowledge." A bit further still: "I wish I could write you a melody so plain / that would [illegible] you dear lady that would consel your pain / for [something blacked out] useless knowledge." And so Dylan has in hand two bits from what will become "Tombstone Blues":

> *Now the medicine man comes and he shuffles inside*
> *He walks with a swagger and he says to the bride*
> *"Stop all this weeping, swallow your pride*
> *You will not die, it's not poison"*

and

> *Now I wish I could write you a melody so plain*
> *That could hold you dear lady from going insane*
> *That could ease you and cool you and cease the pain*
> *Of your useless and pointless knowledge*

In the middle of all this appears a trio of lines—"my sinful mama, you know she moves / like a mountain lion / she's a junkyard princess"—that suggest both "From a Buick 6" and "Lunatic Princess Revisited."

Watching the process as you turn the pages is like seeing a photograph slowly materialize in the developing bath, or maybe a statue freeing itself from the marble block. The two notebooks serve up Bob Dylan live and in color in various hectic portions of 1964 and 1965. You see him in cars, in bars, in airports and gas stations and people's porches and living rooms, maybe with his shades on, smoking cigarettes, meeting interesting people, hearing the radio in the car or the kitchen, turning words and phrases loose from the accumulation in his subconscious and letting them fly around until they find a thermal and float home. The experience is as good as a movie.

"Tombstone Blues" draft lyrics, circa 1965

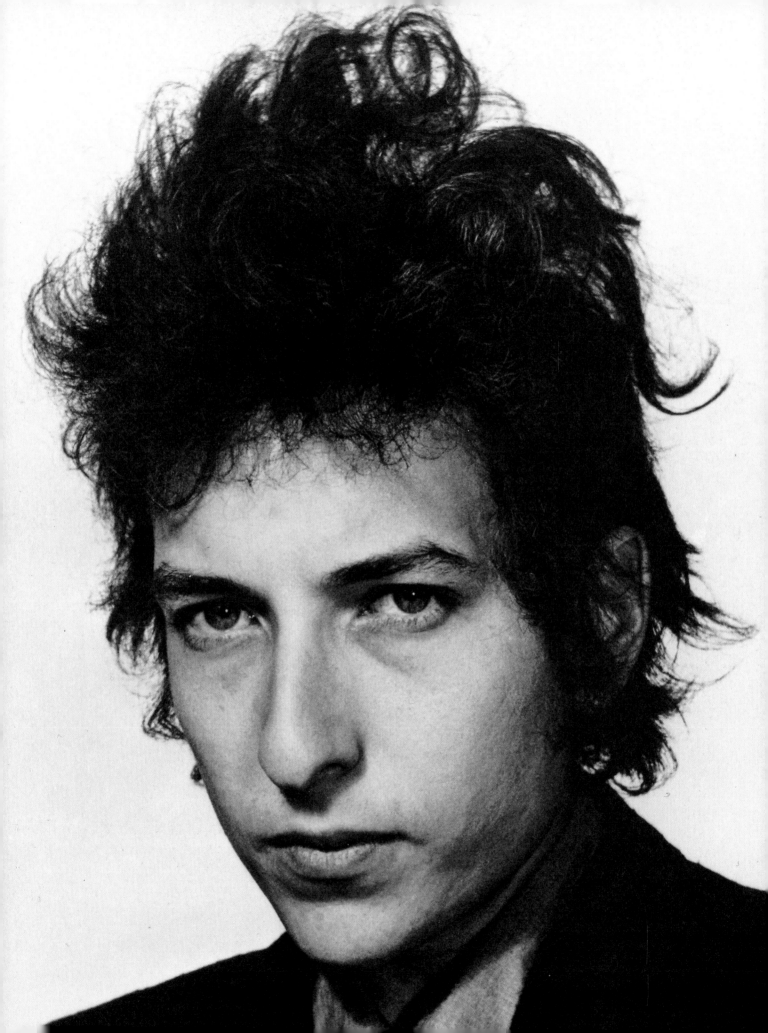

The Sound of the Streets

1965–1966

It was the sound of the streets. It still is.
I symbolically hear that sound wherever I am.

—Bob Dylan, November 1977, Ron Rosenbaum interview, *Playboy*

Bob Dylan, portrait session, 1965. Photograph by Daniel Kramer

Bob Dylan, 1966. Photograph by Barry Feinstein

BRINGING IT ALL BACK HOME

Bob Dylan, *Bringing It All Back Home* sessions, January 1965. Photograph by Daniel Kramer

"SUBTERRANEAN HOMESICK BLUES"

In a *60 Minutes* interview with Ed Bradley in 2004, Dylan described his early writing process:

> *All those early songs were almost magically written.... Well, try to sit down and write something like that. There's a magic to that, and it's not Siegfried and Roy kind of magic. It's a different kind of a penetrating magic.*

The surviving drafts for Dylan's fifth album, *Bringing It All Back Home*, underscore these comments. Musically, the album combines acoustic songs with a new electric band sound that Dylan would continue to explore in the coming year and a half. Dylan's lyrics expand upon the influence of the symbolists and the Beats, introducing a touch of the surreal. The result is uniquely Dylan, yet there is a flow to his writing that can seem uncanny, as if certain images, phrases, or lines have always existed.

The typescript draft for the album's opener, "Subterranean Homesick Blues," overflows with ideas, phrases, and images, with words tumbling over one another. The song is there, however, with only a few handwritten edits and additions.

However, Dylan's gift for the marriage of text and music in performance, evident in the Chuck Berry–inspired "Subterranean Homesick Blues," can be lost in simply looking at words on a page. As Dylan himself said in his Nobel Lecture,

> *Our songs are alive in the land of the living.... They're meant to be sung, not read.*

PAGE 133: "Subterranean Homesick Blues" draft typescript

Look out Kid

xxxxxxxxxxxxxxxxxxxxxxxxxxxxxxxxxxxxxxxxxxxxxxxxxx
xxxxxxxxxxxxxxxxxxxxxxxxxxxxxxxxxxxxxxxxxxxxxxxx
        xxx

    johnny's in the basement/ mising up the medicene
    i'm on the pavement thinking bout the govt
    man in the trnch coat/badge out laid off
    says he's got a bad bill-wants t get paid off
    look out kid/ it's something you did
    god knows when but youre doing it again
    better duck down the alleyway/ looking for new friend
    man in a coonskin cap in the pigpen
    wants 11 dollars bills an you only got ten

    maggie comes fleet foot/ face full of black soot
    talking that the heat put/ plants in the bed but
    the phone's tapped anyway- maggie says that many say
    they must bust in earlymay/ orders from the d.a.
    look out kid it dont matter what you did
but wlak on your tip toes/dont tie no bows/xx better stay away from those
    that carry round a fire hose of the plain clothers
    you dont need a weather man t know which way the wind blows
    keep a clean nose / watch the plain clothes
    Hmm dont wanna be a bum better not chew gum

    gxkxxxkkkx get sick/ get well/ hang aroud the ink well
    ring bell/hard t tell/if anything is gonna sell
    try hard / get barred/ get back back/ write braille
    get jailed/ jump bail/ join the army if you fail

    look out kid/gyoure gonna get get hit
    by users, cheaters, 6 time losers hanging round the theatres
    girl by the whirlpool's looking for a new fool/xx dont follow
        leaders/ kkxkxxxkk watch the parking meters

    get born/ keep warm/short pants/ romance
    learn t dance/ get dressed/ get blessed/ try t be a success
    please her/ please him/ buy gifts xxxxxxxkmdont steal/ dont lift
    20 years of schooling an they put you on the day shift
    look out kid they keep it all hid
    it's nowhere/ all bare/ they just pay your fare there
    frog smxg smog/ thick fog/ they ttell you that it's fresh air
    (dont daxk why but the water well's dry/
    (dont ask why-but you better say goodbye-(better not ask why

ss   candles
    candles
    scandals

    better jump in the manhole/light yourself a candle/
    dont wear scandal, / try t avoid the scandal,
    dont ask why but the
    better say goodbye   be a bum/chew gum/1
    better not start/ they'll just take your head an put t put in
    for the pump dont work cause the vandals stole the handals

"MAVIS"

On the back side of "Subterranean Homesick Blues" are a couple of verses for a song simply titled "Mavis." With a first line that reads "down in chicago there lives a queen," it seems likely that Dylan had Mavis Staples, the great gospel frontwoman of the Windy City–based Staple Singers, in mind.

The group had an early and enduring influence on Dylan after he heard "Uncloudy Day" on the radio as a child.

> *It was the most mysterious thing I'd ever heard. It was like the fog rolling in.*
> *I heard it again, maybe the next night, and its mystery had even deepened.*
> *What was that? How do you make that?*

Although this manuscript was unfinished and ultimately not recorded, Dylan brought it to the January 1965 sessions for the album *Bringing It All Back Home* ("Mavis" is visible on the left side of the music stand).

Bob Dylan (with John Sebastian partially obscured), *Bringing It All Back Home* sessions, January 1965. Photograph by Daniel Kramer

PAGE 135: "Mavis" draft typescript

Mavis

1 down in chicago there lives a queen
  she sings the blues if you know what i mean
  ah mavis

2.xxxxxxxxx i dream she's singing in my sleep but worse
  i wake up thining that i'm in church

3. she sings the blues in a long white robe   like
                                          job globe stone
                                                     down

4.

Photo shoot behind Peter Yarrow's mother's house, Woodstock, NY, March 14, 1965. Photograph by Daniel Kramer

"MAGGIE'S FARM"

Dylan's approach to weaving together multiple, diverse touchpoints has always been an important dimension of his creative process. "Maggie's Farm" exemplifies Dylan's nonconformist roots, updating the sound of the Chicago blues while tying the lyric to a theme that would have had a particular resonance with young fans at the time.

John Cohen, member of The New Lost City Ramblers, noted documentarian, and early Dylan associate, saw another, earlier set of connections in the song, which he detailed in his 1995 interview for *No Direction Home*:

> The idea that the traditional songs gave us excuses and gave us words and ideas and attitudes about life that you could borrow from, that you could build your songs on, that seemed very clear to me. And when Bob sang "Maggie's Farm" I thought he was referring to "Penny's Farm," and when he sang that song in New York, "Living Down in New York Town" ["Hard Times in New York Town"], he just borrowed the melody to "Down on Penny's Farm." "Down on Penny's Farm" is an old sharecropper's song from the rural South.

PAGE 137: "Maggie's Farm" draft typescript

Maggie's ?Farm

1. i aint gonna work on maggie's farm no more (2)
   wake up in the mornign/ fold my hands an pray for rain
   i got a head full of ideas that're drihing me insane
   it's a shame the way she mskes me scrub the floor
   an i aingt gonna work on maggie's farm nomore

2aint gonna work for her brother bill no more
   (2)
      well he gives me a nickel he gives me a dime
      he asks me with a grin if i'm having a good time
      he fine's me eve y time i slam the door
      i aint gonna work for maggie s broghher no more

3. i aint gonna work for maggie's pa no more (2)
   well he puts his cigar out in your face just for kicks
      his bedroom window/ it's made out of bricks
      he's got the national guard standing round the door
   ah i aint gonna wokr for maggies pa no more

4. i aint gonna work for maggies ma no more
      (2)   she talkst ~~to she sll the servants~~ of
   she ~~xkkkxxxxdxxxxxmxkxxkxyxxxxkkxxxxxxxd~~
      ~~gets carried around by~~ servants/ ~~talks~~ of god an man an law
      eveybody says dhe's the brains behind pa
                                        s
      she's (fourty years old but she says he's twenty four
      (she's twenty years old et she claims she's 64

            40 years   24

5. i aint gonna work on maggie's farm no more (2)
      You

   if you aint like everyone else   I try my best + be just the way i am
   they think theyloe been insulted   but everybody wants you t be just like them
   everybody keep track of the   ~~·~~
                                           they say sing while you'r slave
                                           / i just bored

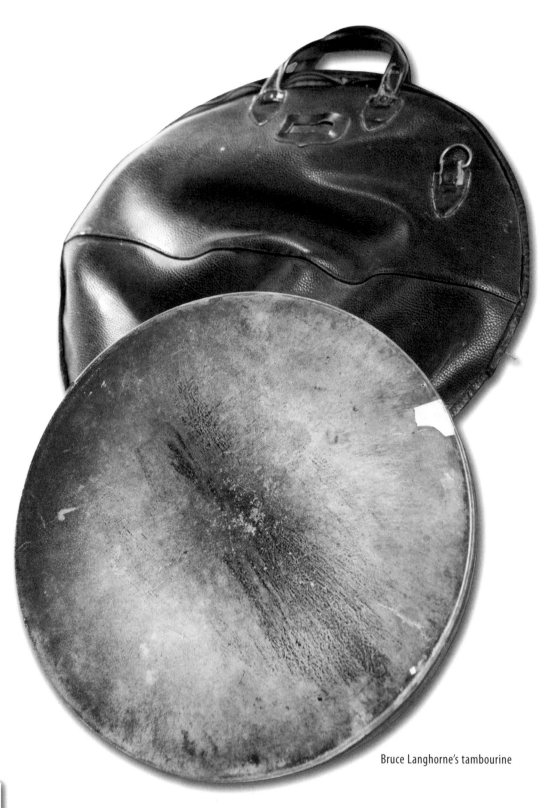

Bruce Langhorne's tambourine

"MR. TAMBOURINE MAN"

Written in February 1964, "Mr. Tambourine Man" went through several iterations before being released on Dylan's March 1965 album *Bringing It All Back Home*. The first existing recording of the song dates to May '64, when Dylan performed the song for Eric von Schmidt at Schmidt's home in Sarasota, Florida. Soon thereafter, Dylan began to play the song live, and he eventually brought the song to the June 9, 1964, session for *Another Side of Bob Dylan*. Although the song was left off that album, Dylan subsequently re-recorded "Mr. Tambourine Man" with the addition of Bruce Langhorne's countermelodies on electric guitar.

In an interview with journalist Cameron Crowe included as liner notes for the 1984 box set *Biograph*, Dylan offered thoughts on the creation of the song:

> *"Mr. Tambourine Man," I think, was inspired by Bruce Langhorne. Bruce was playing guitar with me on a bunch of the early records. On one session, [producer] Tom Wilson had asked him to play tambourine. He had this gigantic tambourine. It was like, really big. It was as big as a wagon wheel. He was playing, and this vision of him playing this tambourine just stuck in my mind. He was one of those characters. I don't know if I've ever told him that.*

Despite being the only other musician on the track, Langhorne wasn't aware he'd been an inspiration for the song until he read those very words in *Biograph*, some twenty years after the song was recorded. Until then, he'd been under the impression that Dylan was referencing Brother John Sellers, the gospel-oriented folksinger who emceed the weekly hootenannies at Gerdes Folk City with tambourine in hand.

Langhorne's own famous "tambourine" was actually a large, 16-inch-diameter Turkish frame drum known as a *daf*, which he'd purchased at Izzy Young's Folklore Center in Greenwich Village. With an animal skin head and jingle bells stapled into the inside of the wooden ring (and a Band-Aid holding together a split in the drum head), the tambourine was one of the Bob Dylan Archive's first acquisitions.

THE SOUND OF THE STREETS

Bob Dylan during the recording of *Bringing It All Back Home*, January 13–15, 1965, at Columbia Records Studio A in New York City. Bruce Langhorne is pictured in the back right with his tambourine. Photograph by Daniel Kramer

American Dream #115

Tom Piazza

(The Interviewer steers his car up a long, winding driveway lined with majestic elm trees, to a three-story stone castle at the top of a hill, where he parks in a gravel space with a sign reading VISITORS. *Stepping out, he pauses and takes in the sweeping views—in one direction a panorama of the Tennessee River as it snakes its way through Chattanooga, and in the other the cozy confines of Boston Harbor. He grabs his voice recorder and notebook out of the back seat, crosses a short footbridge over a moat, approaches a massive medieval wooden door, and rings a cheap-looking, broken plastic doorbell button to its left. Within seconds, the door slowly swings open, and a man well over six feet tall, dressed in a dinner jacket, white tie, shorts, and flip-flops, greets him and wordlessly gestures for him to come in.)*

INTERVIEWER: Thank you so much for inviting me, Mister Piazza; I'm flattered that you made the time, and. . . .

BUTLER: I'm not Mister Piazza. He's in the grand salon, awaiting your arrival. Probably soused by now. Follow me.

(The butler leads the Interviewer down a long, high-ceilinged, dimly lit stone hallway, lined with floor-to-ceiling bookshelves; on the floor in front of the shelves teeter tall stacks of compact discs, cassettes, more books, DVDs, VHS tapes, LPs, 78 records, and folders full of manuscript pages that fall over and spill onto the floor, blocking a clear path. The two men step around these. At intervals, suits of armor stand at attention. At length, the hallway opens into a baronial, high-ceilinged room with a cavernous stone fireplace at one end large enough to park a school bus inside. A school bus is, in fact, parked inside it. Standing in front of the bus, wearing a smoking jacket and ascot, is Tom Piazza.)

TOM PIAZZA: That will be all, Friedrich.

(The butler leaves, and the Interviewer looks around in wonder at the book-lined walls.)

INTERVIEWER: Wow. All these books. . .

PIAZZA: Yes. Lots of books. I use them to insulate the house. Have a seat.

(Piazza gestures toward one of a matching pair of antique velvet sofas facing each other across a stunning Serapi carpet. In the center is a low, six-foot-long oak table supporting a large alabaster bowl filled with shoes. The Interviewer notices, frowns.)

PIAZZA: I hope you had a pleasant drive. Those last ten miles outside of Cheyenne are tough. It's easy to miss the driveway. Do you want anything to drink, by the way?

INTERVIEWER: No, thank you. I'm fine.

PIAZZA: So, okay, you're doing a . . . what. A master's thesis?

INTERVIEWER: It's my PhD dissertation. I'm interrogating the song "Bob Dylan's 115th Dream" as an allegory for the collapse of late-stage capitalism.

PIAZZA: I see. *(He frowns, purses his lips, stares for a few seconds at the table between them.)* Please excuse me for a moment. *(He stands, exits. A few moments later, from a distant room, the sound of raised voices, Friedrich's voice saying "Get back in there; that man is your guest. . ." then sounds of a physical struggle, glass breaking. After a pause, Piazza re-enters the room, holding a towel to his forehead.)*

PIAZZA *(resuming his seat on the couch)*: I'm sorry; I needed to see if the dryer had stopped. Where were we?

INTERVIEWER: My dissertation is on. . .

PIAZZA: Right. Dylan's trip to America. *(Piazza pulls the towel away from his forehead, looks at it, replaces it.)* What's your idea?

INTERVIEWER: My thesis is that Dylan set up a series of metaphors for the oppressive structures encoded in the failing systems of American oligarchical capitalism. Here are the lyrics, typed by Dylan himself . . . I copied them at the Archive.

PIAZZA (*removing the towel from his forehead, revealing a bloody gash near the hairline, he accepts the proffered manuscript page and examines it, at intervals laughing out loud. He then hands it back to the Interviewer.*): Great stuff. As good as Brecht. And the little draft of "Maggie's Farm" on the back. I love all the songs on *Bringing It All Back Home*. Maybe he read from this in the studio. Please go on.

INTERVIEWER: My theory is that images of falling to the ground are rife throughout this indictment of capitalism and imperialism. What's the first thing that happens to the voice in the song? He takes a deep breath and falls down. The "Captain" of the ship—impossibly named the "Mayflower," since the arch-imperialist tool Columbus is seen arriving at the end—immediately puts up a "fort," and commences the classic exploitative process of "purchasing" valuable land from Indigenous peoples with worthless trinkets. The narrator, by the way, at the end, calls himself "Captain Kid," a perfect symbolic representation of the reduction of an adult to the status of a feudal, dependent subject.

PIAZZA: Oh boy. . . (*He picks up a little bell from the table, shakes it twice, sets it back down. Friedrich enters.*)

"Bob Dylan's 115th Dream" draft typescript

PIAZZA: Friedrich, please bring out that plate of herring filets. Also I need a fresh towel. (*Friedrich exits.*) Sorry—please go on.

INTERVIEWER: The narrator, under the sway of the "Captain," proceeds into town, where he picks up a "pay phone"—could there be a better image of the profit motive invading the most private channels of communication?—and a foot comes through the line. Even through the tiniest of apertures, the narrow cord of the telephone, a *foot*—the symbol of oppression and domination—is able to exert its power. . . The owner of a house displaying an American flag opens the door to the narrator, hears the narrator's plea for help, and threatens to "tear him limb from limb" and "break his bones," finally even dismissing the narrator's appeal to Christian charity. He goes into a headquarters for Brotherhood and it is a funeral parlor—clearly symbolizing the death of the societal model of cooperation, and when he leaves the funeral parlor, what happens? A giant bowling ball comes down the road, knocking him—once again—to the ground.

(*Friedrich enters, wearing a Prussian army officer's uniform. He clicks his heels and sets a tray on the table in front of Piazza.*)

PIAZZA: Friedrich. . . First we offer some to our guest, don't we? (*Friedrich bends to pick up the tray, but Piazza stops him.*) Wait one moment. . . (*Piazza leans down close to the tray, examining the contents.*) These aren't herring filets.

FRIEDRICH (*clearly annoyed*): What would you call them?

PIAZZA: They're anchovies. Here—look for yourself.

FRIEDRICH: I don't need to look; I arranged them on the platter. They are herring filets. You caught them yourself on your little "yacht safari" in the Amazon.

"Bob Dylan's 115th Dream" draft typescript

PIAZZA: That was two years ago. And they don't have herring in the Amazon! (*He stands.*)

FRIEDRICH: How dare you question me! (*He pulls a Luger out of the holster at his hip and points it at Piazza.*) I have endured your humiliations long enough!

PIAZZA: Friedrich—Look out! Behind you!

(*Friedrich turns to look; Piazza vaults over the table and tackles him as the Interviewer looks on in horror. Friedrich is easily subdued, and Piazza relieves him of the pistol.*)

FRIEDRICH (*standing up and brushing himself off*): May I have my gun back?

(*Piazza hands Friedrich the Luger, and Friedrich exits.*)

PIAZZA: He freaks out a little when I have guests. Listen, didn't you find anything funny in the song?

(*A loud crash is heard, coming from another room.*)

INTERVIEWER (*visibly disturbed*): Funny? The depiction of misfortune, humiliation, hubris, misunderstanding, and indignity is never funny.

PIAZZA: Really? What do *you* think is funny? (*He places a piece of herring on a cracker and holds it out to the Interviewer, who ignores it.*)

INTERVIEWER: We all must put all of our efforts toward building a new world—one where all structures of exploitation are abolished forever. . . where power relationships are completely dismantled. . . .

PIAZZA: You're going to have a long wait. The world is crazy. America especially. Dangerous, full of possibility good and bad. The contradictions are enough to drive anybody off a ledge. The voice in Dylan's song is free. You get freedom but then you realize you're in a madhouse. You don't think that's funny?

INTERVIEWER: I think it's tragic.

PIAZZA (*nods sadly*): So do I.

INTERVIEWER (*frowning*): Things can't be tragic and funny at the same time. . .

PIAZZA: You ever listen to the blues?

(*Friedrich enters, pushing a cart laden with bottles and glasses.*)

PIAZZA: What was that crash?

FRIEDRICH: One of the camels got loose. Would you and your new friend care for a cocktail before the regiment arrives?

INTERVIEWER (*alarmed*): What is "the regiment. . ."?

PIAZZA (*ignoring the question*): I think that would be delightful, Friedrich. Thank you.

(*Friedrich exits. Piazza stands, pulls a monocle out of a pocket in his smoking jacket, and places it in front of his left eye with some difficulty. From another pocket he extracts a scroll of paper tied with a bright blue ribbon. He unties the ribbon, holding the topmost edge of the scroll in his hands as the remainder unspools to the floor and rolls across the rug, nearly to the fireplace. He clears his throat and begins reading aloud.*)

PIAZZA: Gentlemen. As I stand before you this evening, I am reminded of a long-ago afternoon on which I sat meditating in the forest before a beautiful banyan tree. The soft breeze carried the scent of jasmine through the sun-dappled woods, and a mood of tranquility suffused the scene. As the leaves on the banyan shivered slightly in the gentle breeze, Vishnu appeared, saying, "A Frenchman, an Italian, and an Irishman walked into a bar. As they took their seats, the bartender addressed them, saying, 'Esteemed guests, My wife wished to go on a vacation. "Where do you wish to go?" I asked. "Somewhere I've never been," she responded. To which I said, "How about the kitchen?"' The three guests laughed merrily, nodding and applauding. (*The Interviewer shifts uneasily in his chair. In the distance, the sound of men marching is heard, very faintly.*) 'Perhaps it is just as well,' the bartender went on. 'My wife always wants to make love in the back seat of our car—While I am driving!' The guests laughed loudly and slapped the bar with their hands. The Frenchman said, 'C'est si bon!' The Italian said, 'I'm hungry!' The Irishman said . . .'"

INTERVIEWER: Stop! This is intolerable!

PIAZZA (*throws the scroll on the ground, grabs an andiron from the fireplace, and jumps onto the table*): How are you supposed to live in a crazy world? Every system is unjust! Everybody's shouting "Which side are you on?" The only way to make a perfect society is to get rid of everybody who isn't perfect! Get out the guillotines!

INTERVIEWER (*alarmed*): That's not what I'm saying!

PIAZZA (*wielding the andiron like a harpoon*): You try your best to be just like you are, and everybody wants you to be just like them! They analyze you, categorize you, finalize you, and advertise you! You can't theorize about freedom—you have to *be* freedom. . . . Drink that railroad gin! Shake that dust off your feet! Declare yourself king of infinite space, bad dreams and all. . .

INTERVIEWER: Help! Help!

(*Friedrich, barefoot, runs into the room, sneaks up behind Piazza, and whacks him on the head with a blackjack. Piazza slumps over, rolls off the table and onto the rug. The Interviewer looks down at him in stunned disbelief.*)

FRIEDRICH: Bring me that bottle of akvavit from the cart. He'll be alright.

(*The Interviewer retrieves the bottle and holds it out for Friedrich, looking at the blackjack lying on the floor.*)

FRIEDRICH: You can just set the bottle down there on the rug. I see you like my blackjack. That's a whalebone handle. They don't make them anymore. I hate to have to thump him. It's the only thing to do when he gets started.

INTERVIEWER (*staring down at Piazza*): What made him go crazy?

FRIEDRICH: He read a poem by William Carlos Williams that said, "the pure products of America go crazy," and he just . . . went crazy. You'd better leave before he wakes up. Let me put some of these crackers in a bag for you . . .

INTERVIEWER: No. . . I'll be fine . . . Thank you . . . You don't have to see me to the door . . . (*He exits, quickly. The front door can be heard slamming shut.*)

FRIEDRICH (*Takes a slug from the akvavit bottle*): He's gone. Tense fellow.

PIAZZA (*sits up*): They're all like that now.

(*The sound of knocking can be heard coming from the front door, and they fall silent, listening.*)

FRIEDRICH: That must be your three o'clock, the guy from *Critical Theoretics Review*.

PIAZZA: Bloody hell. (*Sighs deeply.*) Go ahead and let him in.

Bob Dylan and Joan Baez, Club 47, Cambridge, MA,
April 1964. Photograph by Dick Waterman

Original study, circa 1965. Painting by Eric von Schmidt

BOB DYLAN AND JOAN BAEZ CONCERTS, 1965

Although Bob Dylan and Joan Baez had appeared on each other's concerts since 1963, a handful of East Coast Dylan/Baez joint appearances in March 1965 was to be their first (and only) official double bill, as well as their last public performances together until the Rolling Thunder Revue in late 1975.

Baez's manager Manny Greenhill tapped fellow folksinger Eric von Schmidt to create a design for concert posters and flyers to advertise the shows. An accomplished artist and graphic designer, von Schmidt had created the artwork for dozens of albums, primarily for the Vanguard and Pathways of Sound record labels, including those of Joan Baez, James Baldwin, The Blues Project, Reverend Gary Davis, Woody Guthrie, and Cisco Houston.

Von Schmidt, working in the style of French painter Henri Toulouse-Lautrec, used as his subject a photograph Dick Waterman took of Baez and Dylan from a concert at Club 47 in Cambridge, Massachusetts, in April 1964. This study for an Eric von Schmidt painting shows von Schmidt's original conception, with Dylan and Baez mirrored by folksingers Mimi Fariña (Joan's sister) and her husband Dick.

Convention Hall, Philadelphia, PA, concert poster, 1965

Bob Dylan and Joan Baez, New Haven Arena, New Haven, CT, March 6, 1965. Photographs by Daniel Kramer

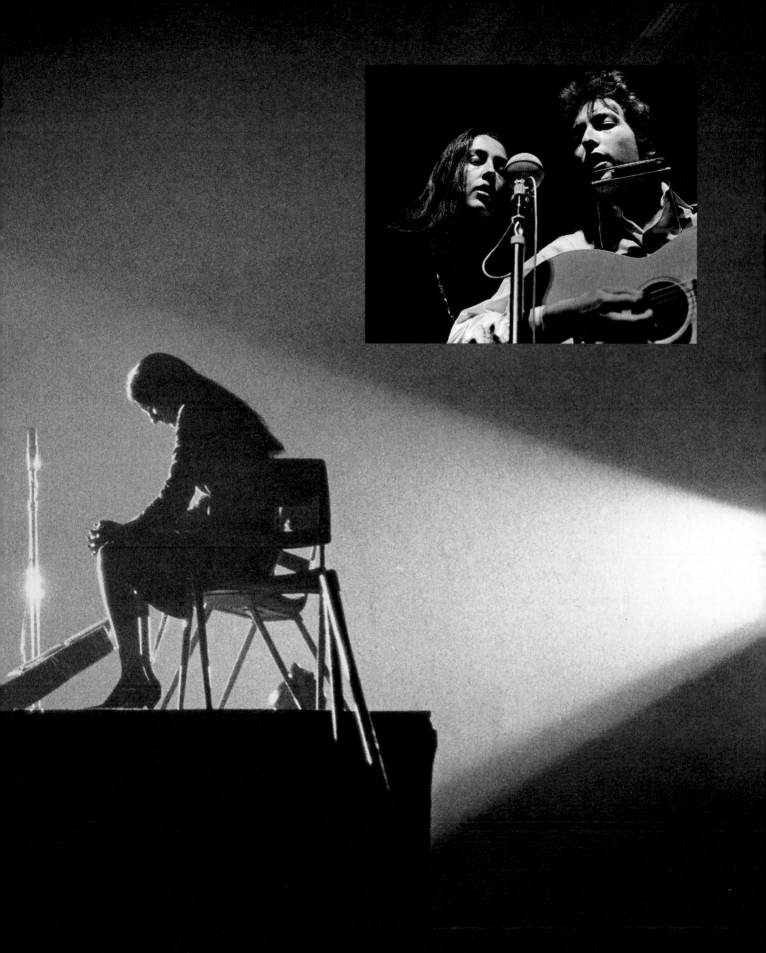

Bob Dylan, New York, February 10, 1965. Photograph by Richard Avedon

THE SOUND OF THE STREETS

New Musical Express, March 26, 1965

Tickets from 1965 UK tour

1965 UK TOUR

Having made his first trip to Great Britain in December 1962 and January 1963, Dylan and his music had always been well received across the pond, and he returned again for a special concert at Royal Festival Hall in 1964 that was recorded by Columbia Records but never issued.

In late April 1965, Dylan returned to the British Isles for a tour that would run through mid-May, closing with a high-profile BBC appearance on June 1, 1965.

Cinema verité pioneer D. A. Pennebaker was along for the ride, filming fourteen days of Dylan's last solo acoustic tour. The ensuing film, *Dont Look Back* (1967), showed the artist at a crucial point in his career and offers glimpses of the mania surrounding him. Starting with its famous opening sequence of Dylan revealing cue cards set to the music of his single "Subterranean Homesick Blues," *Dont Look Back* helped cement the public's image of mid-1960s Dylan as a hip provocateur with an acerbic wit and creativity bursting at the seams.

Shot intimately on Pennebaker's custom 16mm handheld camera, the film documented Dylan as he was performing, writing on his typewriter, dueling with the press, trading songs with Donovan, dealing with mobs of fans, and working through songs for his upcoming albums. The documentary also featured members of Dylan's entourage, including Joan Baez, Marianne Faithfull, Allen Ginsberg, Albert Grossman, Bobby Neuwirth, and Alan Price of The Animals.

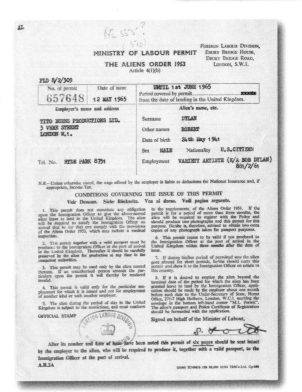

Labor permit for 1965 UK tour

PAGES 152–153: "Subterranean Homesick Blues" from *Dont Look Back*, filmed 1965. Directed by D. A. Pennebaker

Bob Dylan and D. A. Pennebaker (with camera) at the Savoy Hotel, London, April 27, 1965. Photographer unknown

THE BYRDS

Dylan recorded "Mr. Tambourine Man" in January 1965 as part of the sessions for *Bringing It All Back Home*. However, prior to the release of the album that March, the song was making the rounds; an early acetate had gotten into the hands of Jim Dickson, who managed a fledgling group in Los Angeles called The Byrds. The song caught the ear of bandleader Jim "Roger" McGuinn, who, having been enthralled with The Beatles' 1964 film *A Hard Day's Night* (especially George Harrison's twelve-string Rickenbacker), reimagined the song as a sort of Dylan/Beatles mash-up. Dylan had an opportunity to hear the new interpretation on one of his trips to LA, and on March 26, 1965, he made a surprise guest appearance performing the song with The Byrds at the popular Ciro's nightclub on Sunset Strip. As McGuinn later recalled,

> Bob just came up and started jamming with us. There's another picture from that night on the back of our first album. He loved our version of "Mr. Tambourine Man." He and Bobby Neuwirth came to our rehearsals at World Pacific, and they listened to it. He said, "Wow, you can dance to it."

The Byrds released their version of "Mr. Tambourine Man" shortly thereafter in April 1965. Within months the song reached #1 in both the US and UK, launching the "folk-rock" boom of the mid-1960s. It also became the title track to their debut LP on Columbia Records.

While Dylan was in the studio recording "Like a Rolling Stone," photographer W. Eugene Smith shot Dylan and his manager Albert Grossman reviewing a copy of The Byrds' first album a few days before its release on June 21.

The Byrds' second single was another Dylan cover, "All I Really Want to Do," which Columbia rush released on June 14 to compete with the imminent release of Cher's rival cover of the song on Imperial Records. Even as Dylan's songs continued to prove popular and successful for other artists, in 1965 Columbia launched the "No One Sings Dylan Like Dylan!" campaign to promote the singer's own recordings.

Bob Dylan and Albert Grossman, "Like a Rolling Stone" sessions, June 1965. Photograph by W. Eugene Smith

No One Sings Dylan Like Dylan! That's what the excitement is all about. Bob has the fastest-breaking single you've ever seen. Check the charts and watch it climb higher every week! "Subterranean Homesick Blues" ON COLUMBIA RECORDS

"No One Sings Dylan Like Dylan!" advertisement from *Record World*, April 10, 1965

Bob Dylan with The Byrds, Ciro's, Los Angeles, March 26, 1965. Photographer unknown

NEWPORT FOLK FESTIVAL, 1965

The 1965 Newport Folk Festival culminated in Dylan's short but eventful headline performance. Backed by an electric band featuring members of The Paul Butterfield Blues Band (Michael Bloomfield, Jerome Arnold, and Sam Lay), Al Kooper, and Barry Goldberg, Dylan gave a performance that would go down as one of the most consequential concerts in popular music history.

Despite the historic nature of that evening, or possibly because of it, there have been many different accounts of what actually transpired the evening of Sunday, July 25. The following excerpts have been taken from interviews done for the documentary film *No Direction Home*.

BOB DYLAN: *Sometimes there's no sound coming through, so people could get upset about that. Sometimes there's too much sound coming through. I don't think anybody was there having a negative response to those songs, though. Whatever it was about, it wasn't about anything that they were hearing.*

Bob Dylan. Film still from 1965 Newport Folk Festival footage, by Murray Lerner

TONY GLOVER: "Like a Rolling Stone" had come maybe a week or two before. I remember walking around the festival grounds, people had these little transistor radios. And I remember a couple of times hearing "Like a Rolling Stone" come drifting through the air, and I thought that was pretty cool.

Tony Glover.
Photograph by David Gahr

MARIA MULDAUR: The big buzz was that in the second half of the show Dylan was going to perform. And we all knew that he had been rehearsing that afternoon with Butter [Paul Butterfield] and Bloomfield and Al Kooper.

Maria Muldaur. Photograph by David Gahr

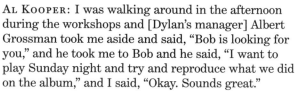

AL KOOPER: I was walking around in the afternoon during the workshops and [Dylan's manager] Albert Grossman took me aside and said, "Bob is looking for you," and he took me to Bob and he said, "I want to play Sunday night and try and reproduce what we did on the album," and I said, "Okay. Sounds great."

We rehearsed on Saturday night in one of those old mansions in Newport, a millionaire's mansion and we were only able to come up with three songs to get it down, so I didn't know what Bob was going to do.

Bob Dylan rehearses with Al Kooper, at right on organ, the afternoon of his headlining performance. Photograph by David Gahr

158

Peter Yarrow checking microphones with Dylan, at right on guitar, during rehearsal. Film still from 1965 Newport Folk Festival footage, by Murray Lerner

Bob Dylan with Michael Bloomfield. Film still from 1965 Newport Folk Festival footage, by Murray Lerner

HAROLD LEVENTHAL: I was backstage and the rumor was that Bob was going to come up with electric instruments. So I hung around to see what was happening. When Bob went up to the stand I was at the steps, and he said to me then, "Where's Pete Seeger?" I said, "He's around somewhere." When he got off the stand he said to me, "Where's Pete Seeger?" I almost said to him, "You don't want to know." Because Pete was very much upset at what happened.

PETER YARROW: [Dylan] got on stage, and he played it, and it was a disaster area. Except for "Maggie's Farm," as I remember, it was incoherent. It wasn't together in terms of time, and not because they were bad musicians, of course, but because they couldn't hear each other well. They didn't have the kind of monitor systems that would allow them to do that, at the time.

BOBBY NEUWIRTH: At some point during that performance at the Newport Folk Festival, the sound system seemed to fry in some way. I remember watching it from out in the audience, with Paul [Rothschild], who was a record producer and a sound engineer himself. Bob's lyrics were relatively inaudible, and that's what caused the restiveness in the crowd.

AL KOOPER: I'm told that people were booing. But I didn't hear any booing.

MARIA MULDAUR: We noticed about a third of the audience was booing, which was unheard of—not in all our days of seeing whatever kind of show we had ever seen, especially for Bob. The other half, us included, were cheering. Then there was another third who didn't know what to do or think.

Bob Dylan and Michael Bloomfield during performance. Film still from 1965 Newport Folk Festival footage, by Murray Lerner

Al Kooper and Bob Dylan during performance. Photograph by David Gahr

Pete Seeger. Photograph by David Gahr

PETE SEEGER: I guess a lot of people felt that Bob was going commercial, but, shucks, he wasn't any more commercial than Burl Ives was.

AL KOOPER: Well, he created a very confrontational performance. He went to the belly of folk music and played loud rock 'n' roll and it was bound to cause some disagreement. But he also only played for fifteen minutes in a show that he was the headliner of in an era where he was the king of folk music.

MARIA MULDAUR: I know he did a couple of songs with the band and then there were these boos and he walked offstage. I believe it was to get his acoustic guitar because I think he only planned to do a few songs with the band. But the audience took it as a capitulation, like they had forced him to go back acoustic.

Bob Dylan closes with "It's All Over Now, Baby Blue." Film still from 1965 Newport Folk Festival footage, by Murray Lerner

John Cohen. Photograph by David Gahr

JOHN COHEN: I know everybody says that Pete Seeger was so angry that he was going to take an ax and chop the cables and turn off the sound that way. But that's not my interpretation. Pete's father was there, Charlie Seeger, and he had a hearing aid and Charlie was very distressed when he couldn't hear things clearly. With all this sound coming from the speakers, Charlie Seeger was quite upset, and I think that affected Pete. So I think he was acting partly on behalf of his father.

PETER YARROW: Bobby was terribly shaken and I ran backstage and he said to me, "What have you done to me?"

I said, "Bobby, here's my guitar. Go onstage and sing." And he went out, and took my guitar, and he did that.

But it was over.

Charles Seeger. Photograph by David Gahr

PETE SEEGER: I never felt that he did move away [from folk music]. Just because Bob was using electric instruments doesn't mean he was moving away. "Maggie's Farm" is just one of the best songs in the world. It's a very real song. At that famous 1965 Newport, I blew my top because the sound was so bad. You could not understand the words, and I was frantic. I said, "Get that distortion out." You could not understand a word. I ran over to the sound system, "Get that distortion out of Bob's voice." "No, this is the way they want to have it." I said, "Goddamnit, it's terrible! You can't understand it. If I had an ax I'd chop the mic cable right now." I was furious. They thought I didn't like the electric instruments.

Postcard from Pete Seeger to Bob Dylan, circa 1985

Bob! Someone just told me that you too think I didn't like your going electric in 1965. I've denied that so many times—I was furious at the distorted sound—no one could understand the words of "Maggie's Farm" and dashed over to the people controlling the PA system. "No this is the way they want it"—this is what I shouted. If I had an axe I'd cut the cable—and I guess that is what got quoted. My big mistake was in not challenging from the stage the foolish few who booed. I shoulda said "Howling [sic] Wolf goes electric, why can't Bob?" In any case, you keep on—

Best Pete

Bob Dylan
c/o Showcase Foundation
P.O. Box 860
Coopers Station
NYC
NY   10003

MARIA MULDAUR: Every night after the concerts George Wien and the festival people would have a party for all the performers. These parties were great—they put us up in these old mansions all over Newport. I remember after this infamous concert we were all excited because the Chambers Brothers were going to be like the party band of that night and they were certainly electric. We went over to the party and they had a big sit-down dinner and all the old guard were sitting at one end of this long, long table all arguing among themselves. I went over and Bob was sitting there wiggling his leg and I said, "Hey, Bob, do you want to dance?" and he looked up at me and said, "I'd dance with you Maria, but my hands are on fire."

In a circa 1985 postcard, folk musician Pete Seeger dispels the myths surrounding his reaction to Dylan's controversial performance as well as notions of authenticity in folk music: "I shoulda said 'Howling [sic] Wolf goes electric, why can't Bob?'"

Leather jacket worn by Bob Dylan during "electric" performance

Bob Dylan in leather jacket, Newport Folk Festival, 1965. Photograph by David Gahr

Documentary filmmaker Murray Lerner shot astounding footage of the Newport Folk Festivals from 1963 to 1965, which he turned into his breakthrough film *Festival!*, released in 1967. These three years of shooting coincided with Dylan's appearances at the festival, giving Lerner a front-row seat to the rise of Dylan's star and his development as an artist. Accordingly, Lerner was on hand during Dylan's 1965 headlining appearance, providing another perspective on what actually happened.

Knowing that his footage of Dylan at Newport was a compelling story on its own, Lerner started editing a standalone film, *The Other Side of the Mirror*, in the late 1960s. (Various elements and edits of Lerner's film exist in the Archive.) Despite the strength of Dylan's performances and the historic nature of the footage, the film was not officially released until 2007.

L–R: Bobby Gregg, Al Kooper, Al Gorgoni, Michael Bloomfield, Frank Owens, Joseph Macho, Jr., Tom Wilson (in control room), Bob Dylan, "Like a Rolling Stone" sessions, June 15, 1965. Photograph by Don Hunstein

"LIKE A ROLLING STONE"

During a June 1965 visit to the Woodstock home of musician Peter Yarrow (of Peter, Paul and Mary), Dylan began to edit a voluminous initial draft of a new song, often cited as between ten and twenty pages or, as Dylan put it, "this long piece of vomit, twenty pages long." This typescript was part of that writing process, with about a verse and a half nailed down and the rest a jumble of images that would largely find their way into the final version of "Like a Rolling Stone." Whether or not the accompanying handwritten manuscript page is related, it was found in a set of papers from the period and shares some language and themes with the song.

While at Yarrow's, Dylan also sat down at the piano to work out a chord progression for the song that would become "Like a Rolling Stone." (The harp, salvaged from Yarrow's upright piano, is part of the Bob Dylan Archive.)

When he entered Columbia Studio A in New York City on June 15, 1965, Dylan led the session musicians from the piano, continuing unsuccessfully to work out the song as a waltz in 3/4 time. Returning the next day, Dylan changed the time signature to 4/4 and switched to guitar. After a brief rehearsal and three takes, the band hit the mark, though they continued for another eleven takes before deciding take 4 could not be bested.

Realizing "Like a Rolling Stone" was an artistic breakthrough, Dylan told CBC Radio in 1966,

> *After writing it, I wasn't interested in writing a novel, or a play, or anything. I wanted to write songs because it was just a whole new category. Nobody's ever really written songs before, really. People have in olden days, but those were sonnets and soft troubadour-type things.*

THE SOUND OF THE STREETS

162

```
once upon a time-you dressed so fine-threw the bums a dime- in your
mine-didnt you/ people'd call-says "beware doll- you bound to fall &
you thought that they were all kidding you/ you used to make fun
about-everybody that was hanging out-now you dont talk so loud-
now you dont seem so proud
             about not being fed in bed butinstead scrounging
youve gone to the finest school-all right-but you only used to
                         your next meal
                    get juiced in it
& nobody's ever taught you how to live on the steet & now
                    you gonna have to get used to it

just another juggler
did tricks for you
youve had all these great theories on life & now you find out they
    dont mean a thing
                                   old friends
youve been blessed by counts these people who who claimed to love
                         now theyre all ashamed of you
                         now theyre all ashamed

you never understood
all your friends that used to brag
all the friends    turned out to be just method actors all in drag
but when you got nothing-you got nothing to lose
youve been shown
you

got it made
you used to have all these precious things-your jewels

kneel

you

when your down like you-there is no room to kneel
youve even
aint it fu i know it hard to discover that
           you really dont know where it's at

when you aint got nothing -you got nothing to lose
youre strength must lie now in your lonesome blues
```

"Like a Rolling Stone" draft typescript

Notes, circa 1965

June 25, 1965

Dear Al:

Because of the somewhat ridiculous
circus in which we find ourselves
regarding Bob and yourself versus
engineering, A & R men, etc., etc.
I am alarmed by what appears to be
a steadily developing pattern of
confusion over our mutual respon-
sibilities.

I feel we have extended ourselves
considerably beyond contractual
provisions to provide an agreeable
working climate for Bob, but in the
light of what has been going on for
the last few months, I am asking that
we sit down as soon as I return from
the Coast (July 6) and come to certain
decisions which I feel must be made.

Until then, the status is quo.

Sincerely,

Kenneth Glancy

KDG:rr

Mr. Al Grossman
Albert Grossman Enterprises
75 E. 55thSt.
New York, N.Y.

Letter from Kenneth Glancy of Columbia Records to Bob Dylan's
manager Albert Grossman, June 25, 1965

Starting in 1965, a shift in Dylan's songwriting led to new habits in the studio. Although Dylan may have had his lyrics written, the session tapes reveal that Dylan often waited until he was in the studio to figure out a song's arrangement. The result was take after take of Dylan working out his new material. With the 2015 release of *The Bootleg Series Vol. 12: The Cutting Edge 1965–1966*, listeners were given the opportunity to pore over the complete sessions of three of Dylan's most iconoclastic and enduring records, including those that produced "Like a Rolling Stone."

The *Highway 61 Revisited* sessions heralded another signifi-cant change in Dylan's recording career, however. Tom Wilson, the Harvard-educated producer whose CV included the likes of Sun Ra, Cecil Taylor, Art Farmer, Simon and Garfunkel, and The Clancy Brothers and Tommy Makem, had been working with Dylan since the *Freewheelin'* sessions. With his relaxed and congenial pro-duction approach on albums like *The Times They Are A-Changin'*, *Another Side of Bob Dylan*, and *Bringing It All Back Home*, Wilson was an integral part of Dylan's growing command of the recording process. However, "Like a Rolling Stone" would be the final Dylan song Wilson would produce.

By the time *Highway 61* sessions resumed on July 29, 1965, just a few days after the furor at Newport, producer Bob Johnston was behind the controls. This letter from Kenneth Glancy, Columbia Records' Vice President of Artists and Repertoire, to Albert Gross-man reflects the uncertainty of the moment. Johnston had only been with Columbia for a few months, and had only a few singles under his belt. However, after finishing the *Highway 61* sessions, he'd remain with Dylan for his next five albums.

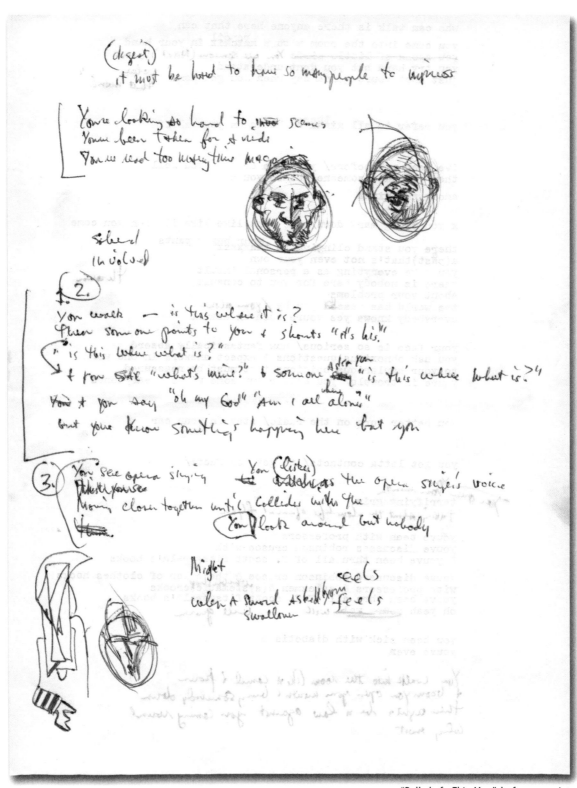

(digest)
it must be hard to have so many people to impress

You're looking so hard to in scenes
You've been taken for a ride
You've used too many this macan

Spend
Involved

2.
You walk — is this where it is?
Then someone points to you & shouts "it's his"
"is this where what is?"
& you say "what's mine?" & someone asks you "is this where what is?"
You & you say "oh my God" "Am I all alone"
but you know something's happening here but you

3. You see opera singing   You (listen)
Twist yourself   to as the opera singer's voice
Moving closer together until collides with you
You look around but nobody

Might   eels
when A sword asked from feels
swallower

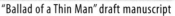

"Ballad of a Thin Man" draft manuscript

"BALLAD OF A THIN MAN"

"Ballad of a Thin Man" is one of those Dylan songs that has meant many different things to many different people, with fans ranging from Black Panther founder Huey P. Newton to Beatle John Lennon. At the heart of the song's ambiguity is its refrain,

> *Because something is happening here*
> *But you don't know what it is*
> *Do you, Mister Jones?*

This handwritten draft, one of two manuscripts in the Archive, largely has the second verse intact before introducing some unused material, including the character of the opera singer, and some put-downs, including "You've read too many Time magazines." While Mister Jones is clearly a composite, with Dylan remarking in 1990, "There were a lot of Mister Joneses at that time," he had a particularly infamous run-in with *Time* reporter Horace Judson in April 1965 while on tour in the UK. Part of their tense exchange is included in the film *Dont Look Back*.

```
Georgia Sam had a bloody nose
& the welfare department wouldnt give him clothes
he asked poor Howard where can i go
& poor Howard said there's only one place that i know

God said to Abraham "kill mea son!"
Abe said "man you must be putting me on!"
God said "no!" & Abe said "what?"
God said "you can what you wish, Abe, but...
next time i come around, you better run!"
Abe said "all right-where you want this killing done?"
God said "on highway 61"

Georgia Sam said "where?please! theyre chasingme...i gotta run!"
& poor howard just pointed with his gun ("that way, son!"
& said "out there...on highway 61"       & he pointed to
```

"Highway 61 Revisited" draft typescript

"HIGHWAY 61 REVISITED"

In 2015, Bob Dylan accepted the MusiCares Person of the Year award with a rare public speech. In generous remarks, Dylan acknowledged impactful people in the course of his career and called out touchstones that influenced some of his most famous songs, including "Highway 61 Revisited":

> *Big Bill Broonzy had a song called "Key to the Highway":*
>
> > *I've got a key to the highway*
> > *I'm booked and I'm bound to go*
> > *Gonna leave here runnin'*
> > *Because walking is most too slow*
>
> *I sang that a lot. If you sing that a lot, you just might write,*
>
> > *Georgia Sam he had a bloody nose*
> > *Welfare Department they wouldn't give him no clothes*
> > *He asked poor Howard where can I go*
> > *Howard said there's only one place I know*
> > *Sam said tell me quick man I got to run*
> > *Howard just pointed with his gun*
> > *And said that way down on Highway 61*

Highway to the Sea: Dylan, Conrad, and the "Tombstone Blues"

Griffin Ondaatje

Where is the sea, that once solved the whole loneliness
Of the Midwest?[1]
—James Wright

Didn't it ever occur to you . . . that I knew what I was doing in leaving
the facts of my life and even of my tales in the background?[2]
—Joseph Conrad's letter to a literary critic in 1921

For me the most amazing thing ever written on Dylan will always be Sam Shepard's four-page chapter entitled "Geography of a Horse Dreamer." The passage appears in the *Rolling Thunder Logbook*, a record of his voyage with that event. A "Logbook" is the perfect word for Shepard's book—as if Dylan's musical troupe journeyed on a chaotic ship across a continent. As they sailed over open highways with Dylan at the wheel of a motorhome, Shepard notes that Dylan, out of the blue, asked him: "Have you ever read Conrad?" Shepard answers he hasn't. Dylan adds: "You should read Conrad."[3] There's a "long pause". . . but that's all Dylan says about the author of *Victory*.

In the early 1990s, sitting in an office cubicle that was hidden by a plastic fern, I was supposed to be reading something job-related but was, instead, reading Conrad's novel *Victory*. On headphones I was listening to a CD of *Highway 61 Revisited*. Just as the song "Tombstone Blues" played, I was finishing the scene in the novel where the outlaw Mr. Jones and his faithful followers Ricardo and Pedro arrive, sun-stroked, in a rowboat in the harbor of Black Diamond Bay (the entrance to the volcanic island in the Java Sea where the book's hero, Axel Heyst, is living with his lover Lena). Suddenly I heard Dylan sing:

> *. . . sends them out to the jungle*
> *Gypsy Davey with his blowtorch he burns out their camps*
> *With his faithful slave Pedro behind him he tramps*

I'd just read a sentence where Ricardo yells "Esclavo!" at the mute follower Pedro.[4] The Spanish word for slave struck me kind of funny—and I remembered something Conrad wrote and flipped quickly to the Author's Note. Sure enough it was there—twice—in Conrad's own words: "faithful Pedro."[5] Suddenly the "faithful Pedro" character from the jungle of Colombia, who is a slave, jumped into Dylan's song as the "faithful slave Pedro" tramping behind Gypsy Davey.

Dylan is known for his mind-jumps in his songs, especially during that period in the 1960s, using references and imagery from all over the place seemingly unconsciously. As he himself said in a 1991 interview, rhymes and images came from "the unconscious frame of mind."[6]

But now I started to consciously look for other connections to Conrad's book. I wondered if the shadowy villain from *Victory*—the "plain Mr. Jones"—had provided some template for the invasive

Mister Jones in "Ballad of a Thin Man." The trace was subtly smuggled under the cover of a common name. It seemed almost unconsciously done. But it was the title "Ballad of a Thin Man" that caught my attention now. Why *Thin Man?* Who's *thin?* I scanned *Victory* for signs. Soon another connection surfaced from Conrad's novel. Mr. Jones

"Tombstone Blues" draft typescript

is described as "thin" numerous times, including once as a "thin man."[7] Revisiting *Victory* recently, I found Mr. Jones described repeatedly as "slender," "lank," "emaciated," "fleshless," "starved," "stalk-like," a "reed," a "pole," and "a skeleton." There are echoes in recollections of Conrad and Dylan themselves. Conrad claimed that he saw a thin man in a hotel on an island in the West Indies in 1875—the man insolently reclined across three chairs in the hot afternoon and his "cadaverous aspect" and "thin shanks" left an "indelibly weird impression" on the young sailor. Conrad recalls: "Mr. Jones (or whatever his name was) did not drift away from me. He turned his back on me and walked out of the room . . ."[8]

A century later Bob Dylan, in a 1965 interview, recalled who his Mister Jones was: "He's a real person. You know him, but not by that name. . . . I saw him come into the room one night . . ."[9]

Somehow, now, when I listen to "Ballad of a Thin Man," it seems the sinister slinking piano chords, played by Dylan, are almost a villain's footsteps creeping up behind Axel Heyst . . . or Bob Dylan.

* * *

THESE CAMEO appearances of "Mr. Jones" and his "faithful slave Pedro" occurred ten years before some of *Victory*'s actors again resurface in Dylan's album *Desire*. A background tide of Conrad's influence flows throughout the 1976 album, and undercurrents between Dylan and the novelist keep tugging at the listener or reader. A drawing of Conrad even washes up on the album's back cover. That image alone holds a clue. A few years before Dylan's Rolling Thunder Revue set sail, Borys Conrad published his memoir *My Father: Joseph Conrad*. It's an affectionate and revealing book. Now, looking at the back cover of *Desire* up close, it's suddenly clear that the pencil drawing is the exact *same* drawing on the cover of *My Father: Joseph Conrad*. Assuming Dylan chose images for the album's collage, it makes you wonder. Dylan reads very widely (as this Archive and books on his work make increasingly clear) and perhaps he even revisited Conrad through the family memoir. Dylan occasionally has intense interest in the childhood origins of fellow artists . . . whether he reads Peter Guralnick's *Last Train to Memphis* (about Elvis)[10] or visits a neighborhood in Winnipeg where Neil Young grew up.[11]

Maybe in the mid-1970s, while choosing the crew for his traveling Rolling Thunder Revue orchestra, Dylan also enlisted Conrad in a more conscious way. As he said in a 1978 interview, he was at that time doing consciously what he "used to be able to do unconsciously."[12] In *Desire* (and *Blood on the Tracks*) Dylan seemed to use Conrad's distinctive technique of shifting perspectives, hopping from one character's point of view to another. "Black Diamond Bay" (written by Dylan and Jacques Levy) telescopes *Victory*'s volcanic island setting and reflects relationships in the book. Other songs on *Desire*—including "Oh, Sister," "One More Cup of Coffee (Valley Below)," "Mozambique," and "Sara"—share an overall seafaring *mood*. Echoes seem everywhere. In *Victory* there is also a traveling orchestra featuring a female violinist with long dark hair (Lena). Even "Romance in Durango" recasts Lena as "Magdalena" in an alternate setting, giving Conrad's lovers a second chance: "Me and Magdalena on the run / I think this time we shall escape." And who knows where the name Rolling Thunder Revue comes from . . . Dylan is said to recall coming up with it when he "looked into the sky" and heard a "*boom* . . . rolling from west to east."[13] But when Mr. Jones interrogates Axel in *Victory*'s climactic scene, the villain and hero are surrounded everywhere by "rolling thunder" as a tropical storm approaches and the volcano begins to blow.

Moreover, before *Desire*, traces of Conrad's *Victory*—although tenuous—drop on the trail in *Blood on the Tracks*. Pedro is an "alligator-hunter" who tracked Axel to his island sanctuary.[14] In Dylan's "Shelter from the Storm," a hounded Christ-like figure is "blown out on the trail / hunted like a crocodile." In "Lily, Rosemary and the Jack of Hearts," Dylan casts a pair of couples in a gambling setting (like the one in *Victory*). The "Jack of Hearts" helps Lily out of the unwanted grasp of Big Jim (a boorish owner of a diamond mine) just as Axel helped Lena escape the harassing and boorish Schomberg (who owns a gambling hotel). And Rosemary, in the "role" of Big Jim's wife, like Schomberg's unassuming wife, facilitates the young female lover's escape. The constant shifting of perspective—and time—feels like Conrad's *Victory*. Dylan credits Norman Raeben (his painting teacher in 1974) as someone who helped him chart a course out of songwriting doldrums.[15] But if we look closely at those layered canvases of songs . . . isn't Conrad's influence also there in the brushstrokes?

Bob Dylan, Contemporary Songs Workshop, Newport Folk Festival, July 24, 1965. Film still from 1965 Newport Folk Festival footage, by Murray Lerner

CONRAD, LIKE a character in one of his books, set out on his first sea voyage in his late teens, when he was "young and had nothing, on the sea that gives nothing."[16] He later wrote in *Youth* that "there are those voyages that seem ordered for the illustration of life."[17] And I wonder sometimes how the origins of artists like Conrad and Dylan—their visions of where they grew up—shaped their journeys outward. Dylan's childhood landscape encompassed the Iron Range, and I thought about this when I saw the word "Blacksmith" in the Archive's draft of "Tombstone Blues." Dylan first sang that a "Blacksmith"—not John the Baptist—spoke to the war leader, the Commander in Chief. The word "Blacksmith" might hold special weight for someone who grew up beside the world's largest open pit iron mine. Blacksmiths forge weapons from iron—and Hibbing's mine supplied iron for America's battleships for both world wars. So a blacksmith in "Tombstone Blues" could suggest military industry forging weapons for war. And seeing the earth torn open daily to make a hole in the ground must be, on some level, gut-wrenching—like having Vulcan tear apart your backyard. "Is there a hole for me to get sick in?" It's possible to project too much on the substitution in lyrics, but as Dylan points out in an exhibit of his own ironwork, he was "born and raised in iron ore country."[18] There's old footage of explosions at the mine in Hibbing that are amazing to see—soil billows up to the sky in massive unfolding red clouds of iron-filled dust. It's oddly beautiful, and resonates with a song on *Planet Waves*, "Never Say Goodbye":

> *My dreams are made of iron and steel*
> *With a big bouquet*
> *Of roses hanging down*
> *From the heavens to the ground*

Conrad suggests youth's gift is that you feel you will "last forever, outlast the sea, the earth."[19] Maybe Dylan also held on to visions from his youth like a compass.

"Tombstone Blues" is like a storm that carries rolling thunder—waves of images and rhymes blow apart the order of things. Static and historical figures clash on a timeline, as if turned on a radio dial. Yet when you listen to the archived audio of Dylan's first performance of "Tombstone Blues" in 1965 at Newport (days before he recorded it for the album), the song drifts gently, with no chorus to anchor it. The chorus is later scrawled over two pieces of paper—and in wavy lines of blue ink we see the lyric "Daddy's in the alley lighting the fuse" crossed out and changed to "Daddy's in the alley looking for food." It's almost as if Dylan defuses the anarchy of the song he's created, grounding its narrator within family and human struggle. Dylan's been labeled an anarchist before—but in "Tombstone Blues" his voice remains a witness and sentinel to chaos and confusion. Like Conrad, his determination to face society's iniquities weathers all storms.

Dylan doesn't need to make his connections to *Victory* known. Among all the writers he talks about in *Chronicles*, Conrad is not mentioned once. Sam Shepard's *Logbook* remains the place Conrad's name is recorded beside Dylan's. But it was Dylan who offered: "You should read Conrad." Other writers like Joan Didion (who claims to reread *Victory* before embarking on her novels) acknowledge the influence, but for Dylan it surfaces in the songs.[20]

When you look at a map of North America and picture anyone growing up in Hibbing, Minnesota, on the Iron Range, you suddenly realize they would be virtually landlocked. Robert Zimmerman lived a thousand miles away from any sea. Any sense of exploration or need to wander restlessly would have to seek a way out.

But in his youth Dylan recalls that his grandmother had a window in her backroom where he "could see Lake Superior . . . freighters and barges off in the distance."[21] Dylan's grandmother had traveled by ship to Duluth from the Black Sea. Conrad, born Józef Korzeniowski in southern Ukraine, was a young foreigner in Singapore when he became first mate on a ship called the *Vidar*. Just as Dylan was known to keep notebooks, Conrad constantly scribbled notes as he sailed in areas in which his earliest works were set. A friend of Conrad's, from those early years, later visited the former seafarer in England in 1909 and told him he'd met old sailing acquaintances of theirs who'd read and *liked* Conrad's books. Conrad, moved, wrote to another friend: ". . .the best of it is that all these men of 22 years ago feel kindly to the Chronicler of their lives."[22]

Dylan is a similarly generous chronicler. We hear it in the line in "Mississippi" when he sings that his ship is sinking: "I've got nothin' but affection for all those who've sailed with me."

* * *

"TOMBSTONE BLUES"

On the afternoon of July 24, 1965, the day before his electric full band set, Bob Dylan played solo acoustic at the Contemporary Songs Workshop at the Newport Folk Festival. In addition to a handful of songs from his previous two albums, Dylan introduced a new one, "Tombstone Blues." In this first version, the song as it would be recorded on *Highway 61 Revisited* was in place, all except for one element.

When Dylan returned to Columbia Recording Studios just five days later and decided to record "Tombstone Blues," the song now had a chorus. Accompanied by the band that had struck gold in "Like a Rolling Stone," including guitarist Michael Bloomfield and organist Al Kooper, the group eased into the song before slowly ratcheting up the tempo. Starting with take 7, other voices begin to pop up on the refrain, tentative and in the background. It's possible that Dylan asked his fellow musicians to join in and, tearing a piece of paper in half, jotted down the words for them to sing along.

Ultimately dissatisfied with the impromptu chorus, on August 3, Dylan brought in The Chambers Brothers to overdub the chorus onto various takes. Those versions remained in the vaults until the 2015 release of *The Bootleg Series Vol. 12: The Cutting Edge 1965–1966*, which presented the complete studio recordings in chronological order.

"Tombstone Blues" draft manuscript

Bob Dylan, acoustic and electric sets at Forest Hills Tennis Stadium, Queens, NY, August 28, 1965. Photographs by Gloria Stavers

FOREST HILLS, 1965

With the 1965 Newport Folk Festival behind him, Bob Dylan inadvertently continued to court controversy when he performed at Forest Hills Tennis Stadium in Queens, New York, on August 28, 1965. *16 Magazine* editor-in-chief Gloria Stavers—who'd photographed Dylan in winter 1963 for a piece that never ran—was on hand to capture Dylan's new approach for his live concerts: In the first set, Dylan would come out with just an acoustic guitar and his harmonica on a rack to deliver a set of songs largely pulled from his most recent albums. After a brief intermission, Dylan would return with a full band to deliver newer material and electric rearrangements of his older songs. Sometimes the performances were well received (as in Austin, Texas); sometimes there would be booing (such as the infamous "Judas" heckle from Manchester, England); oftentimes it was a mix. Despite their initial reception, the dreamy solo acoustic performances and raucous full band sets of 1965 and 1966 now rank as one of Dylan's many highwater marks in the 1960s.

BOB DYLAN AND THE BEATS

ALLEN GINSBERG

Bob Dylan and Allen Ginsberg first met at a December 1963 holiday party thrown by brothers Elias and Ted Wilentz of the 8th Street Bookstore in New York City's Greenwich Village, but they were already fans of each other's work. For Dylan, *Howl and Other Poems* and *Kaddish* were important early influences. As Ginsberg proclaimed in his *No Direction Home* interview, the songs on *The Freewheelin' Bob Dylan* were "a sort of epiphanous moment, hearing a voice that I had never heard before sounding familiar and at the same time totally self-empowered, invented, from another decade than my own, somebody younger."

This photograph taken backstage on November 7, 1964, at McCarter Theatre in Princeton, New Jersey, reveals Dylan and Ginsberg deep in conversation. Also pictured are Ginsberg's partner, the poet Peter Orlovsky (left), as well as radical filmmaker Barbara Rubin and photographer Daniel Kramer (right). Two other photographs of that night, one of Ginsberg, one of Rubin, were featured on the back cover of *Bringing It All Back Home*.

Ginsberg remained one of Dylan's most frequent correspondents until his death in 1997.

L–R: Allen Ginsberg, Peter Orlovsky, Barbara Rubin, Bob Dylan, Daniel Kramer (in mirror), McCarter Theatre, Princeton, NJ, November 7, 1964. Photograph by Daniel Kramer

deare Allen   have listened to Kaddish & read liner notes & also red type on
the back cover where there is you & your Mother & the statues...at first reading
for some reason, i took it like you were justing signing the record for me &
had decided to write a bunch of red lines on the back that that would be nicer
for me than just simply For Bob dylan on the front & that i should Read them
seriously. i must Admit allen, youve Made the strangest

lietenent with the horse in flames

KADDISH

Found among stacks of unsorted manuscript material related to Dylan's novel *Tarantula* was an unfinished letter to poet Allen Ginsberg. Likely written in 1966, the letter was prompted by Dylan's feelings upon hearing *Allen Ginsberg Reads Kaddish*, the recently recorded Atlantic LP of Ginsberg's important poem, *Kaddish*, which was originally published in 1961 by City Lights Publishers.

FELLOW POETS

Dylan and Ginsberg shared a lifelong interest in poetry and literature, and Ginsberg was always eager to share new authors and poets he thought Dylan might like. In an interview for the documentary *No Direction Home*, Ginsberg spoke of Dylan's literary tastes and credentials, as well as Dylan's approach to writing around the time of *John Wesley Harding*:

> [I] brought him a whole bunch of books when he was recuperating in the late '60s, including Emily Dickinson, and Blake, and Rimbaud, and Melville's poetry, I think. Gregory Corso, some Robert Creeley, everything I had in my range at the moment.
>
> I remember him reacting to Rimbaud saying, "How can anybody write anything anymore after Rimbaud?" Not digging Blake so much at the time. I think later on, he got more interested in "I asked a thief to steal me a peach" one of Blake's lyrics.
>
> I got him on the phone one day in late '68, after I'd been talking to Kerouac, who really liked Dylan's work. Kerouac was very chary about his praise, but he liked Dylan's—thought of him as a poet. It was nice that Kerouac recognized it.
>
> I began asking Dylan what he thought his best verse was. Surprisingly, he said, "To live outside the law you must be honest." That was his best verse, best line.
>
> Robert Creeley and I at that time were going over [Dylan's] lyrics trying to figure what was poetry and what was dross? You know, what was filler and what was poetry? We figured one out of every four lines was a line of genius and the rest built up to it. But in that conversation, Dylan was saying that he was now trying to make sure that every line advanced the poetry, so that it was more conscious poetry going forward rather than random and brilliant ideas coming in and out.

In 1969, Ginsberg sent along an audio reel containing his musical renditions of *Songs of Innocence and Experience* by the visionary English poet William Blake, which he recorded with Don Cherry, Bob Dorough, Elvin Jones, Arthur Russell, and Jon Sholle, among others. Produced by Peter Orlovsky and Barry Miles, the album was released on MGM/Verve Forecast in 1970.

Letter from Allen Ginsberg to Bob Dylan, July 9, 1969

L–R: Robbie Robertson, Michael McClure, Bob Dylan, Allen Ginsberg, Adler Place behind City Lights Bookstore, San Francisco, December 5, 1965. Photograph by Dale Smith

L–R: Peter Orlovsky (from behind in braids), Bob Dylan, Sadi Kazi (from behind), Happy Traum, Allen Ginsberg, Jon Sholle, Record Plant, NYC, November 13, 1971. Photograph by Fred W. McDarrah

RECORDINGS AND LIVE PERFORMANCES, 1971

Over two consecutive days in October 1971, Dylan explored the world of improvised poetry in Allen Ginsberg–led groups. On the 30th, he appeared on *FREETIME*, a PBS television program, alongside Ginsberg, David Amram, Gregory Corso, Peter Orlovsky, and Happy Traum. On the 31st, an informal recording that is part of Allen Ginsberg's archives reveals Dylan in a similar ensemble working through musical settings of Ginsberg's and William Blake's poetry. At the end of that recording, Dylan shows the group some chords, perhaps the specific memory that Ginsberg recalled in his interview for *No Direction Home*:

> Peter [Orlovsky] and I were giving a poetry reading in NYU, 1970 or so, and Dave Amram and Dylan came and stood in the back. Dylan later—I didn't know he was there—but later he called me up. And we had been improvising. Peter sang a song about why write your poems down and kill trees when you can give it to the air? I continued the theme, and we were improvising with a bunch of musicians.
>
> Bob called me up and said, "Can you do that?" And I said, "Yeah." So he came over that night and we began improvising, I think, "Vomit Express" or "Going Down to Puerto Rico." I only knew one or two chords, and so he showed me a third chord, so I got my lesson in the third chord, or my indication that there was a third chord, with that one little music lesson.

A little over a week later, Dylan went into the studio with Ginsberg, David Amram, Gregory Corso, Sadi Kazi, Denise Mercedes, Moruga, Peter Orlovsky, Perry Robinson, Arthur Russell, Ed Sanders, Jon Sholle, Surya, Happy and Artie Traum, and Anne Waldman. Holed up at the Record Plant in New York City between November 9 and 17, and again on the 20th (this photo comes from the 13th, and this list of phone numbers in Dylan's hand likely dates to the same period), Dylan contributed to the recordings that made up *Allen Ginsberg: First Blues*, released in 1983 on John Hammond Records.

Notes, circa 1971

ANDY DENIM — 595 158 (652 9906)

Allen Ginsberg — 777 6786

✓ B Neuwirth — 586 8752

Gene Pugach — (201) 935 1035

Allen Jeffreys — 724 9803   West 76th ⑤ᶜ

✓ Carly Simon   725 2066   East 35th

Arthur —   (415) 461 9655   (Cello)

Eric Weissberg   622 9034

✓ Al Kooper   249 7697 ⑥   East 84 ⑤ᶜ bt Park & Lex

Jon Sholle   (NY) 689 0151 (SF) 915 931 8222

David Garr   675 7585

✓ John Lennon   675 8138

✓ David Bromberg   ~~MANNER~~ 787 6188 —   West 85th

1965–1966

Bob Dylan and Allen Ginsberg,
Lowell, MA, November 12, 1975.
Photograph by Ken Regan

VISIT TO JACK KEROUAC'S GRAVE

On November 12, 1975, the Dylan-organized Rolling Thunder Revue of musicians, writers, poets, filmmakers, photographers, and other artists passed through Lowell, Massachusetts. Ginsberg and Dylan used the opportunity to visit Jack Kerouac's grave where they sat, talking about the man and his influence, reading some of the 242 choruses from Kerouac's *Mexico City Blues*, and improvising a few of their own.

In his 1995 interview for *No Direction Home*, Ginsberg revealed that he also tried to get Dylan to bring along fellow Beat writer William S. Burroughs as part of the Rolling Thunder Revue, but it did not come to pass.

WEST COAST BEATS

Noted Italian architect and designer Ettore Sottsass had befriended some of the Beat poets, including Jack Kerouac, Allen Ginsberg, and Neal Cassady, during his inspiration-seeking travels across the United States in the early 1960s. Sottsass and the writer Fernanda Pivano, his wife, subsequently became the conduits for the Beat movement in Italy.

During one such trip, Sottsass happened to be in San Francisco in early December 1965 when Dylan was also passing through town. Although the photos of Dylan at the December 5 gathering of the poets at the City Lights Bookstore might be better known, Sottsass's photos of Dylan, Ginsberg, and Lawrence Ferlinghetti in conversation at a local restaurant offer a more informal glimpse of the artists' relationships. Whether Sottsass's shots are from this particular night, *San Francisco Chronicle* reporter Herb Caen wrote of a similar such evening,

> Early Fri. morning [December 3], into La Tosca on Columbus trooped Folksinger Bobby Dylan, Poets Allen Ginsberg and Laurence [*sic*] Ferlinghetti, Italian Designer Ettore Sott-Sass [*sic*] and a few others—whereupon the waitress took one look at the assorted beards and sandals and announced: "We must maintain some sort of standards around here—out, out, everybody out!" Out they went, muttering and sputtering.

Sottsass later founded the Memphis Group on December 11, 1980. An influential postmodern architectural and design collective, the group drew their name from the fact that Dylan's "Stuck Inside of Mobile with the Memphis Blues Again" from *Blonde on Blonde* played repeatedly in the background of their first meeting.

L–R: Lawrence Ferlinghetti, Allen Ginsberg, Bob Dylan, Peter Orlovsky, Julian Orlovsky, San Francisco, December 1965. Photograph by Ettore Sottsass

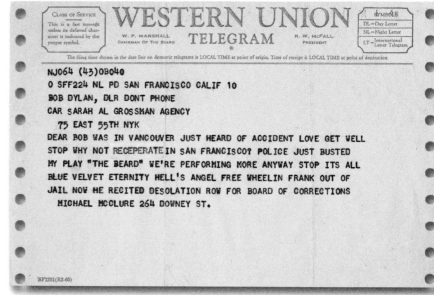

CITY LIGHTS FERLINGHETTI
26 Sept 72

BOOKSTORE
261 Columbus Ave.
San Francisco 94133
362-8193

PUBLISHING HOUSE
1562 Grant Ave.
San Francisco 94133
362-3112

Dear Bob!

I am sending this via Allen, so that you will be sure to get it.

You remember the days when you used to threaten to lay manuscripts & poems on me, and I remember them and am thinking perhaps you would actually like to do the following for a gas: We have a big poetry read-out series – last year we had Voznesensky and →

Yevtushenko – and the latest was Bukowski (see enclosed) – The crowd for Buk was about 600 – for the others 1000 to 2000 – Would you dig doing the same, under the name of Zimmerman – with no mention of Dylan in the advance publicity? Of course, word would get around, but it still wouldn't be a huge mob scene. It would be an event, all right – and – Well, what *have* you done with all that poetry?

love – lawrence.f.

Letter from Lawrence Ferlinghetti to Bob Dylan, September 26, 1972

LAWRENCE FERLINGHETTI

A 1972 letter from poet and City Lights co-founder Lawrence Ferlinghetti, most famous for his poetry collection *A Coney Island of the Mind*, teases unpublished Dylan prose and poems that may be simply lost to time. Since meeting in 1963, Ferlinghetti and Dylan had often discussed publishing Dylan's material via the City Lights imprint, though this never came to pass.

MICHAEL McCLURE

The poet and playwright Michael McClure sent a telegram to Dylan sometime in August 1966. After wishing Dylan a speedy recovery after his motorcycle accident, Mc-Clure noted that on August 8, the San Francisco Police Department had busted his experimental play *The Beard*, arresting the lead actors first under "obscenity" charges, then "conspiracy to commit a felony," before settling on "lewd or dissolute conduct in a public place." (The American Civil Liberties Union took up the case and were ultimately successful in getting the charges dropped.) McClure also mentions that Freewheelin' Frank, the secretary of the increasingly notorious San Francisco Hells Angels, had recently recited the lyrics of "Desolation Row" for the San Francisco Department of Corrections and had been released from jail, though it is unclear whether the Dylan lyrics contributed to his release.

WESTERN UNION TELEGRAM

CLASS OF SERVICE
This is a fast message unless its deferred character is indicated by the proper symbol.

W. P. MARSHALL
CHAIRMAN OF THE BOARD

R. W. McFALL
PRESIDENT

SYMBOLS
DL=Day Letter
NL=Night Letter
LT=International Letter Telegram

The filing time shown in the date line on domestic telegrams is LOCAL TIME at point of origin. Time of receipt is LOCAL TIME at point of destination

NJ064 (43)0B040
O SFF224 NL PD SAN FRANCISCO CALIF 10
BOB DYLAN, DLR DONT PHONE
CAR SARAH AL GROSSMAN AGENCY
  75 EAST 55TH NYK
DEAR BOB WAS IN VANCOUVER JUST HEARD OF ACCIDENT LOVE GET WELL
STOP WHY NOT RECEPERATE IN SAN FRANCISCO? POLICE JUST BUSTED
MY PLAY "THE BEARD" WE'RE PERFORMING MORE ANYWAY STOP ITS ALL
BLUE VELVET ETERNITY HELL'S ANGEL FREE WHEELIN FRANK OUT OF
JAIL NOW HE RECITED DESOLATION ROW FOR BOARD OF CORRECTIONS
  MICHAEL MCCLURE 264 DOWNEY ST.

SF1201(R2-65)

Telegram from Michael McClure to Bob Dylan, August 1966

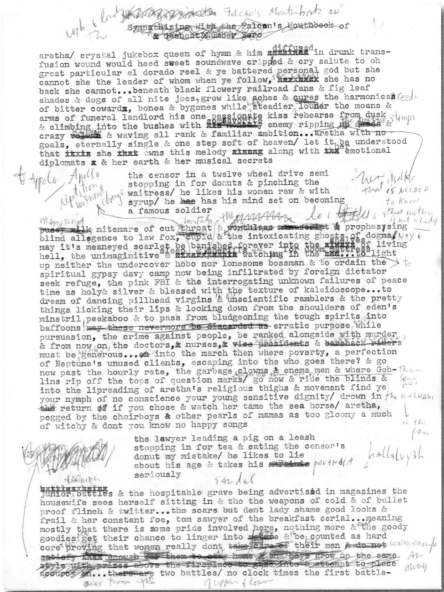

Tarantula opening page, circa 1966

TARANTULA

Although songwriting has always been Dylan's main focus, he has also written in various forms and styles, often blurring the lines between prose and poetry. In the liner notes to *Freewheelin'*, Dylan explained to Nat Hentoff,

> *Anything I can sing, I call a song. Anything I can't sing, I call a poem. Anything I can't sing or anything that's too long to be a poem, I call a novel. But my novels don't have the usual story lines. They're about my feelings at a certain place at a certain time.*

The first (and only) of those novels to be published, *Tarantula*, was begun in early 1965, with Dylan writing in fits and starts. The novel's opening page shown here comes from one of the two full drafts and numerous permutations that are part of the Archive. The structuring of the novel and juxtaposition of different sections is similar to the cut-up method developed by experimental artist Brion Gysin and explored by Beat author William Burroughs. The book's release was delayed following Dylan's motorcycle accident in 1966; it wouldn't be officially published until 1971.

Reflections on *Tarantula*

AMANDA PETRUSICH

In the summer of 1966, Bob Dylan was holed up in Woodstock recovering from a motorcycle accident and attempting to edit *Tarantula*, his first book—a surreal, imagistic, free-associated collection of poetry, prose, and auto-fiction. For Dylan, this was also a period of particular agitation with the press, and with his own self-image. He found the idea that he might be a prophet for the counterculture (an idea that was perpetuated, with equal fervor, by both his devotees and his critics) absurd and paralyzing. He had just finished a tour during which he was routinely booed. The pressures of the gig were getting to him. The precise circumstances of the accident remain somewhat mysterious—maybe a patch of oil, or blinding sun.

It's impossible for most of us to understand how odd and suffocating that kind of adulation (and, more specifically, the expectations that accompany it) might be—how it could scramble a person to be casually imbued with otherworldly qualities, when, in all likelihood, they felt goofy, dumb, and dirty, like everyone else. In *Chronicles: Volume One*, Dylan laments his own anointment. "It had blown up in my face and was hanging over me. I wasn't a preacher performing miracles. It would have driven anybody mad," he wrote. People were breaking into his house in Woodstock at all hours of the day and night, looking for advice, souvenirs, a leg up on something. "I wanted to set fire to these people," he writes. You can feel the vitriol rising in his throat.

The previous year, Dylan had completed a first draft of *Tarantula*, but he'd wanted to make some edits to the pages, and his publisher, Macmillan, was waiting on the final version. They'd already worked up a cover and a title for the book, made some promotional doo-dads (buttons, shopping bags), and sent a few galleys around to potential reviewers. Dylan wasn't ready. He didn't do the edits. People made copies of the galleys, and then copies of the copies, and eventually *Tarantula* forced itself out into the world, despite Dylan's equivocations. The book wasn't officially published until 1971, with an introduction from an anonymous editor. Maybe Dylan had simply given up by then. "Robert Lowell talks about 'free-lancing out on the razor's edge,' and we thought Bob was doing some of that," the editor wrote. "Bob wants it published and so it is now time to publish it."

Tarantula alternate book cover, circa 1971

It's easy to dismiss *Tarantula* as pretentious or illegible or meandering, and at times, it can be all those things—though, in fairness, the same goes for James Joyce's *Ulysses*, or Arthur Rimbaud's *A Season in Hell*, or Gertrude Stein's *Tender Buttons*. Dylan was experimenting with non-linear prose, dismissing the idea that the sentence should be the default building block of every story. This can make *Tarantula* feel thankless and exhausting to read from front to back, particularly if you are intent on scouring its pages for any sort of narrative architecture. Yet it is not so different, fundamentally, from what he was doing on a song like "Subterranean Homesick Blues"— the patching together of disparate ideas and images, trusting that they will coalesce, in the beholder's mind, into something profound.

At its best, *Tarantula* is allegorical and wildly musical. The Archive contains

here lies bob dylan
murdered
from behind
by trembling flesh
who after
jumped on him
for solitude
but was amazed to discover
that he was already
a streetcar &
that was exactly the end
of bob dylan

we sat in a room where Harold, who called himself
he now lies in Mrs. Actually's
beauty parlor
God rest his soul
& his rudeness

Two brothers
& a naked mama's boy
who looks like Jesus Christ
can now share the remains
of his sickness

there is no strength
to give away
everybody now
can just have it back

here lies bob dylan
demolished by Vienna politeness
the cool people can
now write Fugues about him
&
Cupid can kick over his kerosine lamp-
bob dylan-killed by a discarded Oedipus
who turned
around
to investigate a ghost
& discovered that
the ghost too
was more then one person

a handful of typewritten pages—edited drafts of some of *Tarantula*'s more worked-over pieces. For me, one of the most poignant passages of the book appears toward the end, in a section titled "The Vandals Took the Handles (An Opera)." In it, Dylan has written his own epitaph, "here lies bob dylan."

Though the Archive's draft shows that he took to the page with a blue pen, Dylan didn't monkey very much with the original typed verses. The piece already felt lucid and powerful: it functions as a steady, clear-eyed retort to his most hysterical followers, the ones who claimed "to have invented him" yet still failed to understand that he "was more than one person." They swarmed his home, scouring it for information about his life, his work, his accident (and for even more self-serving things, like his phone numbers). By then, he had been eaten up by the entire process, with "no strength / to give away." The epitaph is straightforward and poignant. Dylan feared that he was about to be undone by his own career. He was imagining a moment after his death.

When Dylan won the Nobel Prize, in 2016, it reignited long-smoldering squabbles about what literature means—whether song is poetry (or poetry is song), and who might be more or better entitled to an award celebrating language. These sorts of circuitous arguments have hounded Dylan for nearly his entire career. Though we now think of him as thoroughly canonized, it feels important to remember that he was once dismissed, derided, and misunderstood, too. In his review of *Tarantula* in *The New York Times*, the critic Robert Christgau did not equivocate: "The official appearance of Bob Dylan's *Tarantula* is not a literary event, because Dylan is not a literary figure." Decades later, this still seems like a curious if not irrelevant distinction to make. The documents contained in the Archive reiterate Dylan's intentionality and his watchfulness, particularly regarding his lyrics and other writings; he had serious ideas about how things should sound, look, and feel on the page. *Tarantula* reveals itself over time and with consideration. In that way, it is as deep a piece of literature as anything else he wrote.

AMANDA PETRUSICH

BLONDE ON BLONDE

Blonde on Blonde gatefold, exterior. Photograph by Jerry Schatzberg

"ONE OF US MUST KNOW (SOONER OR LATER)"

"One of Us Must Know (Sooner or Later)" was the first song recorded during the *Blonde on Blonde* sessions to end up on the album, establishing the template for what Dylan later termed "that thin, that wild mercury sound." The song features an incredible performance by pianist Paul Griffin, who had already established his impeccable taste through the stunning countermelodies that are part of the alchemy of "Like a Rolling Stone."

Bob Dylan, *Blonde on Blonde* photo session, 1966. Photograph by Jerry Schatzberg

"One of Us Must Know (Sooner or Later)" draft manuscript

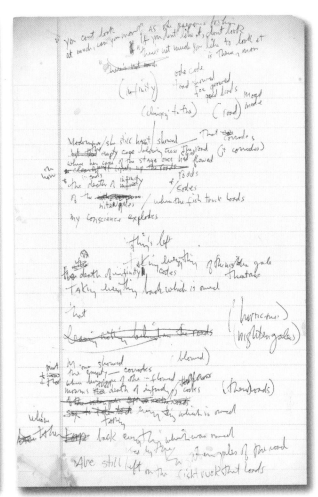

"Visions of Johanna" draft manuscripts

"VISIONS OF JOHANNA"

The dreamlike, impressionistic lyrics to "Visions of Johanna," with their strange confluence of events and characters, both reveal and obscure Dylan's continuing explorations of the boundaries of traditional ballad forms.

On November 30, 1965, Dylan took the song—then with the working title "Freeze Out"—into Columbia Recording Studios in New York City. Accompanied by guitarist Robbie Robertson, organist Garth Hudson, pianist Richard Manuel, and bassist Rick Danko of The Hawks (later The Band), as well as pianist Paul Griffin and drummer Bobby Gregg, Dylan attempted the song across fourteen takes in various arrangements. Unsatisfied with the results, he shelved the song until sessions for what would become *Blonde on Blonde* moved to Nashville the following year.

On February 14, 1966, Dylan recorded "Visions of Johanna" (two false starts, a breakdown, and the master), as the ace local session musicians quickly found the right setting for the song that Dylan had been playing as a solo acoustic number in concerts for the past few months.

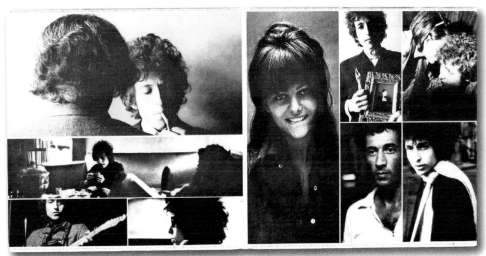

Blonde on Blonde gatefold, interior. Photographs by Jerry Schatzberg

183

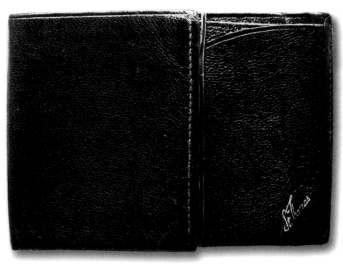

Business card given to Bob Dylan by Otis Redding in April 1966 and found in Dylan's wallet

Bob Dylan's wallet, circa 1966

"JUST LIKE A WOMAN"

Dylan's wallet from around 1966 contained addresses and business cards for poet Adrian Rawlings, photographer Bjørn Larsson Ask, journalist Annette Kullenberg, singer Otis Redding, and many others he met during that time period.

During an interview for *No Direction Home* in 1999, drummer Mickey Jones recounted the circumstances that led to Dylan and Otis Redding meeting for the first and only time during Redding's 1966 residency at the Whisky a Go Go in Los Angeles:

> When I was introduced to Otis Redding by [television host] Lloyd Thaxton, he said, "Otis, this is Mickey Jones. He's the drummer with Bob Dylan." Otis said, "Oh, god. I would give anything to meet Bob Dylan. He's such a hero." I said, "Well we're in the middle of rehearsals right now. We're headin' out in a couple weeks to start a world tour, so we're rehearsing right now, like all night, every night." He said, "Well, I've just opened [a series of concerts at] the Whisky a Go Go, if there's any way you guys could come in."
>
> That night at rehearsal we all took a break and Bob and I were sitting in the little coffee room at Columbia Recording Studios and I said, "So man, you won't believe who I met today: Otis Redding." He went, "Oh, man, I'd give anything to meet Otis Redding." I said, "I can fix that up. He's working the Whisky a Go Go." So he said, "God, let's go down there." I said, "Well, maybe we'll go down for the midnight show."
>
> We went to see Otis's midnight show and we had a blast. Afterwards we went upstairs to the dressing room and out of the door walks Otis Redding. I said, "Otis, we made it after all. I want you to meet Bob Dylan," and [Otis] stuck his hand out. If you look on his album, *In Person at the Whisky a Go Go*, it'll talk about the night that he met Bob Dylan.
>
> I remember Bob picked up an acoustic guitar and he said, "I got a great song for you," and he sat down and played "Just Like a Woman." And Otis Redding said, "You know what? I'll record that. Tomorrow." But he never recorded it, because he got killed in a plane crash not long after that.

THE SOUND OF THE STREETS

184

Bob Dylan at the piano, 1966. Film stills from 1966 European Tour footage, by D. A. Pennebaker

1966 WORLD TOUR

In 1965, Dylan's manager Albert Grossman had agreed for pioneering documentarian D. A. Pennebaker to chronicle Dylan's solo tour of the UK. Dylan and Pennebaker established a collegial relationship, and the resulting film, *Dont Look Back*, became an instant classic upon its release in 1967. Nirvana's Kurt Cobain once called it "the only good documentary about rock 'n' roll."

Never one to miss an opportunity, Grossman sensed the inherent drama of Dylan's new musical direction, and for the following year's tour of the United Kingdom, he decided to simply hire Pennebaker to shoot footage for a film of Dylan's own. Sold to ABC for their *ABC Stage 67* series, Pennebaker's gorgeous color footage was edited by Dylan, Howard Alk, and Gordon Quinn into *Eat the Document*, a nonlinear experimental documentary that intersperses live performances with surrealistic scenes and a taste of the general madness that attended the tour. ABC ultimately rejected the film, and, other than a 1972 debut at the prestigious Whitney Museum, it has rarely been screened.

In 2005, director Martin Scorsese repurposed Pennebaker's vibrant footage for *No Direction Home: Bob Dylan*, the award-winning documentary covering Dylan's early life through 1966. Scorsese ended up dedicating the film to Pennebaker for his "extraordinary contribution."

Contact sheet with D. A. Pennebaker at left and Bob Dylan at right, Stockholm, Sweden, April 1966. Photographs by Björn H. Larsson Ask

PAGE 187:

ROW 1, L–R: John Lennon; Bob Dylan with fans; Dylan

ROW 2, L–R: Dylan; Dylan with Garth Hudson; Mickey Jones

ROW 3, L–R: Robbie Robertson; Bobby Neuwirth; Dylan with producer Bob Johnston at right

ROW 4, L–R: Rick Danko; Dylan with Richard Manuel in mirror; Dylan

ROW 5, L–R: Dylan reads the *Evening Citizen*; Dylan; Garth Hudson

ROW 6, L–R: Dylan at press conference; fans outside concert; John Lennon

Film stills from 1966 European Tour footage, by D. A. Pennebaker

Barry Feinstein photographing Bob Dylan posing with children on Dublin Street in Liverpool, England, May 14, 1966. Film still from 1966 European Tour footage, by D. A. Pennebaker

LIVERPOOL

As Dylan's 1966 tour passed through Liverpool for a May 15 show, Dylan took an afternoon to wander about the bombed-out city. Tour photographer Barry Feinstein and filmmaker D. A. Pennebaker were both on hand, offering different perspectives of the same scenes.

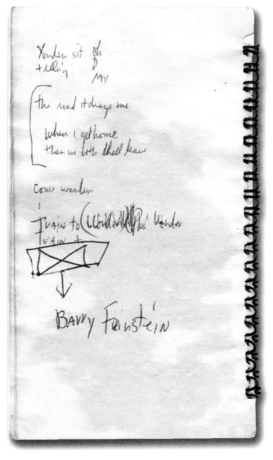

Notebook containing mention of photographer Barry Feinstein, circa 1965

Bob Dylan with children, Liverpool, May 14, 1966. Photograph by Barry Feinstein

PRESS CONFERENCES

By the mid-1960s, press conferences—such as this one at the Hotel Flamingo in Stockholm, Sweden, on April 28, 1966—had become routine for Dylan, a part of the circus that surrounded him wherever he went. Reporters, often with little context or understanding of his music, plied him with questions as they tried to pin him down. In "Interview," an unfinished song written a few years later, Dylan hinted at his feelings for these media events through the lines, "The joint was packed and the flashbulbs popped / I wished I was back in bed." Looking back on the experience for *No Direction Home*, Dylan noted,

> *Well, you had to give absurd answers. When you're in your youth and time's on your side like that you can afford to be just flippant and preposterous with your answers and if they're stupid enough to ask those kinds of questions, you can be stupid enough to answer them.*

An exchange from the May 3, 1966, press conference held at the May Fair Hotel in London gives a taste of the playful back-and-forth that Dylan enjoyed with the media:

INTERVIEWER: Why don't you write protest songs anymore?

DYLAN: *All my songs are protest songs. You name something, I'll protest about it.*

INTERVIEWER: Why do some of your songs bear no relation to their titles?

DYLAN: *Give me an example.*

INTERVIEWER: "Rainy Day Women #12 & 35."

DYLAN: *Have you ever been in north Mexico?*

INTERVIEWER: Not recently.

DYLAN: *Well, I can't explain it to you then. If you had, you'd understand what the song's about.*

INTERVIEWER: What are these film people doing here?

DYLAN: *I don't know.*

INTERVIEWER: Who's the guy with the top hat?

DYLAN: *I don't know. I thought he was with you. I sometimes wear a top hat in the bathroom.*

INTERVIEWER: Will you be meeting the Beatles?

DYLAN: *I don't know.*

INTERVIEWER: What are you going to do in Britain?

DYLAN: *Nothing.*

INTERVIEWER: What about the book you've just completed!

DYLAN: *It's about spiders, called* Tarantula. *It's an insect book. Took about a week to write, off and on. There are three hundred and sixty pages. My next book is a collection of epitaphs.*

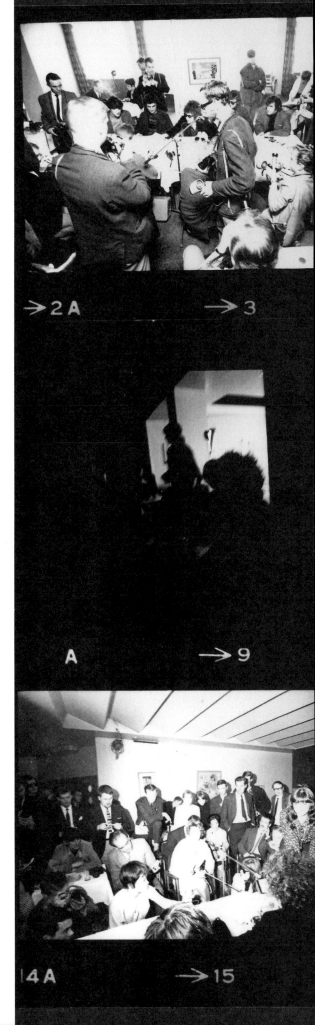

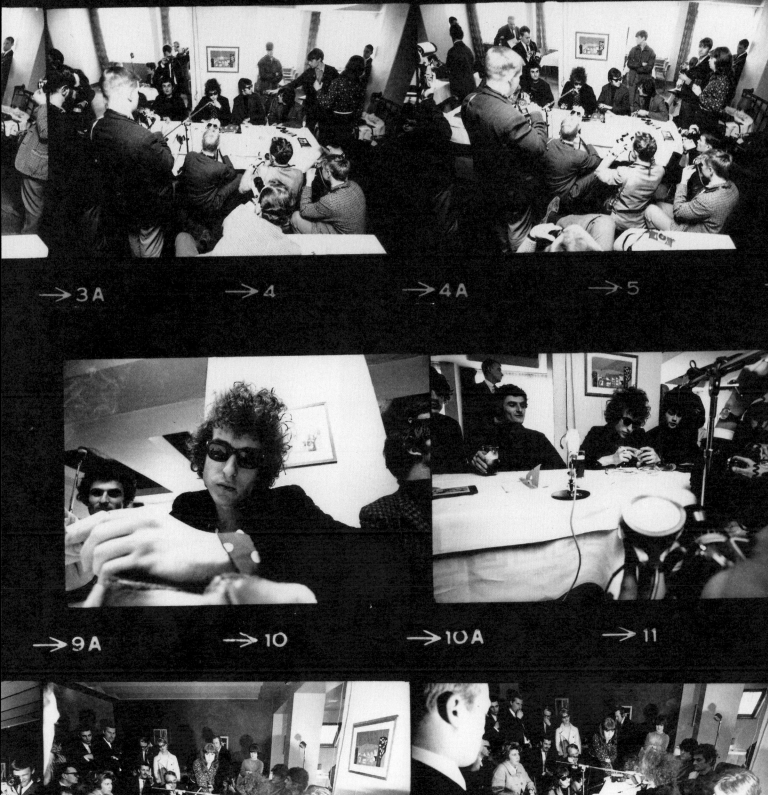

→ 3A → 4 → 4A → 5

→ 9A → 10 → 10A → 11

→ 15A → 16 → 16A → 17

Contact sheet of Bob Dylan's press conference at the Hotel Flamingo in Stockholm, Sweden, April 28, 1966. Photographs by Björn H. Larsson Ask

Dear Paul

In May 1965, at the height of an Anglocentric Dylanmania captured in veritas by D. A. Pennebaker, Dylan did something he has never done before or since; and he did it three times—he filled in questionnaires he was asked to by an impertinent press.

One of those questionnaires was for *New Musical Express*' Lifeline, one was for the Cambridge *Varsity* magazine (which he completed but never returned), and the third one was the girls-only weekly *Jackie*, in which he drew up two long lists of loves and hates. Top of the pops in his list of ten top peeves was: "Writing letters. I just never do that."

Nor was he telling "porkies" (pork pies = lies). The Bob Dylan Archive in Tulsa teems with letters *to* Dylan, but is largely bereft of ones *from* the man. Even outside the Archive, collections of Dylan letters are not so much thin on the ground as completely unknown.

A flurry of letters from 1964 *have* miraculously survived: The one he sent to *Broadside* in January that they published in issue #38; the one he wrote to *Sing Out!* in June that he never sent, but instead ended up among the *Another Side* papers; the four letters he sent to the late Tami Dean, which were later published in the *Telegraph* #16; the spoof letter he wrote on Baez's behalf to her parents that summer, then silence. Unless we count the series of spoof letters he used to break up the blocks of prose in his 1965 "novel," *Tarantula* (at least this time multiple drafts were preserved, and reside in Tulsa).

Fast forward to the summer of 1966, just before the event that will change everything always: Dylan's July 29 motorcycle accident. Dylan has informed his Macmillan editor, Robert Markel, he is hard at work on the galleys of *Tarantula*, but the box of *Tarantula* papers in Tulsa suggest he is already having second thoughts, writing in a quite different style about "Ramona put[ting] our heads in gunny sacks." And then, unexpectedly, we encounter an unfinished letter typed in classic Dylan fashion with minimal punctuation and ampersands galore.

dear paul;   thank you for crawdaddy No. 4 Being sent. have read It 3 times yesterday & 1 today & tonite i hope to dream of Naked Fish...Naked Fish & love of all save that of false dishonor. very gentle piece of explanation point after word CRAWDADDY is probably, You were unAware of, but that is my Business (i.e. -having No-Think-Waste & sex in the rag language & money but being Confined to the apostrophe & the period... MAKE, Knew mistake, everyone but Valentine is at my side & weather is good but still you know, that is an awful big bunch of happy souls upon your body & besides you no i must find Valentine) anyway this leads me to believe that you must knew that all love is equal love & that rock & roll is not only Music-By-The-Love* of-Sound & for the Common-Love* of-Sound (even above & beneath the sound) but also that this kind of music is very fragile music. i'm not sure if i make myself clear but as you

Unfinished letter from Bob Dylan to Paul Crawford, circa 1966

It is addressed "dear paul," thanking him quite specifically for *Crawdaddy* no. 4. Now we are on solid ground. *Crawdaddy*—at least in the first half of 1966—was the crudely mimeographed fanzine Paul Williams, a sophomore at college in Philadelphia, had begun publishing in February of that year, producing what by common agreement was the first rock fanzine (making him the founding father of rock criticism).

Much has been made of Dylan's dismissal of critics in song (notably, "Ballad of a Thin Man" and "Yonder Comes Sin") and sermon (the Royal Albert Hall in May 1966, the religious shows in 1979–80). In reality, he had at times cultivated critics ever since the day he visited the Folklore Center on his first week in New York, and met *Village Voice* writer J. R. Goddard.

Williams had left copies of the first two issues of *Crawdaddy* for Dylan backstage in Philadelphia in February 1966, to be left stunned when Dylan himself phoned him, inviting him "to come to his hotel room that afternoon." Paul found him "friendly and open and talkative . . . even indicating that he felt affirmed by my thesis that rock music was as worthy of being talked about seriously as any other musical form." A bond was established that afternoon.

Dylan duly acknowledges the groundbreaking nature of *Crawdaddy* in the July letter, writing, "there is no magazine around like yours." He also playfully mocks the idea of the writer as critic, not once but twice herein. First, he suggests that "people telling their dreams in dreams" (presumably a reference to those, like himself, whose "thought dreams could be seen") "must seem silly to you as a critic (but youre Really not you no)"; then, at epistle's soon to be suspended end, he playfully berates Paul, "you must write other things too for you know (you must) that this magazine could only expand &. . . ." There it ends.

Sadly, because it was never completed, let alone posted, Paul never saw the letter in question. (Nor did a similar letter, found on another loose leaf from '66, reach Allen Ginsberg, thanking him for an LP of him reading "Kaddish" as he later will, again, in *Renaldo and Clara*.) The most likely explanation—given that *Crawdaddy* no. 4 appeared in mid-July 1966—is that Dylan had his motorcycle accident and became a moderate man.

Though Paul never received Dylan's letter, and thus never knew that Dylan saw him as a writer first, and a critic second, their paths did cross again fourteen years later, and once again he played a crucial role in artistic history. After writing a sincere if skeptical monograph on Dylan's conversion in 1979, titled *Dylan—What Happened?*, Paul found himself invited to spend time with the man at a second series of landmark shows at the Warfield Theatre in downtown San Francisco.

In the intervening fourteen years, Paul had unwittingly taken Dylan's advice and become the writer of New Age lifestyle books like *Das Energei*, handing *Crawdaddy* over to others in the late 1960s as his interests spiraled into broader concerns. But he had never lost his passion for Dylan's work as he found himself and then partner Sachiko "allowed . . . to spend several hours . . . backstage after four of the November 1980 shows. He even . . . told me about another song he was proud of."

That song was "Caribbean Wind," and when Paul and Sachiko attended their fourth Dylan show that week, Paul dropped a note backstage requesting—as Dylan had suggested he could—that he play "Caribbean Wind" that night. He did, but not before a long spoken introduction that namechecked both Lead Belly and Alan Lomax, and explained that he was playing this song because there was "someone important here tonight who wants to hear it." That performance, finally released in 2017, was the one and only live rendition of one of his most important songs, and is perhaps my single favorite Dylan live performance.

Paul would go on to write a three-volume study of Dylan (*Performing Artist*) and a marvelously subjective account of his "rediscovering [of] rock 'n' roll" during the mid-eighties nadir for music, *The Map*. He would even revive *Crawdaddy* in the early 1990s in a format akin to what it had been in the mid-1960s, a mimeographed zine.

Poignantly, he died in 2013, never really recovering from his own cycle accident a few years earlier when, like Dylan '66, he was riding without a helmet; without knowing that Dylan—and those of us who considered him both a friend and a fellow scribe—recognized him as a true writer more often than most of his contemporaries, a perceptive critic most of the time, and an enthusiast always.

Mailbag and mail sent to Bob Dylan, 1966

FAN MAIL

Like many pop icons of his day, Bob Dylan received thousands of fan letters every year. Part of the Archive is a United States Postal Service mailbag stuffed full of largely unopened letters from 1966. Although correspondence from several notable individuals was discovered, such as letters from Minneapolis friend Dave ("Tony") Glover, Andy Warhol associate Gerard Malanga, and television host Ed Sullivan, the majority of the mail was from fans the world over.

Full of offbeat, often charming messages asking Dylan if he likes tuna fish sandwiches or calling him the most famous person after silent film star Fatty Arbuckle, the letters of praise and inquiry were sometimes accompanied by unusual gifts, such as a Ouija planchette, a nail clipper, and a paperback copy of Kurt Vonnegut Jr.'s *Cat's Cradle*.

However, Dylan didn't merely receive letters from younger fans seeking autographs and acknowledgment; his message resonated with those of his generation who lived wildly different lives than his, such as this letter from a soldier in Vietnam who took comfort in Dylan's songs in the midst of the horrors of a war that was beginning to divide the nation.

Dear Bob,

I was listening to a Vietnamese radio station and they played "Blowin in the Wind" by Bob Dylan and there's a magazine here with your address, so I thought I'd drop you a line.

I'm a machine gunner in an Infantry unit. We've been in this Blood drenched country for 5 months. Three of my buddies from my home town (Buffalo, N.Y.) have been killed so far. I've found that the hardest thing to do, isn't keeping alive, as much as it is maintaining normal mentality. I want to live so bad, just to see and touch my family & friends again.

c/o Andy Warhol
231 East 47th Street
New York, N.Y. 10017
5 Oct. '66

Dear Bob, hi!
Wanted to send you the enclosed form photo release, which my publisher tells me I am required to have everyone who will be in my first book of poems, sign. The book will consist of poems I've written for people and movie stills from Andy's screen test series which will accompany each poem. Could you send me the signed release as soon as possible. Do let me know what you've been doing, your songs, poetry, etc. Hope you are well.

All my very best,

Gerard (Malanga)

THE MOTORCYCLE ACCIDENT

In the early morning hours of July 29, 1966, Bob Dylan left the Woodstock home of his manager Albert Grossman on his Triumph Tiger 100. Somewhere between there and his own nearby home, Dylan was involved in a motorcycle crash. Many details surrounding the accident, Dylan's injuries, and his recovery remain a mystery. Dylan himself addressed the incident in *Chronicles,*

Card sent to Bob Dylan by a fan, 1966

I had been in a motorcycle accident and I'd been hurt, but I recovered. Truth was that I wanted to get out of the rat race.

The increasing pressures of fame that Dylan alluded to might be best summed up by the final line of a letter from the sales division of Columbia telling Dylan, "Get well, and thanks for the great product."

Despite his stature as a pop star and public figure, Dylan's accident went unreported until *The New York Times* finally made note of it on August 2, 1966. The contents of the circa 1966 mailbag show just how quickly—and how far—word spread of Dylan's accident. Gauging just from what survives, fans from around the world sent in hundreds of letters and get-well cards.

At the time of the crash, Dylan was slated to go back on the road starting with an August 6 concert at Yale Bowl in New Haven, Connecticut. A handful of other dates are known, including August 13 at Shea Stadium in Queens, New York, and the October 6 Burlington, Vermont, date advertised by this poster. Drummer Mickey Jones recounted what happened next in a 1999 interview for *No Direction Home*:

Later in the summer, we were coming back to New York to do Shea Stadium, and we were going right from Shea Stadium to Moscow. I was gonna come back to New York, two weeks ahead of time, to rehearse for Shea Stadium. It was gonna be Peter, Paul and Mary and Bob Dylan and the band. I had my plane ticket; I was all ready to go back to New York.

One or two days before the flight, I got a call from Bob Dylan. He said "Mickey, I'm in the hospital and we're canceling Shea Stadium." I said, "No kidding, what's up?" He told me he had crashed his motorcycle; he was in traction, in the hospital. I said, "What about Moscow?" He said, "Yeah, we're canceling everything, indefinitely." I said, "Well, man, I'm here, and my prayers are with you. You get well, and we'll do it again. Don't hesitate to let me know."

So that was sorta the end . . .

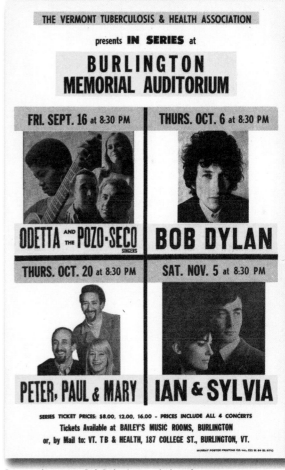

Poster advertising Bob Dylan's canceled performance on October 6, 1966, Burlington, VT

THE SOUND OF THE STREETS

Bob Dylan, Jacob Street, NYC,
January 28, 1966.
Photograph by Jerry Schatzberg

Everybody's Song 1967–1973

*I used to think that myself and my songs were
the same thing. But I don't believe that any more.
There's myself and there's my song, which
I hope is everybody's song.*

—Bob Dylan, February 1968, Hubert Saal interview, *Newsweek*

Bob Dylan, June 1966. Photograph by Frank Dandridge

Bob Dylan, *New Morning* photo session, 1970. Photograph by Len Siegler

Bob:

     Hey well man, Im glad you're alive...if what Time say ks true and the wheel locked, your the only cat I know of whose survived that trip...
     Fractured neck? I guess the only difference between fractured and broken is that when its broke you're dead..you got traction and that whole drag shot? Or can you move around? Laying on your back really messes up your mind--did mine when I had polio...gets you into a whole other world of clock time...wow yes, I still can call back those damned days and I feel for you, no shit...
     Is there gonna be any permanent hassle or will it all heal?
     Did you know Dick Shaw, a teacher cat at the U in English? Went over to his house and his old lady was telling us all about his accident on a bike where his head was split and legs broke and all kinds of graphic gory crap--I had to split--but the main thing is he's okay now, limps a bit and his head healed against all kinds of odds...
     Dave got a BMW 600 cc, and is splitting with Sylvie to NY to record in front of Sept--leaves day after tommorrow...got a tent and everything, Daniel Boone and his 12 string...
     Hugh Brown quit his job and is going back to school he says...hmmm

     Weird thing, some cat said something about you been in an accident, I just ignored kt, cause I heard at least twice before that you were dead (going off a bridge at 90 or something), thenlater some chick said she heard it on the radio, but nobody had any details, like if you wwere dead or alive..so I got up tight trying to find out and couldnt get anything straight for two three days..weird, I was suprised to find that I really could worry about anybody that much anymore--anyhow, I hope it aint as bad as it sounds, and if it ks, I hope it all gets cool soon, no shit--

     So Im gonna do solo gigs and get out there naked and see kf they can cut me up--a target again, all sidemen become invisible unless they give birth to calves on stage maybe...but Ill be frontman and we'll see what happens...contract with Elektra is over, Im a has-been, and so what? Maybe will do solo LP in the future, but its gotta be my way all the way or not at all...time will tell...
     My book still kicks around somewhere in the intestines of Viking Press and I wonder now and then if its being used to keep glass scars off this editors coffee table...
     By the way, whats up with Tarantula? I asked at local bookstore and they said the story is that you're rewriting it again and that they may take it away per the delivery date in the contract and publish in October now whether you're done or not? Can they get away with that shit? Or is that just the usual salesmen "inside" bullshit?
     Why dont you just write it in 26 parts and publish one every three months, like say with a loose leaf binder attachment--build-a-book...
     Hey you ever hear of thsi french book that comes with all the pages loose and you toss it in the air and what ever order you pick them up in, thats the book? Combine that with cuteups, and you'd have a real weird shot, if coherent at all...
     Seems that Elektra wants Koerner to write some pop-like songs and do a session with a whole band--can you see him as a chart maker? I guess its possible--more him than Dave anyhow...
     Hey when ks that ABC special sposed to be? And whats this about a 3 hour movie?
     I see Post exposed you, man them cats are never satisfied if they cant get into every corner and spread it all afound...a sacndal a year and who says that words are waepons?
     Hey you ever read Rhythm Riots & Revolution? Its By David Knobel or some thing--one of the Christian Crusdae books--real crap man--has a flick of you on the cover, artists drawinglike, so you look all sinister and foreign...and very sick inside--folk music ks commy plot, so is rock--folk-rock created by commies to hypnotise the youth and demoralize them for red takeover--very pananoid sick

(over)

Letter from Tony Glover to Bob Dylan, August 17, 1966

A PERIOD OF UNCERTAINTY

Like many of Dylan's friends and associates, Twin Cities–based harmonica player Tony Glover was moved to write after hearing about Dylan's motorcycle accident. His August 17, 1966, letter reads like a state of the union for Dylan's projects, including rumors about his novel *Tarantula* and the ABC film project that would become *Eat the Document*—both left in limbo while Dylan recuperated.

"Dear Landlord" draft manuscript

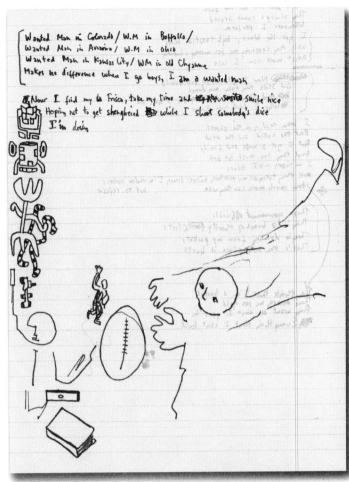

"Wanted Man" draft manuscript

IN THE WOODSHED

The period between 1967 and 1973 is generally considered as Dylan's willful retreat from the public eye, bookended by Dylan's motorcycle accident in 1966 and his return to touring in 1974. Faced with the increasing pressures and demands of fame, Dylan, rather than doubling down on his pugilistic stance of 1965 and 1966, simply left and moved his young and rapidly growing family to Woodstock, New York, then back to Greenwich Village and MacDougal Street in the city, before settling for good in Malibu, California. Instead of delivering an album every six months as was typically expected of pop stars of the day, he made only a handful of albums, a few standalone singles, and sporadic concert appearances, completely on his own terms, setting a precedent for independence that continues to the present day.

Yet even if the world heard less frequently from Bob Dylan, it didn't mean that he was any less active. Dylan was in the woodshed, refining and redefining his art and his relation to it. The time and space afforded by the changes in his new lifestyle opened up avenues for self-expression, and looking across notebooks and manuscripts, sketches and drawings, films and, of course, songs, one can sense Dylan's restless creativity in this period.

The era is defined by a prolific output: lyrics, unfinished stories, bits of dialogues, original epigrams, and other more fragmentary work jostle for space alongside sketches and drawings of faces, instruments, and abstract forms. Dylan's writing style changed from dense, frenetic, abstract pages to a deceptively simple style, and his artwork was defined by repetition as a way of exploring forms. The era reflected an experimenting artist moving through mediums, genres, structures, and styles as a way of exploring a seemingly irrepressible well of ideas. Some made it out to the wider public, as in the case of the lyrics to "Dear Landlord" from the 1968 album *John Wesley Harding*, or "Wanted Man," written for Johnny Cash, who recorded it in 1969 at San Quentin State Prison. However, most of Dylan's writings and drawings from this era never reached the public eye.

Bob Dylan at piano with Richard Manuel (top); David Boyle, Tiny Tim (in hat), Manuel, Dylan playing cards (middle); Dylan (bottom), Woodstock, NY, circa 1967. Filmmaker unknown

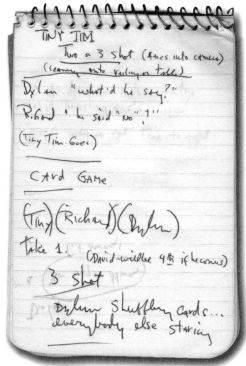

Editing notes, circa 1967

WOODSTOCK, 1967

While editing D. A. Pennebaker's footage from the 1966 tour with Howard Alk and Gordon Quinn, Dylan filmed additional scenes in and around Woodstock with Paul Stookey (of Peter, Paul and Mary) and Tiny Tim, along with Richard Manuel, Garth Hudson, and Rick Danko. Little of the accompanying sound for this footage survives, so it's unknown whether it is related to *Eat the Document* or an independent concept entirely. (It's also worth noting that the 1968 experimental film *You Are What You Eat*, directed by Dylan's friend Barry Feinstein, features many of the same principles.) But what is clear is that they were conceived of as distinct scenes such as the card game sequence identified in these editing notes.

The Basement Tapes sessions audiotape box, 1967

American Federation of Musicians dues report
for *The Basement Tapes* recording sessions

THE BASEMENT TAPES

After the conclusion of the 1966 World Tour, new sets of concert dates were being booked. But Dylan's July 29, 1966, motorcycle accident brought that to a sudden end.

With their future plans now in flux, members of his backing band, The Hawks (soon to be renamed The Band), found places to rent near Dylan. Guitarist Robbie Robertson moved to a place around Woodstock, New York. In February 1967, bassist Rick Danko, organist Garth Hudson, and pianist Richard Manuel moved into a house in West Saugerties dubbed Big Pink because of its eye-catching, salmon-colored siding.

With Dylan on the mend, they all began to play music informally in early 1967, first in the "Red Room" at Hi Lo Ha, Dylan's Byrdcliffe home, before moving into Big Pink, where Garth Hudson had organized an ad hoc studio in the basement using two stereo mixers, a tape recorder borrowed from Dylan's manager Albert Grossman, and a set of microphones borrowed from Peter, Paul and Mary. Between June and October 1967, the ensemble made over 120 recordings including traditional songs, covers, and a set of original material that showed the vast reaches of Dylan's imagination, a healthy dose of humor, and a wide range of shared musical influences.

SANTA FE

Santa Fe,
Dear, dear, dear, dear, dear, Santa Fe.

My woman needs it ev'ryday

She promised this a-lad she'd stay,

She's rollin' up a ~~lot of~~ *lotta* bread

To toss away.

She's in Santa Fe,

Dear, dear, dear, dear, dear, Santa Fe.

Now she's ___*opened ?*___ up a ~~happy~~ *shappy* home,

She's proud, but she needs to roam,

She's ___*2 beats gonna write herself a ~~letter~~ a rainbow poem*___ ~~up a happy home~~ *have some foam* *(7 Beats)*

She's ___*even gonna let me* ~~roam ?~~___

In Santa Fe.

Santa Fe,

Dear dear, dear, dear, Santa Fe.

Since I'm ~~a~~ *never* gonna cease to roam,

I'm never, never far from home,

~~A~~n' I'll never, ever, ~~ever roam~~ *scratch my comb*

To ~~xaxx~~ *sail away* (?)

~~She's all feel bad too don she don't feel badglad~~ *We almost been had*

No, no, no, no, doggone, don't feel *so* bad

She's the worst thing I've ever had   *long legged*

Sh~~es~~ a bad ___*4 Beats* ~~by at last~~ *under grad*___

She's over cause ___*she sleeps in my pad* *4 Beats*___ glad

She's never disappeared so bad

when I'm
~~I'm well~~ away

Very few original manuscripts for the songs from *The Basement Tapes* sessions are known to exist. Instead, this version of "Santa Fe" comes from the files maintained by Dylan's music publishing company. Part of their process for copyrighting new Dylan songs involved transcribing the lyrics from an existing recording and sending them to Dylan for his handwritten corrections and edits, meaning that the recorded version of the song might contain different lyrics from the copyrighted version. Such was the case when "Santa Fe" was copyrighted in 1973, though that difference wouldn't be known until the 1967 recording was officially released on *The Bootleg Series Volumes 1–3 (Rare & Unreleased) 1961–1991*.

Following the success of cover songs like Peter, Paul and Mary's "Blowin' in the Wind," and The Byrds' "Mr. Tambourine Man," Dylan and Grossman formed a new music publishing company called Dwarf Music in 1966. The following October, they compiled a publisher's demo of fourteen Dylan originals to shop to prospective artists, which were taken from the sessions that yielded *The Basement Tapes*.

Bob Dylan, *The Saturday Evening Post* photo session, Woodstock, NY, 1968. Photograph by Elliott Landy

As artists began to cover the new songs, hits started to emerge. Peter, Paul and Mary released their version of "Too Much of Nothing" in November 1967. In January 1968, Manfred Mann had a hit with "Quinn the Eskimo (The Mighty Quinn)." That April, Julie Driscoll with Brian Auger and the Trinity released "This Wheel's on Fire," which went to the top of the UK singles charts and got them a spot on Top of the Pops. The Byrds followed with their own version of "This Wheel's on Fire," which appeared on their 1969 album *Dr. Byrds and Mr. Hyde*, produced by Bob Johnston. Additional covers emerged from the likes of Fairport Convention, Ian & Sylvia, and The Band themselves. At the height of the psychedelic '60s, Dylan had created a counterweight—a new roots-based musical style that in many ways anticipated what today is referred to as Americana.

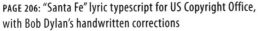

"Quinn the Eskimo (The Mighty Quinn)" sheet music, as performed by Manfred Mann, 1968

PAGE 206: "Santa Fe" lyric typescript for US Copyright Office, with Bob Dylan's handwritten corrections

PAGE 209: Maquette for *Dylan* poster, circa 1967. Artwork by Milton Glaser

Contact sheet, April 1967. Photographs by Don Hunstein

MILTON GLASER'S "*DYLAN*"

With their star absent from the public eye amid news of a motorcycle accident in Woodstock, Columbia Records began preparing *Bob Dylan's Greatest Hits*. Although the circumstances surrounding the accident and the extent of Dylan's injuries were the subject of widespread public speculation, the label needed to circumnavigate the uncertainty surrounding their star while drumming up positive press for their forthcoming release. One of their solutions was for Columbia's art director John Berg to commission up-and-coming graphic designer Milton Glaser to design a special poster for inclusion with the LP release.

Taking inspiration from a 1957 self-portrait of the similarly mercurial visual artist Marcel Duchamp, Glaser added a rainbow mane of curly hair that drew upon the art nouveau, modernist, and burgeoning 1960s counterculture movements. (Dylan was also thinking of Duchamp, though later in this period, writing in a circa 1972 notebook: "Marcel Duchamp quit painting at 30 to become a chess player. He's got one year on me already.")

The simple text, "Dylan," was a font of the artist's own creation. The result not only became a classic piece of Dylan iconography, but also an enduring work of graphic art that is in the collections of major art museums around the world, including in the permanent collection of The Museum of Modern Art. (Glaser would go on to a distinguished career that included his most famous design: the "I Love NY" logo.)

Although the poster solved some of Columbia's woes, Dylan's absence meant they

had no new photos to use for promotional purposes. Shortly after the album's March 27 release, they turned to staff photographer Don Hunstein to organize a photo shoot showcasing the Glaser poster, featuring a young, mod-looking woman using the poster as a prop. Essentially a gag setup, the photo shoot—which in black-and-white lost the vibrancy of Glaser's original work—yielded results that were perhaps so immediately unsatisfying that the photos were rarely, if ever, used.

Self-Portrait in Profile, 1957. Artwork by Marcel Duchamp

Greatest Hits advertisement from *Jazz & Pop*, October 1967

EVERYBODY'S SONG

FOLLO
STAT
FOR
CROPPI
AND
SIZE

12 1/2 x

14 1/4 x

"As I Went Out One Morning" from *Writings and Drawings*, published 1973. Drawing by Bob Dylan

"John Wesley Harding" 45 rpm single, Scandinavia, 1968

Reflections on "As I Went Out One Morning"

JOHN DOE

So many musicians are guilty of wishing they had written Bob Dylan songs. Maybe it's sort of sad? I admit being guilty of wishing I had written many of his songs but particularly the entire *John Wesley Harding* record. It turns a corner and reveals a completely new world to the listener. A world where mystery, servitude, and a wide-open land fill your eyes and heart.

At the Bob Dylan Archive, 3×5-inch spiral notepads contain much of the source material for this record, and most of it is fragmentary. A line or two here and there, many of which are rewritten for the final record. No full pages of lyrics from that period remain in the many boxes of this section of the Archive. It seems fitting, since those songs are equally filled with space punctuated by stark images of flight and pursuit. All the writing in those notepads is consistent with that imagined world where people travel by foot and the telegraph or railroad may be the most modern development. Nonetheless, notepads are universal in that they also contain lists of mundane pieces of the author's life. Sketches and drawings drift in and out and surround some of the poetic wanderings. There's even dimensions and a sketch of a living room rug in addition to lyrics to a few old country and western songs. Maybe here's where Bob is wishing he wrote someone else's song?

Recordings for *John Wesley Harding* fall into a few categories. There's one where the song is fully realized and only one or two takes are needed. "John Wesley Harding" and "The Ballad of Frankie Lee and Judas Priest" fall into that group. It's quite obvious that they captured what the song needed to say, so why cut it again? Then there are songs like "All Along the Watchtower" or "Drifter's Escape" where the tempo and structure stays virtually the same, and several takes are looking for "the one." What's interesting here is that almost all of the takes could be master takes. Everyone is playing at the top of their game, and their leader sings and plays like his life depends on it. It all seems to be going by very fast.

Then there are a couple songs like "As I Went Out One Morning," where everything evolves as each take is laid down in succession. At first it's a slow waltz, which is abandoned after one take and changed to 4/4 time. It still stays much slower than its final version, but the difference between take 1 and take 2 is startling. It's hard to emphasize how radical the transformation is on this particular song. Listening to each in the progression allows you to hear that evolution. The counter-melodies from the electric bass and harmonica change bit by bit to give it the heart and backdrop for the scenes to play out. There's very little chatter on tape before each take regarding what to do; "what if you try this?" or "how many bars between this verse and the next?" There isn't much need for lengthy discussions. They figure it out by playing and seem eager to keep the velocity. And when it's done, it's done. The final take—which is only take 4—is what we know as the final version. How fortunate for us that they made the effort to find a fully realized version that keeps the urgency of a first or second take.

L–R: Rick Danko, Bob Dylan, Robbie Robertson, Carnegie Hall, January 20, 1968. Photograph by David Gahr

WOODY GUTHRIE TRIBUTE, 1968

On January 20, 1968, Dylan played A Musical Tribute to Woody Guthrie at New York City's Carnegie Hall, his first public performance since the end of his 1966 World Tour. Guthrie's manager, Harold Leventhal, had organized the event as a benefit for the US Committee to Combat Huntington's Disease, the ailment that led to Guthrie's passing three months earlier. In a 1999 interview for *No Direction Home*, Leventhal recalled how Dylan's involvement came to pass:

> [Dylan] called me the day that Woody had died—he'd probably heard it on the radio—and he said to me that, "You should run a benefit or some kind of affair in recognition of Woody, and please let me know and I'll be there." I said at this point we hadn't made any decisions. That was in October. It came later on in January that we did hold a memorial meeting and Bobby came down. He used The Band as a backup. It was marvelous.

Dylan performed at both the afternoon and evening shows, backed by Robertson, Danko, Manuel, Hudson, and Helm. Their arrangements of Guthrie's "I Ain't Got No Home," "Dear Mrs. Roosevelt," and "Grand Coulee Dam" reflected the sound they'd worked up in the basement at Big Pink over the course of the previous year. Dylan also appeared in the ensemble finale of "This Land Is Your Land" alongside Judy Collins, Ramblin' Jack Elliott, Richie Havens, Country Joe McDonald, Odetta, Tom Paxton, Pete Seeger, and Woody's son Arlo Guthrie. The concerts were recorded, and songs from Dylan's afternoon performance were included on the 1972 album *A Tribute to Woody Guthrie*.

L–R: Bob Dylan, renowned Indian sitarist Ravi Shankar, and tabla player Alla Rakha at a dinner party organized by Shankar, circa 1968. In August 1971, Dylan performed at the Concert for Bangladesh, which George Harrison and Shankar organized. Photographer unknown

Bob Dylan and Harold Leventhal at Ravi Shankar's dinner party, circa 1968. Leventhal was an early supporter of Shankar's music, and promoted the sitarist's first concerts in New York City. Photographer unknown

SING OUT!
THE FOLK SONG MAGAZINE
VOLUME 18 NUMBER 4 OCTOBER/NOVEMBER, 1968 $1.00

EXCLUSIVE INTERVIEW WITH BOB DYLAN
INTERVIEW WITH BUKKA WHITE
TEN YEARS WITH THE RAMBLERS
WORDS & MUSIC TO "MR. BOJANGLES,"
"THE WEIGHT" AND OTHERS

Sing Out! magazine, with Bob Dylan's painting on cover, 1968

EARLY ARTWORK

Dylan began experimenting with painting after receiving his first set of paints in May 1968 as a twenty-seventh birthday gift. Dylan turned to his neighbor, the artist Bruce Dorfman, for some pointers, and Dorfman later recalled that Dylan counted Vermeer, Monet, and Van Gogh as early influences. However, Dylan soon became enamored by another modernist painter. That summer, Dylan had attended the *Rousseau, Redon, and Fantasy* exhibition at the Guggenheim Museum, which featured the works of Henri Rousseau, Odilon Redon, Marc Chagall, Giorgio de Chirico, James Ensor, Paul Klee, Joan Miro, and Francis Picabia. As poet Michael McClure, who accompanied Dylan to the museum, later recalled, Dylan "had eyes for nothing but the Chagall. Chagall was *the* meaningful world for him."

Although Dylan's artistic endeavors were largely for his own satisfaction, a handful of Dylan's earliest paintings ended up gracing the covers of The Band's 1968 debut album *Music from Big Pink*, the October 1968 issue of *Sing Out!*, and, later, his 1970 album, *Self Portrait*. Additionally, his drawings from this time period were later included in his first volume of collected lyrics, *Writings and Drawings* (1973).

SING OUT!

The October 1968 issue of the foundational folk-music magazine *Sing Out!* notably featured one of Dylan's early artworks on the cover, a painting of a guitar player. Yet it was the contents inside that many purchased the issue for, an "exclusive," extensive interview with Bob Dylan.

Over the course of three sessions in June and July 1968, Dylan sat down with Happy Traum and John Cohen, old friends from his Greenwich Village basket-house days, for a candid interview. As much a conversation among peers about the nature of being an artist as it was an attempt to put Dylan on the stand, the interview stood in stark contrast to Dylan's interactions with interviewers during his '65 and '66 press appearances. Dylan talked openly and honestly about a number of topics, including his work on *Eat the Document*, his place in the music industry, interacting and relating to fans, songwriting and musical genres, his influences, his feelings on recent advances in recording technology and studio effects, the war in Vietnam and Dylan's place as a "political" songwriter, and writing *Tarantula*.

John & Penny Cohen
Rd. 1 Tompkins Corners
Putnam Valley, N. Y.

Dear Bob & Sarah

     I want to say thanks again for helping us out with the interview for Sing Out. I hope it does what it should for the magazine. On seeing the cover, I am glad to have gone through all the fuss-because it is a wonderful painting... perhaps someday- I can work out a trade of some sort with you- painting for painting/ or photographs or something... Since I last saw you I've been to California & North Carolina- and bumped into Roger (JIm) McGuinn. He's married, has a kid, and sends regards... I had a good visit with him and taped another interview for Sing Out while I was at it.

     In North Carolina I (hopefully) finished my film of Dillard Chandler- he is a very strange man indeed- and is somewhat the opposite of the rest of America.

     Anyhow, I've decided to have a sort of party for the people from Sing Out at my house next Sat. Oct. 19 - And would like to invite you & Sarah and any kids you want- Happy is driving here with his family- so you could travel with him. I guess there'll be music as well, for the Pennywhistlers are coming- as well. Hope you can make it- we're planning on the afternoon& evening .

     In any event, I'm hoping to see you again soon...

     best, and how's the new kid?

Letter from John Cohen to Bob Dylan, postmarked October 14, 1968

Music from Big Pink album cover, 1968. Painting by Bob Dylan

SKAO 2955

MUSIC FROM BIG PINK

On September 15, 1965, Dylan arrived in Toronto on a tip from Mary Martin, one of Albert Grossman's employees. Knowing that Dylan was searching for a steady group of musicians to execute his new electric music, Martin had recommended a group called The Hawks, a name taken from their line of work backing up rockabilly hellraiser Ronnie Hawkins. Impressed with what he heard, Dylan booked guitarist Robbie Robertson, pianist Richard Manuel, organist Garth Hudson, bassist Rick Danko, and drummer Levon Helm. From late September 1965 through May 1966, this group of musicians, though often absent Helm, would accompany Dylan at his polarizing concerts around the world.

When Helm reentered the fold at the tail end of the 1967 *Basement Tapes* sessions, The Hawks soon reconfigured themselves as The Band and began to define a new musical direction.

Dylan's stamp of approval came in several ways. It was at his insistence that the group's iconic song, "The Weight," was published in the October 1968 issue of *Sing Out!* magazine, which featured his own interview and cover art. More visibly, though, Dylan contributed a painting to the cover of their debut album, *Music from Big Pink*, released on July 1, 1968. The artwork, an image of what Helm described as "five musicians, a roadie, and an elephant," was integrated into a layout done by fellow Woodstock resident and *Greatest Hits* poster designer Milton Glaser.

Bob Dylan, Woodstock, NY, 1968. Photograph by Elliott Landy

EVERYBODY'S SONG

Notebook, late 1960s

On April 9, 1969, when devoted Dylan fans returned home from their local record store with a copy of the newly released *Nashville Skyline* in hand, they were in for a big surprise. Dylan had gone country.

Yet country music had always been a staple of Dylan's listening, going back to his days listening to the Grand Ole Opry and other country programs on the nation's clear channel radio stations. (These notebook pages from the late 1960s show some of the current songs that had caught Dylan's ear.) And although he had been recording in Nashville since 1966 with the same musicians who graced the country hits of the day, Dylan had never so fully adopted the stylistic markers of the genre.

Musically and lyrically, the songs were simpler, the sound adorned by a pedal steel guitar. But perhaps most arresting was Dylan's voice, a kind of country croon. Even Allen Ginsberg was struck by Dylan's "new deep-voiced album," when he first heard it at Arlo Guthrie's apartment in Greenwich Village. remarking that it "sounds like Bing Crosby half the time."

This foray into country music, like his later explorations of gospel music and other American traditions, would resonate in various ways for years to come. In fact, since 1992 Dylan has featured one of the canonical country instruments, a steel guitar, in his touring band.

PAGE 218: "I Threw It All Away" draft manuscript

PAGE 219: Bob Dylan, *Nashville Skyline* cover photo, Woodstock, NY, 1969. Photograph by Elliott Landy

(I used to hold)

1. Once I held her in my arms
   And she said she would stay
   I treated her cold, I had treasure untold
   I gave it all away
   (Repeat)
   I was cruel, I treated her like a fool

2. Once I had mountains in the palm of my hand
   And rivers that flowed through every day
   I must be was mad / I didn't know just what I had
   I gave it all away
   But I was blind to what I had and could call mine
   I gave it all away
   (threw)

Just what I was doin I can't say
But the reason I am hurting
I know now for certain
Your heart will soon be hurting

(
The same one that you've got today
but I grew restless and (had to travel on)
I gave it all away

And never give it away
                              (her who you
So if you've found someone gives all your love
keep her to your heart, dont let her stray
(take) There's thousands boys just waiting for a chance at what you have
       Don't go throwing it away

                    Whatever was driving me
(One thing for certain is that soon you will be hurting
 If you throw it all away

Okey, Catch 'm at the bullfight
  "   Put 'm in the moonlight
  "   watch 'm on the will fight
  "   fool 'm in the cool night

Johnny catch a rabbit
  "   "   " beer
  "   "   " in no cow
                hair
  "take it downtown
  "   a wife
Stay naked for the
    rest of your life

Love is all there is / It makes the world go round
love only love and that is all (will keep you satisfied
And no matter how we feel / we can't ever stop this when
                                about
                                it   one can never live without it

Neither fool-boy so you'll fall
         take a tip from some(body) who has tried

love will make the world go round
that's one thing for sure

Dear Bob and John:

We understand that each of you performs a duet with the other on one song to be included in the other's next album. We also understand, and this will confirm, that each of you has agreed that he will not receive any royalties in respect of his performance on the other's album.

If the information or our understanding is not correct, please get in touch with me as soon as possible.

Hopy you and your families are well.

Kindest personal regards.

Cordially,

Dick

Mr. John Cash
Caudell Drive
Hendersonville, Tennessee

Mr. Bob Dylan
Box 125
Bearsville, New York

February 26, 1969

MRA/af

Letter from Dick Asher of Columbia Records to Bob Dylan and Johnny Cash, February 26, 1969

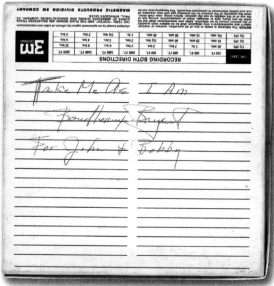

"Take Me as I Am" publishing demo from songwriter Boudleaux Bryant

The sessions for *Nashville Skyline* ended with a loose, two-day collaboration between Dylan and country legend Johnny Cash, featuring another special guest (and Cash's fellow Sun Records alum), the guitarist Carl Perkins. As the tape rolled, the pick-up group performed a variety of their own songs, as well as a smattering of country, gospel, and folk material. A brief clip of Dylan and Cash performing "One Too Many Mornings" can be seen in director Robert Elfstrom's 1969 film, *Johnny Cash: The Man and His Music*.

Nashville Skyline opened with a Dylan/Cash duet of "Girl from the North Country," a song first released on *The Freewheelin' Bob Dylan*. Cash also contributed the album's liner notes in the form of a poetic tribute to his longtime friend, titled "Of Bob Dylan"; Cash won a Best Album Notes GRAMMY for these notes in 1970.

Dylan would repay the favor just a few months later by reprising their duet alongside two other numbers on the first episode of *The Johnny Cash Show* on ABC.

EVERYBODY'S SONG

Bob Dylan on the set of *The Johnny Cash Show*, May 1, 1969.
Photograph by Al Clayton

3. Savile Row.
LONDON.

Dear Bobbie,
Thanks for Nashville Skyline, it
is beautiful. Love to You All.
George Harrison

Letter from George Harrison to Bob Dylan, circa 1969

Nashville Skyline was successful both artistically and commercially. The album was well received by fans and friends alike, with personal notes coming from Beatle George Harrison and music publisher Artie Mogull (who signed Dylan to his second music publishing contract). *Nashville Skyline* also spawned the Top 10 hit single, "Lay, Lady, Lay," his highest-charting single since "Like a Rolling Stone" in 1965.

But more importantly, the album was part of a cultural shift in the perception of Nashville that started when Dylan first began recording *Blonde on Blonde* there in 1966. Speaking to this moment, country singer-songwriter Kris Kristofferson later observed, "The country scene was so conservative until he [Dylan] arrived. He brought in a whole new audience. He changed the way people thought about it— even the Grand Ole Opry was never the same again."

THE WIG & PEN has done the impossible— the food's even better!

London
Saturday,
August 30, 1969
No. 27,254   5d.

Evening News

DANCING AT
Tiddy Dols
See Amusement Guide

Isle of Wight
FESTIVAL
SPECIAL

A living legend is back in Britain for the great pop fiesta

THE DAY OF DYLAN

Thousands take the road to the isle

By PETER COLE

TOMORROW evening, around eight o'clock, a small, flimsy, tousled haired man will mount the festival stage at Woodside Bay. And at last the long silence will be broken. Bob Dylan will be back.

After all the rumours and counter-rumours, the talk about motor-cycle accidents and the gossip of that quiet man who lives up in the Big Pink, north of New York, we shall at last see him.

And nothing else will matter except the sound. Because Dylan is much more than a living legend; he is first and foremost a singer and a writer. That's all that counts.

There are those who would denigrate the legend but I am not one of them. And, doubtless, there won't be many among the thousands and thousands here on the Isle of Wight.

Role as spokesman

It has been said that Dylan only exists because he is needed; the times in which he lives demand a spokesman. And upon Dylan has fallen that role. But this is equally true of all great artists—they are produced by the times in which they live just because they are of the times in which they live.

So when Dylan sang "The times they are a changin'" we knew they were; but we wanted somebody to say it. And when Dylan sang "Blowing in the wind" he was articulating the frustrated idealism of the

ban the bombers and the New Left.

Dylan has grown through the protest bit—affected no doubt by his long period on his back after the accident—into the new Dylan of Nashville Skyline.

Now he seems much more together. He is strongly influenced by country and western music and sings not of war but of love.

Denied a message

He has always denied any intentional "message" in his songs. He has left others to read in what they will. Which they have, endlessly. And why not?

And Dylan, shy, quiet and withdrawn as he is, recluses in the hills with his wife and his children, writing.

But tomorrow night he will sing for us. Not just for half an hour but for three or four. We are very lucky.

On the back page, your guide map with more star pictures and story

THE CHANGING FACE...

This is how Bob Dylan appeared to his fans, during his last tour of Britain in 1965.

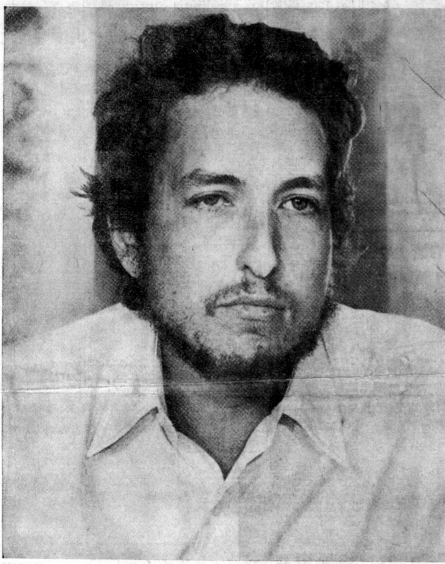

BOB DYLAN : the recluseful folk singer who has finally emerged from his home in Big Pink, New York, to appear once again in front of his British fans.

Now meet the members of The Band ...

Isle of Wight Festival ticket order form, 1969

ISLE OF WIGHT FESTIVAL, 1969

On August 31, 1969, Dylan headlined the Isle of Wight Festival, which was his largest public appearance in three years. It had taken organizers Ray and Ronnie Foulk weeks of negotiations to convince Dylan to perform at the relatively obscure event, but ultimately he signed on, responding to the island's cultural history and particularly its associations with the celebrated poet Alfred, Lord Tennyson.

Arriving on the island, Dylan holed up with The Band at Foreland Farm in the village of Bembridge to spend the week rehearsing. George Harrison also visited, fueling speculation that The Beatles might make a special appearance with Dylan. That wouldn't be the case, but the media frenzy surrounding Dylan's performance—and Dylan's reaction to it—inspired Harrison to write "Behind That Locked Door," which he released on his triple-album solo debut *All Things Must Pass* the following year.

In advance of Dylan's performance, other VIP guests showed up on the island, including John Lennon, Yoko Ono, Ringo Starr, Keith Richards, Françoise Hardy, Syd Barrett, Elton John, and Jane Fonda. The press eagerly covered all of these arrivals, inflating expectations for what was to come.

In his cream-colored suit, closely cropped hair, and new voice, the Bob Dylan of 1969 presented much differently than the Dylan whose last UK appearance had been in the frenzied days of his 1966 tour. Clearly still in the country spirit of his latest recording, Dylan and The Band drew heavily on material from *Nashville Skyline* and *John Wesley Harding*, though they also dipped into older songs such as "Like a Rolling Stone." A handful of Isle of Wight songs were selected for the following year's *Self Portrait* album (the full concert was not released until 2010). Dylan did not return to the stage for another two years.

"Minstrel Boy," a then-unreleased song that had been recorded as part of 1967 sessions that produced *The Basement Tapes*, was perhaps the most unexpected song Dylan performed at the Isle of Wight. Dylan liked the live performance enough to release it on *Self Portrait* in 1970. This handwritten manuscript is part of the files maintained by Dylan's publishing company, and was likely written out when the song was copyrighted around the time of the release of *Self Portrait*. However, the lyrics differ from the 1967 version (which only has one verse), the 1969 Isle of Wight performance, and a subsequent version published in the 1973 book *Writings and Drawings*.

PAGE 222: *Evening News* (London), August 30, 1969

"Minstrel Boy" draft manuscript

BOB DYLAN AND THE BEATLES

On Friday, August 28, 1964, journalist Al Aronowitz took Bob Dylan to the Delmonico Hotel in New York City to meet The Beatles for the first time.

They next crossed paths in London on May 9, 1965, when, after a day of filming the feature *Help!*, The Beatles attended Dylan's Royal Albert Hall concert and later visited Dylan at his suite at the Savoy Hotel.

Having established a friendly relationship, Dylan invited the group to his 1966 shows at Royal Albert Hall. After Dylan's May 26 show he visited John Lennon at Kenwood, the latter's home in Weybridge outside London. The next day, filmmaker D. A. Pennebaker captured the pair on their return to the city. That night, Lennon and George Harrison attended the final show of the tour and afterwards Dylan, Paul McCartney, and The Rolling Stones visited Dolly's nightclub.

For five of the most famous people in the world, these early meetings would be the start of lifelong camaraderie punctuated by compliments and occasional collaboration.

Bob Dylan's notes on hotel stationery, including Albert Grossman's and John Lennon's phone numbers, 1965

JOHN LENNON

During 1965 and 1966, as Dylan's UK tours afforded the opportunity to get to know John Lennon, the lines of influence blurred as Lennon penned the Dylan-inflected "Norwegian Wood" and Dylan responded with the "Norwegian Wood"-esque "Fourth Time Around."

Dear Editor:

Re Eileen Strong's interesting suggestion in the November SING OUT! that Bob Dylan and John Lennon are really one person.

Look at the picture of Lennon on the cover of his book, In His Own Write, and then look at the picture of Dylan on his first Columbia LP and draw your own conclusions.

And even more significant! HAS ANYONE EVER SEEN THEM TOGETHER? I intend to investigate further and ask Joan Baez, who is the only person I know who knows both.

Sincerely,
Ralph J. Gleason
San Francisco, Calif.

Editor's Note: Let the reader decide for himself.

Bob Dennon   John Lylan

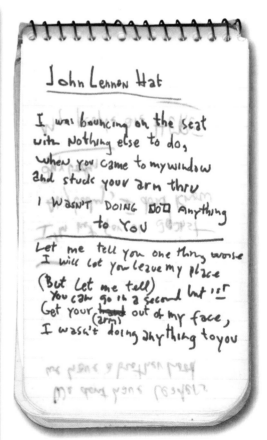

ABOVE: Notebook, late 1960s

LEFT: Journalist Ralph Gleason's letter to the editor, *Sing Out!*, 1965

224

Bob Dylan and George Harrison, Concert for Bangladesh, Madison Square Garden, NYC, August 1, 1971. Photographer unknown

GEORGE HARRISON

A testament to their budding lifelong friendship, George Harrison visited Dylan in Woodstock over Thanksgiving 1968. Upon his return to the UK—in a thank you note addressed to "Tiny Montgomery," the titular character of a *Basement Tapes* song that was making the rounds—Harrison told Dylan he enjoyed the film (presumably a cut of *Eat the Document*). He also sent Dylan the chords for a song they'd written together, "Thingymubob," as well as an accompanying lyric "And I'm glad to hold you in my arms / I'd have you anytime." When Harrison released his first post-Beatles solo album, *All Things Must Pass*, in 1970, "Thingymubob"—now called "I'd Have You Anytime"—was the opening track.

During the same visit, Dylan and Harrison made a short recording of "I'd Have You Anytime" and another song, "Nowhere to Go" (also called "Every Time Somebody Comes to Town"). However, rumors have circulated about another song called "Ramblin' Woman," which Harrison attempted as part of The Beatles' *Let It Be* sessions in January 1969. Throughout the course of those sessions, Harrison led the group through several Dylan covers including "I Threw It All Away" (a song that Harrison must have learned from Dylan the previous November because Dylan hadn't recorded it yet).

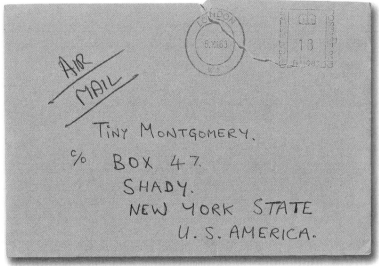

Envelope for letter from George Harrison to Bob Dylan, postmarked December 5, 1968

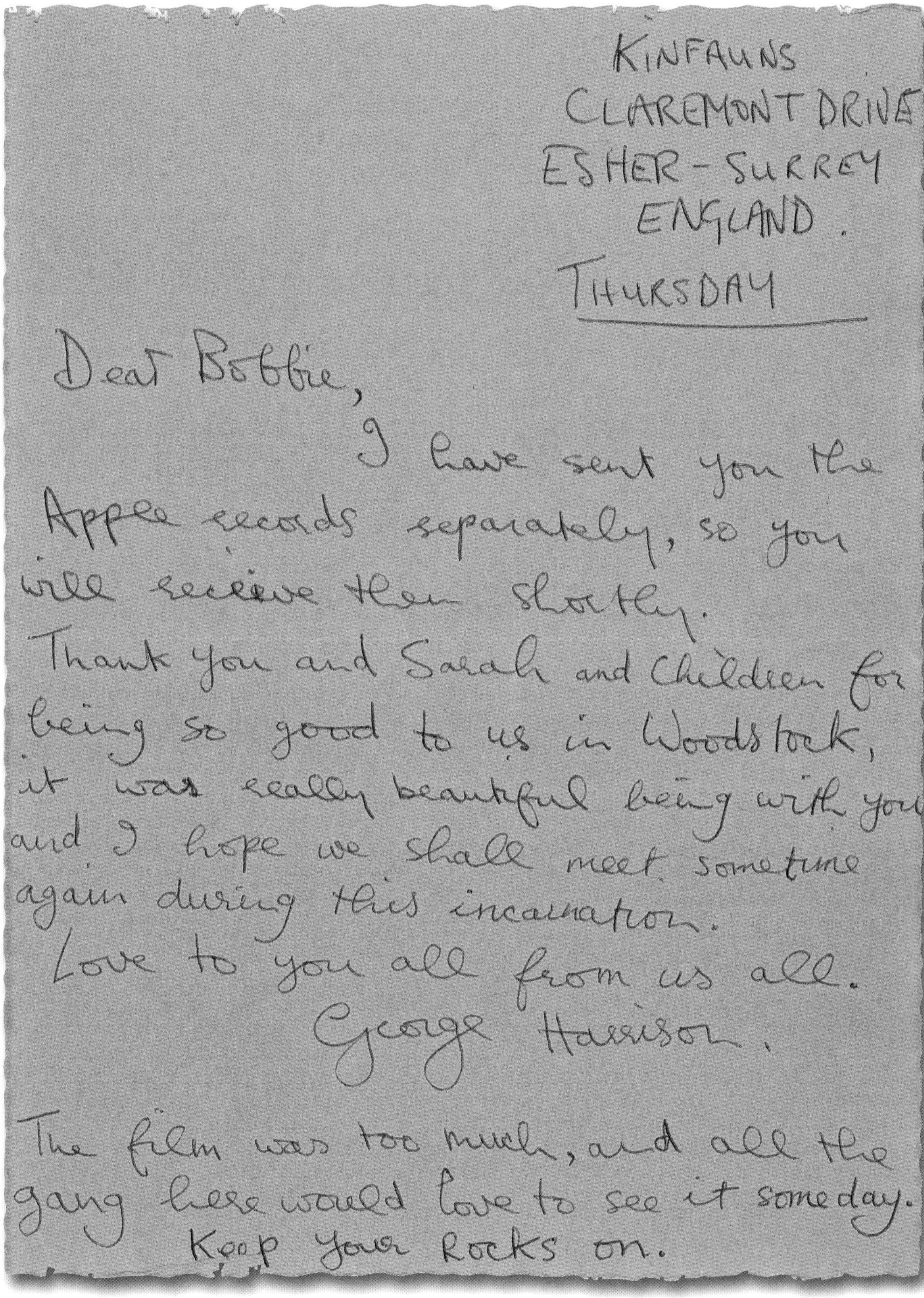

KINFAUNS
CLAREMONT DRIVE
ESHER - SURREY
ENGLAND.
THURSDAY

Dear Bobbie,

I have sent you the Apple records separately, so you will recieve them shortly.

Thank you and Sarah and Children for being so good to us in Woodstock, it was really beautiful being with you and I hope we shall meet sometime again during this incarnation.

Love to you all from us all.

George Harrison.

The film was too much, and all the gang here would love to see it someday.

Keep your rocks on.

Letter from George Harrison to Bob Dylan, postmarked December 5, 1968

Dear Bobbie,

THINGYMUBOB is

Maureen — E to / C#⁷ / F#ᴹ Aᴹ / to E

the middle was   E for 4 beats

A flat 4 beats

C#m. 4 beats to B⁷.

_____

and I'm glad to hold you in my arms

I'd have you anytime.

Love to You All.

George.

Ringo Starr with Bob Dylan, Isle of Wight, 1969. Photograph by Stephen Goldblatt

RINGO STARR

In August 1969, when Dylan played the Isle of Wight Festival, he had occasion to connect with The Beatles once again. John Lennon and Yoko Ono, George Harrison and Pattie Boyd, and Ringo and Maureen Starkey made the trek, hanging backstage, and watching the special one-off performance from among the excited festivalgoers.

Starr would go on to perform with Dylan on a few occasions, including at the 1971 Concert for Bangladesh and as part of sessions for Dylan's 1981 album *Shot of Love*.

HEART OF MINE
vocals and piano - Bob Dylan
2nd vocal - Clydie King
drums - Jim Keltner, Chuck Plotkin
bass - Donald "Duck" Dunn
organ - Wm "Smitty" Smith
guitar - Ron Wood
Tom Tom - Ringo Starr

Shot of Love LP inner sleeve (detail), 1981

PAUL McCARTNEY

Although Paul McCartney was unable to attend the Isle of Wight because of the birth of his first child, he sent Dylan this Christmas card in 1969. Despite their different styles, the two musicians have remained mutual admirers of each other's works. Dylan turned up at McCartney's return to live performance, the Wings Over the World tour, in 1976 (an extra backstage pass that Dylan used to jot down some notes is in the Archive). In a 2007 interview for *Rolling Stone*, Dylan expressed his admiration for the former Beatle,

I'm in awe of McCartney. . . . He can do it all and he's never let up. He's got the gift for melody; he's got the rhythm. He can play any instrument. He can scream and shout as good as anybody and he can sing the ballad as good as anybody. . . . Just everything and anything that comes out of his mouth is framed in a melody.

Christmas card from Paul McCartney to Bob Dylan, 1969

Mal Evans's Apple Corps address, 1969

Bob Dylan and The Beatles' personal assistant Mal Evans,
Isle of Wight, 1969. Photograph by Stephen Goldblatt

Telegram from Peter Fonda and Dennis Hopper
to Bob Dylan, April 1969

EASY RIDER

While selecting music for the
1969 counterculture classic
Easy Rider, Dennis Hopper
and Peter Fonda decided
they wanted to use Dylan's
"It's Alright, Ma (I'm Only
Bleeding)" from *Bringing It
All Back Home*. After they
were unable to secure rights
to Dylan's version, Hopper
and Fonda turned to Roger
McGuinn of The Byrds to
record a cover version of the
song, which they included in
the film alongside a Mc-
Guinn original with a Dylan
connection. McGuinn later
recalled that, when Hopper
and Fonda were courting
Dylan to write a theme song
for *Easy Rider*, they screened
the film for him. Although
Dylan wasn't interested in
contributing, he did jot down
some lines, saying "Give this
to McGuinn, he'll know what
to do with it."

Bob Dylan and Dennis Hopper backstage,
1974. Photograph by Barry Feinstein

EVERYBODY'S SONG

Bob Dylan, *Self Portrait* sessions, Columbia Studio A, Nashville, May 3, 1969. Photograph by Al Clayton

EVERYBODY'S SONG

Bob Dylan and Bob Johnston, May 3, 1969. Photograph by Al Clayton

SELF PORTRAIT

After the country sounds of *Nashville Skyline*, Dylan changed course again with *Self Portrait*, a collection of folk songs, originals, and live performances from the 1969 Isle of Wight Festival. Despite the album's idiosyncrasies and a mixed critical reception, *Self Portrait* demonstrated Dylan's enduring star power, topping at #4 on the *Billboard* 200 and #1 on the *Cash Box* and *Record World* album charts. Even more surprising is that the album spawned a hit single, the wordless "Wigwam," which went to #41 on the *Billboard* Hot 100 chart and would go on to become an instrumental hit in a number of countries including Germany, the Netherlands, Switzerland, and Belgium.

In 2013, *Self Portrait* was given an opportunity for reappraisal with the release of *The Bootleg Series Vol. 10: Another Self Portrait (1969–1971)*. Adding outtakes and alternate takes, stripping away overdubs, and providing additional context, *Another Self Portrait* emphasized the period as a strong return to musical roots that Dylan obscured on the original version of the album.

L–R: Delores Edgin, Dottie Dillard (partially obscured), Bob Dylan, May 3, 1969. Photograph by Al Clayton

Self Portrait alternate cover mockup, 1970. Photograph by John Cohen

In 1970, John Cohen photographed Bob Dylan at his townhouse in Greenwich Village and near Cohen's farmhouse in Putnam Valley, New York. A selection of the photos was used to mock up a potential album cover for Dylan's *Self Portrait* album, released June 8, 1970. However, Dylan decided to use a portrait he'd recently painted rather than the Cohen photos. In a 1984 *Rolling Stone* interview with Kurt Loder, Dylan recalled,

> *And then I did this portrait for the cover. I mean, there was no title for that album. I knew somebody who had some paints and a square canvas, and I did the cover up in about five minutes. And I said, "Well, I'm gonna call this album Self Portrait."*

Self Portrait artwork offset lithography printer's progressive proofs, 1970

Self Portrait album cover. Painting by Bob Dylan

Huey Digs Dylan

GREGORY PARDLO

"As you probably know from our Chairman Bobby Seale's book," Huey Newton writes in a letter to Bob Dylan dated August 24, 1970, "your music has always meant a great deal to the Black Panther Party." The letterhead places the Party headquarters at an Oakland, California, address in the now gentrified Prescott neighborhood. In the top left corner of the page, the brawny feline, the familiar logo of the BPP, stalks its prey. The fresh face of young Bobby Hutton decorates the top right corner. Recruited at 16, Hutton was the Party's first treasurer and its first casualty. The teenaged Crispus Attucks of the Black Panther Party, Hutton, half-dressed and holding his hands in the air to show that he had no weapons concealed, was shot twelve times by Oakland police. The left margin of the page lists members of the Central Committee: Minister of Defense Huey Newton; the aforementioned Chairman Bobby Seale; Kathleen and Eldridge Cleaver as Communications Secretary and Minister of Information respectively. Other offices listed include Chief of Staff, Field Marshall, and a host of ministries, some of which are still vacant. Filled and unfilled, the loftiness of all the offices listed evokes the gothic scale of the Party's ambitions.

Letter from Huey Newton to Bob Dylan, August 24, 1970

Addressed to a Prince St. Station post office box in Manhattan, the letter thanks Dylan for being interested, as Newton has learned "from a number of sources," in performing a benefit concert for the Party's legal defense. Seale and a handful of his fellow Black Panthers were standing trial in New Haven on conspiracy charges. Along with the Vietnam War, the New Haven trials topped the popular list of grievances in the ferment of student activism in 1970. Newton, himself only recently released after two years in prison, inveighs against government agents and "the superhuman crew" railroading Seale to "the heart attack machine," lyrics from Dylan's "Desolation Row" woven knowingly into his appeal for Dylan's help.

The future Oakland mayoral candidate Bobby Seale published *Seize the Time* earlier that year with Random House, a major New York publisher. *Seize the Time* tells the Black Panther Party's origin story. In a chapter titled "Huey Digs Bob Dylan," Seale describes the scene at their attorney's house where the BPP produced their official newspaper. "The brothers had some big earphones," Seale writes, and they

PAGE 237: Huey Newton with *Highway 61 Revisited*, Berkeley, CA, 1970.
Photograph by Stephen Shames

would get halfway high, loaded on something, and they would sit down and play this record over and over and over, especially after they began to hear Huey P. Newton interpret that record. They'd be trying to relate an understanding about what was going on, because old Bobby did society a big favor when he made that particular sound. If there's any more he made that I don't understand, I'll just ask Huey P. Newton to interpret them for us and maybe we can get a hell of a lot more out of brother Bobby Dylan, because old Bobby, he did a good job on that set.

Apparently, Newton had a penchant for stream-of-consciousness lectures—an improvisational style of cultural critique—using Dylan's lyrics as a kind of Rosetta stone to translate what, at the time, were mysterious and oppressive social forces. I like to think Newton's rhetorical style derived, along with Dylan's lyrics, from a shared wellspring of American creative imagination.

Dylan's notorious non sequiturs, his enigmatic locutions on and off the wax that practically tied reviewers' and interviewers' shoestrings together under the table made up a form of poetry the Black Panthers could relate to: irreverent, associative, and slippery. Take, for example, Dylan's acceptance speech for the Tom Paine award at the Emergency Civil Liberties Union's Bill of Rights Dinner in 1963. Dylan chastised the "old people" in attendance because they were the kind of people who would

> talk about Negroes, and they talk about black and white. And they talk about colors. . . . There's no black and white, left and right to me anymore; there's only up and down and down is very close to the ground. And I'm trying to go up without thinking about anything trivial such as politics.

Initially, Dylan announced that he wasn't accepting the award on anyone's behalf. There was no reason he should, but because he found it necessary to disavow any allegiance suggests that these thoughts were on his mind. He ended his speech by indeed accepting the Tom Paine award on behalf of James Forman, a civil rights activist, Executive Secretary of the Student Nonviolent Coordinating Committee (SNCC), and, later, one-time member of the Black Panther Party.

How does a folk artist avoid such a trivial thing as politics? It is a problem for an artist of any kind, let alone one in thrall to the expressive energy at the core of American culture, an expressive energy with a history of inspiring escapes, revolts, and transmitting the news of the day without

notice by overseers; an expressive energy that can alchemize field hollers and the moans of misery into three chords blooming from a circle of fifths.

In his acceptance speech, Dylan also lamented that because many African Americans were wearing suits at the March on Washington where Dylan had performed just a few months earlier, they didn't look like any of his friends. He later rethought much of what he said in his speech that night. In a letter—an epistolary poem, really—of apology to the Emergency Civil Liberties Union for his rambling and confounding acceptance speech, he clarified,

> if a Negro has t wear a tie t be a Negro
> then I must cut off all ties with who he has t do it for.
> I do not know why I wanted t say this that nite.
> perhaps it was just one of the many things in my mind
> born from the confusion of my times.

It should be noted that seated next to Dylan and seen chatting conspiratorially with him in the many photos of that evening was James Baldwin, dressed respectably in a jacket and tie, a bright carnation in his lapel. Whether or not Dylan was put off by the decorum of this much older man of letters, it is clear Dylan preferred the company of the laboring folk whose collective imagination fertilized the American Dream. He wanted to fine-tune his conception of America's bedimmed and marginalized working classes. He was grasping for the comfort of his people. To rise above trivial politics was to tune in to a language that only the like-minded could hear—a code, a kind of jive born of shared moral outrage.

This commonality, a history of moral outrage, created a poetic language Dylan and the Black Panthers all understood. It was a language conveyed not so much in words as in its manner of expression, with a clarity of meaning evolved in response to unspeakable racial terror in America. For Dylan, it offered a way to rise above the logic of difference that the "old people's" culture was founded upon, the logic that produces the social, cultural, sexual, and religious divisions that inhibit the free flow of imagination. While Dylan abhorred inhibitions, he may have found race nonetheless bedeviling. From his earliest protest song, "The Death of Emmett Till," to his 2001 homage to the scholar Eric Lott's book on blackface minstrelsy in America, *Love and Theft*," and beyond; from his veneration of Black musicians like Miles Davis to his secret marriages to Black gospel singers, African American people and culture hold a flame that Dylan returns to again and again.

* * *

A 1966 interview with Sandra Suffolk for the British magazine *Queen* reportedly began with Suffolk asking Dylan how much money he wanted to make. "All of it," he said. This wasn't mere avarice. Wherever Dylan finds he can't commandeer the machinery of exploitation, he'll throw wrenches into it, as he did during this interview. One of the more innocuous photos taken by Jerry Schatzberg made its way onto the original gatefold sleeve of the 1966 album *Blonde on Blonde*. Another image, however, shows Suffolk wearing a Guy Fawkes–style hat, standing to Dylan's right. She clutches an issue of the magazine that employs her. Her right hand obscures the face on its cover, but leaves the name of the magazine clearly legible. Dylan, on the other hand, holds an issue of *Life* magazine with Sammy Davis Jr., Harry Belafonte, and Sidney Poitier poised on the cover. A cigarette pins Dylan's right hand to the top corner of the magazine while his left hand clips the lower corner. One wonders who staged this self-conscious tableau. The jive, that subversive poetry, is evident here, too, in Dylan's posture. He's holding the magazine as if it were proof of life in a kid-

PAGE 238: L–R: [unidentified], Clark Foreman (giving award), Bob Dylan, John Henry Faulk, James Baldwin, Tom Paine Award ceremony, Emergency Civil Liberties Committee's Bill of Rights Dinner, December 13, 1963. Photographs by Ted Russell

GREGORY PARDLO

napping photo. He *wants* us to see it clearly. Surely, it was a coincidence that that particular issue of *Life* was near at hand, but how better to stymie what would otherwise be for Suffolk and *Queen* an unambiguous endorsement than by calling our attention instead to three of the most accomplished African American entertainers then alive? The coffee table in this apartment holds a porcelain tea service. A ceramic soup tureen sits on top of a stack of leather-bound books. One of the books belonging to the set is on the floor next to what might be Suffolk's spiral notebook. The layout here is important because of the conversation it forms with an iconic photograph of Huey Newton at home in Berkeley shortly after his release from prison.

In Stephen Shames's 1970 photograph, Newton is shirtless and buff as the day he walked free from the Alameda County Courthouse, having done two years in prison until an appeals court overturned his manslaughter conviction. The photograph captures him in his living room. Among the seven books stacked on the coffee table beside him, only two are identifiable. Thumb index notches suggest the book at the bottom is a dictionary. On top is a copy of *Seize the Time*, face down. The stack

Bob Dylan with James Baldwin, ECLC Bill of Rights Dinner, December 13, 1963.
Photograph by Ted Russell

is surrounded by newspapers, a sculpted horse figurine, a box of tissues. Wes Montgomery's eponymous 1970 album is on the floor behind him. Sunlight from the window hazes Newton's left side, giving sheen and crisp lines to the wide fronds of the potted fiddle leaf fig tree that seems to laurel Newton grandly around his shoulders. Even shirtless in crisp white flap-pocketed jeans, Newton looks every bit the bourgeois intellectual—cultured, educated, fit—that he is, minus the suit and tie. He is holding a copy of *Highway 61 Revisited* as if it were proof of life, and, in some ways, it is. "One of the nice things about being out on the street again," Newton writes in the letter to Dylan, "is that, in the few free moments I've had, I've been able to sit back and listen to your records again." I imagine the record player spinning on top of the cinder block shelf that runs below the window and just outside the frame of the photograph, sounds of the street percolating through the screened window, mixing with the lyrics: *Because something's happening here / But you don't know what it is / Do you, Mister Jones?*

Dylan's father, Abram Zimmerman, was 8 years old and living in Duluth, Minnesota, in June of 1920 when the John Robinson Circus came to town. If Abe didn't see the show, he would have been unavoidably familiar with the details of the lynching that brought the circus to an ignominious end. An unsupported and secondhand accusation of rape resulted in the arrest of six Black men out of a lineup of 150 circus employees. Of the six arrested, Isaac McGhie, Elmer Jackson, and Elias Clayton were dragged from the jail, beaten, and hanged in the center of town from a streetlight by a raging mob. The lynching drew a substantially larger crowd than the circus. From their truck, men dragged a noose through town, shouting "C'mon, join the necktie party!" Such a meager enticement attracted no less than six thousand citizens to the jail. In his autobiography, Roy Wilkins of the NAACP, who was 19 years old at the time and living in neighboring St. Paul, detailed events of that night. According to Wilkins, the mob attempted to saw through the bars of the jail cell for over an hour. Failing to overcome that barrier, they improvised a battering ram and drove it through the 16-inch exterior brick wall. If Abe Zimmerman did not identify with the mob, he may have been so unfortunately empathetic as to identify with the men who sat inside the cell waiting while the mob pooled its intellectual resources to prise them from their relative safety. And if Abe Zimmerman identified with those men inside the cell, the story he related to his son was likely to leave an emotional scar, as it would traumatize anyone inclined to value the fundamental tenets of human society.

The famous postcard from the hanging of the three circus employees needn't be described in any detail. Suffice to say it shows a throng of freaks grinning with delight at their diabolic enterprise. Some enterprising soul seized the opportunity to mass-produce it. It sold widely. "Desolation Row," the song Newton quotes in his letter to Dylan, in case anyone needs reminding, begins, "They're selling postcards to a hanging, they're painting the passports brown / the beauty parlor is filled with sailors, the circus is in town." Sadly, there's no record of Newton interpreting these lyrics.

"What the hell is a geek?" Bobby Seale asks Huey Newton in *Seize the Time*.

"A geek is usually a circus performer," Newton replies, and imagines the performer as a trapeze artist who can't work because of an injury. "So the circus feels very sorry for him and they give him a job." Newton goes on:

Bob Dylan with James Baldwin, ECLC Bill of Rights Dinner, December 13, 1963. Photograph by Ted Russell

> They put him into a cage, then people pay a quarter to come in to see him. They put live chickens into the cage and the geek eats the chickens up while they're still alive. . . . But these people who are coming in to see him are coming in for entertainment, so they are the real freaks. And the geek knows this . . . what Dylan is putting across is middle-class people or upper-class people who sometimes take a Sunday afternoon off and put their whole family into a limousine, and they go down to the Black ghettoes to watch the prostitutes and watch the decaying community. They do this for pleasure, or for Sunday afternoon entertainment. . . . What is the one-eyed midget? He screams and howls at Mr. Jones. Mr. Jones doesn't know what's happening. Then the one-eyed midget says, give me some juice or go home. And this again is very symbolic of people who are disadvantaged. They're patronizing Mr. Jones, the middle-class people.

For several pages, Seale channels Newton channeling Dylan, a common understanding running through them all, connecting them like dots, like a line scribbled by the needle of a polygraph that is searching for an ever-elusive baseline of meaning, the machinery of oppression trembling at the sound of their poetry.

NEW MORNING

COLLABORATION WITH ARCHIBALD MacLEISH

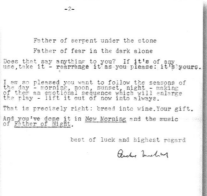

Letter from Archibald MacLeish to
Bob Dylan, July 4, 1969

In April 1969, theatrical producer Stuart Ostrow and director Peter Hunt had just opened the musical *1776* on Broadway to rave reviews, and were looking for their next project. With the initial intention of translating Dylan's just-released album *Nashville Skyline* to the stage, Ostrow reached out to Dylan through Clive Davis at Columbia Records. Plans for the collaboration soon changed, however, and Pulitzer Prize–winning modernist poet Archibald MacLeish was brought in to develop a script for which Dylan would compose original music. Ostrow later recalled that he thought "coupling the Republic's poet laureate and America's balladeer was a unique invitation to young and old audiences."

Based on the Stephen Vincent Benét short story "The Devil and Daniel Webster," the musical told the tale of Jabez Stone, a farmer from New Hampshire who sold his soul to the devil only to try to get out of the deal with the help of renowned nineteenth-century lawyer Daniel Webster. Hunt eventually retitled the musical *Scratch*, after the name of the devil in Benét's story.

By that June, Dylan had written "New Morning" and "Father of Night," and on October 17, he journeyed to Conway, Massachusetts, to visit MacLeish. MacLeish's strong creative vision for the play dominated the collaborative process, however, and Dylan decided to repurpose the songs for his next album, *New Morning*. As Dylan framed it in *Chronicles*:

> *Archie's play was so heavy—so full of midnight murder. There was no way I could make its purpose mine, but it was great meeting him, a man who had reached the moon when most of us scarcely make it off the ground.*

Scratch was ultimately produced, running from May 6 to 8, 1971. Rather than original compositions, the play featured well-known Dylan songs.

"THE MAN IN ME"

Based on a working set list of songs for *Scratch*, it appears that "The Man in Me" is one of the songs that had been originally written for the production. This lyric draft of the song comes from a notebook also containing lyrics to "If Dogs Run Free," "Winterlude," and fragments of "Father of Night."

Parts of the sessions for *New Morning* were videotaped on very early Portapak equipment, likely by Dylan's friend Terry Noble. Among all the footage in the Archive, this particular video is unique in that it captures Dylan recording the exact version of a song that appeared on an album.

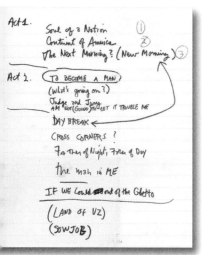

Notes for *Scratch*, circa 1969–70

EVERYBODY'S SONG

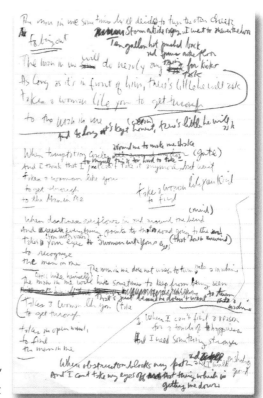

"The Man in Me"
draft manuscript

New Morning photo session, 1970.
Photograph by Len Siegler

Princeton University OFFICE OF THE DEAN OF STUDENTS
408 WEST COLLEGE
PRINCETON, NEW JERSEY 08540

November 16, 1970

Mr. Bob Dylan
P.O. Box 36
Prince Station
New York, New York 10012

Dear Bob:

Thank you very much for the marvelous record which you sent
last week, so thoughtfully inscribed. It's a fine recording, and
we are all cheered to have it echoing around the house. I wish
I had something equally good to send you, but alas I don't.

I enjoyed meeting you last June, and I hope the occasion at
Princeton was as pleasant for you as it was for us to have you.
Thank you once again for your record, with all best wishes,

Yours sincerely,

Neil L. Rudenstine

NLR/mde

Bob Dylan with Coretta Scott King, Princeton University, June 9,
1970. Photograph by William E. Sauro

Letter from Princeton Dean of Students Neil L. Rudenstine to
Bob Dylan, November 16, 1970

"DAY OF THE LOCUSTS"

On June 9, 1970, Dylan was awarded an honorary doctorate in music by Princeton University alongside
civil rights leader Coretta Scott King and journalist Walter Lippman. Although he was reluctant about
accepting the award, he later relented and traveled to the ceremony with his wife and musician David
Crosby (formerly of The Byrds), donning the cap and gown provided to him for the auspicious occasion.

This was Dylan's first award ceremony since he received the Tom Paine Award in December 1963 at
the annual Bill of Rights dinner organized by the National Emergency Civil Liberties Committee. Dylan,
who was joined on the dais that evening by the dinner's keynote speaker James Baldwin, was given
the award in recognition for his "distinguished service in the fight for civil liberty." Dylan's off-the-cuff
speech perplexed and offended many in attendance, particularly his comments about sympathizing
with President John F. Kennedy's assassin Lee Harvey Oswald. In fact, his speech caught the attention of the FBI, with his Oswald comments ending up in his girlfriend Suze Rotolo's personal FBI file.

The New York Times ran an article on the very day of the Princeton ceremony about the impend-
ing arrival of Brood X, the seventeen-year cicadas that had been spreading northwards. However,
the insects had already arrived in New Jersey, and they'd drowned out most of the day's proceedings.
Dylan, described by the master of ceremonies as "one of the most creative popular musicians of the
last decade," was further exasperated when it was said that "Although he is now approaching the per-
ilous age of 30, his music remains the authentic expression of the disturbed and concerned conscience
of young America." Dylan memorialized the event in the song "Day of the Locusts," which he recorded
two months later on August 12, the last song recorded for *New Morning*.

EVERYBODY'S SONG

Princeton University honorary doctorate ceremony, June 9, 1970.
Photographer unknown

WHEN I PAINT MY MASTERPIECE

WORDS AND MUSIC BY BOB DYLAN

"WHEN I PAINT MY MASTERPIECE"

"When I Paint My Masterpiece" dates to the March 1971 sessions that were Dylan's first collaboration with Tulsa's Leon Russell, who produced and played piano on the song. Yet Russell was not the only Tulsa connection to the sessions: bassist Carl Radle and drummer Jim Keltner originally hailed from the city, and guitarist Jesse Ed Davis was also an Oklahoman. (The group was rounded out by guitarist Don Preston and backing vocalists Claudia Lennear and Kathi McDonald.) The all-star band delivered a stunning version of the song, with Keltner's subtle timekeeping deserving special note. To break in the new band, Dylan ran through a handful of tunes, including "Spanish Harlem," "I'd Just Be Fool Enough (To Fall)," "That Lucky Old Sun," "Lady's Man," "Blood Red River," and "Alabama Bound," before recording "Watching the River Flow," which he released as a single that June.

Despite the incredible performance on "When I Paint My Masterpiece," the song ended up almost as an afterthought with its inclusion as an additional track on *Bob Dylan's Greatest Hits Volume II*, released in November 1971. However, the song took on a life of its own. Two months earlier, The Band had released their version of the track on their fourth album, *Cahoots*. By 1972, Jerry Garcia had adopted the song, which would figure prominently in the Grateful Dead's 1987 shows, including those with Dylan. Artists like Elliott Smith, Emmylou Harris, and Haruomi Hosono have also subsequently covered the song.

Dylan has performed the song numerous times since recording it. During the 1975 leg of the Rolling Thunder Revue, Dylan opened his set singing the song as a duet with Bobby Neuwirth, and a rewritten version was the opening track on Dylan's critically acclaimed 2021 livestream concert *Shadow Kingdom: The Early Songs of Bob Dylan*. Reflecting on "When I Paint My Masterpiece" in 2020, Dylan said,

> It's grown on me as well. I think this song has something to do with the classical world, something that's out of reach. Someplace you'd like to be beyond your experience. Something that is so supreme and first rate that you could never come back down from the mountain. That you've achieved the unthinkable. That's what the song tries to say, and you'd have to put it in that context. In saying that though, even if you do paint your masterpiece, what will you do then? Well, obviously you have to paint another masterpiece.

"When I Paint My Masterpiece" lyric typescript for US Copyright Office, with Bob Dylan's handwritten corrections

WHEN I PAINT MY MASTERPIECE

Oh, the streets of Rome are filled with rubble
Ancient footprints are everywhere
You can almost think that you're seein' double
On a cold, dark night on the Spanish Stairs.

Got to hurry on back to my hotel room
Where I've got me a date with Botticelli's niece
~~Yup~~ she promised that she'd be right there with me
When I paint my masterpiece.

Oh, the hours that I've spent inside the Coliseum
Dodging lions and wastin' time
Oh, those mighty kings of the jungle, I could hardly stand to see 'em
Yes, it sure has been a long, hard climb.

Train-wheels runnin' through the back of my memory
~~As the daylight hours do increase~~ When I ran on the hilltop following a pack of wild geese
Someday, everything is gonna be smooth like a rhapsody
When I paint my masterpiece.

I left Rome and landed in Brussels ~~on a plane ride~~
~~With a picture of a tall oak tree by my side~~ so bumpy that I almost cried
Clergymen in uniform and young girls pullin' muscles
Everyone was there and nobody tried to hide.

Newspapermen eating candy
Had to be held down by big police
Someday, everything is gonna be diff'rent
When I paint my masterpiece.

bridge

This is the way Bob sing it on new recording.

This was copyrighted as an alternate version - music varies also in meter, melody, Rhythm, Harmony, key, and modulation

247

CONCERT FOR BANGLADESH, 1971

The Concert for Bangladesh Japanese movie poster, circa 1972

In 1971, George Harrison and his mentor, the revered Indian musician Ravi Shankar, masterminded a benefit concert to aid the refugee crisis resulting from the Bangladesh Liberation War (March–December 1971). In a struggle for independence from Pakistan, more than fifteen million refugees fled the province of East Pakistan (now Bangladesh) into neighboring India, while Pakistan's army committed genocide on the ethnic Bengali people.

Harrison and Shankar held their benefit at Madison Square Garden on Sunday, August 1, 1971, with a two-concert extravaganza (a matinee at 2:30 p.m. and an evening concert at 8 p.m.). Among the performers at the concert were Ringo Starr, Eric Clapton, Billy Preston, Leon Russell, Badfinger, and Indian sarod prodigy Ali Akbar Khan. It also featured a rare appearance from Bob Dylan, his first since the 1969 Isle of Wight Festival.

Approximately 40,000 people attended the concerts, and Harrison and Shankar were able to raise nearly $250,000 from ticket sales alone. The concerts were recorded and filmed and were released as a single LP, a three-album box set, and a concert film, which was released in the spring of 1972. By 1985, more than $12 million had been raised through sales of the albums and documentary.

September 1, 1971

Mr. Bob Dylan
36 Prince Street Station
New York, New York

Dear Bob:

Thank you for all your help.

Hare Krsna

George

George Harrison

Apple Records Inc., 1700 Broadway, New York, N.Y. 10019 Telephone (212) 582-5533

EVERYBODY'S SONG

Letter from George Harrison to Bob Dylan, September 1, 1971

George Harrison and Bob Dylan, Concert for Bangladesh, Madison Square Garden, NYC, August 1, 1971. Photograph by Henry Diltz

Tarantula bootleg edition, published by the *Georgia Strait* underground newspaper, 1970

Dylan's first book, *Tarantula*, is an experimental collection that combined stream-of-consciousness writing with recurring literary themes throughout. Written in 1965 and 1966 (though some of his experimental typescripts date to 1964), the abstract, often surreal stories in the book bear similarities to the prose poetry that graced the back cover of *Bringing It All Back Home* and *Highway 61 Revisited*.

Although the book's original publication was slated for 1966, Dylan's motorcycle accident that July led to an initial postponement that stretched into a five-year delay. While the book languished in publishing limbo, bootleggers found copies and began to release their own versions of the book in the burgeoning underground press. Despite attempts to stem the flow, the book, like the recordings that became *The Basement Tapes*, found wider and wider circulation.

The Vancouver-based *Georgia Strait*, a preeminent Canadian countercultural magazine, published one of the rarest bootleg editions. After testing the waters by printing excerpts of *Tarantula*, the magazine received cease-and-desist letters from Dylan's lawyers. Yet that did not dissuade them. The *Strait* went all in, publishing the full book *and* the correspondence with Dylan's lawyers as a supplement to their December 2–9, 1970, issue. In 1971, Macmillan published the first authorized edition.

Tarantula Canadian advertisement, circa 1971

Photographer Jerry Schatzberg first shot Dylan during the July 1965 sessions for *Highway 61 Revisited*, and the pair developed a rapport that continued for the next nine months. Schatzberg's images were featured in the *Saturday Evening Post*, *The Bob Dylan Song Book*, and, most famously, the cover and album artwork of *Blonde on Blonde*. These images shaped the public's perception of Dylan and have continued to do so ever since. (One of Schatzberg's 1965 portraits of Dylan, titled *Edenic Innocence*, adorns the exterior of the Bob Dylan Center.)

When *Tarantula* was finally prepared for publication in 1971, Schatzberg's mid-60s portraiture was a natural choice. This mounted print appears to have been shooting art for an alternate version of the book's dust jacket.

Tarantula alternate book cover, circa 1971

Bob Dylan, 1965. Photograph by Jerry Schatzberg

"Hi Bob, It's Tony"
The Dylan/Glover Interviews

ANNE MARGARET DANIEL

From 1969 to 1971, Tony Glover recorded a series of telephone calls with Bob Dylan. Glover, an old friend of Dylan's, did so with Dylan's knowledge and permission, and ultimately sought to write an article for *Esquire* based on the later conversations. The article never came to pass, and Glover kept the recordings until his death in 2019. These audiocassettes were sold in a series of separate auction lots in November 2021. The earliest group of these phone calls, made from January to June of 1969, were grouped together as Lot 5029, and commanded a final price double that of any of the other lots: $10,664.00. The auction catalog description will tell you why; in these conversations, Dylan and Glover

> discuss the "Basement Tapes," new LPs, the local music scene, covering standards, record sales, [Dylan's] album *Nashville Skyline* and duets with Johnny Cash, singles of "I Threw It All Away" and "Lay Lady Lay," and bands like The Doors and Creedence Clearwater Revival. In these conversations with an old friend, Dylan is at ease—a departure from the cautious tone typically struck with journalists during this period. With candid thoughts on his own work and the music industry at large, these phone calls offer a fascinating look into Dylan's mind at a time when he was the most elusive star in America.

More than this, though, the conversations show two things: Dylan's wide-ranging knowledge of music and his constant interest in new releases and in the music business itself; and what a good and caring friend he is. The first is well known after his *Theme Time Radio Hour* show made it evident, but the second receives little testimony from those close to Dylan, since they do not talk about it. His charitable contributions and activities have received little press, though Dylan's 2015 MusiCares award was for his commitment to philanthropy as well as his artistic achievements, and all sales from his 2009 album *Christmas in the Heart* have gone to worldwide charities providing meals to those in need. However, his private acts of kindness generally remain just that.

Tony "Little Sun" Glover, born David Curtis Glover, and Bob Dylan, who was still Robert Zimmerman then, met in Minneapolis in 1959 or 1960, when Dylan was a sometime student at the University of Minnesota, and Glover was playing guitar and an epic blues harmonica in the coffeehouses and bars of Dinkytown. Born in Minneapolis in 1939, Glover at 20 was already a fixture of the local music scene. The intermittent band he would form with Dave "Snaker" Ray and "Spider" John Koerner as a blues and folk trio remained influential until their last performance together in November 2002. Glover was also a popular late-night DJ on KDWB Radio, sharing new music and old cuts he loved with Minneapolis in the smallest hours of the morning; and a music writer whose articles appeared in magazines including *Sing Out!*, *Creem*, *Crawdaddy*, *Hullabaloo*, and *Rolling Stone*.

Dylan left for New York City and swift, meteoric fame in January 1961. Glover stayed in Minneapolis, but the men remained in touch as the sixties unfurled. These phone calls began in January 1969, when it was very cold in the Catskill Mountains of Woodstock, New York—where Dylan, his wife Sara, and their fast-growing family were living at the time—and even colder in the Twin Cities.

TG: . . . how's the weather there?

BD: *Very cold.*

TG: Yeah, it's about 15 below here. . . . Just had about 15 inches of snow.

BD: *Oh yeah? Wow.*

Minnesota boys know from snow. There's a lot of meteorological comparison as the conversations go on; Glover is pretty envious when Dylan announces in their next call, in February, that he's just back from a "great" vacation in Jamaica.

New music, old favorites, and what they're working on are at the heart of every phone call. Even when Dylan has a new album coming out—they discuss *Nashville Skyline* in great detail—or when he's been recording in Woodstock with friends—he sends Glover an early cassette of songs from the 1967 *Basement Tapes* sessions—Dylan solicitously steers the discussion to Glover's interests and gigs every time. He is not guarded with Glover, and talks freely about many things. Dylan is clearly keen on their friendship as an equal thing.

Among the bands they talk about are The Doors, with whom Glover had played in Minneapolis in 1968. Their mentions of the Los Angeles–based psychedelic kings lead to an interesting intimation of an idea for a road show composed of Dylan's neighboring friends and acquaintances—just what he would put together in 1975 and call the Rolling Thunder Revue.

Bob Dylan with Tony Glover and Mimi Fariña, Viking Hotel, Newport, RI, July 1964. Photograph by John Byrne Cooke

ANNE MARGARET DANIEL

BD: *They're moving up to Woodstock.*

TG: The Doors are? Good grief.

BD: *Somebody told me last night.*

TG: God, everybody's gonna be up there—time to move out, right?

BD: *Well I tell ya, they got so many musicians around here that it's like you could take a whole show on the road, you know? Just people that live around here...*

Woodstock surely had an all-in-the-family feel back then. Glover speaks longingly of coming out himself: "That's sorta my dream, to get into the woods or the hills up there and go into the city once in a while to take care of business." Dylan had moved to Woodstock after spending considerable time at the Bearsville compound of his manager, Albert Grossman. Albert's wife Sally Buehler Grossman had introduced her good friend Sara Lownds to Dylan, and the couple married in 1965; the Grossmans supplied the Dylans with a place to live before they found their own house in the area. Robbie Robertson was living in

D: Hey, theres a name man, you should xxxxxx play some Josh White—

T: Ive got some on an old LP where Sonny Boy Williamson was playing sideman harp on a few things, I may play some of that—either that or the real old stuff with Sonny Terry and Leadbelly, his other stuff I dont care a whole lot for.....I dunno, you know of any good rock things?

D: Well theres that group Creedence Clearwater...whats the name of that group?

T: Creedence Clearwater Revival

D: Yeah, they do some good things—

T: Ahh—who was it? Solomon Burke I think just put out Proud Mary which they did...not bad, makes more sense when he tells a story—

D: Oh, did you hear Wilson Picketts version of that Steppenwolf song? Get out on the highway?

T: Really??

D: Whats that song? "Head out on the highway, looking for intentions—"

T: Born To Be Wild

Tony Glover interview with Bob Dylan, transcript, 1969

one of the Grossmans' cottages in 1969, as is evinced by Dylan giving Glover his phone number there. He, Garth Hudson, Richard Manuel, Rick Danko, and Levon Helm (recently returned from a couple of years in Arkansas, New Orleans, and Los Angeles) had toured with Dylan and would do so again. In 1967 they were recording his songs, some co-written with Danko and Manuel, and old ballads alike in almost daily sessions in a variety of venues, but most famously in the basement of a big pink frame house in Saugerties.

However, by early 1969 Dylan was emerging, quietly and infrequently, from the basement and the woods. He had been traveling to Tennessee to work on his newest record, *Nashville Skyline*. "My new record is the best. . . . I'm real proud of this new record we got coming up." When Glover reminds him "that's what you said about *John Wesley* [*Harding*] too," Dylan laughs. "Ah, not like this one. This one does it." Glover has one question for him: "Is Johnny Cash on it?" Always a keen critic, Glover doesn't pull punches when he picks up the new album:

> my lady really likes it too, she says this is the first album she's really been able to understand the words on. . . . My favorite cuts are "To Be Alone With You," "Lay Lady Lay," that's about my most favorite one—if I had to pick one cut that'd be the one, and "Tonight I'll Be Staying Here With You," really dig that too. But all of it, sorta, generally— the only thing is, man, it's too short— it seems like it's over before it's halfway through[.]

Glover started his radio show that spring, after taking classes and getting his Federal Communications Commission license, excited about the "bread" of $165 a week, which he described as "the most money I ever made in my life on a steady basis." Dylan was full of support and advice for him, recommending the name for both the DJ and the show: "Tony Clover. . . . Cruising with Clover. . . . Yeah! That sounds good to me, man. If I was just switching around the dial and I heard 'Cruising with Clover,' that'd be where I'd listen." Glover was amused by the echo of "Crimson and Clover," released in 1968 by Tommy James and the Shondells, and used the name for his show. Dylan wanted to know what people thought: "Cruising with Clover . . . did it go over?" Listening to the tape, I thought of Dylan's 2018 change to the lyrics of "When I Paint My Masterpiece," a song that was first released by The Band in 1971. "Sailin' around the world full of crimson and clover / Sometimes I feel like my cup is running over," Dylan sang, and continues to sing today in live performances— and I wonder if he recalled the name he'd given to that first radio show of his friend. Glover played his favorite tracks from Dylan's new album late at night, and Dylan always wants to know about the reception: did people call in? Did they like the songs?

Dylan is not self-referential, though. He's always engaged in other artists' music, recommending The Flying Burrito Brothers and Hank Williams Jr., and a little incredulous when Glover tells him that The Rolling Stones have recorded Hank Snow's "I'm Moving On," a song he knows well:

> BD: *Did they do that?*
> TG: Yeah, I think it was on "December's Children" maybe.
> BD: *"Big eight wheel a rollin down the track / means your true loving daddy ain't coming back"?*
> TG: Yeah, maybe not exactly those words, but that song—they do it bottleneck style, sorta rock-country. I think it's a live recording they did at a concert.
> BD: *Ray Charles did it too.*

He's intrigued by Johnny Winter and "that group Creedence Clearwater," and loves Wilson Pickett's cover of "Born to Be Wild." When Tony wants to play the unreleased "Million Dollar Bash" live, Bob says sure, and walks Tony (inaccurately!) through the lyrics Glover can't make out from *The Basement Tapes* version:

> TG: Let's see, I got "That big dumb blonde with her wheel gorged, totaled a friend of hers"?
> BD: *Yeah, I think so.*
> TG: "with his checks all forged"
> BD: *Yeah.*

"Are you ever gonna record with them?" Glover insists of The Band, telling Dylan he'd "really like to hear that." Dylan says he doesn't know. They later return to the idea, though, and Dylan is thinking about it now:

> TG: I wish sometime you would record with them, I'd like to put in my vote for it, if it works out.
> BD: *Yeah, well you mean that easy going kind of music?*
> TG: Yeah, it's so nice, so mellow . . . I see what you mean about radio play, it's sorta like a relaxed party thing.
> BD: *Yeah, well that's all it is. You can do those kinda things in a garage, you know? And that's what it's gonna sound like.*

Bob Dylan and The Band: the original garage band, years before "garage band" became a recognized term in the music business. The Band would be all over Dylan's music in 1973 and 1974—thanks, perhaps, to this conversation with Glover.

After his death in May 2019, Patti Smith described Tony Glover as a "man with an unshakable personal code," and, as you listen in on his phone calls with Dylan, her words ring true. Glover does not flatter or ask for things, except for the "basement tape" Dylan had already offered to send him. He is honest in his opinions of other musicians, and of Dylan's own songs, and always ready to defend those opinions good-humoredly but firmly. His voice is happiest when he is sharing news with Dylan, telling him of interesting music he hasn't yet heard or of recording sessions among friends back in Minneapolis or out in California, and talking about their respective careers. From the easy balance in their voices and words, you'd never know that one man had a string of gold records and was an international music superstar, and that the other was a radio disc jockey well known in Minnesota and folk circles, but not widely outside these places. As Dylan said in his telegram, when he thanked Glover for writing the liner notes to *The Bootleg Series Vol. 4: Bob Dylan Live 1966, The "Royal Albert Hall" Concert* (1998), "YOU WERE THERE. STILL ARE. AND ALWAYS WILL BE."

Glover won the ASCAP/Deems Taylor Award for those liner notes. The telegram Dylan sent him in congratulations was snapped up for $1,200 in the auction; Glover's entire collection, from his Dylan-related items to inscribed books, magazines, records, musical instruments, photographs, and other recordings, garnered almost half a million dollars. The cassette tapes of the 1969 telephone calls and Glover's transcriptions have now been donated to the Bob Dylan Archive. It is my hope that the other Glover tapes, and similar materials, will follow—and end up housed together, as Tony Glover kept them safely and for so long, where they belong for good.

        So, to the mian point here; Playboy was interested in seeing the interview-
t first mainly for their paperback book branch--when I told them to forget that,
they said that they had a precedent of never repaeting an interview subject--
but....so they sent me a ticket to fly to Chicago. Did that, met the cat
and sat in his office while he read it. As I more or less expected in front
he siad he didn't feel they could use it. I pressed him for reasons, and
he was the most explicit of any editors yet. He said that while it would be
of great interest to Dylan "students" and fans, it would probably just bore
their general audience. Even tho it is revealing etc, it's revealing only
to someone who knows the Dylan history. He tlaked about the previous Playboy
interview and said that what made that valid was that it was a shared put-on
--that nothing much was revealed there, but it was done in an entertaining
style, a style that captured a reader where content might not.

        All in all, the impression I get from all the various editors is that
Dylan has become a bit too normal for their readers tastes.
        To which I say, the hell with that bullshit--it is a good interview, a
lot is said there--people seem to dislike it because of what it isn't rather
than what it is...an old routine, right?

        So, the only thing I plan to do with it now it just put it in a drawer
and wait. Maybe someday somebody'll come looking for a piece and you can
turn them on to this...I'm only sorry that we both spent so much fruitless
time and effort on it...but what the hell...it was interesting and I learned
a lot about the weird-ities of magazine editors anyway...

        Unless you want to do something really bizzare with it like give it to
this high school cat who puts out a mimegraphed rock fan paper, sort of like
the old Little Sandy Review--hes a real enthusiastic rock cat, and it would
really be a flip...

        Seriously tho, I'll just stash it away in the closet for the time being
and won't do anything else with it unless I hear from you, or if any brainstorm
hits I'll check with you first...

Letter from Tony Glover to Bob Dylan, July 8, 1971

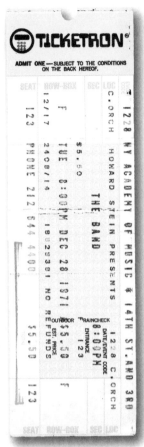

Bob Dylan's ticket for The Band's concert at the NY Academy of Music

SURPRISE APPEARANCE WITH THE BAND, 1971

On December 31, 1971, at the end of The Band's New Year's Eve concert at New York City's Academy of Music, Dylan made an unexpected onstage appearance for an encore of four numbers: "Down in the Flood," "When I Paint My Masterpiece," "Don't Ya Tell Henry," and "Like a Rolling Stone." Although the set was unrehearsed, with *Rolling Stone* reporting that "Dylan and the boys in The Band huddled before each song to work out chords and impromptu arrangements," the cheers from three thousand stunned attendees seemed proof enough that the musicians had hit the mark.

EAT THE DOCUMENT

After the filming of D. A. Pennebaker's documentary during Dylan's 1965 tour, manager Albert Grossman seemingly saw the 1966 tour as an opportunity to continue in the visual medium.

Grossman sold the idea to the execs at ABC, who planned to air the film on their new series called *ABC Stage 67*, a prime-time arts and culture series that featured hour-long dramas, musicals, documentaries, and comedies starring the likes of Lauren Bacall, Ingrid Bergman, Truman Capote, Laurence Olivier, Robert Mitchum, Peter Sellers, and many other big-name stars.

D. A. Pennebaker was brought in to direct the shoot, and Howard Alk, his wife Jones Alk, and Bobby Neuwirth all came along to assist in various capacities. The result was nearly seventy thousand feet of film shot in glorious color, both aesthetically beautiful and historically important.

Shooting the tour may have been the easy part, though, as a series of complications hampered the film's progress. First Dylan was in a motorcycle accident, so Pennebaker made an hour-long film from the footage,

Film stills from *Eat the Document*, released 1972. Directed by Bob Dylan from 1966 European Tour footage, by D. A. Pennebaker.

titled *Something Is Happening Here*. Dylan rejected that film for being too similar to *Dont Look Back*. Then Dylan and Howard Alk began editing the film that became *Eat the Document* from the outtakes of Pennebaker's film into something presentable for the network.

Ultimately it was rejected, but the stories behind why it was rejected differ. Many believed the network execs felt it was too avant-garde for a mainstream television audience. Alk recalled that one person commented, "What city are we in? What's happening?" However, *ABC Stage 67* executive producer Hubbell Robinson later gave a different reason: in the fall of 1966 Dylan didn't have a finished film in hand, and there simply wasn't time to get it on the network's spring slate of shows. Before the existing cut could be satisfactorily re-edited, the program *ABC Stage 67* was canceled in May 1967 after just twenty-six episodes. Dylan continued to work on the film throughout the late 1960s, and his deep engagement in the creative and editing process is reflected in the several notebooks and file folders full of notes. In one notebook, there is a tantalizing mention of the address of Alfred Hitchcock, who might have put a very particular slant on the film's experimental narrative. There are also various iterations of the film synopsis as it evolved from *Document* into *Eat the Document*.

Dylan spoke eloquently about the difficulties of making the film and the narrative solutions that emerged in the 1968 *Sing Out!* conversation with fellow documentary filmmaker John Cohen:

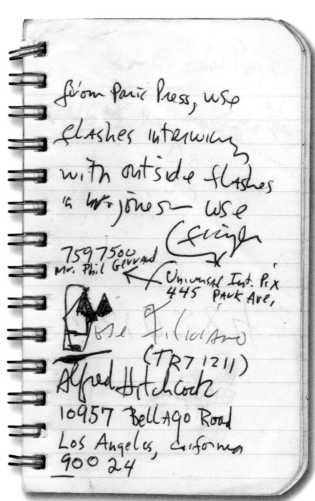

> *What we had to work with was not what you would conceive of if you were going shooting a film. What we were trying to do is to make a logical story out of this newsreel-type footage . . . to make a story which consisted of stars and starlets who were taking the roles of other people, just like a normal movie would do. We were trying to do the same thing with this footage. . . . And we were very limited because the film was not shot by us, but by the eye, and we had come upon this decision to do this only after everything else failed. And in everything else failing, the film had been cut just to nothing. So we took it and tried to do it this way because it was a new method and it was new to us, and we were hoping to discover something. And we did.*

Eat the Document made its big screen debut in 1971 at the Academy of Music in New York City, a screening that was organized by The Band's manager John Taplin, before enjoying a short run in 1972 as part of the New American Filmmakers Series at the Whitney Museum. Despite interest from distributors, cinemas, museums, and—as with everything Dylan does—bootleggers, *Eat the Document* has never been officially released and has remained largely unseen for more than fifty years.

Notebook containing editing notes for *Eat the Document*, mid to late 1960s

THIS
SHEET
IS
NOT
TO
BE
GIVEN
A
NUMBER
OF
HIS
OWN!

Pennybaker's Film of Albert Hall Inside
JHH

Outside - coming in - the
Stage - piano - me cha cha - Richard over me at piano -
Mr Jones minor playing hymn - my hands - trilling - scale -
(not especially good film until later notified here on this proper)
too fast - slow - "Rainy Day Women" - bad picture - g'mes standing
me walking to mike + back past band to table -
"Another emergency" Fred Perry /

weigh in
weighless
Garth / .... into for soundtrack / picture of
perry again - "what we wanna do - coupled you see ..."
Garth still playing - Alderson & Perry talking -
Richard's hand playing piano - bass playing
all alone & mikey talking - bass stops - Garth
again
(Fly Trapeze)

drunk film
+ Garth - fall midsensal songs -
men looking into piano - different men at this
point
Robbie (white guitar) playing to hisself -
not good film) he playing down for second -
waltzy & looking - me going into darkness
talk to Alderson - up to mike - (Garth sluty)
playing
Cut to Open Hall now - acoustical guitar check

to size and position as in advertisement

STRIP INTO

RETURN TO: Sussman & Sugar, 24 West 40th St., New York 18

Client VN325 Pub. TBR
Date 7/8 Size 12 x 3

"Writings and Drawings by Bob Dylan"

WRITINGS AND DRAWINGS

In 1973, Knopf published *Writings and Drawings*, a landmark volume that was the first authorized collection of Dylan's lyrics. Predominantly made up of song lyrics from his first, self-titled album (1962) through *Bob Dylan's Greatest Hits Vol. II* (1971), the book also compiled then unreleased songs such as "Tell Me, Momma" from the 1966 tour, as well as examples of his other written output including liner notes and concert programs. Notably, several manuscripts that are now part of the Bob Dylan Archive were included in the volume, including an early typescript draft of "Subterranean Homesick Blues" (then titled "Look Out Kid!") and the typescript of "Field Mouse from Nebraska," which was used for the book's end papers.

Originally titled *Words*, the book went through the design stages before Dylan decided to change course. A few years earlier, he had begun a series of whimsical and at times sardonic illustrations, which he collected under the name "Morris Zollar Wants to Know." The titular character—a sort of Mister Jones figure—could be found throughout asking inane questions about Barry Goldsmith, tattoo parlors, and "the Nashville Skyline Rag." From the more than one hundred illustrations in the series, Dylan selected eighteen that corresponded to particular song lyrics of his, and retitled the book *Writings and Drawings*. For an artist famously reluctant to explain his art, these visual interpretations are mischievous companions to the written word, and in some regards, perfect foils to those who obsessed over Dylan's every word. (In 2018, Dylan would take the idea in an entirely different direction with the *Mondo Scripto* art series.)

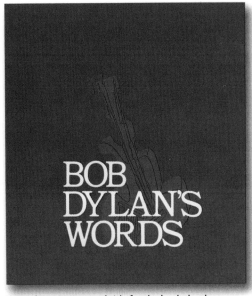

Unused concept art and title for the book that became *Writings and Drawings*, circa 1973

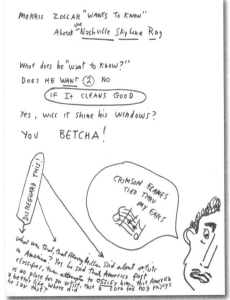

From the "Morris Zollar Wants to Know" series, circa early 1970s. Drawing by Bob Dylan

"Guitar," circa early 1970s. Drawing by Bob Dylan

PAGE 260: *Writings and Drawings* advertisement production art, circa 1973. Photographer unknown

PAT GARRETT & BILLY THE KID

Pat Garrett and Billy the Kid lobby card, 1973

THE FILM

Although films had always been one of Dylan's passions and inspirations, director Sam Peckinpah's 1973 Western *Pat Garrett and Billy the Kid* was Dylan's first foray into Hollywood filmmaking. Screenwriter Rudy Wurlitzer, an acquaintance, asked Dylan to write music for the film, and Peckinpah, moved by a performance of the song "Billy," offered him a role. Filmed on location in Durango, Mexico, during late 1972 and early 1973, in *Pat Garrett and Billy the Kid,* Dylan played the role of "Alias," a mysterious friend of Billy the Kid.

In an unpublished writing in the Archive from soon after the film was released, Dylan acknowledged the great work that Peckinpah did in bringing the story to the screen:

> *Regardless of its flaws, Sam Peckinpah's* Pat Garrett and Billy the Kid *is THEE [sic] Billy the Kid movie. Don't let anyone tell ya different. It's hard enough to take a story which no one knows and make sense of it on the screen. But to take one where everyone knows the outcome from the beginning has to be a monumental undertaking—Sam said it was his hardest since* Ride the High Country.

EVERYBODY'S SONG

THE SOUNDTRACK

In the midst of the film's production, Dylan repaired to CBS Discos Studios in Mexico City for the first soundtrack recording session. Subsequent sessions in California at Burbank Studios proved to be more productive: all but one of the songs from the soundtrack came from these dates. Dylan's handwritten credits for the album reflect the fact that the sessions were filled with familiar faces from across his career, including Bruce Langhorne, Roger McGuinn, Booker T. Jones, Jim Keltner, and Russ Kunkel.

In a September 2022 interview with Keltner conducted by the Bob Dylan Center, the drummer recalled the experience of recording the soundtrack and, in particular, "Knockin' on Heaven's Door":

> "Knockin' on Heaven's Door" was recorded on a soundstage at Warner's, so it was a big room. In those days, they didn't do it like today where you watch a little screen. In this case it was the wall. It was massive. The first thing that hit me was the changes, the song really talked to me. It had those changes that just haunt you and then the words were killing. It's Dylan, how else do you describe it? It was him describing a scene, only in this case we're actually seeing the scene. We're not having to conjure it up by just the lyric. This actress, Katy Jurado, she's crying because her husband is dying at the edge of the river, Slim Pickens, the actor. She's crying and Bob's singing that song, "Mama, put my guns in the ground." It gets me, just talking about it after all these years. I was crying and I was amazed that I was crying and playing, and pretty soon I thought, "Don't blow this!"
>
> Sure enough, we got the take. With Bob, it's very fast. You don't do more than a couple of takes maybe. That was a really amazing gift to me, to do my thing on a song that was so beautiful and to be surrounded by really great players. Though playing with Bob, it almost didn't matter who else was playing because I hooked right in with him.

Pat Garrett & Billy the Kid soundtrack credits, 1973

METRO · GOLDWYN · MAYER Presenta

"PAT GARRETT Y BILLY THE KID"
con
JAMES COBURN
KRIS KRISTOFFERSON
BOB DYLAN

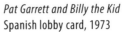

Pat Garrett and Billy the Kid
Spanish lobby card, 1973

1967–1973

"Knockin' on Heaven's Door" sheet music, 1973

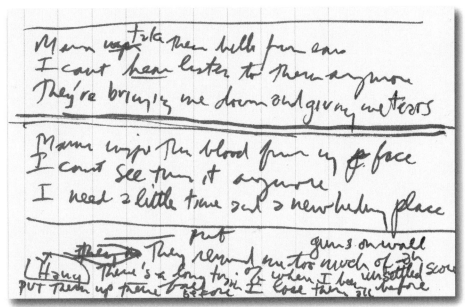

"Knockin' on Heaven's Door" draft manuscript, 1975

"KNOCKIN' ON HEAVEN'S DOOR"

Columbia subsequently released "Knockin' on Heaven's Door" as a single, which ended up reaching the Top 10 in several countries. Since then, it has become one of Dylan's most iconic and well-loved songs, living on through innumerable cover versions including those of Antony and the Johnsons, Bryan Ferry, Eric Clapton, Roger McGuinn, and Television. However, it was the massive hit version by Guns N' Roses that brought the song back into the popular consciousness perhaps more than any other; after including the song in their live sets beginning in 1987, they released the song as a single for their 1991 album *Use Your Illusion II*.

Dylan himself has also revisited the song across his career, rewriting or adding new verses and finding new resonances within the song's understated simplicity. This is part of a process of revision and rearrangement with his songs that Dylan has continued to this day. In a 1980 interview, he explained,

> *It's a very fine line you have to walk to stay in touch with something once you've created it. . . . Either it holds up for you or it doesn't.*

Although he'd recorded the song in February, by late 1973, Dylan revisited "Knockin' on Heaven's Door," most likely in advance of his forthcoming tour with The Band. These particular lyrics were not used, and the verse Dylan ended up singing on the tour went,

> *Mama wipe the blood from my face*
> *I'm sick and tired of the war*
> *Got a lone black feelin', and it's hard to trace*
> *Feel like I'm knockin' on heaven's door*

In 1975, as Dylan rehearsed older material for the Rolling Thunder Revue, he turned once again to the words of "Knockin' on Heaven's Door." With the addition of the "Mama wipe the blood from my face" verse from this manuscript, the song became a highlight of each Rolling Thunder Revue concert.

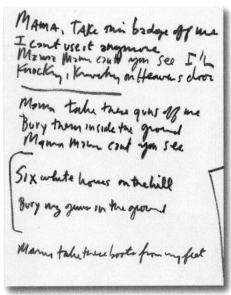

"Knockin' on Heaven's Door" draft manuscript, 1974

PAGES 268–269: *Self Portrait* alternate album cover mockups, 1970. Photographs by John Cohen

The Constant State 1974–1978 of Becoming

An artist has to be careful never really to arrive at a place where he thinks he's at somewhere. . . . You always have to realize that you are constantly in a state of becoming, and as long as you can stay in that realm, you'll sort of be alright.

— Bob Dylan, 2005, interview, *No Direction Home: Bob Dylan*

Bob Dylan, 1974. Photograph by Barry Feinstein

L–R: Bobby Neuwirth, David Blue, Ronee Blakley, Bob Dylan, the Other End, NYC, 1975.
Photograph by Ken Regan

1974 tour concert tickets

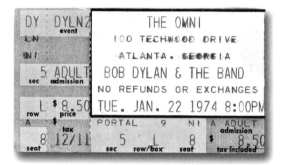

L–R: Robbie Robertson, Rick Danko (obscured), Bob Dylan, Levon Helm, 1974.
Photograph by Barry Feinstein

BOB DYLAN AND THE BAND 1974 TOUR

Aside from some special one-off performances, Dylan had not staged a full-scale tour since 1966. In the intervening eight years, the world of rock 'n' roll touring had changed dramatically. When Dylan toured in 1966, he was revolutionary for bringing along a custom sound system built by engineering whiz Richard Alderson, who was fixing and soldering the equipment as the band circled the globe. (At that time, The Beatles were still playing through stadium PA systems on their final tour.) Now in the early 1970s, touring was big business, and operations had scaled accordingly.

For Dylan's return to touring at the start of 1974, he reunited with The Band, booking a forty-concert, thirty-date, twenty-one-city tour that traveled to arenas across the United States and Canada. When the tour was announced in November 1973, it generated a tremendous amount of excitement among fans and the media, with Dylan landing on the cover of *Newsweek*.

L–R: [unidentified], Barry Imhoff, Bob Dylan, Rick Danko, 1974. Photograph by Barry Feinstein

L–R: Bob Dylan, Robbie Robertson, Rick Danko, 1974.
Photograph by Barry Feinstein

List of
potential
songs for
1974 tour

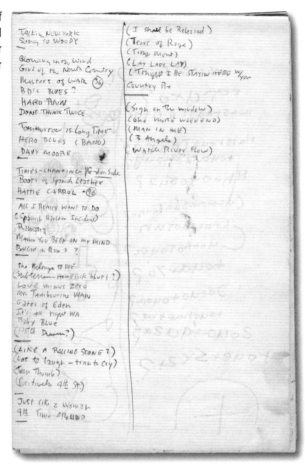

Over the course of a couple weeks in December 1973, Dylan
and The Band rehearsed for the tour at Village Recorders
in Los Angeles. The tour would present Dylan an opportunity to reimagine his back catalog, which set a precedent
for rearranging and rewriting that has become a hallmark
of his live performances ever since.

Dylan and The Band used the first show, in Chicago on
January 2, 1974, to work out the kinks; in the remaining
concerts they alternated sets and ended with a joint finale.
Although the set list remained fairly static, there were surprises and highlights throughout the tour. An appearance of
the previously unreleased early 1960s song "Hero Blues" was
one of the former, while there would be Watergate-weary
cheers nightly when Dylan sang the line "Even the President
of the United States sometimes must have to stand naked"
during "It's Alright, Ma (I'm Only Bleeding)."

Despite the commercial success of the tour, which
grossed nearly $5 million, Dylan felt underwhelmed and
disconnected musically. Reflecting on his experience of the
tour in 1985, Dylan told Cameron Crowe,

> *I think I was just playing a role on that tour,*
> *I was playing Bob Dylan and The Band were*
> *playing The Band.*

THE CONSTANT STATE OF BECOMING

Bob Dylan at Ford's Theatre, Washington, DC, 1974. Photograph by Barry Feinstein

When the tour passed through Washington, DC, Dylan took the opportunity to visit the art of the Phillips Collection and Ford's Theatre, site of the assassination of President Abraham Lincoln in 1865.

Tour '74 was an attraction not only for Dylan fans; Dylan's friends and associates came out to see the live performances as well. Songwriter John Prine turned up in Chicago for the first shows of the tour, and Joan Baez, Warren Beatty, Carole King, Jack Nicholson, and Ringo Starr attended the final shows at the Los Angeles Forum. In New York, with Dylan headlining the legendary Madison Square Garden, the guest list included everyone from Miles Davis, to John Lennon and Yoko Ono, to Dylan's old friends the Baileys.

On February 4 in St. Louis, Missouri, Leon Russell made a surprise appearance during Dylan's evening concert. According to fan reports, the pianist and producer wandered onstage, put his cowboy hat on Dylan's head, and then, despite Dylan's gesture towards the microphone, walked back offstage leaving the audience in rapturous applause.

BOB DYLAN/THE BAND

Appearing At:
Missouri Arena

Monday, February 4

6:00 & 10:00 p.m.

Leon Russell and Bob Dylan, Missouri Arena, St. Louis, February 4, 1974. Filmmaker unknown

THE CONSTANT STATE OF BECOMING

Bob Dylan with Amedeo Modigliani's portrait of Elena Povolozky, Phillips Collection, Washington, DC, 1974. Photograph by Barry Feinstein

Notably, Dylan made a special stop of his own after a performance in Atlanta, Georgia, to pay a visit to future president Jimmy Carter at the Governor's Mansion, the start of a special friendship. Speaking about that first meeting in a 2020 documentary, Dylan said,

When I first met Jimmy [Carter], *the first thing he did was quote my songs back to me. And that was the first time I realized my songs had reached into basically the establishment. He put my mind at ease by not talking down to me and showing me a sincere appreciation of the songs I had written.*

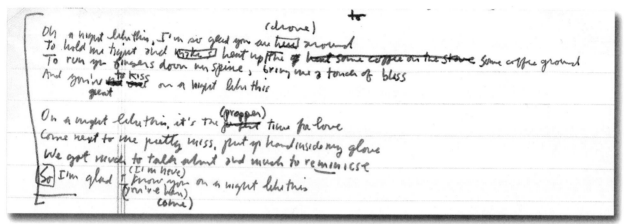

"On a Night Like This" draft manuscript

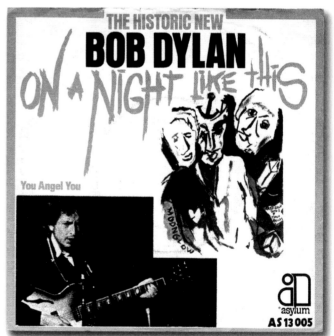

"On a Night Like This" 45 rpm singles, Spain and Netherlands, 1974

THE CONSTANT STATE OF BECOMING

In mid-1973, around the time that they were planning Tour '74, Bob Dylan briefly left Columbia Records and signed with Asylum, a label founded two years earlier by David Geffen and Elliot Roberts. When signing with the fledgling label, Dylan had agreed to compile a live album from the tour, which became *Before the Flood*. Yet Geffen felt that the tour would be stronger if Dylan had a new album to promote. Luckily, Dylan had a set of new songs, as he recounted in an unpublished manuscript:

> *We were living outside of Los Angeles in 1973. I bought a house that belonged to the great sportswriter Jim Murray. . . . After he cleaned out, I went into his abandoned work studio and immediately wrote about twelve or fifteen songs in about three days.*

In mid-November 1973, Dylan and The Band convened at Village Recorders in Los Angeles to lay down tracks for the album that would become *Planet Waves*. As is typical of Dylan's working method in the studio, the group worked quickly to find the right feel, trying out various arrangements before a master take was captured. The case of "On a Night Like This" showcases how sympathetic a set of musicians Dylan had in The Band. Each surviving take explores a different dimension of the song, moving easily and convincingly between the blues, honky tonk country, and New Orleans funk before landing in the accordion-driven Cajun territory of the final arrangement.

To show how different the recording industry was in the early 1970s, the final session for *Planet Waves* was November 14, 1973, and the album was mixed, mastered, manufactured, and on the shelves by January 17, 1974. In fact, the album was supposed to be released two weeks earlier to coincide with the start of Tour '74, but a last-minute title change from *Ceremonies of the Horseman* to *Planet Waves*, and the addition of liner notes by Dylan (drafts of which are in the Archive), led to delays. *Planet Waves*—with the enduring classic "Forever Young" as its literal centerpiece in two different versions—proved worth the wait, going to #1 on the *Billboard* album chart.

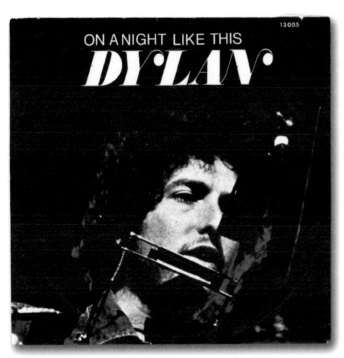

"On a Night Like This" 45 rpm singles, Yugoslavia and Italy, 1974

Bob Dylan, 1974. Photograph by Barry Feinstein

Reflections on "Dirge"

RAYMOND FOYE

I hate myself for loving you ...

—BOB DYLAN

In what is certainly Dylan's most arresting opening line since "Positively 4th Street"—"You've got a lotta nerve to say you are my friend"—the singer lays bare the tangled roots of ardor. In a simple line of six words, love and hate are boldly struck as two sides of the same coin. In this Dylan has an illustrious forebear—the Roman poet Catullus (circa 84–circa 54 BCE). While it was Sappho who first "invented" love in Western poetry, it was Catullus who invented hate: castigating friends, lovers, and lesser poets, with invective always pointed, sometimes playful, captivating readers to this day:

> *Odi et amo, quare id faciam fortasse*
> *Nescio, sed fieri sentio et excrucior.*
> —Catullus, *Carmina LXXXVI*

> I love and I hate, why you ask?
> I do not know, but I feel it, and I am in hell.

The entire poem is a single elegiac couplet: eight verbs, no adjectives, no nouns. The concision is stunning, as is the scansion and choice of words: *excrucior* alludes to a crucifixion. That Catullus wrote it about his best friend's wife, well, *nihil sub sole novum*: there is nothing new under the sun. In his own way Dylan achieved something as new in popular songwriting as Catullus did in lyric poetry, when he stripped the sugar coating from the genre and committed such searing and honest sentiments to vinyl and airwaves.

Catullus's influence in English poetry from the sixteenth to the twentieth century is all-pervading; no classical poet holds a place of equal importance with the possible exception of Virgil and Ovid (and on both poets Catullus was a primary influence). In American poetry, Edna St. Vincent Millay, Ezra Pound, Louis Zukofsky, Allen Ginsberg, and many others are in his debt. (I recall Dylan carefully quizzing Ginsberg about Catullus in his dressing room backstage at Roseland Ballroom in New York in 1994; he also asked about several William Blake aphorisms.)

Although her poetry has a poised and formal air that suggests a conservative sensibility, Edna St. Vincent Millay (1892–1950) was anything but. She was openly bisexual, a feminist, a political maverick, and an occasional morphine addict. She was also so popular a poet that practically any literate person in America in the 1940s and '50s would have been familiar with her work. Like the rhyming ballads of Poe, many of her poems literally sing off the page:

> If I could have
> Two things in one:
> The peace of the grave,
> And the light of the sun ...
> —"Moriturus"

(You'll understand ~~some day~~)
(This time, that time & No Time)

G. C' dorn

I hate myself for loving you, the weakness that it showed
You were just a painted face on a trip down suicide Road
The stage was ~~set~~, the lights blew out, the ~~actors~~ couldn't tell
I hate myself for loving you & I'm glad the curtain fell
dead clerk ~~rang~~ a bell   dead clerk rang the bell
The whole damn thing exploded & I'm glad the curtain fell ——

I hate myself for loving you, the need that was expressed
And the mercy that you showed me, that's what I hated best
But his tveol turns in/out itself ~~and~~ love is bound to win,
In kind of golden Deeds ~~~~ the angels play with sin

(Try myself on my mind)   it's part of my nature to be wild
(with a deck of cards)
Strong minded individuals never show their cards
(Sings)   (trumpets) he sings the song
Leonard Cohen, he talks of train depots and men forever stripped
Playing out his folly while his clock is being (whipped)
(with a tag which bears his home) slipped
(like a stone in orbit, He revolves, ~~around~~ inside the game
I hate myself for loving you, and it's a dirty rotten shame
strong medicine indeed   He's beaten til he's tame
Then ~~are~~ those who want to be whispered to, I don't think
I'm of them
In an age of fiberglass, I'm looking for a gem
Strong medicine indeed (when) these in time of no regret
The empty mirror upon the wall ain't showed me nothing yet
Lust   (empty mirrors) (says no one's out of debt)
I've paid the price of loneliness at least I'm out of debt
is the sickness, strong medicine is the cure
I can't recall a useful service you've ever performed for me
You've taken but you've given ~~~~ and now I'm going free
I hate myself for loving you, but I won't fall no more
It's over, you go on your way   it just something that can't be
I'm going far and going wide and I'm going by myself —   helped
Happiness ain't bought in stores or rented thru the mail (like a suit)
You can't buy happiness in stores or get it from the moon
You can't see it on museums walls
When the ~~~~ is a ~~~~ you got to ~~~~
I hate myself for loving you, now get outta here you bitch (written)

Her poem "Dirge Without Music" begins:

> I am not resigned to the shutting away of loving hearts in the hard ground.
> So it is, and so it will be, for so it has been, time out of mind . . .

I don't know if Dylan knew this poem when he wrote *his* "Dirge," but the concluding phrase in the second line will certainly catch the attention of his closer readers. It is easy to imagine Dylan reading "Dirge Without Music," with its weird blend of the amorous and the funereal, and deciding to add the music. In any case, Millay's skill at cadence and rhyme, her love of paradox, her adroit shifts between metaphor and direct speech, and her defiant stance towards society are all qualities Dylan shares as a lyric poet.

* * *

"Dirge" has been a perennial favorite of Dylan fans down through the years, first and foremost for its words of truthful vengeance. It also contains a staggeringly virtuosic guitar accompaniment by Robbie Robertson, more duel than duet, full of stabbing melody lines, played with an attack that spotlights the stark drama of the lyrics. It is Robertson's finest hour—all the more remarkable given that it was only the second of two takes, of a song he'd never heard before.

"Dirge" also belongs to that special category in Dylan's oeuvre: the piano song, an occasion where Dylan's under-appreciated rhythmic skills always come to the fore. Dylan's rhythm, while always natural, is never ordinary. Rooted in the blues and early New Orleans jazz, the key is syncopation: shifting time by placing stresses where they normally would not occur, occasionally moving the downbeat, and frequently stressing notes not on the beat. (Dylan achieves something similar when he opposes the guitar and harmonica during solos, but the percussive nature of the piano makes the effect far more pronounced.) At the same time there is also a skillful use of rubato in his vocal phrasing—borrowing time from one bar while giving it back in the next, without disrupting the overall rhythmic flow. It is something Dylan does spontaneously, to great expressive effect, and it is one of the reasons why his recorded performances still seem so fresh: the listener is right there with the

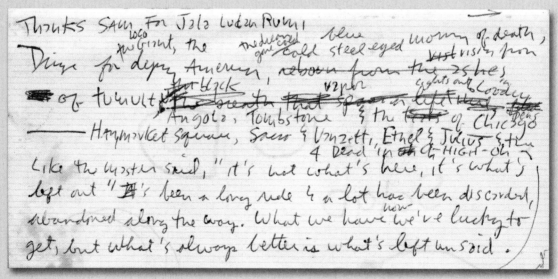

Unpublished *Planet Waves* liner notes, draft manuscript

singer in the moment of creation. This unique rhythmic sense was also at the heart of The Band's musical style, and is one of the reasons they were such a perfect fit for him.

*   *   *

The manuscripts in the Bob Dylan Archive in Tulsa pose far more questions than they answer, as one would expect of their creator. The most frequently asked question about "Dirge"—"Who is the song about?"—has no better answer than David Crosby's reply when I asked him who was Guinnevere? "Songs are seldom about one person," he said. To which I might add, they are sometimes not about any person, except the songwriter.

But often the Tulsa manuscripts do clarify nagging textual questions that fans have wondered about over the years: in "Dirge," does he actually say, "Like a slave in Ovid, who's beaten till he's tame," rather than the line given in the songbooks, which is often thought to be mis-transcribed as "Like a slave in orbit . . ."? Not only would Ovid be a satisfying literary reference, it would make perfect sense in the context of his *Amores*, where the poet decrees, "Desire rules, as a master rules his slaves." Naturally I rushed to find that line. Sorry, it's "orbit." But I did find the following verse, wherein I think lies the key to the song:

> *Leonard Cohen, he ~~chases~~ sings of ~~Birds~~ Freedom and man forever stripped*
> *playing/acting out his folly while his back is being whipped*
> *Laughing in his cell (Laughing to his cell mate)*
> *Like a slave in orbit . . .*
> *There are those who want to be worshipped to, I'm not one of them. . . .*

As it turns out, Leonard Cohen is the animating spirit behind the song, which makes perfect sense, since if you want darkness, he's the perfect guide. The working drafts attempt to nail him down in a variety of ways:

> *Leonard Cohen he ~~talks~~ sings of ~~trumpets~~ train depots and man forever stripped*
> *Playing out his folly while his back is being whipped*
> *Like a slave in orbit, he revolves around inside the game*
> *With a number or a name . . .*

In the final song, all of this is simply boiled down to: "Heard your songs of freedom . . ." The name-check has been erased. Mr. Cohen has served his purpose. And as Dylan writes in those still-unpublished liner notes about "Dirge": "What we have now we're lucky to get, but what's always better is what's left unsaid."

*   *   *

In "Dirge," as in "Positively 4th Street," Dylan is telling somebody off, or "needling them," as he more gently (and punningly) phrased it in a 1965 press conference. And he clearly relishes doing so, as a draft of the first line attests:

> *I hate myself for loving you, the need that was expressed*
> *and the mercy that you showed to me, that's what I hated best . . .*

Robbie Robertson remembers the song as originally titled "Dirge for Martha," addressed to a woman who had accused Dylan of going soft, after he played her the track of "Forever Young." True or not, in the discarded song-by-song liner notes in Tulsa, Dylan makes it clear just who is on the receiving end of this song:

> *Dirge for dying America, the dream gone cold, cold blue steel eyed women of death, rising from the ashes of tumult black vapor, lights out [. . .] Haymarket Square, Angola, Tombstone, Saco + Vanzetti, Ethel + Julius + the 4 Dead in Oh-HIGH-Oh. Like the Master said, 'it's not what's here, it's what's left out.' It's been a long ride and a lots been discarded, abandoned along the way . . .*

What strikes me as especially interesting about "Dirge," based upon an examination of the manuscripts, is that Dylan seems to be doing the exact reverse of his normal writing process, where he usually begins with the most personal and specific details of a situation and then gradually writes them out, such that the trajectory goes from the personal to the general. In "Dirge" the flow is reversed: Dylan begins with the general and evolves into the personal. What we assumed was a song about an old flame is in fact a song about his country. And as we know from Dylan's interviews in Scorsese's Rolling Thunder Revue film, the American Bicentennial for him was an ominous time, full of portent.

Time and again while researching in Tulsa I find my long-standing interpretation of any given album to be diametrically opposed by the drafts and fragments in the notebooks. I always considered "Dirge" to be the exception to an otherwise upbeat and buoyant album, full of fond childhood memories, and exquisite haiku-like nature imagery of his Minnesota youth. Yet Dylan's notes and drafts for *Planet Waves* reveal virtually the entire album to be a dark lament for a country where things have gone seriously wrong, "ten years of decadences" as Dylan calls it in his notebook. Although the album title *Planet Waves* has always been considered an allusion to Ginsberg's 1968 City Lights book *Planet News*, I couldn't help but think what was really on Dylan's mind was Ginsberg's next book, *The Fall of America: Poems of These States, 1965–1971*, published in April 1973, seven months prior to the recording of *Planet Waves* (November 1973). *The Fall of America* is Ginsberg's prophecy of the undoing of the American empire at the hands of a war machine that runs on money and political corruption, a landscape poisoned from chemicals and fossil fuels, psychically scarred from the holocausts of the Native Americans and the African slave trade, and the burlesque of the media dumbshow eager to turn it all into entertainment.

The abandoned liner notes to "Dirge" continue:

> *Drink to it, another bottle of rot gut, and gonareah exploding from Yankee stars, wither the white rider on the Mississippi River + the poison factory. Down another bottle of Tequila and thank your Yankee stars for the gonhorea exploding into the 21st century. Twisted skeleton remnants of the shabby past . . .*

And Mr. Dylan is only getting started, but you get the idea.

In the highly truncated liner notes that were eventually printed on the back cover of the album, Dylan refers to the "Gone World," a reference to another of his Beat heroes. Lawrence Ferlinghetti's first book, *Pictures of the Gone World* (1955), deals with many of the same themes as *The Fall of America*, albeit from a gentler, wittier, more surrealist angle, yet no less pointed. One wonders if in the end Dylan didn't favor this approach to Ginsberg's Old Testament wrath.

"What's that I hear now ringing in my ears?" Phil Ochs sang. To which Dylan answers to himself: "Could it be the bold new authoritarian anthem?" And then, in a typical moment of "It's Alright, Ma" levity, he informs the imaginary listener:

Is this the death of America? Or the sprouting of a new land, the suggestion of a new beginning? Well, whatever, rest easy, it is the sound of no more than the phono . . .

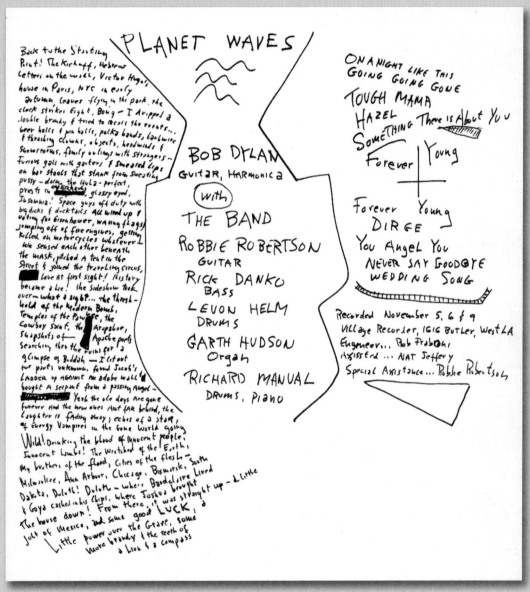

Planet Waves songbook featuring back cover of album, with Dylan's original liner notes

L–R: Dennis Hopper, Arlo Guthrie, Melvin Van Peebles (obscured), Melanie, Bob Dylan, Dave Van Ronk, Larry Estridge, Friends of Chile benefit concert, Felt Forum, NYC, May 9, 1974. Photograph by Marcelo Montealegre

Bob Dylan's program for Friends of Chile benefit concert

Friends of Chile benefit concert ticket stub

THE CONSTANT STATE OF BECOMING

Bob Dylan (holding guitar at right), Friends of Chile benefit concert, Felt Forum, NYC, May 9, 1974. Photograph by Marcelo Montealegre

FRIENDS OF CHILE BENEFIT CONCERT, 1974

Folksinger Phil Ochs, after hearing about the plight of political prisoners in the wake of the brutal September 11, 1973, Chilean coup, began making plans for a Friends of Chile benefit concert at Madison Square Garden's Felt Forum, to be titled "An Evening with Salvador Allende." For Ochs, the benefit concert had personal resonance: he'd met Chilean folksinger Víctor Jara during a June 1971 trip to Chile with Yippie "leader" Jerry Rubin and Stew Albert and performed with him for Chilean miners in the remote mountains of the country.

Held on May 9, 1974, the benefit featured an all-star cast, including Argentinian saxophonist Gato Barbieri, Arlo Guthrie, folksinger Melanie Safka, actor and musician Melvin Van Peebles, and Dave Van Ronk. Political activist Daniel Ellsberg attended, as did former Swedish ambassador to Chile Harald Edelstam. Dennis Hopper emceed the event and recited Allende's last speech and a Pablo Neruda poem that had been included in the concert program. The Living Theatre, the New York–based experimental theater troupe, reenacted in graphic detail the torture methods Pinochet's soldiers used against the citizens of Chile. Pete Seeger read the last poem Jara ever wrote, "Somos Cinco Mil" ("We Are Five Thousand"), which the martyred folksinger had written while he awaited his fate alongside thousands of other political prisoners held captive at the Estádio Nacional.

Rumors circulated that Dylan was to be in attendance, though after being pegged as a "protest singer" in the early 1960s, he had largely given up performing for political causes. Dylan agreed to perform at the last minute. Tickets, which had been slow to sell, sold out almost immediately. Backstage, the atmosphere was festive, as old friends reconnected over copious amounts of wine, which contributed to an overall freewheeling time onstage. Dylan sang Woody Guthrie's "Deportee," with Arlo Guthrie, "North Country Blues," and "Spanish Is the Loving Tongue," and he closed out the brief set with "Blowin' in the Wind," joined onstage by Melanie, Ochs, Seeger, Van Ronk, and others.

I'm Learning It These Days Richard Hell

Time flies by like a great whale
And I find my hand grows stale at the throttle
Of my many faceted and fake appearance
Who bucks and spouts by detour under the sheets
Hollow portals of solid appearance
Movies are poems, a holy bible, the great mother to us
People go by in the fragrant day
Accelerate softly my blood
But blood is still blood and tall as a mountain blood
Behind me green rubber grows, feet walk
In wet water, and dusty heads grow wide
Padré, Father, or fat old man, as you will,
I am afraid to succeed, afraid to fail,
Tell me now, again, who I am?

—Ted Berrigan, Sonnet XXXIV, from *The Sonnets*

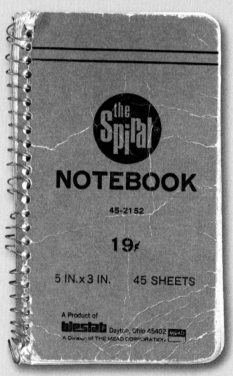

Blood on the Tracks notebook, circa 1974

One can't imagine that Bob Dylan has been afraid of success or failure. His confidence appears to abide. As this reporter wrote in a notebook when mulling the lyrics to songs on *Blood on the Tracks*: They're sad, even heartbreaking, but he always lands on his feet—that's what makes him Bob Dylan.

Many things make him Bob Dylan, as many things make anybody, but one that definitely sets him apart is that he always lands on his feet. His doubts are just opportunities to sing.

> The gods demand of the system that a certain number of people sing, like the birds do, and it somehow was given to me to be one of those people—and I mean I did have a choice—I could have decided not to, to be a truck driver or a filmmaker. But I like doing that, and I feel that probably the major reason I write is because the gods might destroy . . . the whole thing could fall apart. I lift my voice in song. I lift my voice in song.

—Ted Berrigan, from documentary film
Poetry in Motion, as quoted by Ron Padgett
in his book *Ted*

Regarding the above intro/epigraph sonnet: it's a collage (all the poems in Berrigan's *Sonnets* are) that reflects *Blood* and Bob, but unintentionally or by chance or because of the secret shapes of things—it was composed not later than 1963—which is how many of the greatest things happen, including lines and effects of Bob Dylan's lyrics. The audience creates the work as much as the artist does.

I, or "I," wrote about Dylan once before, in 2005, for a music magazine that asked for a few lines about a favorite of his songs. My choice was "You're a Big Girl Now" from *Blood on the Tracks*, a number that can still choke me up. I chose it because it was the song of his I knew that best exemplified his bewildering powers by having such a distance between its extreme emotional impact and the banality of its lyrics. How can those silly words be so affecting? "Time is a jet plane, it moves too fast." Where is the poetry in that? The metaphor is clumsy and the observation commonplace. But in the song it breaks your heart.

What kind of relationship is there between good poems and good song lyrics? I thought I'd research further in the Bob Dylan Archive by checking the drafts to "You're a Big Girl Now" to see if I could find out anything about his wording decisions.

The notebooks were enjoyable, though the thing that most seemed to set them apart from other good writers' notebooks was a kind of abundance. Bob is just more of everything. I still have to smile in wonder to think that the Bob Dylan from when I was a teenager has copped the Nobel Prize in Literature and also now has a whole institution in place to hold and make available his notebooks and tape archives and related artifacts. I remember reading a few years ago somewhere that Dylan is the most documented person who ever lived, which surprised me, if only for a minute—but who could guess Nobel Prize? It *is* like he's Jesus, living for us, as perhaps has occurred to him, in resentment or not, in various contexts.[1]

The notebooks for *Blood on the Tracks* are small and spiral-bound, pocket-sized. The writing is tiny and can be crowded, but usually quite legible. My personal favorite two moments in the two known *Blood* working notebooks (there's a third in the Morgan Library that mostly contains neatly penned fair copies of each song) were these: "I don't care if I never see another Bergman film"[2] and "If Marcel Proust could see me now / He wouldn't be ashamed."[3] (There's such a homely, Dylan feel to this one—it's pure Dylan.)

There's another great spot where he goes, "It's like this:" and then gives a full play-by-play of a baseball game's final half inning, the bottom of the 9th, which had commenced at 5–0 and concluded 5–4[4] . . . Is it love-life allegorical? (I'm sorry—don't snap at me, BD . . .)

The most personal sounding entry, apart from the lyrics themselves (the notebooks have scattered diaristic-seeming entries, lists of various types, and stray phone numbers, etc., as well as—primarily—lyrics-in-progress) was this passage:

> *For a short time, I found you and you*
> *found me. Those were the best days.*
> *Days of youth. (Days of Glory, of inner*
> *struggle) A time when we didn't know*
> *or care who we were. We walked in*
> *the woods, in a world of our own.*
> *I was a the child and you were the Madonna.*
> *It would be a while before*
> *the Man and the Madonna* [?—word indistinct] *would enter,*
> *before the structured roles would*

change our beings. How did
it happen? Before we would find it
necessary to fit into the structure. Now
we live to catch up with ourselves but
where are we that we are so far apart
from ourselves, from what we used
to be, from what we used to have and find so natural.[5]

In a way, in its poignancy and feeling for the truths of an affair, that's the most poetic passage in the pair of notebooks. It reminds me of Rilke a little. With Dylan you can never be sure, but the lines sound like they come directly from his inner being, way less guarded and metaphorical and heterogeneous and parable-istic and carnivalesque than his songs, but as if it could be the un-tempered underlying meaning of a song. Who would not be moved by what he says there? That's another thing about Bob—he has that curse, like Jack Kerouac and Lester Bangs, of feeling like a friend to a great proportion of the people who respond to him at all.

As it happens, "You're A Big Girl Now" turned out to be one of the least documented of the drafts of *Blood* material in the Archive. There's one piece of paper that is mostly just a series of end rhymes, presumably made to help him recall all the lines as he first tried singing it. The only difference from the recorded song in that memory aid is that on the record "in somebody's room" is, on the paper scrap, a bed rather than a room.

The remaining compositional trace of the lyrics in the Archive's *Blood* notebooks looked like this:

You're
Too Big For YOUR Pants [?] *BRITCHES, Baby*
BIG GIRL: "It's a the price I have to pay"

[along the right margin:]

Time is a
jet
plane
fast last
I can
change
I swear

[back to page proper:]

A change in the weather can even be extreme
But the changing of horses in the middle of the stream
is taking a chance, babe—[6]

So much for any enlightenment about how those lyrics succeed despite being clichés. (Though the word-music is strong, as usual from Dylan, with internal rhymes and alliteration, etc., and in the performance of course a whole lot of the power comes from the melody and playing and the vocal delivery.) Bob is into the traditions, is the best I can say, and he trusts his instincts. He's not the first to be unfazed by familiar tropes—in fact J. L. Borges, unjustly forsaken by the Nobel committee, made a strong case for them. He pointed out that over and over throughout history the same metaphors appear in great literature, whether it is an identification of stars with eyes or dreams with life. Then there's time as swift, conversations short and sweet, and leaving a lover like changing horses in midstream.

The rhyme scheme and construction of the song are interesting and scrupulously symmetrical. Each verse is six lines. The first and final couplets rhyme, but the middle one disrupts dramatically with a cry of emotion that isn't rhymed and includes those double whales of "oh!": The form of the stanzas vividly embodies their emotional content. The song is emotionally complex, which is another exceptional ability of Bob's and perhaps a thing he values more than technical issues like the ordinarily inadvisable use of clichés. And of course it's not as if he is a weak writer who typically resorts to them. He trusts his instincts and we can only learn from that. Say he's Jesus, a prophet: we should follow his example by figuring out the areas where our instincts are most trustworthy and spend as much time there as possible, learning.

> *I was burned out from exhaustion, buried in the hail*
> *Poisoned in the bushes and blown out on the trail*
> *Hunted like a crocodile, ravaged in the corn*
> *"Come in," she said, "I'll give you shelter from the storm"*
>
> —Bob Dylan, "Shelter from the Storm" from *Blood on the Tracks*

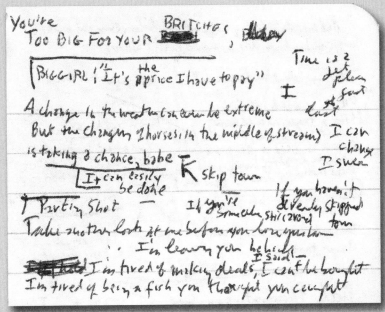

Blood on the Tracks notebook, circa 1974

BLOOD ON THE TRACKS

Dylan closed out 1974 by writing and recording *Blood on the Tracks*, an album that is widely regarded as a masterpiece. During a summer spent on his Minnesota farm in 1974, he worked on the songs, filling every space of three small pocket notebooks with his already tiny handwriting, as can be seen in the lyrics to "Idiot Wind" from the blue *Blood* notebook. Words, phrases, and ideas jostle for space, building into songs that run into one another on the page. The energy of Dylan's inspiration is palpable, as is his work ethic and master craftsman's touch. "You're Gonna Make Me Lonesome When You Go" features one of Dylan's go-to songwriting tools: lists of words he could rhyme, including many of his clever, ever-so-off rhymes. "Shelter from the Storm," on the other hand, seems to have emerged almost fully formed, with few emendations, echoing the flashes of inspiration Dylan later recalled experiencing with many of his songs from the early 1960s.

After working on them for some months, Dylan previewed his new songs for a number of friends and fellow artists, including David Crosby, Stephen Stills, and Graham Nash, as well as bluegrass musician Peter Rowan. Dylan did the same with *Highway 61 Revisited* guitarist Michael Bloomfield, but with the intention of potentially drafting him to play on the record. Bloomfield, however, struggled to find a place in this particular batch of songs, later saying, "They all began to sound the same to me; they were all in the same key; they were all long." Bloomfield wasn't entirely wrong. Dylan had been experimenting with a particular open tuning that he used for many of the songs on the album, which on the one hand gave the guitar a more open, ringing sound, but on the other hand limited the number of usable, different chords.

Alternate treatment of original photograph used for *Blood on the Tracks* cover artwork. Photograph by Paul Till

PAGE 298: Alternate treatment of original photograph used for *Blood on the Tracks* cover artwork, Maple Leaf Gardens, Toronto, May 10, 1974. Photograph by Paul Till

I had a job in the Great North Woods
Working as a cook for a spell
But ~~I never~~ the hours were just too much for me
And one day the axe fell
So I drifted down to LA
where I [reckoned] met my cousin Chuck
Who got me a job in an airplane plant
loading cargo on to a truck ~~(out pour)~~   close
But all the while, I was ~~alone~~, the past was far behind
And I seen a lot of women but you never escaped my mind
and ~~I~~ we grew

                                        promised to another man

And she turned to look at him and said this aint the end.
Keep your eyes ~~on~~ don't forget me   we'll meet ~~someplace~~ again
                              [Don't]
on the ~~there is~~ nothing else has gone between us & we've bound to meet again
for too much

She was dancing in a topless place, I stopped in for a beer
I see the side of her familiar face, in the spotlight so
        Aint kept Hello she said.   Clean
Thought (you) looking at the side of her face
              (There was [
Hello Never [
              I made joke, ~~she didn't laugh~~ but I studyed
    I must admit I was a little uneasy when she bent her
                   down to tie the lace(s)   face
Later on, I got ~~up~~ to go [🚬]   I was attracted   familiar
She was ~~tending~~ ~~train~~ when I turned around, asked me for face
                              leaning and   my hair like her
And later on she called to me, across the crowd
    I thought you were would say hello, I thought
    ~~we~~ And later on, I got up to leave   to myself out loud
          ~~come~~ out of nowhere ~~to leave~~ she said me, what's your ~~name~~
    She was standing!   pretty pretty much the same

And now we're reached the end of the rope, the circle's come to an end
                                                          changing
        And now we've meeting again I
Now
Screwed it into the fender sayin Montreal   Northwoods
                                                 workering 125 ↓
                                                   3 cook
Anew did know   It was   just too much as a cook
        when we were going to / stay just too like work   for 3
                                                 one day   spell   the 2x2

I remember how little time we had, we either busy or stoned
Running too fast and every thing we planned always had to be postponed
You   tell me
But noting that you even did even had to be explained
        he meant   meant to get stuck
                                           body
She was dancing in a topless place, somepl   complex
Noting that you
        I just couldn't make that seem too explained
            as a couple of lovers washed away , I couldn't   much of a fuss
How we singly met that smoky nite (in) away , I couldn't
In the kitchen of the joint   help but
We always did feel the same   think
but we saw it from a different point   of us

We were always —

She was married when you first met soon to be divorced
You helped her out of a jam I guess but you used too
                                                 a little much
And you drove that car as far as you could,   force
                                    abandoned it out west
And yz split up one dark sad night both agreeing
                                               it was best
And she turned around to look at you
As you were walking away
And deep inside her heart she knew
Yu'd meet again some day

        Others — on the needle

Track sheet from *Blood on the Tracks* sessions, A&R Studios, NYC, September 17, 1974

With the workshopped songs in hand, Dylan booked four days of studio time at New York City's A&R Studios from September 16 through the 19th, with Phil Ramone engineering. When the first day of tracking started, Dylan hadn't booked other musicians to play on the tracks; rather, it seems as if he conceived of the record as an acoustic album with occasional accompaniment. John Hammond, who attended the sessions, stated for a November 1974 *Rolling Stone* article by Larry Sloman: "Bob said to me, 'I want to lay down a whole bunch of tracks. I don't want to overdub. I want it easy and natural.' And that's what the whole album's about. Bobby went right back to the way he was in the early days and it works."

Dylan tried out this stripped-down, scaled-back concept for several takes of a few different songs before multi-instrumentalist Eric Weissberg was brought in to contribute. Weissberg, in turn, recruited members of his band Deliverance (named after the 1972 film they scored) to add to the tracks. Other musicians joined as well, including guitarists Charlie Brown and Barry Kornfeld, keyboardist Thomas McFaul, bassist Tony Brown, drummer Richard Crooks, and Buddy Cage, the pedal steel player from New Riders of the Purple Sage. However, after the first day Dylan decided to let most of the musicians go; he kept only Brown and Cage, and, enlisting pianist Paul Griffin, had them overdub parts onto certain tracks.

With thirteen masters in the can, he felt the record was completed, and he assembled a version of the album. However, after sitting with the recordings, Dylan decided he needed to re-record some of the songs. In late December, just after the holidays, he holed up at Studio 80 in Minneapolis and worked out new full band arrangements for five of the songs: "Tangled Up in Blue," "Idiot Wind," "If You See Her, Say Hello," "You're a Big Girl Now," and "Lily, Rosemary and the Jack of Hearts." Joining him during the sessions were Bill Berg, Tony Brown, Gregg Inhofer, Kevin Odegard, Peter Ostroushko, Billy Peterson, and Chris Weber.

THE CONSTANT STATE OF BECOMING

In addition to changing the arrangements and overall feel of the songs, Dylan had rewritten some of the lyrics, playing with first- and third-person pronouns to make the subject of the songs ambiguous. Dylan later recalled,

> *I guess I was just trying to make it like a painting where you can see the different parts, but then you also see the whole of it. With ["Tangled Up in Blue"], that's what I was trying to do . . . with the concept of time, and the way the characters change from the first person to the third person, and you're never quite sure if the third person is talking or the first person is talking. But as you look at the whole thing it really doesn't matter.*

Released on January 20, 1975, *Blood on the Tracks* ended up going to #1 on the *Billboard*, *Cash Box*, and *Record Weekly* album charts. Over time, the record has gone double platinum, with over two million copies sold.

Bob Dylan, 1974. Photograph by Barry Feinstein

Tangled

JOY HARJO

Every age has its prophets and troubadours, the singers of trouble, love, and the tangled story we humans make as we journey from birth to death, from the Earth to the stars and back. Dylan began in the footsteps of Woody Guthrie, then veered to stand and sing his original take on the story of our generation. By 1975, the year the album *Blood on the Tracks* was released, and the tune "Tangled Up in Blue" caught the ears of so many, there was more than enough trouble with conflict in Vietnam, the Khmer Rouge massacres, apartheid in South Africa, and the aftermath of Wounded Knee. Anna Mae Pictou Aquash, the American Indian Movement warrior, was found dead: shot in the head in a ditch, gone for months.

The lyrical ballad-like poemsong of "Tangled Up in Blue" is a kind of chorus of different lives—each crafted around a transformative moment revealed in the ordinary details out of which our living unwinds. Each story is gathered with the hook phrase "tangled up in blue," which is more than just a catchy set of words for the trick of it. Blue could be the blue light emerging momentarily after twilight, to signal the dark. It is the color of the auric field, that which moves between spirit and earthliness. It is a cord that connects us to history, the history we make within our individual story, that connects us with family, a community, a country, an age: a generation. We are tangled up in blue.

Dylan often changed the stanzas as he performed and recorded the song through the years, adding and subtracting. I appreciate that kind of form as the stories are always changing. We change the way we tell them, we experience them differently, as we move through time and history.

The way I speak or spoke about Dylan, or any artist of his age, is different now than it was when I was 16 years old and my ears were young.

Of his song, Dylan responded, "There's a code in the lyrics, and there's no sense of time . . . yesterday, today, and tomorrow all in the same room, and there's very little you can't imagine not happening." In other words, these "Tangled Up in Blue" lyrics make a kind of equation of memory. Words are given momentum by emotional fervor. Each soul exists in shimmering memory, and memory does not stand still. It is constantly moving within us, through us, with or without us, so that perhaps we are ultimately creations of time. Perhaps memory has created us, perhaps it shifts time by an ache of loneliness or a sigh of awe at unbelievable beauty found at closing time in a bar at the edge of nowhere, or at the click of a key in the ignition to say goodbye to goodbye when we had just made love to a miracle.

In one memory I am at Indian school in a Navy peacoat, my long dark hair hiding my face. I have a pen in my hand copying out "Blowin' in the Wind" longhand on one of those spiral-bound tablets with green lined paper. I copy "The Times They Are A-Changin'," and sing it to myself under the tall cottonwoods on the Indian school campus.

It will be years before I find my voice. I will find it in the soundscape of my generation. We listened to the changing times on the radio, carried transistor radios and listened under the blankets at night to the voices of history and to the singers of love and heartbreak. We played music, danced under light shows, stars, to living music whose resonant sound patterns still cling to the trees, to memory, as we tangled up in blue.

We were bent by history, defined by it, even destroyed by it, but like others of my generation, beset by violence and tragedy, we were inspired by Dylan and other singers and players who lifted our spirits, who inspired us to pay attention and keep going through the story that we are making, all of us. Dylan reminded us in his poemsongs that every one of us has a story. "Tangled Up in Blue" could essentially be a holographic poemsong, each verse a fractal of an immense story, a mirror, a memory we left behind in a diner booth.

The sky is blue as I listen to "Tangled Up in Blue" in downtown Tulsa, next door to the Oklahoma Jazz Hall of Fame. I turn up the music. My girlhood is just miles up the road. Blood tales run through our bones, like these streets made of the unspeakable.

In this moment in history, we are witness to unprecedented and illegal moves to destroy democracy, to erase equality and undermine human rights based on false premises of sexism, racism, culturalism for greed. In these tangled times, we need the words of the poets, the singers, the prophets to move in the direction of vision and truth, away from repression and repressive acts that undermine the collective human spirit, away from the false stories that support the destruction of earth, the undermining of female power which in a healthy society stands hand in hand with male power.

Now the radio I am listening to is digital. I miss the crackle of signal, the scratch of needle on vinyl, but the need for what we find in the music is the same. I bring my restless spirit, disturbed by the blood on the tracks of history, to the altar of music. Love threads through every sung vowel of becoming.

"Tangled Up in Blue" 45 rpm single, Spain, 1975

"Tangled Up in Blue" 45 rpm single, Japan, 1975

JOY HARJO

THE BASEMENT TAPES

Following the string of authorized cover versions—and hit singles—spawned by Dylan and The Band's 1967 recording sessions in the basement of Big Pink came *Great White Wonder*. Released in July 1969, and widely considered rock 'n' roll's first bootleg, the double album signaled the opening of the unauthorized Dylan floodgates that would eventually lead the Recording Industry Association of America to call Dylan the most bootlegged artist of all time. *Great White Wonder*, which was named after its blank white gatefold cover, featured seven songs from *The Basement Tapes* sessions, as well as songs sourced from various private tapes and radio and television broadcasts.

By the time of its release in 1975, *The Basement Tapes* had become an exemplar of what critic Greil Marcus would later call "The Old, Weird America." Designer Reid Miles's concept behind the album's artwork speaks to this very idea: Dylan and The Band are just additional characters populating a world of their creation.

The official release of *The Basement Tapes* seemed only to fuel the desire to hear everything from the sessions. Nearly forty years later, fans got their wish. In 2014, *The Bootleg Series Vol. 11: The Basement Tapes Complete* was released, featuring every track that was recorded, sourced from organist Garth Hudson's original audio reels.

The Basement Tapes gatefold artwork proof, 1975

THE BASEMENT TAPES

L–R: John Hammond (foreground), Scarlet Rivera, Rob Stoner, Bob Dylan, Chicago, September 11, 1975. Photographer unknown

THE CONSTANT STATE OF BECOMING

THE WORLD OF JOHN HAMMOND, 1975

On September 10, 1975, well over a decade since he'd been dubbed "Hammond's Folly," Bob Dylan gathered with a stellar troupe of musicians in Chicago to honor the career of the legendary John Hammond, who was retiring from the music business. A talent scout and producer with a keen ear and moral compass, Hammond had spent forty-five years signing, producing, and championing a roster of musicians that reads like a who's who of twentieth-century jazz, blues, folk, and rock performers: Count Basie, Mike Bloomfield, Charlie Christian, Leonard Cohen, Aretha Franklin, Babatunde Olatunji, Pete Seeger, Bruce Springsteen, Big Joe Turner, and, of course, Bob Dylan.

Hammond had been a stalwart supporter of African American musicians from very early on in his career, helping to persuade Benny Goodman in the early 1930s to hire Black musicians, including Charlie Christian, Lionel Hampton, and Teddy Wilson. In 1938 and 1939, Hammond organized two landmark concerts before an integrated audience at Carnegie Hall titled From Spirituals to Swing. These concerts included performers such as the Count Basie Orchestra, The Golden Gate Quartet, Big Bill Broonzy, Sister Rosetta Tharpe, Lester Young, and Sonny Terry, who was on hand for the 1975 tribute. Hammond also released the first compilation LP of Robert Johnson's music titled *King of the Delta Blues Singers* on Columbia Records in 1961, which helped lead to the rediscovery of the Delta blues musician's largely forgotten legacy after his death in 1938 by musicians including Bob Dylan.

Hosted by Columbia Records president Goddard Lieberson and Atlantic Records principal Jerry Wexler, *The World of John Hammond* television special featured performances from more artists whose careers Hammond had helped along. The first segment focused on Hammond's jazz legacy, and featured performances by Marion Williams, Helen Humes, Benny Goodman with Teddy Wilson, George Benson, Red Norvo, Jo Jones, and Milt Hinton, as well as historic footage of Bessie Smith and Billie Holiday. The second segment expanded to include blues and folk, with performances by the trio of Teddy Wilson, Milt Hinton, and Jo Jones, followed by performances by Sonny Terry, John Hammond Jr., and Bob Dylan.

The World of John Hammond special, which was produced as part of WTTW's *Soundstage* series, was Dylan's first television appearance since *The Johnny Cash Show* in 1969. Backed by bassist Rob Stoner, drummer Howie Wyeth, and violinist Scarlet Rivera, Dylan ran through "Hurricane" and "Oh Sister," which had not yet been recorded, and "Simple Twist of Fate," from *Blood on the Tracks*.

Rivera, a Chicago native who had been born Donna Shea, had met Dylan six weeks earlier, on June 30, when Dylan spotted her carrying a violin case. After a brief audition at Dylan's Greenwich Village studio, Rivera joined Dylan's entourage at the Bottom Line, where he made a surprise appearance backing Muddy Waters. Later they visited the Brooklyn home of Dylan's old friend Victoria Spivey.

L–R: Roger McGuinn, Joni Mitchell, Ramblin' Jack Elliott, Joan Baez, Bob Dylan, Steven Soles, Bobby Neuwirth, Ronee Blakley, Forum de Montréal, December 4, 1975. Photograph by Ken Regan

ROLLING THUNDER REVUE, 1975

Bob Dylan, 1975. Photograph by Ken Regan

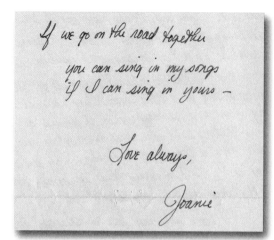

Letter from Joan Baez to Bob Dylan, November 24, 1971

In 1971, Joan Baez wrote to Dylan, floating the idea of them doing a duo tour for charity. Although that tour didn't come to pass, Baez and Dylan did cross paths several times in the years leading up to the Rolling Thunder Revue, including at the Tour '74 shows at the Los Angeles Forum and in early 1975 at the SNACK benefit concert in San Francisco.

Rolling Thunder Revue "Sold Out" poster, 1975

Feeding off the revitalized energy that could be felt in New York City's Greenwich Village, Dylan decided to gather musicians, poets, playwrights, filmmakers, and other artists to form what would become known as the Rolling Thunder Revue.

Across thirty shows from October 30 to December 8, 1975, Dylan and his caravan would travel through small towns in the Northeast, showing up, playing live concerts with little to no advance warning. Arriving at a place like Worcester, Massachusetts, they'd advertise and sell tickets in the afternoons and perform that evening. Along the way, there'd be additional stops, such as Plymouth Rock, the Dream Away Lodge, Tuscarora Nation Indian Territory, and Gordon Lightfoot's house. A crew would be on hand to film the proceedings, some scenes highly scripted, others improvised and inspired by the moment. In stark contrast with the tightly formatted 1974 tour, the Rolling Thunder Revue would be open and evolving.

Starting with a core group of musicians who had recently been part of the *Desire* recording sessions, Dylan's backing band organically developed and expanded as friends and colleagues old and new were invited to participate. Playwright Jacques Levy, who had co-written most of *Desire* with Dylan, was brought in to direct the stage show. Dylan reconnected with Joan Baez, Bobby Neuwirth, and Ramblin' Jack Elliott. Roger McGuinn of The Byrds signed on, as did poet Allen Ginsberg. Playwright Sam Shepard was brought in to work on a script for the film. Fresh off the success of Robert Altman's film *Nashville*, actress-singer Ronee Blakley was enlisted. A then unknown T Bone Burnett was part of the group, as was Mick Ronson, guitar hero from David Bowie's backing group The Spiders from Mars. Special guests dropped in throughout the tour, and Joni Mitchell, so taken with the experience after a few performances, stayed on for the full run.

In a 1995 interview for *No Direction Home*, Allen Ginsberg recalled his experience watching Dylan during the tour:

> I listened night after night as he sang. What struck me was that he became at one, or identical with, his breath. In English the word "spirit" / "spiritual" comes from "spirit," "spiritus," which is Latin for "breath" or "breathing." Dylan had become a column of air, so to speak, at certain moments, where his total physical and mental focus was this single breath coming out of his body. He was giving his whole body—his whole focus and concentration—like a form of yoga where everything around was subordinated to the projections through the spirit into the air of the intelligence of the words.
>
> Onstage he had this ten-foot-square area where he was absolutely free to do anything he wanted. He was totally free to be the magician, and to exhale his spirit, or to sing with his entire body and mind. There's a line in Rimbaud: "to possess truth in one soul and one body." Dylan had found a way to be like a shaman with all of his intelligence and consciousness focused on his breath.

The Rolling Thunder Revue was a much-celebrated artistic triumph, then and now. The legend and influence of that tour continues to resonate, not least because of the incredible film footage that was shot. Dylan would eventually edit this footage into 1978's *Renaldo and Clara*, but more recently it was used to great effect in the 2019 film documentary *Rolling Thunder Revue: A Bob Dylan Story by Martin Scorsese*.

Rolling Thunder Revue handbill, 1975

PAGES 314–315:
CENTER: Rolling Thunder Revue curtain; CLOCKWISE FROM TOP LEFT: Bob Dylan at Tuscarora Reservation, NY; Dylan with *Crystal Magick* by Carlyle A. Pushong; Joan Baez and Dylan; Scarlet Rivera, Roger McGuinn, Dylan; Aboard Phydeaux, the tour bus; Allen Ginsberg, Peter Orlovsky, Dylan, Sam Shepard, Lowell, MA; Mick Ronson, Baez, Rob Stoner, Dylan, Rivera, Seacrest Motel rehearsals, Falmouth, MA; Ronee Blakley (left) and Joni Mitchell (with guitar) backstage; Dylan; Revue wardrobe; Backstage; Performance, Plymouth, MA; Rivera, Jacques Levy, Howard Alk (with camera), Dylan, Stoner, T Bone Burnett, Steven Soles, Ronson (sitting), S.I.R. Studios, NYC; Revue finale. Photographs by Ken Regan

L–R: Bruce Springsteen, Karen Darvin, John Prine, Bob Dylan, Veterans Memorial Coliseum, New Haven, CT, November 13, 1975. Photograph by Ken Regan

Rolling Thunder Revue performers and crew, December 1975. Photograph by Ken Regan

THE CONSTANT STATE OF BECOMING

Bob Dylan and Patti Smith, NYC, October 1975. Photograph by Ken Regan

Alongside the other musicians, poets, writers, and artists fulfilling their various duties, Ken Regan was brought onboard as the tour's official photographer, capturing the chemistry on and off the stage and documenting a new era of Dylan iconography.

In an interview for the Bob Dylan Center, Roger McGuinn reflected on being part of the Rolling Thunder Revue:

> We went on the road with this caravan of different vehicles. Bob had a red Cadillac Eldorado convertible that he liked, and we had a GMC motorhome called the Green Machine. Then there was Phydeaux, which was Frank Zappa's tour bus that he had converted from an old Greyhound bus into a modern rock 'n' roll tour bus with a suite in the back and bunks in the middle and a couch, galley, and TVs. I'd never seen anything like it at the time.
>
> So we just went up and down the East Coast with this thing and it was a four-and-a-half hour show. Joni Mitchell joined us, Arlo Guthrie. We got to Toronto and Gordon Lightfoot was there. We went to Leonard Cohen's house for dinner in Montréal. We stayed at these great resorts because we couldn't fit so many people into a regular hotel. It was the best two-month party I've ever been to.

Joan Baez and Bob Dylan, 1975. Photograph by Ken Regan

DESIRE

Desire sessions with Eric Clapton (obscured, second from left) and Bob Dylan with Emmylou Harris (center at microphones), Columbia Studio E, NYC, July 28, 1975. Photograph by Ruth Bernal

Bob Dylan and Jacques Levy, Columbia Studio E, NYC, July 28, 1975.
Photograph by Ruth Bernal

Dylan's seventeenth studio album, *Desire*, came together in the spring of 1975 in New York City. At the time, the emergence of punk in the city had brought the scene to a new inflection point, with Dylan taking in at least one performance of The Patti Smith Group at the Other End. Dylan began writing songs with an eye towards assembling a band when serendipity took its course, as he noted in an unpublished manuscript,

> *Scarlet [Rivera] was crossing 2nd Avenue and Rob Stoner was playing with Bobby Neuwirth. Jacques Levy was standing on Bleecker St. and we went and wrote up a lot of songs in a short time. Marta Orbach was talking about Joey Gallo and I was thinking about Hurricane Carter. Emmylou [Harris] came by and we sang "Oh, Sister" and "Catfish" was tried at least once a night.*

Dylan found himself a songwriting partner in playwright and lyricist Jacques Levy, with whom he co-wrote all but two of the songs on *Desire*. Meanwhile, Dylan began to assemble a group of his own with bassist Rob Stoner (courtesy of an introduction from Bobby Neuwirth) and violinist Scarlet Rivera. A spare but propulsive sound began to emerge, colored by Rivera's violin, which provided the ensemble, and subsequently the album and the Rolling Thunder Revue, with a mysterious accent to match the drama of the Dylan/Levy lyrics.

Yet even as Dylan took steps towards forming a working group, he also invited session musicians to participate in the recording process. There was an initial session with members of Dave Mason's band in early July. Then after a break of two weeks, more than twenty musicians showed up to the July 28 session, including guitarist Eric Clapton (one of five guitarists present) and singer Emmylou Harris. However, over the following few days of recording, the group was pared down until it was essentially the core group of musicians who would accompany Dylan on the upcoming Rolling Thunder Revue. In the end, the sessions produced *Desire*, an album that received critical acclaim, topped the *Billboard* charts, and remains an essential entry in Dylan's catalog.

"Isis" typescript draft with
Jacques Levy's phone number
on back

```
I MARRIED ISIS ON THE FIFTH DAY OF MAY,
BUT I COULD NOT HOLD ONTO HER VERY LONG,
SO I SADDLED MY PONY AND RODE STRAIGHT AWAY,
FOR THE WILD, UNKNOWN COUNTRY WHERE I COULD NOT GO WRONG.

I CAME TO A PLACE OF DARKNESS AND LIGHT,
THE DIVIDING LINE RAN THROUGH THE CENTER OF TOWN,
I HITCHED UP MY PONY TO A POST ON THE RIGHT,
WENT INTO A LAUNDRY TO WASH MY CLOTHES DOWN.

A MAN IN THE CORNER APPROACHED ME FOR A MATCH,
I KNEW RIGHT AWAY HE WAS NOT ORDINARY,
HE SAID ARE YOU LOOKIN FOR SOMETHIN EASY TO CATCH,
I SAID I GOT NO MONEY, HE SAID THAT'S NOT NECESSARY.

WE SET OUT THAT NIGHT FOR THE COLD IN THE NORTH,
I GAVE HIM MY BLANKET, HE GAVE ME HIS WORD,
WHEN I SAID WHERE WE GOIN, HE SAID WE'D BE BACK BY THE FOURTH,
I SAID THAT'S THE BEST THING THAT I'VE EVER HEARD.

I WAS THINKIN 'BOUT DIAMONDS, I WAS THINKIN 'BOUT GOLD,
I WAS THINKIN 'BOUT MANSIONS AND JEWELS IN A BOX,
AS WE RODE THROUGH THE CANYONS, THROUGH THE DEVILISH COLD,
I WAS THINKIN 'BOUT ISIS AND THE WORDS THAT SHE TALKS.

HOW SHE TOLD ME THAT ONE DAY WE'D MEET UP AGAIN,
AND THINGS WOULD BE DIFFERENT THE NEXT TIME WE WED,
HOW SHE TOLD ME TO HANG ON AND BE HER TRUE FRIEND,
I STILL CAN'T REMEMBER THE BEST THINGS SHE SAID.
```
my mind is still filled with the things that she said
```
WE CAME TO THE PYRAMIDS ALL IMBEDDED IN ICE,
HE SAID THERE'S A BODY I'M TRYIN TO FIND,
IF I CARRY IT OUT, IT'LL BRING A GOOD PRICE,
'TWAS THEN THAT I KNEW WHAT HE HAD ON HIS MIND.

THE WIND IT WAS HOWLING AND THE SNOW WAS OUTRAGEOUS,
WE CHOPPED THROUGH THE NIGHT AND WE CHOPPED THROUGH THE DAWN,
WHEN HE DIED I WAS HOPIN IT WASN'T ████████ CONTAGIOUS,
BUT I MADE UP MY MIND THAT I HAD TO GO ON.

I BROKE INTO THE TOMB AND THE CASKET WAS EMPTY,
THERE WAS NO JEWELS, NO NOTHIN, I FELT I'D BEEN HAD,
THEN I SAW THAT MY PARTNER WAS JUST BEIN FRIENDLY,
WHEN I TOOK UP HIS OFFER I MUST'VE BEEN MAD.

I PICKED UP HIS BODY AND DRAGGED HIM INSIDE,
THREW HIM DOWN IN THE HOLE AND PUT BACK THE COVER,
I SAID A QUICK PRAYER AND I FELT SATISFIED,
AND RODE BACK TO MY ISIS, MY FRIEND AND MY LOVER.

SHE SAID WHERE YOU BEEN AND I SAID NO PLACE SPECIAL,
SHE SAID YOU LOOK DIFFERENT, I SAID THAT'S OKAY,
SHE SAID YOU BEEN GONE, I SAID THAT'S ONLY NATURAL,
BUT I'M BACK HERE WITH YOU -- ██████████████
```
she said I thought you'd come back   I SHE SAID YOU MIGHT AS WELL STAY *said I might as well stay*
```
TRUE LOVE NEVER GOES WRONG, BODY TO BODY IT'S ALWAYS THE SAME,
SO NEVER SAY NO WHEN YOU HEAR A LOVE SONG,
IT'S ALWAYS ON PURPOSE AND PART OF GOD'S GAME.
```

*Jacques Levy
677-1342*

"ISIS"

The cinematic narrative in the ballad of "Isis" was a perfect foil for
Dylan's enigmatic new sound and quickly became a highlight of the
Rolling Thunder Revue. This typescript with handwritten edits has a
few notable differences from the final version, most prominently a tag
at the end. On the reverse is co-writer Jacques Levy's phone number.

THE CONSTANT STATE OF BECOMING

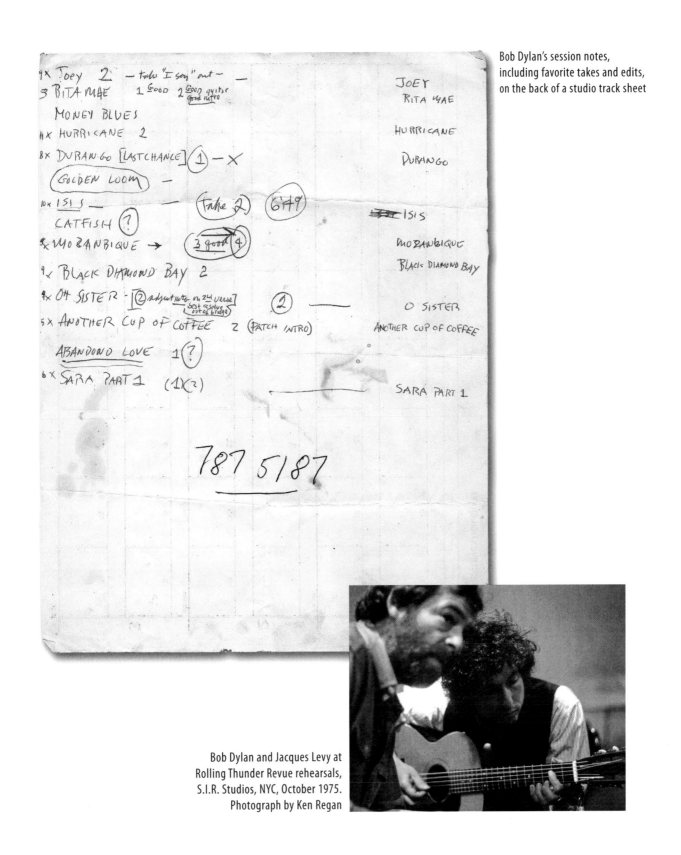

Bob Dylan's session notes,
including favorite takes and edits,
on the back of a studio track sheet

Bob Dylan and Jacques Levy at
Rolling Thunder Revue rehearsals,
S.I.R. Studios, NYC, October 1975.
Photograph by Ken Regan

Eric Clapton and Bob Dylan, Columbia Studio E, NYC, July 28, 1975.
Photograph by Ruth Bernal

"ABANDONED LOVE"

On July 3, 1975, after joining Ramblin' Jack Elliott at the Other End for renditions of Woody Guthrie's "Pretty Boy Floyd" and the classic "How Long" blues, Dylan took a solo turn testing out a new song called "Abandoned Love."

Later that month, on July 31, Dylan brought the song into the studio and recorded it in two takes, though he ultimately left it off *Desire* in favor of the gangster ballad "Joey." "Abandoned Love" was finally released on the career retrospective *Biograph* in 1985, the same year The Everly Brothers covered the song.

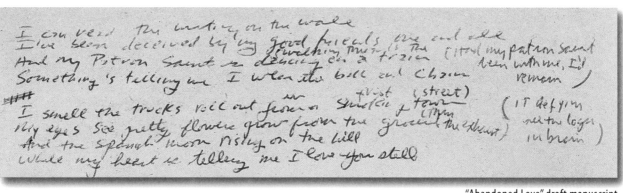

"Abandoned Love" draft manuscript

Songs of Redemption--6

Who woulda thought he'd say it, so everybody finally know him,
same soul crying vulnerable caught in a body we all are?--enough
~~xxxxxxxx~~ Person revealed to make Whitman's ~~xxxx~~ nation weep.
And behind it all the vast lone space of No God, or God, mindful
conscious compassion, life time awareness, we're here in America
~~xxxx~~ at last, redeemed. O Generation, ~~get to work!~~ *Keep on working!*

> Allen Ginsberg
> Allen Ginsberg
> York Harbor, Maine
> 10 November 1975

Allen Ginsberg and Bob Dylan, Lowell, MA,
November 3, 1975. Photograph by Ken Regan

1

Songs of Redemption

Hurricane, the only innocent Hurricane, protest song:
Pro (in favor) + Attest (testify for) the character case of
Boxer Mr Carter framed on bum rap Passaic County N.J. whom
Dylan minstrel visited in jail. Doctor Poet W.C. Williams
dying nearby said "A new world is only a new mind", & spent life
redeeming pure North Jersey language so later poets could sing
"tough iron metal" talk rhymes

ITALICS
> "They want to put his ass in stir
> They want to pin this triple mur-
>   der on him
> ...He coulda been the champion of the
>   wooorld--"

& end plain as day

ITALICS
>   "... Shame!
>   to live in a world where Justice is a game! "

so every Paterson kid will know News furthermore that

ITALICS
>   "Ruben sits like Buddha in a 10 foot cell."

Big daily ~~xxx~~ Announcement, song'll hit streets Supreme Courts'll
have coughed & weeped, Reuben Carter sprung pray God if there's
One in America--familiar harmonica pierces ears that just
heard about "criminals with suits & ties..."

All
further
italics
>   Old Bards & Minstrels rhymed their years' news on pilgrimage
> road--Visitations town to town singing Kings' shepherds' Cow boys'
> & lawyers' secrets--Good Citizen Minstrel truth's instantaneously
> heard, Big Sound in conscious generations. Local newsboy-prophet

"SONGS OF REDEMPTION"

On November 10, 1975, while the Rolling Thunder Revue was in York Harbor, Maine, poet Allen Ginsberg wrote the liner notes for Dylan's forthcoming *Desire* album, which he titled "Songs of Redemption." The signed six-page typescript with Ginsberg's handwritten edits is the final version of the text that would appear on the album's inner sleeve.

Allen Ginsberg's hand-edited liner notes for *Desire*, November 10, 1975

325

"Hurricane" 45 rpm single, Japan, 1975

RUBIN "HURRICANE" CARTER

In 1975, Dylan learned of the case of Rubin "Hurricane" Carter, a middle-weight boxer whose promising career had been stopped by a wrongful triple murder conviction. As detailed by Carter in his 1974 autobiography, *The Sixteenth Round: From Number 1 Contender to Number 45472*, Dylan was moved by Carter's life story and the injustice of his imprisonment. In response, Dylan and Jacques Levy penned "Hurricane," detailing the evidence of the case alongside the episodes of racism and racial profiling that led to Carter's conviction. Although the song was originally recorded in July 1975, Dylan re-recorded it on October 24, during rehearsals for the Rolling Thunder Revue. Rush-released as a single in November, the song would develop into a searing centerpiece of the tour.

"Hurricane" draft manuscript

THE CONSTANT STATE OF BECOMING

And <u>thats</u> what I wanted to tell you this afternoon! What you
are searching for has been found . . .

Rubin

Letter from Rubin Carter to Bob Dylan, October 19, 1979

Since their first meeting, Dylan and Carter remained in touch, with Carter making an appearance in the 2019 film *Rolling Thunder Revue: A Bob Dylan Story by Martin Scorsese*. As Carter noted in that film,

Bob has always been searching. Every time I see him now, and we don't see each other frequently, but every time I see him I ask Bob, "Have you found it yet, Bob?" And Bob says, "Yeah, I found it." But I know he hasn't, because he keeps searching.

Rubin "Hurricane" Carter and Bob Dylan, Correctional Institution for Women, Clinton, NJ, December 7, 1975. Photograph by Ken Regan

Ronee Blakley and Rubin Carter with reporters, Correctional Institution for Women, Clinton, NJ, December 7, 1975. Photograph by Ken Regan

THE NIGHT OF THE HURRICANE

As the Rolling Thunder Revue wound its way back to New York City, they made a stop at the Correctional Institution for Women in Clinton, New Jersey, where Rubin Carter was then being held. Accompanied by the press, Dylan visited with Carter, and the ensemble performed an abridged set for the inmates, one that included "Hurricane."

On December 8, 1975, the first leg of the Rolling Thunder Revue concluded with The Night of the Hurricane at Madison Square Garden. An all-star benefit that also included appearances from Roberta Flack, Coretta Scott King, Richie Havens, and Muhammad Ali (who called Rubin Carter, still in prison), the evening raised nearly $100,000 for the Hurricane Trust Fund to pay for Carter's legal defense. Robbie Robertson of The Band also showed up to play on "It Takes a Lot to Laugh, It Takes a Train to Cry."

A second benefit concert was held at the Houston Astrodome on January 25, 1976, with Stevie Wonder, Isaac Hayes, Dr. John, and Shawn Phillips also on the bill.

Thanks in part to the raised public profile of Carter's case, he was granted a new trial in 1976. Although reconvicted, he continued to appeal the case. Carter was finally freed in 1985, with the trial judge noting the case had been "predicated upon an appeal to racism rather than reason, and concealment rather than disclosure."

PAGE 328: CLOCKWISE FROM TOP:
Bob Dylan, Rob Stoner, Ronee Blakley, Steven Soles, Night of the Hurricane; Performance at Correctional Institution for Women, Clinton, NJ; Performance, Night of the Hurricane; Muhammad Ali calls Rubin Carter from the stage, Night of the Hurricane. Photographs by Ken Regan

PAGE 329: CLOCKWISE FROM TOP:
Coretta Scott King; Roberta Flack; Robbie Robertson with Bob Dylan, Night of the Hurricane; Muhammad Ali and Dylan backstage, Night of the Hurricane; Rubin Carter with Joan Baez at Correctional Institution for Women, Clinton, NJ; Working out the set list backstage at Correctional Institution for Women, Clinton, NJ. Photographs by Ken Regan

Bob Dylan at left with bugle leading the Rolling Thunder Revue at The Breakers, Newport, RI, November 1975. Photograph by Ken Regan

Rolling Thunder Revue poster, 1976

ROLLING THUNDER REVUE, 1976

In the spring of 1976, Dylan organized another leg of the Rolling Thunder Revue tour, which would travel across the South and Southwest featuring a slightly different group of musicians. Notably, Texan Kinky Friedman joined the Revue as a headliner, substituting for Ramblin' Jack Elliott, who didn't turn up until the penultimate show of the tour in Fort Collins, Colorado. There, during his solo turn, Bobby Neuwirth recognized Elliott in the sea of faces and literally pulled him onto the stage.

On this second leg of the Rolling Thunder Revue, Dylan approached the show differently, adding new repertoire (originals and covers), revising arrangements, and rewriting lyrics. "Seven Days" is the only new song that Dylan introduced in 1976. Performed live only six times on the second leg of the Rolling Thunder Revue, the song saw its first official release on the Ronnie Wood album *Gimme Some Neck* in 1979. One of Dylan's live versions, taken from an April 21, 1976, show in Tampa, Florida, was eventually released as part of *The Bootleg Series Volumes 1–3 (Rare & Unreleased) 1961–1991*. In the spring of 1996, at a dozen shows across the United States, Canada, and Europe, Dylan unexpectedly—and briefly—revived the song as part of his set lists.

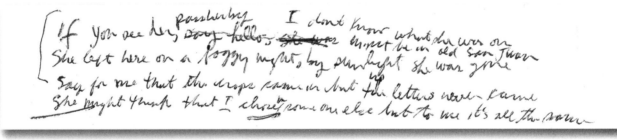

"If You See Her, Say Hello" draft manuscript, 1976

"IF YOU SEE HER, SAY HELLO," 1976 VERSIONS

Dylan played "If You See Her, Say Hello" twice during the 1976 leg of the Rolling Thunder Revue, each time with a different set of rewritten lyrics from the *Blood on the Tracks* original. This version, where she might be in "old San Juan," bears similarities to a version of the song that Dylan performed in Lakeland, Florida, on April 18, 1976.

Bob Dylan
Hard Rain

New!

Bob Dylan
Hard Rain

including:

Shelter From
The Storm

Lay, Lady, Lay

Blowin' In
The Wind

Maggie's Farm

I Pity The
Poor Immigrant

Idiot Wind

On Columbia Records • Cassettes, & 8-Track Tapes

Hard Rain advertisement, 1976

LIVE ALBUM

The two official releases documenting the tour were both called *Hard Rain*. One was a live album with songs selected from two May 1976 concerts (Fort Worth, Texas, and Fort Collins, Colorado). The tour featured the first live performances of *Blood on the Tracks* material like "You're a Big Girl Now" and "Shelter from the Storm," both of which were included on the live album. Demonstrating the strengths of the 1976 band, the former plays with dynamics to amplify the emotional register, and the latter is a slashing interpretation featuring Dylan's only live performance on slide guitar.

At the final show of the tour in Salt Lake City, Dylan is even rumored to have performed the epic "Lily, Rosemary and the Jack of Hearts." Unfortunately, no soundboard recording survives, as the tour's sound system had been returned after the Fort Collins performance, and the borrowed one had no recording equipment.

"Stuck Inside of Mobile with the Memphis Blues Again" (live) 45 rpm single, Portugal, 1976

Hard Rain promotional material, Japan, 1976

TELEVISION SPECIAL

The hour-long concert special *Hard Rain* was Dylan's first and has never been rereleased since its initial broadcast on NBC in September 1976. Composed of highlights from the Fort Collins performance, some of which appeared on the *Hard Rain* album, the concert climaxes with a stunning close-up performance of "Idiot Wind" as intense and moving as any of Dylan's work before or after.

Hard Rain television special, Hughes Stadium, Fort Collins, CO, May 23, 1976. Video stills by TVTV

The Last Waltz invitation, 1976

"The Last Waltz"
Welcome

We hope you enjoy spending Thanksgiving with us here at Winterland. We'd like to let you know what arrangements have been made to make sure that everyone is served dinner, comfortably. Here's the order of events:

When you enter the lobby, you have two choices. You may proceed to the main floor, or to the balcony. The same Thanksgiving dinner will be served on both levels.

On the main floor, tables have been set up so you may sit for dinner. After you've finished, please clear your place so that another person may sit down. Upstairs, you may sit in the balcony seats after getting your dinner at the buffet tables on the mezzanine. After your meal, please take care to discard your plates: ushers will be circulating with trash bags to assist you.

For the vegetarians among you, special meatless dishes have been prepared. They will be served at a table at the end of the right aisle on the main floor.

Beginning at 5:00 p.m., the 38 piece Berkeley Promenade Orchestra will be playing. A formal dance floor has been set up in front of the stage for your dancing pleasure. We welcome you to dance with us until 8:00 p.m., when the dance floor and the tables will be cleared in preparation for the 9:00 p.m. concert. After the concert, you are again invited to enjoy the dance music of the Berkeley Promenade Orchestra. We hope that our visiting artists will join us during these festivities.

We thank you for your courteous cooperation in making this a day to remember. It could only happen in San Francisco, and that's because of you.

Happy Thanksgiving! Happy listening! Happy Waltzing! Enjoy!

Cheers!
Bill & All the other Turkeys

THE LAST WALTZ

The Band performed their final concert on Thanksgiving Day, November 25, 1976, at the Winterland Ballroom in San Francisco. Organized by Bill Graham, and dubbed The Last Waltz, the concert featured an all-star cast of friends and collaborators, including Paul Butterfield, Bobby Charles, Eric Clapton, Neil Diamond, Dr. John, Muddy Waters, Ronnie Hawkins, Van Morrison, Joni Mitchell, and Neil Young. Bob Dylan also turned up, and together with The Band they blazed through four songs from across their shared history. The evening ended with everyone coming to the stage for a poignant rendition of Dylan's "I Shall Be Released." Director Martin Scorsese, who would later work with Dylan on two documentary films, shot the historic proceedings for a film of the same name. *The Last Waltz* was selected for the National Film Registry of the Library of Congress in 2019.

In recognition of the holiday, Thanksgiving dinner was served to attendees before the show.

RENALDO AND CLARA

As the Rolling Thunder Revue began to take shape in 1975, Dylan hired a film crew to capture the action and brought in playwright Sam Shepard to help write a script. After the second leg of the Revue ended in late May 1976, Dylan and Howard Alk began editing the footage. The result was *Renaldo and Clara*, which melded musical performances, scripted scenes, and documentary footage into a four-hour-long film. *Renaldo and Clara* translated Dylan's continuing interest in shifting perspectives, the elusive boundaries of truth and fiction, and character studies into the visual language of film. But at its core was Dylan's music. As Dylan explained in a 1978 *Rolling Stone* interview,

> *You know what the film is about? It begins with music—you see a guy in a mask* [Bob Dylan], *you can see through the mask he's wearing, and he's singing "When I Paint My Masterpiece." So right away you know there's an involvement with music. Music is confronting you.*

In an interview done for the Bob Dylan Center in 2019, writer Larry "Ratso" Sloman shared a story about the genesis and reception of his own chronicle of the Rolling Thunder Revue, *On the Road with Bob Dylan*:

When the tour was over, people wanted to hang out in New York. Bob, McGuinn, and I went to the Other End and the jukebox came on and somebody played three Byrds songs in a row. And Bob turned to McGuinn and said, "Hey Roger, you didn't do your best songs on this whole tour." Then "Like a Rolling Stone" came on—this is the song that changed my life—I said, "Bob, you didn't do your best songs on this tour." And Bob said, "What about you? What did you do? I didn't read one article. Why don't you go home and write?" So that's what I did. I went home and I wrote, and I was up there transcribing all these tapes myself because I'm not set up to do this, typing up on a manual typewriter, all the notebooks. I have like thirty-five notebooks where I'm just taking notes like Hunter Thompson.

I finished the manuscript and I sent a copy to Bob and Howard Alk, who were out in Malibu editing *Renaldo and Clara*. A couple of days later I came home and I saw there was a message on an answering machine from Howard Alk. He said, "Ratso, you did it, man. None of us thought you could, but I read the book in one night, Bob read the book in one night, and we just love it. We think it's great." So I was thrilled. Later I asked for a quote and Bob gave me that quote on the cover, "the War and Peace of rock and roll."

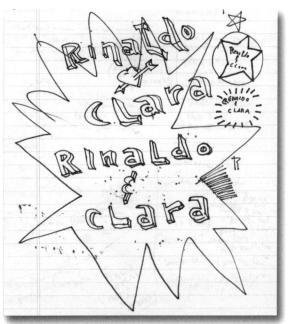

Bob Dylan's handwritten notes on *Renaldo and Clara*, circa 1977

Renaldo and Clara theatrical poster, Italy, 1978

After Dylan spent most of 1977 editing *Renaldo and Clara*, the finished film was released on January 28, 1978. After short theatrical runs in New York, Los Angeles, and select cinemas around the world, all of which received largely negative reviews, the film was shelved. Although the film was subsequently cut down to a two-hour version that focused more on the remarkable musical performances, it too enjoyed only a short release period before it was pulled from distribution. Even though *Renaldo and Clara* remains in the vault, the film has been subject to reappraisal and, like much of Dylan's more misunderstood work, has generated a more favorable response in the context of his long career.

Renaldo and Clara ticket, Japan, 1978

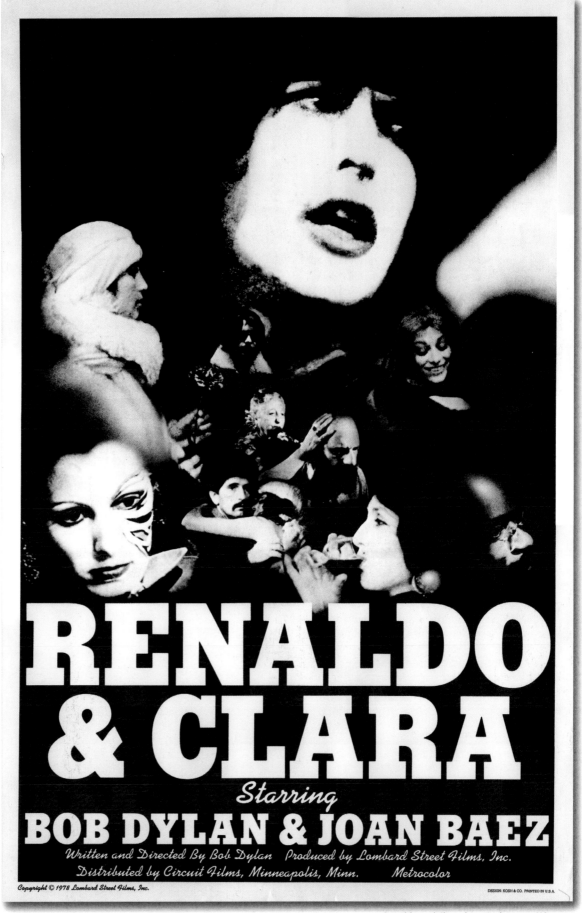

Renaldo and Clara theatrical poster, US, 1978

Audiotape box for January 11–12, 1978, rehearsals

1978 RUNDOWN REHEARSALS

Rundown Studios was a rehearsal space and recording studio Dylan maintained in Santa Monica, California, between 1977 and 1982. Outfitted by Arthur Rosato and Joel Bernstein, who had been part of Dylan's road crew in 1976, the two-level converted office space provided Dylan with a stable base of operations. Auditions and rehearsals were extensively taped between late 1977 and the end of 1981, providing a thorough record of Dylan's musical activities during a particularly creative period.

Among the musicians who attended the 1977–78 rehearsals were Rolling Thunder stalwarts Rob Stoner and Howie Wyeth, jazz pianist Walter Bishop Jr. (perhaps the only musician to play with both Dylan and jazz icon Charlie Parker), Jesse Ed Davis (who had played on "Watching the River Flow" back in 1971), and former Wings drummer Denny Seiwell. Eventually Dylan arrived on a sound that leaned towards adult contemporary pop and featured, for the first time, a saxophonist and back-up female vocalists.

The band Dylan assembled—which would accompany him on much of the 1978 tour and serve as the core group for the *Street-Legal* sessions—included Billy Cross (lead guitar), Alan Pasqua (keyboards), Steven Soles (rhythm guitar and back-up vocals), David Mansfield (violin and mandolin), Steve Douglas (saxophone, flute), Rob Stoner (bass), Bobbye Hall (percussion), Ian Wallace (drums), and Helena Springs, Jo Ann Harris, and Debbie Dye (background vocals).

Bob Dylan with guitar, Hong Kong International Airport, 1978. Photograph by Joel Bernstein

BOB DYLAN AT BUDOKAN

1978 tour poster, Japan

The more I think about it, the more I realize what I left behind in Japan - my soul, my music and that sweet girl in the geisha house - I wonder does she remember me? If the people of Japan wish to know about me, they can hear this record - also they can hear my heart still beating in Kyoto at the Zen Rock Garden - Someday I will be back to reclaim it.

Bob Dylan

Liner notes for *Bob Dylan at Budokan*, 1978

Between February and December 1978, Dylan embarked on his first world tour since 1966. Backed by an eleven-piece band, he performed 114 shows across four continents, with stops in Australia, New Zealand, the United Kingdom, Europe, the United States, and Canada.

The tour began with Dylan's first visit to Japan. On February 17, Dylan gave a press conference at Tokyo's Haneda International Airport in advance of eleven dates in the country. Released in Japan in August 1978, with a worldwide release in April of the following year, *Bob Dylan at Budokan* eventually went platinum in Australia, and gold in the United States and Canada.

Bob Dylan waiting for a train, Japan, February/ March 1978. Photograph by Hirosuke Katsuyama

Bob Dylan signing autographs; in performance at Nippon Budokan Hall, Japan, March 1978. Photographs by Hirosuke Katsuyama

STREET-LEGAL

Shortly after arriving in Los Angeles after the Far East leg of the 1978 tour, Dylan and his band returned to Rundown Studios in Santa Monica. There, between April 25 and May 1, they recorded Dylan's eighteenth studio album, *Street-Legal*, with Don Devito producing.

After a month break, the band returned to the road, beginning a seven-day residency at Universal Amphitheater in Los Angeles before embarking upon their UK and European leg of the tour. On June 15, the day of their first concert, *Street-Legal* was released.

"Baby, Stop Crying" was released as the album's first single on July 31, 1978. The songs continue to captivate in the 21st century, with "New Pony" and "Señor (Tales of Yankee Power)" having been artfully covered by The Dead Weather and Willie Nelson, respectively.

Bob Dylan, 1978. Photograph by Morgan Renard

```
long distance-tears- woman touch-drifting
neon light-cows-lonesome bell tone-bathed
prince, convinced-upward, heart- ashes & dust he predicted to us-dreams apart
babe in the arms-golden haired stripper on stage- wind back
```

"Where Are You Tonight? (Journey Through Dark Heat)" draft typescript

"WHERE ARE YOU TONIGHT? (JOURNEY THROUGH DARK HEAT)"

Dylan typed out a set of phrases and images that became building blocks for the epic "Where Are You Tonight? (Journey Through Dark Heat)," which concluded *Street-Legal*. Like many other songs on the album, the song employs vivid prophetic and apocalyptic imagery.

> sixteen years-sixteen banners united
> over the hills where the good sheherd grieves
> desperate men - desperate women divided
> spreading their (wings) (lips)(tongues) (words) neath the falling
> leaves
>
> fortune calls-I stepped forth from the shadows
> To the marketplace, merchants & thieves hungry for power
> My last deal gone down-she was smelling sweet like the meadows
> Where she was born-on midsummer's eve near the tower
>
> The cold blooded moon-the captain watching the celebration
> sending his thoughts to a beloved maid
> Whose ebony face is beyond communication (imagination)
> the captain is down but still believing that his love will be repaid
>
> They shaved her head-she was torn between Jupiter & Apollo
> A messenger arrived-hound dogs on his trail (on 2 black nightengal)
> I seen 'm on the steps & I couldnt help but follow
> follow her down past the fountain where she lifted her veil (they)

"Changing of the Guards" draft typescript

"CHANGING OF THE GUARDS"

Some critics have taken "Changing of the Guards" as autobiographical, noting that the "sixteen years" that open the song would mark the beginning of Dylan's recording career in 1962. However, the rich visual imagery Dylan uses throughout the song makes its subject difficult to pin down, with Dylan himself commenting soon after the album's release,

> *It means something different every time I sing it. "Changing of the Guards" is a thousand years old.*

L–R: Jerry Scheff, Jo Ann Harris, Alan Pasqua, Carolyn Dennis, David Mansfield, Bobbye Hall, Steve Douglas, Bob Dylan, Billy Cross, Helena Springs, Ian Wallace, Steven Soles, 1978. Photograph by Morgan Renard

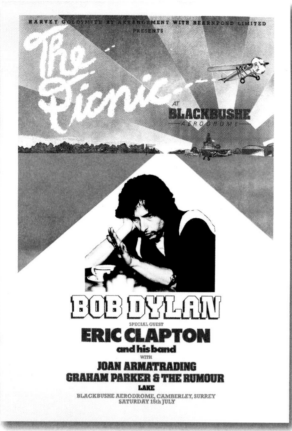

"The Picnic at Blackbushe" concert poster, 1978

THE PICNIC AT BLACKBUSHE

On Saturday, July 15, Dylan gave his final show on the European leg of his 1978 World Tour at the Blackbushe Aerodrome in Camberley, Surrey, England. Dubbed The Picnic at Blackbushe by promoter Harvey Goldsmith, the gig was not only the largest show of Dylan's career, but it was also the largest paid one-day concert in UK history: 250,000 people were said to have been in attendance, including Ringo Starr, Barbara Dickson, John Cooper Clarke, members of The Clash, comedian Billy Connolly, actress Jenny Agutter, and Bianca Jagger.

Dylan headlined the concert and was supported by Eric Clapton, Joan Armatrading, and Graham Parker & the Rumour, with the bands Merger and Lake kicking off the day's events. Dylan's headlining set included thirty-four songs that kept the audience transfixed for nearly three hours.

THE CONSTANT STATE OF BECOMING

Blackbushe Aerodrome, Camberley, England, July 15, 1978. Photograph by Morgan Renard

PAGE 346: TOP TO BOTTOM: Bob Dylan and Billy Cross at soundcheck; Set list on amplifier; Dylan (second from right) backstage; Guitars for the tour; Dylan in performance, Europe, 1978.

PAGE 347: Bob Dylan, Europe, 1978.

Photographs by Morgan Renard

List of new songs, circa late October/early November 1978

1978 TOUR, NORTH AMERICA

As Dylan's world tour made its way across the United States and Canada between September and December of 1978, he began to write a number of new songs with lyrics scribbled on hotel room stationery and workshopped by the band during any extra time left over at soundchecks. "More than Flesh and Blood Can Bear" and "Legionnaire's Disease" are two such songs, whereas "She's Love Crazy" is a Tampa Red classic from 1941 that Dylan performed throughout the European and North American legs of the tour. Dylan even debuted "Do Right to Me Baby (Do Unto Others)" on December 16 in Hollywood, Florida, the final date of the tour, foreshadowing his new gospel direction.

PAGE 349: Bob Dylan, 1977.
Photograph by Annie Leibovitz

Surviving in a Ruthless World 1979–1987

The Seventies I see as a period of reconstruction after the Sixties, that's all. That's why people say: well, it's boring, nothing's really happening, and that's because wounds are healing. By the Eighties anyone who's going to be doing anything will have his or her cards showing. You won't be able to get back in the game in the Eighties.

—Bob Dylan, December 1977, Jonathan Cott interview, *Rolling Stone*

Bob Dylan, 1984. Photograph by Ken Regan

L–R: Fred Tackett, Mary Elizabeth Bridges (obscured by tambourine), Gwen Evans, Bob Dylan, 1980. Photograph by Arthur Rosato

SLOW TRAIN COMING

In the midst of a grueling year-long world tour in 1978, Bob Dylan experienced a religious awakening. Speaking from the stage at a November 27, 1979, concert at San Diego's Golden Hall, Dylan recounted his moment of epiphany during a concert a year earlier in that same city, on November 17, 1978.

> *Towards the end of the show someone out in the crowd knew I wasn't feeling too well. I think they could see that. They threw a silver cross on the stage. . . . I looked down at that cross. I said, "I gotta pick that up." So I picked up the cross and I put it in my pocket. . . . I brought it backstage and I brought it with me to the next town, which was out in [Tempe] Arizona. . . . I was feeling even worse than I'd felt when I was in San Diego. I said, "Well, I need something tonight." I didn't know what it was. I was used to all kinds of things. I said, "I need something tonight that I didn't have before." And I looked in my pocket and I had this cross.*

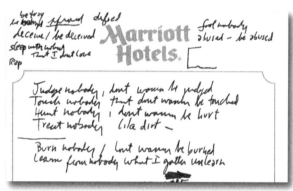

"Do Right to Me Baby (Do Unto Others)" draft manuscript, circa December 1978

Dylan's first public expression of his newfound faith came during the final show of the 1978 World Tour on December 16, when he debuted "Do Right to Me Baby (Do Unto Others)," an original gospel song riffing on the Golden Rule. By that point he had been working on the song that would become "Slow Train" for a couple of months. The first known recording of "Slow Train" is from an October 5 soundcheck in Largo, Maryland, and there are two early drafts from Denver, where Dylan played on November 6. Dylan continued to work on the song throughout the tour, and the image of the "slow train" continued to take on different meaning and relevance.

Slow Train Coming was recorded between April 30 and May 4, 1979, at Muscle Shoals Sound Studio in Alabama. With famed producer Jerry Wexler at the helm, the album featured Dire Straits guitarist Mark Knopfler, as well as several musicians who would make up the core of Dylan's band over the next two years, including bassist Tim Drummond and backing singers Carolyn Dennis, Helena Springs, and Regina McCrary.

Released on August 20, 1979, *Slow Train Coming* featured nine new tracks including the singles "Gotta Serve Somebody," "Man Gave Names to All the Animals," and "Slow Train." Although the critical response was mixed, largely because of Dylan's explorations of Christian themes, the album reached #3 on the US *Billboard* charts soon after its release. Jann Wenner, co-founder of *Rolling Stone*, called the record "one of the finest records Dylan has ever made."

```
1. sometimes/ i feel so outnumbered/
   i get weary from slings & ar rows that i'm dodgin'

   bridges burnin/ i'm turnin & tossin/ crossin
      thru the darkness with cat's eyes watchin'

 & there's a slow train a-comin up around the bend
```

"Slow Train" draft typescript

"Man Gave Names to All the Animals" 45 rpm single, Japan, 1979

BACK ROW, L–R: Pick Withers, Tim Drummond, Bob Dylan, Mark Knopfler
FRONT ROW, L–R: Gregg Hamm, Barry Beckett, Jerry Wexler, Muscle Shoals
Sound Studio, Sheffield, AL, April/May 1979. Photograph by Dick Cooper

"GOTTA SERVE SOMEBODY"

Released as a single with the B-side "Gonna Change My Way of Thinking," "Gotta Serve Somebody" was Dylan's first hit song in years, reaching #24 on *Billboard*'s Hot 100, and remaining on the charts for twelve weeks. He debuted the song on *Saturday Night Live* on October 20, 1979, his first and only performance on the long-running show. The song earned Dylan his first-ever solo GRAMMY award (Best Rock Vocal Performance, Male), and he performed it for the awards ceremony, on February 27, 1980, in what was his first-ever GRAMMY performance.

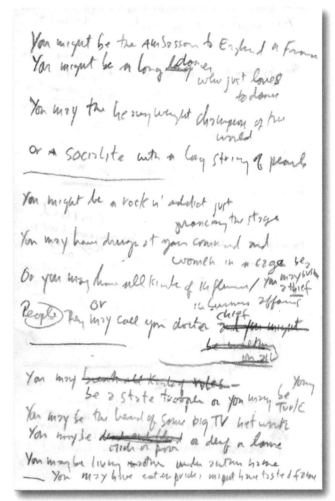

"Gotta Serve Somebody" draft manuscript

"Gotta Serve Somebody" remains one of Dylan's most enduring songs, with dozens of cover versions by artists such as Patti Austin, Charlie Daniels, Etta James, Willie Nelson, and Mavis Staples. The song was also prominently featured in an episode of HBO's award-winning show *The Sopranos*. Dylan has continued to perform the song live as part of his 2023 concerts.

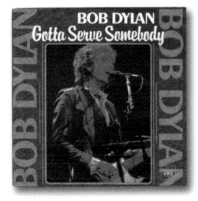

"Gotta Serve Somebody" 45 rpm singles, Netherlands, France, Spain, 1980

Slow Train Coming album art concept

Slow Train Coming album art concept. Designed by
William Stetz, drawing by Catherine Kanner

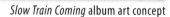

Slow Train Coming album art concept

To develop the proper iconography for *Slow Train Coming*, Bob Dylan engaged a relatively unknown photographer and graphic designer named William Stetz, who later recounted that the only direction he was given to come up with the visual theme was from Dylan playing him the album. After exploring several directions, Stetz eventually landed on the right concept, and he hired illustrator Catherine Kanner to execute the final drawing.

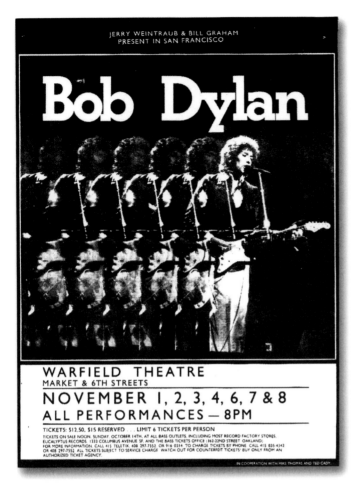

WARFIELD THEATRE
MARKET & 6TH STREETS

NOVEMBER 1, 2, 3, 4, 6, 7 & 8
ALL PERFORMANCES — 8PM

TICKETS: $12.50, $15 RESERVED . . . LIMIT 6 TICKETS PER PERSON

TICKETS ON SALE NOON, SUNDAY, OCTOBER 14TH, AT ALL BASS OUTLETS, INCLUDING MOST RECORD FACTORY STORES,
EUCALYPTUS RECORDS, 1333 COLUMBUS AVENUE SF. AND THE BASS TICKETS OFFICE (862-22ND STREET OAKLAND).
FOR MORE INFORMATION, CALL 415 TELETIX, 408 297.7552, OR 916 0314 TO CHARGE TICKETS BY PHONE. CALL 415 835.4342
OR 408 297.7552. ALL TICKETS SUBJECT TO SERVICE CHARGE. WATCH OUT FOR COUNTERFEIT TICKETS! BUY ONLY FROM AN
AUTHORIZED TICKET AGENCY.

IN COOPERATION WITH MIKE THOMAS AND TED CADY.

Concert tickets, 1979

Warfield Theatre advertisement,
1979

WARFIELD THEATRE, 1979

In late October 1979, Dylan began assembling a band for his upcoming tour. Bassist Tim Drummond stayed
on board following the spring sessions for *Slow Train Coming* and was joined by keyboardist Spooner Oldham,
who was part of the famed Muscle Shoals Rhythm Section. Drummer Jim Keltner, who had worked with
Dylan on several different occasions throughout the 1970s, was brought in to round out the rhythm section.
After a series of auditions, Fred Tackett of Little Feat was hired to play lead guitar. Gospel singers Helena
Springs, Mona Lisa Young, and Regina McCrary, a Nashville native whose father sang in the legendary
gospel quartet The Fairfield Four, provided support. Intriguingly, the rehearsals also featured a horn section
that Tackett remembered as being led by trumpeter Marcus Belgrave of Ray Charles's band. Although
the horn section was ultimately left behind, the band was tight after nearly a month of rehearsals when it
opened at the Warfield Theatre in San Francisco on November 1, 1979.

Over fourteen shows in sixteen days, Dylan and his new band debuted his new gospel sound. His backing
singers opened the show, setting the tone, and although fans were aware of his new musical direction, it still
came as a surprise when Dylan only performed his new gospel songs at each concert. Most controversially,
Dylan preached from stage. In an interview with the Bob Dylan Center, Fred Tackett remembered some of
the audience reactions to the shows:

> There were a lot of people that were very supportive of what he was doing. A lot of people who were
> born-again Christians were extremely supportive, but then there were a lot of Bob Dylan fans that didn't
> like it at all. The best thing I saw was this one guy in the front row who had a big white poster board that
> said, "Jesus loves your old songs." The shows were very controversial. We had people like [atheist activist]
> Madalyn O'Hair protesting, and a guy dressed in white with a cross, I mean, a literal full cross walking up
> and down in front of the theater. It was all very exciting.

Bob Dylan, Portland, OR, January 1980. Photograph by Arthur Rosato

SAVED

Photograph used for the revised *Saved* album cover, taken April/May 1980. Photograph by Tony Wright

Nine months after recording *Slow Train Coming*, Dylan returned to Muscle Shoals Sound Studio in Sheffield, Alabama, to record another album with producer Jerry Wexler. Between February 11 and February 15, 1981, Dylan channeled the energy of a tent revival into the nine tracks that would appear on his twentieth album, *Saved*.

Saved continued Dylan's exploration of gospel-infused music with lyrics exploring religious themes. "Solid Rock" and the title track "Saved" were gospel rave-ups, whereas "Pressing On" and "What Can I Do for You?" were soulful ballads. "In the Garden" was a song Dylan continued to perform long after its initial recording, frequently featuring the song in set lists from 1986 to 1991 and again in 1994 and 1995.

Renowned visual artist Tony Wright was commissioned to provide art direction. His front cover concept featured a pastel painting of a divine hand reaching down from the heavens to touch the outreached hands of the multitudes. In 1985, a new cover design was developed, featuring an enhanced version of one of Wright's photographs from the inner sleeve of the album.

pressing on for the high calling of the Lord

"Pressing On" draft manuscript

"PRESSING ON"

"Pressing On" was well known to Dylan fans as the intense closing number of his sets during the late 1979 and early 1980 tours. Another of Dylan's gospel songs that has become a classic, it has been covered by Antony and the Johnsons, Chicago Mass Choir, Glen Hansard, Alicia Keys, and John Doe, whose version Dylan called "a once-in-a-lifetime recording."

L–R: Mona Lisa Young, Regina McCrary, Bob Dylan, Clydie King, Terry Young, Muscle Shoals Sound Studio, Sheffield, AL, February 1980. Photograph by Dick Cooper

"SAVED"

Dylan drew upon whatever was at hand to jot down lyrics when inspiration struck, including the back of a bank deposit slip belonging to the parents of keyboardist Spooner Oldham in Muscle Shoals, near where *Saved* was recorded.

Saved alternate cover art concept. Artwork by Tony Wright

Saved original album cover. Artwork by Tony Wright

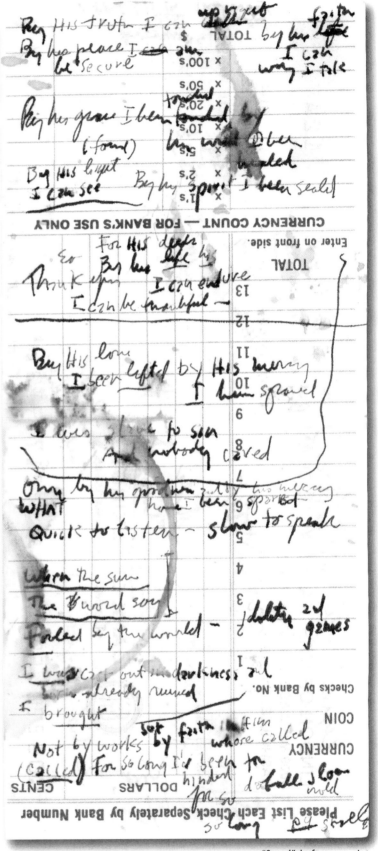

"Saved" draft manuscript

361

TOURS, 1980

Dylan embarked on two tours in the first part of 1980, in January and February and again in April and May, bringing his gospel show across the United States and Canada. As the tour went on, Dylan began to introduce new songs, including "Cover Down, Pray Through," "I Will Love Him," and "Ain't Gonna Go to Hell for Anybody." He continued to revise the last song over the course of the year to the point of nearly completely rewriting it when he performed it in shows that November and December as part of his Musical Retrospective tour.

Over four nights in mid-April, Dylan video-taped his concerts in Toronto, followed by two nights in Buffalo, New York, for a concert special that was never finished. Capturing his gospel band at one of their peaks, the footage sat largely unseen until it was revisited as *Trouble No More: A Musical Film*, produced as part of *The Bootleg Series Vol. 13: Trouble No More 1979–1981* in 2017.

PAGE 362: TOP: Bob Dylan, April/May 1980. Photograph by Tony Wright

PAGE 362: BOTTOM: L–R: Bob Dylan, Tim Drummond, Regina McCrary, Mona Lisa Young, Mary Elizabeth Bridges, Gwen Evans, Clydie King, April/May 1980. Photograph by Tony Wright

BELOW: Tim Drummond, Regina McCrary, Mona Lisa Young, Gwen Evans (obscured), Bob Dylan, Clydie King (obscured), Terry Young, April/May 1980. Photograph by Tony Wright

11/6

```
SERVE SOMEBODY
SENOR        ~ (Simple twist of fate)
ROLLING STONE
WALK AROUND HEAVEN   (CITY OF GOLD)
GIRL FROM THE NORTH COUNTRY
AIN'T GONNA GO TO HELL
ABRAHAM, MARTIN & JOHN
KEEP IT BETWEEN US
BLOWING IN THE WIND
¿?? DO RIGHT)   (GROOM STILL WAITING)
COVENANT WOMAN    Abraham Martin & John
SLOW TRAIN            keep it between US
JUST LIKE A WOMAN
( HARD RAIN)
(FALLING IN LOVE)
CARRIBEAN WIND
(WHAT CAN I DO)
SOLID ROCK
IN THE GARDEN


EXTRA:

SAVING GRACE      RAMONA
SAVED
I BELIEVE IN YOU
WHEN YOU GONNA WAKE UP
Saved by the Grace of your love
We just disagree
REGINA:   FALLING IN LOVE


RAMONA        (I SAW THE LIGHT)
```

Set list notes, November 1980

WARFIELD THEATRE, 1980

Dylan returned to the Warfield Theatre at the beginning of his 1980 tour, which was billed as *A Musical Retrospective*. From mid-September through the end of October, Dylan and his group rehearsed at Rundown Studios in advance of the tour, working through older material from his catalog as well as newer songs such as "The Groom's Still Waiting at the Altar" and "Every Grain of Sand" (both later released on 1981's *Shot of Love*), and the unreleased "City of Gold." Dylan and the group also ran through an eclectic mix of cover songs, including Neil Diamond's "Sweet Caroline," Willie Nelson's "Sad Songs & Waltzes," and "Rainbow Connection."

Although this slate of cover songs didn't make it to the live sets, one did: "Abraham, Martin and John," originally made famous by Dylan's old friend Dion. Dylan's version, done at the piano as a duet with Clydie King, was a standout of the tour. In 2019, on the occasion of her death, Dylan paid tribute in a short eulogy: "She was my ultimate singing partner. No one ever came close. We were two soul mates."

Among the new songs that Dylan debuted during the Warfield concerts was one of his great unfinished works: "Caribbean Wind." Dylan has performed the song live exactly once, supposedly at the request of music critic and *Crawdaddy* editor Paul Williams. (Although Dylan recorded the song during 1981 sessions for *Shot of Love*, a version was not released until the 1985 retrospective *Biograph*.)

The Warfield shows featured numerous musical guests, including Jerry Garcia, Roger McGuinn, Maria Muldaur, and Mike Bloomfield, in one of his last-ever performances.

Bob Dylan, Warfield Theatre, San Francisco, November 1980. Photograph by Richard McCaffrey

```
      chorus.....& them carribean winds still blow
                  from mexico to mexico to curecuo
                  from chinatown to the furnace of desire
              & those distant ships still sail the sea (of liberty)
                  on iron waves so bold & free
                  bringin all them who are near to me
                  nearer to the fire


                                           (Hair brown)
   1. she was from haiti, intense & extreme extreme & intense
      i dont think she'd ever knew innocense known innocense
      i was playin' a show in miami at the teatre of mystery

      i tol' her 'bout jesus, told her 'bout the rain
      she told me & 'bout division, tol' me the pain
      that had risen from the ashes & xxx abided in her memory
                                                          refugee
      was she a virtuous woman, i really cant say   / throwout gypsy
      something about her said "trust me anyway"
      as the days turned to minutes & the minutes turned back into hours
                       be sleeping & the nite
      i pretended to listen & he thought i was
      but i was just paying attention like a rattlesnake does
      when he hears footsteps tamplin on the flowers


   2. our shadows drew closer til they touched on the floor
      they sat at a table with their backs to the door (itinevant wonders for
      preachin' obscenities, expectin the waiting for the night to arrive    )

      he was well connected but her heart was a snare
      & she had left him to die in there
       but i knew i could get him out while he still was alive
```

"Caribbean Wind" draft typescript

If You See Her on Fannin Street ALEX ROSS

"Prayed in the ghetto with my face in the cement": few Dylan songs nail down their subject and mood so emphatically in the opening line. "The Groom's Still Waiting at the Altar" stems from the so-called gospel period, but it does not traffic in uplift and salvation. Instead, it memorializes a dark, twisted night of the soul. The live version trundles onward into some of the most savagely self-lacerating imagery of Dylan's career:

> Heard the last moan of a boxer, seen the massacre of the innocent
> Felt around for the light switch, became nauseated
> Just me and an overweight dancer between walls that had already deteriorated

As so often in Dylanland, naturalistic scenes intermingle with visionary ones. The biblical massacre of the innocent intrudes upon a prizefight. We could be at the rundown casino of Herod the Great, where the protagonist has shacked up with Salome's obese sister.

This apocalyptic blues stomp in A minor has a ghostly, marginal presence in the Dylan canon. It was written in the summer of 1980, before a late-fall run of West Coast shows, including a twelve-night stand at the Warfield in San Francisco. Dylan sang it five times in the course of the tour: on November 13, 15, 16, and 19, in San Francisco, and on November 25, in San Diego. Despite several vibrant renditions with celebrity guitarists—Carlos Santana, Jerry Garcia, and, most spectacularly, Michael Bloomfield—the song then vanished from Dylan's live set, never to return. A recording was made during the *Shot of Love* sessions, but it was unaccountably omitted from the original vinyl album. After it found airplay as the B-side to the "Heart of Mine" single, it showed up on the *Shot of Love* compact disc.

If, as the record suggests, Dylan never felt entirely happy with "Groom," a simmering uncertainty about the lyrics may have been the cause. Countless Dylan songs have undergone fluctuations over the years, but "Groom" is more turbulent than most. The apparent first sketch is written on a piece of paper with MEMO at the top, in large stencil letters. This and all subsequent drafts lead off with the words "Prayed in the ghetto." Here it goes on: ". . . groped around for the answer, / Heard the last moan of a boxer, got friendly with an overweight dancer." Another option is "Spent my last dollar on an overweight dancer."

Following the venerable blues tradition, the song broods over a failed relationship, this time with an elusive woman named Claudette: "Don't know what I could say 'bout Claudette that wouldn't come back to haunt me / I finally had to give her up 'bout the time she began to want me." Like many other objects of Dylanesque affection, she has lifted up stakes and absconded to points unknown: "Don't know about Claudette, she could be in the mountains or prairies / be respectably married or running a whorehouse in Buenas Aries" [*sic*]. These lines vary little through later drafts and in the various recorded renditions, although on *Shot of Love* Dylan devises a looser, more playful rhyme for "Buenos Aires": ". . . ain't seen her since January."

At the same time, the first draft gestures toward themes of fame and public incomprehension, of the kind that figure in *Blood on the Tracks*, especially "Idiot Wind." An alternate version of the first

MEMO

(~~formerly~~) she was pleasing me – only her, the birds & bees and me –
Certainly

1. prayed in the ghetto – groped around for the answer (spent my last dollar on) (pulled a train)
heard the last moan of a boxer – got friendly with an overweight dancer
felt around for the light switch – became nauseated
saw my picture in ~~the~~ a news paper – outdated
(became so nauseated. (light switch) thought lightning would strike me
Saw my picture in a newspaper, didn't look anything like me)

CHORUS
cant find her or forget her, cant remember or forgive her and I cant fault her (got to remember to forget her)
~~Carnally~~ Carnaly she's nothing but talk, spiritually she like the rock of gibralter
If you see her on Fannin Street, tell her I still think she's neat
And that THE GROOM'S STILL WAITING AT THE ALTER

2. There were warriors who smelled like women – planning out robbery (into charity) and
mistaking my shyness for aloofness, my silence for snobbery
Never did get the message, dont even know if one was sent to ME
About the madness of becoming what one was never meant to be

I cant even learn that small baby –

3. NEVER CARED if we were loved, just wanted to be respected
Among thieves and among children, we were always accepted
I pawn all my feeling, cast down imaginations
got tired of people bringing God's name into every sense less conversation

4. Dont know what I could say 'bout Claudette that wouldn't come back to haunt me
I finally had to give her up 'bout the time she began to want me
(we had all kinds of hangers on – who would let the fruit go rotten
dont know where she came from but I heard she picked cotton)
(she had an ex husband who let his fruit go rotton
(what he was trying to learn, she'd already forgotten   get
(what she was trying to learn, IS already forgotten

5. Locked into a time zone with a slightly high temperature (cleaning out stables)
I see fools acting out their (beliefs) consciences (checking their watches – I see wise men standing
round like furniture (tables)
there's a wall between you and what you want and you got to leap it
Tonight you got the power to take it but tomorrow you wont have the power to keep it

6. Never did feel comfortable around lawyers and politicians
guess it depends which side you're on and I dont like to make quick decisions   becoming
Dont know about Claudette, she could be in the mountains or prairies (running a ranch a dude
be respectably married or running a whore house in Buenos Aries   in the prairie)

"The Groom's Still Waiting at the Altar" draft manuscript

ALEX ROSS

Mike Bloomfield guest appearance (right with guitar) with Bob Dylan (far left), Warfield Theatre, November 15, 1980. Film still by Bill Pagel

verse reads: "became so nauseated thought lightning would strike me / saw my picture in a newspaper, didn't look anything like me." The most piercing of these lines have an autobiographical ring:

> *There were warriors who smelled like women (into charity) and planning out robbery*
> *Mistaking my shyness for aloofness, my silence for snobbery*
> *Never did get the message, don't even know if one was sent to me*
> *About the madness of becoming what one was never meant to be*

Shy people the world over can recognize the syndrome of coming across as aloof when one is merely afraid. One can only imagine what it's like to be a shy person who is cast as some sort of world-historical savior.

The first line of the "shyness" verse, the one that sets up the rhyme with "robbery," causes the most trouble. In later drafts the warriors became "gamblers," then "dream peddlers." Once Dylan begins singing the song live, he introduces new variations each night, never singing the line the same way twice. Highwaymen and hitmen enter the picture, pushing women or pushing hell-raising, sometimes wanted on murder charges. In the *Shot of Love* sessions, the words change yet again: "Try to be pure at heart, they arrest you for robbery." Perhaps this is why Dylan failed to find satisfaction in the song: he never found the right setup for his brilliant diagnosis of the psychology of shyness. None of these robbery scenarios quite gels.

Fruitful or not, the frenzy of revision evident in eight pages of drafts makes clear that "Groom" has particular resonance for Dylan. As in the *Blood on the Tracks* notebooks, alternatives proliferate above the lines and in the margins. He finds another image for the nauseous opening tableau: "Pictures moved on the walls—chairs & tables vibrated." He lists back-up rhymes for "nauseated":

estimated, decorated, depreciated, imitated, celebrated, hesitated, duplicated, dominated, illustrated. On the back of one page he alludes intriguingly to the "city of the cross near the Hotel St. Cloud"—perhaps a premonition of the brooding St. James Hotel in "Blind Willie McTell." One entire verse goes by the wayside:

> i can tell about midnight by the way the trees begin to bend
> that life ain't like a mountain railroad—sometimes the tracks came to a dead end
> i can think the unthinkable but i'm losing my admiration
> for people bringing God's name into every senseless conversation

The conflict between secular and sacred agendas in the gospel phase is reaching a breaking point. Dylan's lifelong resistance to being defined makes another swerve inevitable.

The five live performances of "Groom" are ferociously intense, even if the singer tends to get a little lost in his baroque new lyrics. (On November 13, Claudette ends up making two trips to Buenos Aires.) The Bloomfield version is in a category of its own—one of the peaks of the entire live archive. At the outset, there's some uncertainty whether the guitarist is going to join in. Dylan says: "If Michael is still out there—you wanna play on this? Where are you sitting, Michael?" When he gets no answer, he goes on: "Can't seem to find Michael, so, ah, we're gonna to start anyway." Someone chimes in: "He's coming, he's coming." It takes a minute or so for Bloomfield's sinuous figuration to kick in: we hear the first characteristic lick after "Never did get the message." The electricity that springs up between singer and guitarist is immediate and tremendous. At one point, a revved-up Dylan shouts, "Whoa Mike!" Heartbreakingly, this was Bloomfield's final live performance with Dylan; he died just two months later.

When it came time to record "Groom" for *Shot of Love*—an ill-fated album that resulted in the suppression of two other great songs of this period, "Caribbean Wind" and "Angelina"—Dylan undertook a full-scale rewrite, not necessarily for the better. He backtracks on the lurid material of the first verse: "Felt around for the light switch, felt around for her face / Been treated like a farm animal on a wild goose chase." Fresh images of disaster crop up, though they border on cliché: "City's on fire, phones out of order / They're killing nuns and soldiers, there's fighting at the border." Some blatant religious sermonizing is tried out and then thankfully dropped: "The communists were falling, capitalists were crawling / the hand of God is moving—Jesus is calling." All the same, the finished take has a crisp, driving energy. For whatever reason, it's transposed from A minor to the odd key of B-flat minor.

The lyrics continued to fluctuate even after the final take had been set down. When a transcript was sent to Dylan for purposes of establishing copyright, the editorial pen came out once again. In one case, he simply corrects a misheard lyric: it's "you got to leap it," not "you got to leave it." But he also has second thoughts about his earlier edit of the light-switch moment: "became nauseated" is restored to its place of honor. The subsequent line undergoes a further mutation: "She was walking down the hallway while the walls deteriorated." Even if Dylan is destined to sing the song no more, he is still turning over its tumultuous imagery in his mind, seeking the perfect snapshot of spiritual chaos.

SHOT OF LOVE

On August 28, 1981, Dylan released his twenty-first album, *Shot of Love*, mixing secular and religious themes. Sessions for the album occurred in fits and starts in a number of locations with a few different producers before Dylan settled on Chuck Plotkin, who had recently produced Bruce Springsteen's *Darkness on the Edge of Town* (1978) and *The River* (1980). The bulk of the recording took place at Plotkin's Clover Recorders between April 23 and May 15. Dylan, who also co-produced the album, brought in a raft of musicians to play on the sessions, including Mike Campbell, Danny Kortchmar, Steve Ripley, Fred Tackett, and Ronnie Wood on guitar, Tim Drummond and Donald "Duck" Dunn on bass, Carl Pickhardt, Willie Smith, and Benmont Tench on keyboards, and Jim Keltner and Ringo Starr on drums and percussion. Carolyn Dennis, Clydie King, Regina McCrary, Madelyn Quebec, and Jennifer Warnes added vocals to the album.

Dylan included ten new songs for the record, including "Every Grain of Sand" and the title track "Shot of Love." Bumps Blackwell, who oversaw the early breakthrough recordings of Little Richard, produced the album's title track. Dylan later told *New Musical Express* that "Shot of Love" was his "most perfect song. It defines where I am spiritually, musically, romantically and whatever else. It shows where my sympathies lie. It's all there in that one song."

In fact, on multiple occasions, Dylan has referred to the whole album as his favorite.

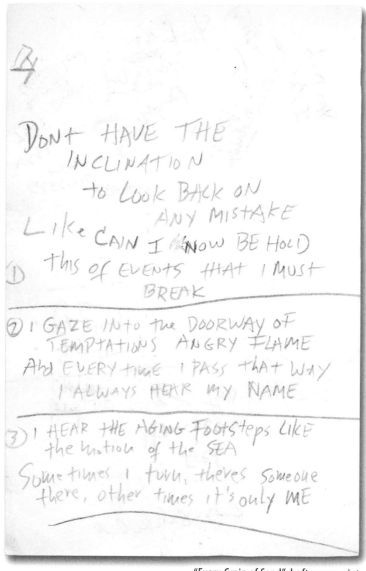

"Every Grain of Sand" draft manuscript

Bob Dylan, Europe, 1981. Photograph by Howard Alk

"LENNY BRUCE"

On the torn edge of this typescript are the lyrics to the song "Lenny Bruce." An ode to the subversive comedian, the song references a long-ago meeting. (A notebook Dylan carried with him in early 1964 contains an address for Bruce.)

In an interview with the Bob Dylan Center, guitarist Danny Kortchmar described the first time he heard the song "Lenny Bruce" and what it was like to play on *Shot of Love*:

We were [at Rundown Studios] for two or three days before we moved to Clover Studios, which is where the album was finished. One day Bob came in and said, "Oh, I wrote this tune last night," and he sat down and played "Lenny Bruce Is Dead." Fantastic song. Benmont [Tench] and I just looked at each other, astonished, thinking "You wrote that *last night*?" That's one of Bob's unheralded tunes, a great, great song. It's perfect, really.

```
dead man, dead man               every grain of sand
shot of love                     angelina
you changed my life              the groom is still waiting at the al
need a woman                     love that's pure
property of jesus                carribean wind
                                       lenny bruce is dead. he didn
                                  commit no crime/ he just told
                                  like it was but that was lon
                                  your time called him a sick
                          xaxwaaxxaxxaaxxaa comedian
poison pen                             they got to put label
biting the hand that feeds you        folks...cause they wa
cruel jungle                             to be like shirts
got two shirts, gimme one             but lenny was real &
getting away with murder              funny joke
                                  lenny bruce is gone
                                    & those that killed him
punk surfer               (lenny bruce is dead...but his ghost li
comet of vomit            on & on....
over there                never did get no golden globe awar
lenny bruce               never did make it to synanon
bill collector            he was an outlaw...that's for
                          more than an outlaw than you ever
                          lenny bruce is long gone
strange noise             but his spirit lives on & on
phenomenon
needle in the haystack
womansville               maybe he had some problems. mayb
vaccuum cleaner             some things he couldnt work ou
needle in the haystck     but he sure was funny & he sure
junky in the yard         the truth & he knew what he was ta
ganster on the corner       about
face all torn & scarred   but he never robbed no church
going deeper than the botton  nor cut off any babies he
can you find the way to my lenny  but he xxixxxxxxxxxxxxxxxxxxxxxx
or must i draw you a diagram  just took folks that hide all
                          & shined a light in their beds
                            lenny bruce is over the hi
                          he was just somebody that ha
                                  killed
```

"Lenny Bruce" draft typescript

L–R: Fred Tackett, Steve Ripley, Bob Dylan, Tim Drummond (obscured), Madelyn Quebec, Carolyn Dennis (obscured), Clydie King, 1981. Photograph by Howard Alk

Concert advertisement, England, 1981.
Photograph by Howard Alk

TOURS, 1981

Following the recording of *Shot of Love*, Dylan set out on
a world tour. Joining the 1980 iteration of the group was
Steve Ripley on guitar and Madelyn Quebec, who added
a fourth voice to Dylan's backing chorus. Having played
together for nearly two years as a working unit, the band
was incredibly responsive to Dylan's musical direction.
After some warm-up shows in mid-June 1981, Dylan barn-
stormed across Europe in June and July before returning
to embark on a tour of the United States and Canada in
October and November. On this second leg, organist
Al Kooper returned to the band for the first time since
1965, and Arthur Rosato joined as a second drummer.

The filmmaker Howard Alk, who had worked with
Dylan on *Eat the Document* and *Renaldo and Clara*, took
thousands of photographs and filmed select musical
performances during the tour.

Dylan continued to use Rundown Studios for part of
1982, including an Allen Ginsberg recording session on
February 23. He soon began to wind down his activities
there, marking the end of an era.

L–R: Fred Tackett, Steve Ripley, Bob Dylan, 1981. Photograph by Howard Alk

ROW 1, L–R: Bob Dylan in performance; Eric Clapton, Dylan, George Harrison backstage at Earls Court, London; Jim Keltner

ROW 2, L–R: Steve Ripley with Dylan; Clydie King, Regina McCrary, Madelyn Quebec; Fred Tackett, Tim Drummond

ROW 3, L–R: Ripley; Dylan in performance, Europe; Ripley, Dylan, Carolyn Dennis, Drummond, soundcheck

ROW 4, L–R: Dylan, Bad Segeberg, West Germany; Tour bus; Dylan backstage, Europe

Photographs by Howard Alk

1979–1987

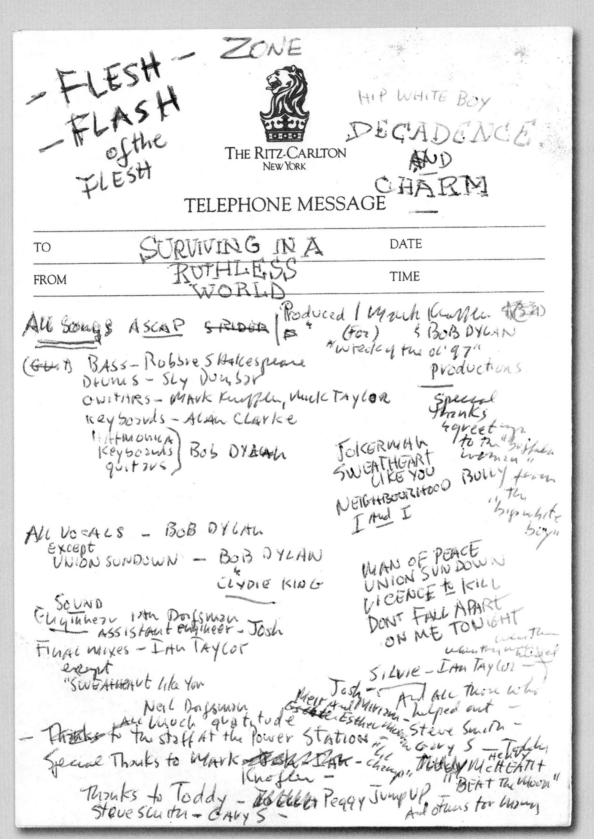

Infidels album credits and other notes, 1983

Widescreen

TERRY GANS

I've had thirty years of "Dylan dreams." Not every night. Maybe once or twice a year. In color. Very detailed and specific. Kind of a dreamed, real-life Harry Dean Stanton in the video for "Dreamin' of You."

The dreams almost always follow a progression:

I'm in a record store. One wall is brick. A low wooden wall separates the shop floor from the stairway behind me as I look through a bin of LPs. In the Dylan assortment I find several albums I've never seen before. They seem to be recent releases on the actual Columbia label. Maybe I've been aware of these song titles, but I've never seen them or heard them. It's an odd familiarity. I can almost but not quite make out the intriguing titles, or lyrics printed on the back. Something always distracts my focus on them. I want to hear these songs. Then I wake up. It all seems so real, so true at the instant of waking. But solving the mystery will have to wait for another dream. Doesn't everybody have these dreams?

In July 2018, I walked into the Dylan Archive in Tulsa. My goal was to see if there was information in the written and recorded materials from 1982–83 to help me understand what led to the remarkable 1983 *Infidels*—the album that was and the one it might have been. I wanted to see if what I found could lead to an article or book, or if the album and the already known outtakes were the sum total of what there was. I'd previously written on what had been available since the mid-80s and didn't want to kick that dog around again. There was indeed more—a lot more—and the visit resulted in the book *Surviving in a Ruthless World: Bob Dylan's Voyage to Infidels*.

At the Archive, the initial batch of materials I requested included several boxes of folders of lyric drafts. There were also two small notebooks. I swear I heard a whisper: "Son, this ain't a dream no more—it's the real thing."

The first "real thing" was the folder of writings for what became "Don't Fall Apart on Me Tonight." That first instant my (white-gloved) hand touched the ink from the hand of the man that roiled the water, it was an emotional moment. But it was a moment. Throughout, I remained aware of the privilege of being able to work with these primary materials. But once the awe of the instant passed, I became immersed in what research is—work. The feeling became one of responsibility to the artist and potential future readers to do the job properly.

I had a wealth of material to work with. Sometimes there were more than twenty typewritten drafts of a song. Sometimes, there were a few words written on a matchbook cover. All of it required attention. A few months earlier the great historian Robert Caro had shared one of the principles that guided him in his research. It was branded into Caro's work ethic by Alan Hathway, his first managing editor: "Just remember," he said. "Turn every page. Never assume anything. Turn every goddamn page." No one else is Robert Caro, but the rule applies to all of us.

I worked with the drafts and listened repeatedly to about seventy hours of session and reference tapes. Hard work and a labor of love and blood and sweat. No tears, though. All the material was remarkable.

All of it had the kind of impact upon me I recalled from when I saw *Hondo* in 3D, or *20,000 Leagues Under the Sea* in CinemaScope in the mid-50s. Up until then, the movies I saw were in a standard 4:3 aspect ratio (the same as all televisions until home theater appeared in the 1980s).

With new widescreen films, the theater curtains closed after the previews and then reopened wider than this boy had ever seen. While the action was mostly still in the middle, there were details and objects on the left and right sides that added detail and depth to the picture.

And that is what the archival documents and recordings brought to *Infidels*. Here was Alan Clark moving between piano and organ. The Mark Knopfler guitar in the left channel and Mick Taylor in the right working to capture the right sound for each song. I could hear Dylan changing lyrics on the fly, or read the word-by-word variations as he typed or wrote or scrawled on whatever was handy.

And out on the edges of this *Infidels* picture were two 2 × 4-inch spiral-bound notebooks. If these did not contain the genesis of the project, they figured in its thematic and lyrical gestation and delivered a CinemaScopic parting of the curtains and the 3D depth to view the finer points of creativity. More than a historic leather jacket or an oversized tambourine, these little artifacts recorded Dylan's thoughts contemporaneous with the creation not just of some of the songs, but of the spirit of the album to come. The artist played with parts of lyrics and riffs. The second line in the notebooks, "I was telling myself, 'Ain't nothing worth stealing in here,'" made it into an *Infidels* outtake and survived for the following album.

The notebooks recorded lyric musings, travel diaries, rough song drafts, track listings, snatches of philosophy, to-do lists, musicians' names (Michael Jackson, Pink Floyd, Steve Cropper, Duck Dunn, Willie "Smitty" Smith, and Ian Wallace).

Dylan seemed to have paper and pen at the ready. Like a butterfly collector, he always had his net at hand. Never should a fragile, fluttering thought escape. What reads to be sixteen separate lines of perhaps overheard chatter comprise a single page. That's my guess as to what he wrote down, but I can't know for sure.

Certainly, the lyric writing in the notebooks preceded Dylan's work in the studio. How this work contributed to the recorded songs is part of the artistic process we can only glimpse and contemplate. He could have already been working on some of the songs, and just writing may have advanced the effort. Or he could have referred to the notebook pages later to remind himself. He did keep them, and they survived to form a part of the Archive, adding details for a researcher nearly forty years later.

My search for the broader story of *Infidels* was focused and essentially single-minded. If one doesn't have a defined task, you do not gain entry to the Archive at this point. It is not a place for a wandering fishing expedition. Second, there is so, so much written and recorded material, and the temptation to satisfy curiosity is so strong, that discipline is required to do the best work and get the research completed.

I did stray, however, late on a Saturday afternoon when the Archive and Bob Dylan Center hosted a visiting poet and journalist. I had spent six hours on task and was a little fatigued. To wrap up the day, I requested a file tangential to the ones identified as 1982–83. The organization of all the material in the Archive was still being perfected, and some *Infidels* writings had shown up in other boxes. It was worth a shot.

I found a few more drafts of "Too Late," but there were also some tantalizing writings apparently from 1977. (Let me say now that my belief is that there is no "Holy Grail" to unlocking the mystery that is Bob Dylan. There is no single "AHA!" moment. But there are many "aha" discoveries.)

I discovered several unknown song sketches. One was a first-person account of a "romantic" assignation; one was a recitation of another person's shortcomings and presumed motivations. Then I got to the evidence that what had been rumored in 1978 was factual.

Guitarist Steve Soles told reporter Robert Hilburn in 1978 that Dylan had visited him the year before and played ten or twelve songs. He had not and did not record them, and they served to help him work out his feelings about the end of his marriage. They were described by Soles as "dark and chilling." One title was given as "I'm Cold." Dylan himself referred to these songs to Hilburn in May 1978: "I had some songs last year which I didn't record. They dealt with that period as I was going through it. For relief, I wrote the tunes. I thought they were great. Some people around town heard them. I played them for some friends. But I had no interest in recording them."

There can be singular joyful moments of discovery in research. When I found lyrics that ended each verse with "because I'm cold," and maybe I shouted "Eureka!" I know everyone in the next room looked up. "Listen," I said, "It's cold in the morning and it's cold at night." While we can wish for the added satisfaction of finished lyrics or even a recording of it in song form, as Dylan sang in 1978 in a revised "The Man in Me": "Oh what a wonderful feeling, just to know that you really exist."

So, what lesson did I learn? Never pass up the chance for extra work on a Saturday. And maybe some of those dreams are real.

* * *

Draft manuscript, circa 1977

"I'M COLD"

Between 1976 and 1977, Dylan publicly performed only one new song, "Seven Days," which found its way onto the set lists of several 1976 Rolling Thunder Revue performances. Dylan wouldn't tour again until 1978, spending much of 1977 editing his film *Renaldo and Clara*. Yet Dylan was still working on new songs. Early drafts for one song, which contains the refrain "I'm Cold," were discovered in a notebook dating to this time period.

INFIDELS

Dylan's 1983 album *Infidels* occupies a particular place in his discography, seen by many fans and critics as both a return to form and a missed opportunity, with outtakes that are as beloved as the album itself. Critics' reviews were mixed upon its release: Writing for *The New York Times*, Stephen Holden called *Infidels* "a disturbing artistic semirecovery by a rock legend who seemed in recent years to have lost his ability to engage the Zeitgeist," though he admitted that it "may be the best-sounding album Mr. Dylan has ever made." On the other hand, Christopher Connelly of *Rolling Stone* said it was the "best album since the searing *Blood on the Tracks* nine years ago."

Coming at the tail end of Dylan's engagement with gospel music, *Infidels* continued Dylan's investigations of morality, albeit through less of a black-and-white lens. Here the focus is not just on the human condition, but on more personal themes of love and loss, as well as external ones, especially politics. On a handwritten draft for the album's credits, Dylan wrote a working title for his new album: "Surviving in a Ruthless World."

```
1. ᛉᚲᚢᛞᛁᛜᚷᚲᛁᛜᚲᛏᚺᛖᚲᚲᛁᚲᛖᚱᚲᛖᛊᛏᚲᚺᛁᛜᚷᚲᚠᛁᚲᚺᚲᚲᚲᛁᛏᚲᚺᚲᚣᛟᚢᚲᚲᚺᚲᚾᛞᛉ
   standing out over the waters & casting your bread while the eyes of the
                   idol with golden head are glowing
   distant ships sailing into the ᛁᛉ mist- you were born with a snake in
                      both of your fists -while a hurricane's blowing
   freedom just around the corner for you
   but with truth so far off, what good will it do
                   REFRAIN

2. so swiftly the sun sets in the sky-you rise up & say goodbye to no one
   no store bought shirt for you on your back - one of your women must sit
                      in the shack & sew one
   shedding off one more layer of skin
   keeping one step ahead of the persecuter within
                   REFRAIN
                            Yur can walk on the
3. youre a man of the mountains-a-den of the clouds-maniplater of crowds-
                      youre a dream twister
   youre going to sodem & gomorah but what do you care? aint nobody there
                   would wanna marry your sister
   scratching the world with a fine tooth comb
   a king among nations- youre a stranger at home
                   REFRAIN
```

"Jokerman" draft typescript

"JOKERMAN"

The opening track from *Infidels*, "Jokerman" encapsulates Dylan's new melding of the spiritual and the political. He was inspired by the religion, music, and culture of the Caribbean while traveling on his boat the *Water Pearl* in the early '80s. He later recalled in a 1984 *Rolling Stone* interview:

> *"Jokerman" kinda came to me in the islands. It's very mystical. The shapes there, and shadows, seem to be so ancient. The song was inspired by these spirits they call jumbis.*

"Jokerman" represents one of the densest series of drafts in the entire Archive. Over the course of some seventeen versions, Dylan weaves together a dense web of vivid allusions and metaphors, eliciting "a shadowy world" of "nightsticks and water cannons, tear gas, padlocks, Molotov cocktails and rocks behind every curtain."

Dylan brought in guitarist Mark Knopfler of Dire Straits (who had played on the 1979 album *Slow Train Coming*) to co-produce *Infidels*. Working out of the Power Station, one of New York City's premier studios, Dylan and Knopfler used new digital recording technology by the 3M company, which allowed them more flexibility with overdubs in later stages of making the album.

Between April and May 1983 they completed nine tracks for the album. However, after Knopfler departed in June for a Dire Straits tour, Dylan continued to work on the album, rewriting and overdubbing songs as well as changing the album's sequence. Although the released version had more of Dylan's own vision than the one he shared with Knopfler, Dylan later praised Knopfler's involvement, noting,

> *He helped make this record in a thousand ways, not only musically, which in itself would have been enough.*

SURVIVING IN A RUTHLESS WORLD

```
i seen the arrow on the doorpost
saying this property condemned
all the way from from new orleans
to jerusalem
i traveled thru east texas
where many martyrs fell
i know nobody can sing the blues
like blind willy mactell
```
I heard the hooded see
quiet
```
i sang a song at sundown
with my foot upon a fence
the stars above the barren trees
were my only audience
them charcoal gypsy maidens
can strt strut their feathers well
but nobody can sing the blues
like blind willy mctell
```

"Blind Willie McTell" draft typescript

Bob Dylan and Mark Knopfler, Power Station,
NYC, 1983. Photographer unknown

"BLIND WILLIE McTELL"

Soon after the release of *Infidels*, alternate takes and outtakes found their way into the world, shifting opinions on the album yet again. As the bootleg material from the sessions started to circulate, fans and critics alike got their first taste of the songs that had hit the cutting room floor, like "Foot of Pride" and "Blind Willie McTell."

Yet for Dylan, the songs were incomplete. "Blind Willie McTell," which is now considered a classic, wasn't released until the 1991 archival box set, *The Bootleg Series Volumes 1–3 (Rare & Unreleased) 1961–1991*. Even though Dylan's handwritten edits reveal the song's elements beginning to fall into place, he later told *Rolling Stone*,

L–R: Bob Dylan, Sly Dunbar, Robbie Shakespeare,
Mark Knopfler, Mick Taylor, Power Station, NYC, 1983.
Photographer unknown

> It was never developed fully, I never got around to completing it. There wouldn't have been any other reason for leaving it off the record. It's like taking a painting by Monet or Picasso—goin' to his house and lookin' at a half-finished painting and grabbing it and selling it to people who are Picasso fans.

"Foot of Pride," the searing indictment of human vanity set to a modified twelve-bar blues, was another song left off *Infidels* only to be released on *The Bootleg Series Volumes 1–3*. Dylan tried the song, originally titled "Too Late," in a variety of different musical arrangements over two days of tracking exclusively dedicated to the song. Eventually, Dylan would go back to the drawing board, rewriting and retitling it "Foot of Pride."

Although Dylan himself has never performed the song live, Lou Reed gave a blistering version during Columbia Records' *30th Anniversary Concert Celebration* held at Madison Square Garden on October 16, 1992.

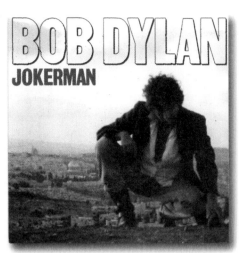

L–R: Paul Sapounakis,
Hurricane Fund
co-organizer; George
Lois, Hurricane Fund
executive director
(in a Hurricane Fund
t-shirt); Bob Dylan,
Veterans Memorial
Coliseum,
New Haven, CT,
November 13, 1975.
Photograph by
Ken Regan

"JOKERMAN" MUSIC VIDEO

At the time *Infidels* was released, the twenty-four-hour music video channel, MTV, was in its early heyday, and any artist who wanted their music heard was expected to make a promotional video. Although Dylan was familiar with the medium—the D. A. Pennebaker–directed "Subterranean Homesick Blues" is widely considered one of the first music videos—he hadn't yet entered the fray until the videos for "Sweetheart Like You" and "Jokerman."

At the suggestion of promoter Bill Graham, George Lois, the legendary Madison Avenue ad man, was brought in to direct the video for "Jokerman." Lois was no stranger to MTV; he was responsible for the classic "I Want My MTV" ad campaign, which found its way into Mark Knopfler's lyrics for Dire Straits' "Money for Nothing." He was no stranger to Dylan, either, having met him at the Hurricane Carter benefit almost a decade earlier.

Working with Lois on the video's concept was Larry "Ratso" Sloman, who wrote the tour memoir *On the Road with Bob Dylan* about his time with the Rolling Thunder Revue. Together they decided to intercut footage of Dylan lip synching to the song on a soundstage with still images that related to the song's lyrics.

Released on March 27, 1984, the video went on to be widely praised and shown on air, despite its six-minute length. Dylan, however, was initially uncertain about doing a video in the first place and was perplexed at its positive reception, as Larry Sloman later recalled in an interview with the Bob Dylan Center:

> We start shooting the video and Bob is singing along, and the whole time he's got his eyes closed. So after each take, George would pull me aside and say, "Ratso, you gotta get him to open his eyes." So after each take, I'd go out there and say, "That was good, man. That was good. You think maybe you could open your eyes a little bit?" And he'd say "No problem." And there's another take. Eyes closed. Another take. Eyes closed. George is getting beside himself. He says, "He's gotta open his eyes!" So finally, after maybe seven takes I go over and I say, "Bob, they love it, but George really wants you to open your eyes when you're singing the chorus." And Bob goes, "I'm trying."
>
> So then we shoot this last take, and he starts singing, and now he's like squinting and his eyes are half open. And he's singing the chorus, and he gets to the end of the chorus and he just opens his eyes and stares at the camera. And it was like, chills. It's like those piercing baby blue eyes, this charisma is just burning.
>
> After we finished the video, George showed it to Columbia and they went crazy. They're over the moon. They think this is the greatest video they ever saw. A few days later I got a phone call from Bob, and he said, "Larry, the video is good, but I don't know about me in it."
>
> So the video comes out, Bob now goes to tour in Europe, and the video comes out and they show it on MTV and it goes into like, sub-lunar rotation because it's so long. So I fly over to Europe on vacation, where Bob is playing, and I get to the venue and they bring me backstage. Bob says, "Hey Larry, how you doing?" I said, "Great. You're not gonna believe this, but Friday Night Videos just made 'Jokerman' the video of the week and the *LA Times* says it's one of the greatest videos ever made." And Bob pauses and he goes, "Well, either I'm crazy or the world's crazy."

PAGE 385: Bob Dylan, "Jokerman" music video shoot, 1984.
Photographer unknown

Bob Dylan, Mark Knopfler, Mick Taylor, Alan Clark, Robbie Shakespeare, Sly Dunbar, Power Station, NYC, May 1983. Film stills from unused promotional footage, directed by Albert and David Maysles

THE MAYSLES BROTHERS

These film stills are from a set of unfinished music videos shot by renowned documentary filmmakers Albert and David Maysles at the Power Station in New York City while Dylan was recording *Infidels*. The footage features Dylan playing along to "Don't Fall Apart on Me Tonight," "License to Kill," and "Neighborhood Bully," accompanied by the studio band he'd assembled: guitarist and co-producer Mark Knopfler and keyboardist Alan Clark of Dire Straits, former Rolling Stone guitarist Mick Taylor, and rock-solid reggae rhythm duo Sly Dunbar and Robbie Shakespeare on drums and bass respectively. The format proved too forced at the time and remained in the vaults until the project was revisited as part of the promotion for the 2021 release, *The Bootleg Series Vol. 16: Springtime in New York 1980–1985*.

L–R: Liberace, David Letterman, Bob Dylan. Photographer unknown

L–R: Bob Dylan, J. J. Holiday, Tony Marsico, *Late Night with David Letterman*. Photographer unknown

LATE NIGHT WITH DAVID LETTERMAN, 1984

On March 22, 1984, Dylan made a rare television appearance, performing on *Late Night with David Letterman* in one of his few activities promoting his new album *Infidels*. Dylan was accompanied by a trio of young, relatively unknown musicians, with whom Dylan had been privately rehearsing at his home in Malibu since late 1982: bassist Tony Marsico and drummer Charlie Quintana of the LA-based Chicano punk band The Plugz and guitarist J. J. Holiday. In their only public appearance as Dylan's backing group, they performed in front of a live television audience three songs: blues legend Sonny Boy Williamson II's "Don't Start Me to Talkin'" followed by "License to Kill," and ending with a ferocious version of "Jokerman."

In an interview with the Bob Dylan Center, Holiday and Marsico shared their recollections of the gig:

TONY MARSICO: For some reason, something must have hit Bob. A lot of punk stuff. The Clash were happening at the time.

J. J. HOLIDAY: We talked about The Clash in rehearsals.

MARSICO: I think he just got a bug right after he did *Infidels* and I'm guessing that's why he called us up because we were just green. We were a ragtag bunch of guys. I mean we weren't studio guys yet. It was pretty weird how someone like Dylan would take a chance on three punks and bring us into the fold. That guy could get any musician he wanted.

HOLIDAY: I remember going backstage on the [Letterman] show. We were talking like, "How many verses are there? Is there a solo?" He goes, "No, if it's going well, we'll keep it going. And if it's not, I'll signal you. We'll cut it off."

MARSICO: On national TV, right?!

HOLIDAY: I do say "Jokerman" was rehearsed enough.

MARSICO: That was all rehearsed. The only thing that wasn't rehearsed was the roadie giving him the right harmonica.

HOLIDAY: There's a variety of stories there, but Dylan just walked around and said, "Keep playing." I had no intention of stopping. But you can see him on camera quickly trying to get his harmonica.

MARSICO: He went from guy to guy across the stage going, "Keep going! Keep going!" Cause we didn't know, and the cameraman got really confused, and the red lights are flashing here, one camera's over there, and nobody knows who to focus on. Charlie, who's behind the drums, started cracking up laughing because we're in the middle of this chaos going on onstage. If you watch the video, Bob is at the back of the stage throwing his arms up in the air.

HOLIDAY: Hey, it was one of those things that could have happened at any gig. It just happened to happen on national television. . . . I always say our second gig would have been stellar.

David Letterman had only been the host of his own show for just over two years when Dylan first appeared on the program in March 1984. The world-famous pianist and larger-than-life cultural icon Liberace had a cooking segment on the show, where he and Letterman made his famous "Liberace Individual Egg Casserole." When asked about Dylan, Liberace praised him, saying, "He has a statement to make in music, and he does it very well, and we've missed him—he's been away too long."

Dylan performed on Letterman's show more than any other in his career. As part of the *Late Night with David Letterman* Tenth Anniversary Special at Radio City Music Hall, on January 18, 1992, Dylan performed "Like a Rolling Stone," and in November 1993, Dylan returned to *Letterman* (now on CBS) to perform "Forever Young." Dylan made his final appearance on *Letterman* on May 19, 2015, David Letterman's penultimate show before he retired. Dylan performed a moving version of "The Night We Called It a Day," from his album of standards, *Shadows in the Night*, released earlier that year. In his introduction, Letterman called Dylan "the greatest songwriter of modern times."

FROM TOP TO BOTTOM:

Liberace and Bob Dylan

Bob Dylan and Paul Shaffer

L–R: Tony Marsico, Paul Shaffer, Steve Jordan, Charlie Quintana, J. J. Holiday

Bob Dylan and Calvert DeForest (Larry "Bud" Melman)

L–R: Tony Marsico, Bob Dylan, Charlie Quintana, J. J. Holiday

Photographer unknown

1984 European Tour poster

1984 European Tour program

Between May 28 and July 8, 1984, Dylan embarked on a stadium tour of a dozen European countries, consistently playing to some of the largest audiences of his career. Although advertised in some locales as the *Infidels* tour, Dylan's shows featured only a handful of songs from his latest album, though Dylan took the opportunity to revise some of his older material.

A live record, *Real Live*, compiled from the final three shows of the tour at St. James' Park in Newcastle, Wembley Stadium in London, and Slane Castle in Ireland, by producer Glyn Johns showcased some of these updated versions. Despite mixed reviews, the new, radically reworked solo acoustic version of "Tangled Up in Blue" garnered particular praise. Dylan agreed, later remarking, "On *Real Live* it ["Tangled Up in Blue"] is more like it should have been. I was never really happy with it."

Carlos Santana joined the tour as an opening act, making guest appearances during the final few songs of Dylan's set nearly every night. His distinctive guitar playing is displayed on the version of "Tombstone Blues" selected for *Real Live*. Other guests joined Dylan onstage throughout the tour, including Joan Baez, Van Morrison, Bono, French singer Hugues Aufray, and Chrissie Hynde of The Pretenders.

Concert ticket, Barcelona, June 28, 1984

Bob Dylan, Slane Castle, Ireland, July 8, 1984. Photograph by Ken Regan

Two Possible Lies and the Truth

MICHAEL ONDAATJE

"If I were a writer how I would enjoy being told the novel is dead. How liberating
to work on the margins, outside a central perception."

—DON DELILLO

"Isn't it always like this? Something uncontrollable becomes the hero. . . ."

—BRENDA HILLMAN

"I find people long to get to know me in five minutes. Between you and me I am
not deep, but very wide, and it takes time to walk around me."

—HONORÉ DE BALZAC

"Rinehart . . . Rinehart—I'm a most indifferent guy!" This is a line that appears a few times as a lead-in to the chorus in a jazz number played by Count Basie's band. It was sung by his lead singer, Jimmy Rushing. When eventually asked the meaning of the repeated line, Rushing said that every evening, in the apartment block he lived in, a woman on street level would yell out at the top of her voice "Reinhardt! Reinhardt!" And every night there never was a response. Whether this was the true source of the line or not, it feels just perfect, reliable, full of dramatic possibilities. . .

What I love about Dylan is the huge range of sources in the music he knows. He will cover Brendan Behan's great prison song "All Along the Banks of the Royal Canal," and Elizabeth Cotton's "Shake Sugaree." He will recreate and re-energize, with just a few verbal changes, the plot, narrator, and characters in "Delia's Gone." Politically and artistically he is a communal writer with a vast democratic sense of musical history. We witness it most clearly in his *Theme Time Radio Hour*—a celebration of the sources of music, ancient and modern, that he grew up with.

And there is in him that important artistic aspect of *loitering*—a quality that we see occurring in the great collages of Kurt Schwitters and the photographs of Robert Frank. You discover this quality in the early drafts of his songs, even in those that will emerge eventually as spare and meticulous. The sources of so many of those songs are a far-ranging thicket of phrases, tones, altering rhythms, questions, uncertainties evident during the construction and shaving down of a song, where even a character or set of lines will often in the end emigrate to another song a year or two later. He always allows himself that open door somewhere. Everything, anything, is possible during the progress of a song or poem. Just as one can look at a great poem like "The Art of Losing" by Elizabeth Bishop and be almost appalled by those first few drafts, but by the end recognize the evolving craft that makes it a great and meticulous villanelle. So many of Dylan's rough drafts written on hotel room stationery show that wayward collage-like history of his songs, always curious in their search for a possible new way out. So that in "Brownsville Girl," which he wrote with Sam

Shepard, he'll yell out in the middle of one of the verses—hilariously uncalled for!—"If there's an original thought out there, I could use it right now!"

A few years ago, I managed to get to see Balzac's house in Paris, now a museum, and discovered there the novelist's scrawled over and rewritten pages. It looked like a similar raucous prose style at work. There were even wonderful note-like drawings which seem almost maps of discovery that he could perhaps follow in the story he was working on—just as in the past an artist such as Brueghel would use map makers to help him structure a canvas. Dylan, even in his almost barely verbal emotion of a love song, such as "This Dream of You," will hide in an almost minimal haiku-like repetition where the longing is simply stated again and again and again until it cannot move away from the singer. "This curiously home-made pact," as Robert Creeley describes writing.

Along with this cautious intimacy Dylan, after beginning with a solitary piano, will then and only then, looking out from the St. James Hotel, step into the landscape and plot of a song. In "Blind Willie McTell" the plot *is* the landscape, that alone he steps into, with a few chords of his piano.

> *See them big plantations burnin'*
> *Hear the cracking of the whips*
> *Smell that sweet magnolia blooming*
> *See the ghosts of slavery ships*

"Blind Willie McTell"—my friend the poet C. D. Wright always thought—should be America's national anthem.

* * *

There has always been a deep affection and even influence between poems and song, film and paint, even novels and cooking. To make a pompous qualitative distinction of status between one art form and another is absurd, as well as being often self-protective. My favorite line of literary criticism by a French critic is "The best bacon omelets I have eaten in my life have been with Alexandre Dumas."

So I'll end with a small anecdote by the writer Bobbie Louise Hawkins in a piece she wrote called "The Elevation of Terre Haute Is 50 Feet."

> When you come to Terre Haute's city limits there's a metal sign, and stamped into the metal you can read: "Terre Haute Indiana, elevation 50 feet. The birthplace of Paul Dresser who wrote 'The Banks of the Wabash.'"
> Terre Haute was also the birthplace of Theodore Dreiser. The city made some choice to forget about Dreiser who was indecent. He supposedly wrote dirty books and seduced young girls and got ruined by his excesses. He was the ninth child in a poor family in the poorest part of the town. His brother Paul changed his name to Dresser during the Great War. Dreiser was too German. Paul Dresser also wrote "My Gal Sal." But for the sake of the record it was not Dresser who wrote "The Banks of the Wabash," it was his brother, the novelist Theodore Dreiser, the author of *Sister Carrie* and *An American Tragedy*, the twisted lecher, who could never look the other way, whose birth was attended by the graces. It was Theodore Dreiser who wrote the words Terre Haute still holds in memory.

> Oh, the moonlight's fair tonight along the Wabash
> From the fields there comes the breath of new mown hay
> Through the sycamores the candle lights are gleaming
> On the banks of the Wabash far away.

MICHAEL ONDAATJE

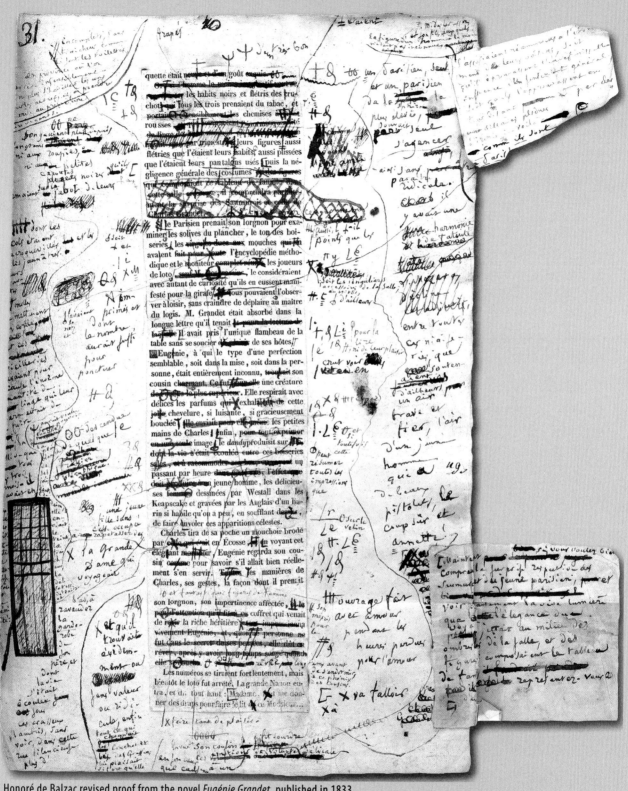

Honoré de Balzac revised proof from the novel *Eugénie Grandet*, published in 1833

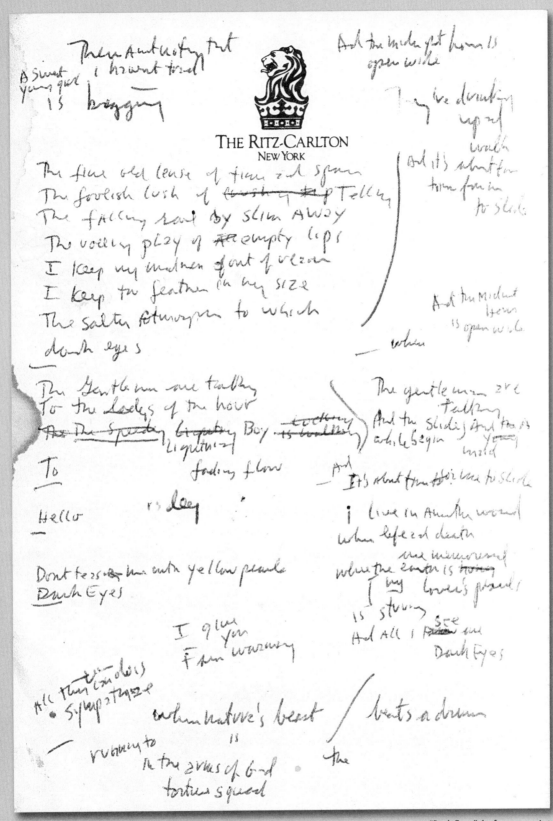

"Dark Eyes" draft manuscript

MICHAEL ONDAATJE

EMPIRE BURLESQUE

Released on June 10, 1985, Dylan's twenty-third studio album, *Empire Burlesque* reflected the sound of the 1980s in its production. Recorded between July 1984 and March 1985, the album featured numerous guest musicians, including Mike Campbell, Benmont Tench, and Howie Epstein from Tom Petty and the Heartbreakers, Ronnie Wood, Al Kooper, Jim Keltner, and many others. Dylan produced much of the record himself, with hip-hop, dance remix, and New Wave producer Arthur Baker assisting with mixing the album.

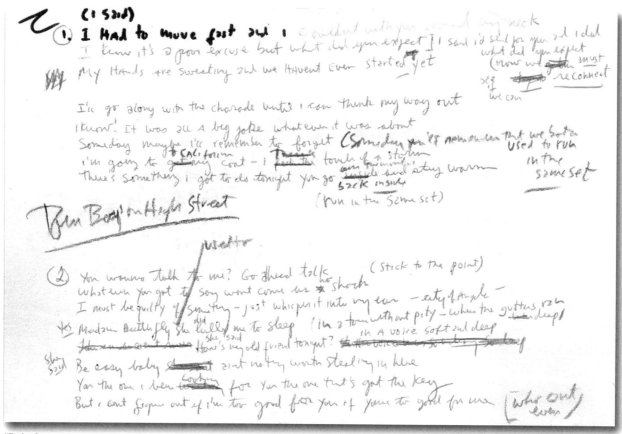

"Tight Connection to My Heart (Has Anybody Seen My Love)" draft manuscript

"TIGHT CONNECTION TO MY HEART (HAS ANYBODY SEEN MY LOVE)"

The album opener "Tight Connection to My Heart (Has Anybody Seen My Love)" was originally conceived and recorded as "Someone's Got a Hold of My Heart" for *Infidels*. However, in the interim Dylan had completely rewritten the song for *Empire Burlesque*. One draft was written on a Ritz Carlton hotel notepad, dating to Dylan's stay in New York during the recording of the album. Although Dylan rarely performed the song live, he demonstrated the song's versatility and depth in showcasing the song as an acoustic number during his legendary Supper Club shows in 1993. Acclaimed theater director Conor McPherson similarly reinvented the song as a mournful ballad as part of his critically acclaimed *Girl from the North Country* musical.

PAGE 397: Bob Dylan, Power Station, NYC, 1985.
Photograph by Deborah Feingold

SURVIVING IN A RUTHLESS WORLD

"WHEN THE NIGHT COMES FALLING FROM THE SKY"

Upon its release, some critics panned *Empire Burlesque* as "Disco Dylan" because of its synths, electronic drums, and overall '80s sound, with "When the Night Comes Falling from the Sky" as a case in point. Originally recorded as a fast-paced rocker featuring Stevie Van Zandt and Roy Bittan of Bruce Springsteen's E Street Band, the version of the song ultimately selected by Dylan and producer Arthur Baker was done in the style of contemporary dance tracks. The song was even given a 12-inch promotional release to take into the clubs. Although released as a B-side in the United States, "When the Night Comes Falling from the Sky" was selected for its own release internationally. The UK 7-inch single features a rare alternate edit and mix of the song.

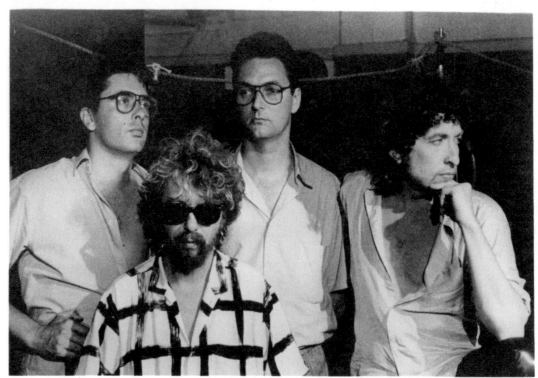

During production of the promotional video "When the Night Comes Falling From the Sky," the second single from the album EMPIRE BURLESQUE, are, from left: Co-director Mark Innocenti, executive director/performer Dave Stewart of Eurythmics, co-director Eddie Arno, and Columbia recording artist Bob Dylan. (Photograph: Peter J. Carni)

BOB DYLAN

"When the Night Comes Falling from the Sky" music video publicity photo, 1985. Photograph by Peter J. Carni

Bob Dylan at Leo Tolstoy's estate Yasnaya
Polyana, USSR, July 1985. Filmmaker unknown

L–R: Bob Dylan, Robert Bly, Seamus Heaney,
USSR, July 1985. Filmmaker unknown

SOVIET UNION, 1985

In July 1985, Soviet poet Yevgeny Yevtushenko invited Bob Dylan to Moscow to attend the 12th World Festival of Youth and Students. Prior to that, their paths had almost crossed for years. In April 1962, Dylan performed at a concert benefiting the VIII World Youth Festival of Peace and Friendship in Helsinki, Finland; Yevtushenko attended the festival later that year. In 1964, Dylan namechecked Yevtushenko in his liner notes for *The Times They Are A-Changin'*. And in 1972, Dylan attended a dinner at the New School in Yevtushenko's honor, sitting at a table with poet Gregory Corso and author Kurt Vonnegut Jr.

On July 25, 1985—twenty years to the day since his controversial Newport Folk Festival performance—Dylan performed before an audience of internationally renowned poets at the Central Lenin Stadium. Although no full recording survives, Dylan reportedly played "Blowin' in the Wind," "The Times They Are A-Changin'," and "A Hard Rain's A-Gonna Fall." While in the USSR, Dylan also visited the estate of Russian author Leo Tolstoy at Yasnaya Polyana, located a few hours from Moscow, where, according to his recounting of the visit in *Chronicles: Volume One*, a tour guide let him ride the great Russian writer's bicycle.

COLUMBIA DAILY SPECTATOR   Tuesday, April 10, 1962

THE UNITED STATES FESTIVAL COMMITTEE, INC.
(to send participants and a cultural presentation to the VIII World Youth Festival
of Peace and Friendship in Helsinki, Finland — July 1962)
Presents **A FOLK AND JAZZ CONCERT**

Alix Dobkin   •   Pete Seeger   •   Bob Dylan
Archie Shepp and His Jazz Sextet   •   Jerry Silverman
Cecil Taylor   •   Perry Robinson & His Jazz Combo

Wednesday Evening   April 25, 1962   at 8:30 P.M.
at PALM GARDENS   310 W. 52nd Street (8th Ave.)
Contribution $2.75   Students $1.75
For tickets call or write: United States Festival Committee
460 Park Ave. So., N.Y. 16   MU 6-0182

Concert benefit advertisement, *Columbia Daily Spectator*, published
April 12, 1962

Bob Dylan, Central Lenin Stadium, Moscow, July 25, 1985.
Videographer unknown

399

L–R: Lou Reed, Bob Dylan, Tom Petty, Randy Newman, backstage at Farm Aid, Champaign, IL, September 22, 1985. Photograph by Deborah Feingold

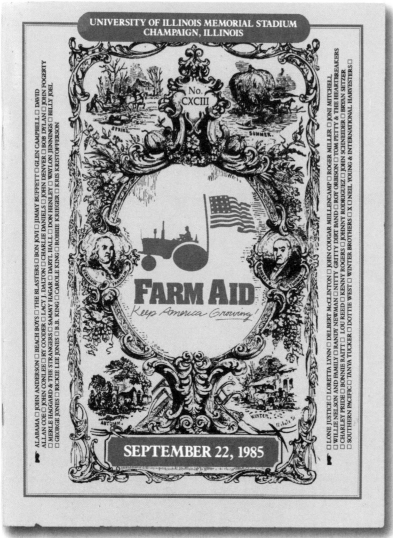

UNIVERSITY OF ILLINOIS MEMORIAL STADIUM
CHAMPAIGN, ILLINOIS

No. CXCIII

FARM AID
Keep America Growing!

SEPTEMBER 22, 1985

Farm Aid concert program, 1985

FARM AID, 1985

Performing to a worldwide audience thought to exceed one billion people as part of the Live Aid concert benefiting famine relief in Ethiopia, Dylan took a moment after the "Ballad of Hollis Brown," his tale of rural poverty, to also acknowledge the plight of the American farmer. The idea resonated with fellow performer Willie Nelson, and he ran with it.

About two months later, on September 22, 1985, Dylan took the stage in Champaign, Illinois, for the first inaugural Farm Aid concert. Backed by Tom Petty and the Heartbreakers—their first performance together—Dylan delivered a short set that also notably featured a guest appearance from Willie Nelson.

PAGE 401 (TOP): Farm Aid, 1985.
Photograph by Steve Kagan

PAGE 401 (BOTTOM): Bob Dylan and Tom Petty, Farm Aid, 1985. Photograph by Ebet Roberts

Bob Dylan and David Bowie, *Biograph* release party, Whitney Museum, NYC,
November 13, 1985. Photograph by Vinnie Zuffante

On November 7, 1985, less than six months after the release of *Empire Burlesque*,
Dylan once again changed the landscape of the music business with the release of his
fifty-three-track box set *Biograph*. Released as a five-LP, three-cassette, or three-CD
set, *Biograph* was a collection of previously released tracks, studio outtakes and demos,
unreleased songs, and live performances from some of Dylan's most critical concerts.

Former *Rolling Stone* music critic and author of the book *Fast Times at Ridgemont
High* Cameron Crowe provided the liner notes, with an exclusive wide-ranging interview
with Dylan. The thirty-six-page booklet provided fans with rare or never-before-seen
photos spanning Dylan's career. The set reached #33 on the *Billboard* charts and provided a blueprint for Dylan's long-running, award-winning archival box set series
The Bootleg Series.

PAGES 404–405: Bob Dylan, 1985. Photograph by
David Michael Kennedy

403

The Gunfighter's Never Ending Tour

ROBERT M. RUBIN

"If there's an original thought out there, I could use it right now."

—BOB DYLAN

"Brownsville Girl" opens with a two-stanza reference to Henry King's Western movie *The Gunfighter* (1950):

> *Well, there was this movie I seen one time*
> *About a man riding 'cross the desert and it starred Gregory Peck*
> *He was shot down by a hungry kid trying to make a name for himself*
> *The townspeople wanted to crush that kid down and string him up by the neck.*
>
> *Well, the marshal, now he beat that kid to a bloody pulp*
> *As the dying gunfighter lay in the sun and gasped for his last breath*
> *Turn him loose, let him go, let him say he outdrew me fair and square*
> *I want him to feel what it's like to every moment face his death.*

Peck's actual onscreen words as he dies are: "If I was doing you a favor I'd let 'em hang you right now—and get it over with. But I don't want you to get off that light. I want you to go on being a big tough gunny. I want you to have to see what it means to have to live like a big tough gunny. So don't thank me yet, pardner. Just wait. You'll see what I mean."

The gunfighter is the transitional love object of the American frontier. He renders himself obsolete in the process of taming it for decent folk: think John Wayne yielding to Jimmy Stewart in *The Man Who Shot Liberty Valance* after secretly saving his life. ("When the facts become legend, print the legend.") Lose the law and order gloss and what you are left with is a guy who, once he achieves a certain level of success, narrowly defined—killing rather than being killed in a series of theatrical confrontations—must keep moving just to avoid more pointless showdowns. To paraphrase Robert Warshow, we don't know what he does all day, where he sleeps, or the particulars of what he stands for . . . just that he's "psychically troubled and isolated in his profession by something 'dark' in his nature or past."[1] As originally envisioned by André de Toth, from whom King took over the directing reins, the gunfighter is, according to Richard Slotkin, "a killer celebrity who finds himself trapped in the role and reputation he has spent his life seeking."[2] Sound familiar? Want more? He's at "the center of a public fantasy life so powerful that those in its spell had to seek to become and, failing that to destroy, the idealized figure."[3]

The gunfighter remains an enduring metaphor for artists, especially musicians. Alto players constantly tried to knock Charlie "Bird" Parker off his perch. Hendrix blew Clapton away in London with "Killing Floor" after inviting himself on stage to "sit in." Young guns were always coming for Dylan. Having owned the sixties, he was a sitting duck by the eighties. He *was* Jimmy Ringo. Is *The*

Gunfighter the Western Dylan wished he had made, or at least the one he felt like he was trapped in?

Dylan was obsessed with Billy the Kid. A decade earlier he had elbowed his way into Sam Peckinpah's *Pat Garrett and Billy the Kid*. Screenwriter Rudy Wurlitzer recalled Dylan thought he was some sort of reincarnation of William Bonney (Richard Gere would play a Dylanesque Billy in *I'm Not There*). Peckinpah loved Dylan's music, but there was not much room for him onscreen. (Ironically, Kris Kristofferson, featured as Billy the Kid, had been an aspiring tunesmith sweeping up at Columbia's Nashville studios when *Blonde on Blonde* was recorded.) To squeeze Dylan in, Wurlitzer made him a stuttering printer's assistant who happened to be a skilled knife fighter. He called him Alias. ("Brownsville Girl": "The only thing for sure we knew about Henry Porter was that his name wasn't Henry Porter.") The neophyte actor was frustrated by Peckinpah's rather unorthodox comportment on set, as well as his own marginality to the actual making of the movie apart from its soundtrack. He was already a celebrated singer/songwriter. What he really wanted was to be a Western movie star.

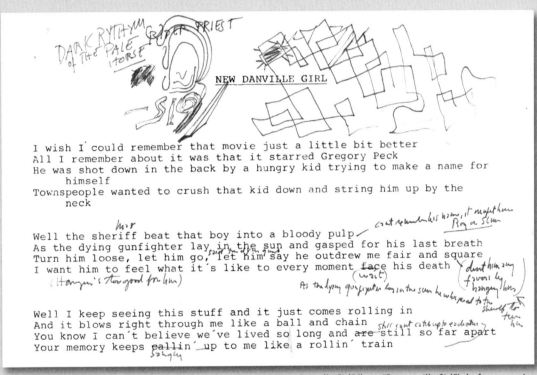

"New Danville Girl" (later "Brownsville Girl") draft manuscript

Shortly after the movie came out, Sam Shepard was hired to write a screenplay while traveling with Bob and the Rolling Thunder Revue. Dylan might have had some kind of Western in mind, but *Renaldo and Clara* didn't quite fit that bill. In 1975, Shepard was a cult figure, along for the ride. A decade later, brought on again for "Brownsville Girl," he's a Pulitzer Prize winner for . . . wait for it . . . *True West*. Shepard midwifed a screenplay for a metaphysical road movie, in the form of lyrics to a "long take" pop song, the whole shooting match triggered by the memory of a *noir* Western.

The narrator of "Brownsville Girl," while able to recall and recount aspects of the film in some detail, has a harder time situating himself in it. ("I can't remember why I was in it or what part I was supposed to play" / "I don't remember who I was or where I was bound.") Even when he places himself directly in the movie's narrative, it's not clear what's going on: "Well they were looking for somebody with a pompadour." In *The Gunfighter*, the young punk Hunt Bromley, whom we first meet in the barber chair, has a thick mop of natural curls. So who's the pompadour? Elvis in *Flaming Star*? Remember, Dylan briefly owned Warhol's *Double Elvis* before trading it to his manager for a couch. Can we call Dylan's haircut—at least the iteration he sported at Newport when he achieved electric outlaw status—a pompadour? Is he flashing on the moment when Pete Seeger et al. turned on him? When he's "cornered in the churchyard" (here we are far from the action of the original movie), is he referring to his "Christian" period and its less than enthusiastic critical reception? Who knows, and who really cares. The song is a ticket to a lucid dream. You put yourself in it, like Dylan does with *The Gunfighter*, and see where it takes you.

Jimmy Ringo is doomed, but Dylan is redeemed. He hung up his guns but not his spurs. Bob can walk into any bar in America and knock back a few fingers of Heaven's Door without constantly having to check the exits. "Brownsville Girl" heralds the "late" Dylan to come, a unique genre in which all music—not just his but everybody's, from Blind Willie McTell to Frank Sinatra—emerges from and melts back into memory, and is made new again. With *"Love and Theft,"* and everything that came after, Dylan elevated himself back up into a category of one. In a musical landscape littered with undead legacy acts, he is a Living National Treasure.

NORTH CAROLWOOD DRIVE
LOS ANGELES, CALIFORNIA 90077

March 17, 1995

Ms. Marcy Holloway

Austin, TX   78736

Dear Marcy Holloway,

As I write this note of appreciation, I am listening to Bob Dylan's Brownsville Girl.

Dylan and Pete Seeger are two American originals, both favorites of mine.

I had heard Brownsville Girl years ago, but I'm listening now from a fresh, though more distant perspective. I'm pleased, and honored to think that something I did in 1949 or '50, made a strong impression on Dylan, and that he expressed it in this powerful ballad.

Thank you for your letter, and for reminding me.

All good wishes.

Sincerely,

Gregory Peck

Letter from Gregory Peck to Marcy Holloway, March 19, 1995

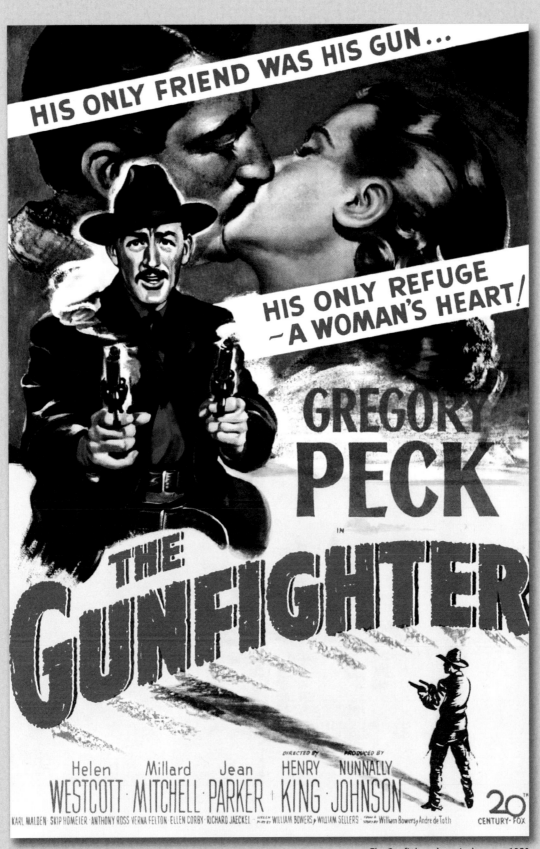

The Gunfighter theatrical poster, 1950

ROBERT M. RUBIN

BOB DYLAN WITH TOM PETTY AND THE HEARTBREAKERS

Tom Petty and Bob Dylan, Los Angeles, April 10, 1986.
Photographer unknown

Frankfurt, West Germany, concert poster, September 28, 1987

TRUE CONFESSIONS / TEMPLES IN FLAMES TOURS

In 1986 and 1987, Bob Dylan embarked on two highly successful tours collaborating with Tom Petty and the Heartbreakers. True Confessions, the first tour, had legs in the United States and Australia, the latter of which produced the HBO television concert special *Hard to Handle*. In 1987, after a tour with the Grateful Dead, Dylan reconnected with Petty and company for an inspired series of performances across Europe dubbed the Temples in Flame tour.

Guitarist Mike Campbell recounted the experience of playing with Dylan in an interview with the Bob Dylan Center,

> Playing with Bob, I learned so much about spontaneity and about thinking on your feet. The Heartbreakers at that time weren't doing much improvisation. We had our songs and we played them pretty much like the record—maybe at the end we might stretch out a solo, but we were pretty much playing the program. With Bob it wasn't that way at all. It was kind of anarchy in a way, a beautiful anarchy where we would rehearse a song a certain way and it might be like the record, but it might not. So we learned it the way he was doing it and we'd think, "Okay, that's how we're gonna do it," but when we'd get to the gig, he might decide to change it yet again. I thought he was just so brave to take that chance in front of an audience and just trust that they're gonna stick with him. More often than not, something better would happen.

True Confessions tour backstage pass, 1986

Hard to Handle set list notes, February 1986

HARD TO HANDLE

On a notepad from the Sebel Townhouse Hotel in Sydney, Australia,
Dylan worked through the potential
set list for *Hard to Handle*, his first
television concert special in a decade.
At the time, the production was the
largest 35mm multi-camera shoot in
Australian history, and a generation
of young Australian filmmakers who
would go on to distinguished careers
participated.

Film stills from *Hard to Handle*, Entertainment Centre, Sydney, February 24–25,
1986. Directed by Gillian Armstrong

411

COLLABORATIONS

Beyond the electricity of Bob Dylan and Tom Petty and the Heartbreakers' concert performances, several songs also came out of their years working together. Dylan and Petty co-wrote "Got My Mind Made Up," which ended up on Dylan's 1986 album, *Knocked Out Loaded*. Dylan, Petty, and Mike Campbell co-wrote the song "Jammin' Me," which Tom Petty and the Heartbreakers released as a single. And in their only joint appearance on a studio recording, they cut "Band of the Hand (It's Hell Time Man!)" for the Michael Mann film of the same name. The latter, produced by Petty, featured Fleetwood Mac's Stevie Nicks among the backing vocalists.

Tom Petty and the Heartbreakers never really escaped Dylan's orbit, returning to the fold at various times to offer their unique musical services. In 1988, Dylan and Petty were part of the supergroup The Traveling Wilburys, releasing two critically acclaimed and commercially successful albums. Following that group's demise, the two rarely collaborated again, though Dylan and Petty remained musical comrades-in-arms.

Upon Petty's sudden passing on October 2, 2017, Dylan said, "It's shocking, crushing news. I thought the world of Tom. He was a great performer, full of the light, a friend, and I'll never forget him." Shortly thereafter, at an October 21 concert in Broomfield, Colorado, Dylan performed Petty's classic "Learning to Fly" as an encore.

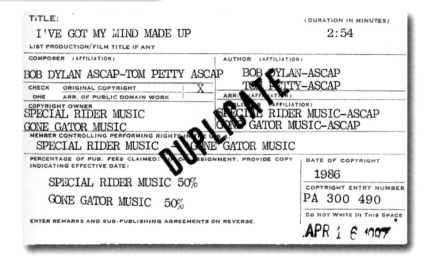

"Jammin' Me" and "I've Got My Mind Made Up" label copy cards

"Jammin' Me" 45 rpm single, 1987

It's Hell Time Man!

JEFF SLATE

There he was. Bob Dylan.

At 19, I'd already fallen in and out of love with the man I knew as the "voice of his generation" a few times. As a young kid, I'd inherited my brother's copy of *Greatest Hits*, with its shadowy, enigmatic cover—a shot of Dylan in profile, harmonica to his lips—with a stray copy of *Greatest Hits II*, sans sleeve, jammed inside. But my diet in those days mainly consisted of The Beatles, The Kinks, The Who, Elvis Presley, and even Bread and Paul Revere and the Raiders, so Bob Dylan was a bit of a leap. But then one day I traded some firecrackers for a copy of The Byrds' *Mr. Tambourine Man,* and I found my way back to the source.

The great run of '60s albums—*The Times They Are A-Changin'*, *Another Side of Bob Dylan*, *Bringing It All Back Home*, *Highway 61 Revisited*, and *Blonde On Blonde*—soon found their way into my collection, as did the live album with The Band, *Before the Flood*, as well as the mind-bending *Blood on the Tracks*, and its sister album *Desire*, as did the bootleg *The Great White Wonder*, which I thought was a copy of The Beatles' "White Album" when a middle-aged neighbor gave it to me, saying, in an uncharacteristically serious tone, as he handed it to me, "You've got to listen to this, man."

To be fair, I wasn't sure what I was listening to. I was a pre-teen and out of my depth, to be sure.

By 13, I'd picked up the bass and had joined my first band. For fledgling musicians, Dylan's music remained more than a little intimidating. We could pull off "Summertime Blues" and "My Generation," and even "Cold Turkey," but Dylan's songs, with *all those words*, seemed beyond our limited capabilities.

By college, in the 1980s, I was playing what were left of the Greenwich Village haunts where Dylan had cut his teeth, as well their grungy successors, often armed with only an acoustic guitar, often playing Dylan's hits to get the attention of the drunken tourists.

Now, on July 16, 1986, standing in front of me, in the dark, cavernous Madison Square Garden, was Dylan, wearing a white vest—with his bare arms showing—leather pants with large silver studs down the sides, fingerless gloves and what looked to me, way off in row F of section 338, to be an earring. He'd already played a mercurial mix of classics, covers, and new songs with Petty, who had then taken center stage and wowed the crowd with "Listen to Her Heart," "Think About Me," "The Waiting," and an extended "Breakdown." Alone, with only an acoustic guitar, Dylan surveyed the crowd for what seemed like forever. The tension was palpable.

The collaboration had come about almost as a lark. Dylan had mentioned at Live Aid, in July 1985, that he hoped "some of the money that's raised" could be used "to help pay the mortgages on some of the farms," during an acoustic set backed by Keith Richards and Ronnie Wood. That set about a chain of events that led to the first Farm Aid concert, the following September. Dylan was, of course, invited, but he needed a band. Manager Elliot Roberts mentioned Tom Petty and the Heartbreakers and, by all accounts, Dylan thought it was a good idea.

"He called me and said he needed a band, and was thinking of getting John Cougar's band," recalls Heartbreakers' guitarist Mike Campbell. "I said, 'Don't do that. You should get my band.' It was kind of cheeky of me, but I thought we could do it better."

In fact, the pairing of Dylan with Petty and his Heartbreakers was a match made in rock 'n' roll heaven. Dylan's version of "Baby, Let Me Follow You Down" was the first song Campbell ever learned on the guitar, and his seminal 1965 single "Like a Rolling Stone" had a similar impact.

"When he put that out, my life changed, in terms of, 'Wow, he's singing about me. I can relate to everything he's saying,'" Campbell recalls.

Keyboardist Benmont Tench had already worked with Dylan in the early '80s.

"The first session I did for him was the song 'Caribbean Wind,' which ended up on the *Biograph* box set," Tench recalls. "It was beautiful. But the session didn't work out. A few months later I got a call to work on *Shot of Love*. I played a little piano, and Bob played some piano. The songs were 'The Groom's Still Waiting at the Altar'

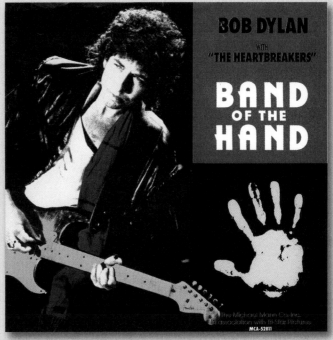

"Band of the Hand (It's Hell Time Man!)" 45 rpm single (front), 1987

and 'Every Grain of Sand.' I was very, very present and aware for those sessions. That's a very under-appreciated record, and a very special record."

Dylan was joined by Campbell and Heartbreakers bassist Howie Epstein on 1985's *Empire Burlesque*, and Petty had crossed paths with the legend over the years, so while the pairing was a bit unusual—Petty and company were stars in their own right—their roots rock style and aesthetic no doubt fit in nicely with Dylan's.

With Farm Aid under their belt, plans for a tour were hatched. Both Tench and Campbell recall the pre-tour rehearsals as hard work, but more fun than the band had had in ages.

"It was good for the Heartbreakers, because it was at a stage when we were a little stale," recalls Campbell. "Bands go through those stages, when you've been together for years, and we were at a point where a little of the sparkle was gone. We needed a break from just doing the routine. I think it was good and really fun and healthy for Tom, too, to be in a band and not have to be 'the guy,' and just be part of the band, and play guitar and sing a little bit, but not have to be on the mic all night long. So it revitalized our band. Playing with Bob was the real deal and very educational. We toured a long time with him. Around the world, basically. But we had a blast."

Still, they were working with Bob Dylan, which Campbell was reminded of on the first day of rehearsals.

"It was incredible, because we did a whole bunch of songs that we never did in the set," he says. "We did folk songs, blues songs, some of his more obscure songs. And I had a little Superscope Ghettoblaster that I used to record the rehearsals with the Heartbreakers, so I could go back and study it and make notes. So I had my recorder on the piano, and he walked over at one point and asked, kind of dejected, 'You got tapes too?' And I said, 'Well, this is just for me.' He looked at me like, 'Okay, I guess I can trust you.'"

"He pulled out songs that I knew, but I didn't know the ins and outs of, and then there'd be some beautiful song from the 1700s that I'd never even heard of, or he'd play something I hadn't that had been a hit for Carl Smith in the fifties," recalls Tench excitedly of the "education" he says he and his fellow Heartbreakers got working with Dylan. "I want to say he's a school, but he's not a school. Because school is something that you dread. He's a musician, he's a singer, he's a writer. He's got the knowledge accumulated. He opened my mind up to a lot of other kinds of music. And it opened my mind up to disabusing myself of the notion that I knew anything about where this guy was at."

Soon they were on the road, first in the Far East and Australia—where the famed *Hard to Handle* HBO special was filmed—and in Festival Studios in Sydney, with Petty producing, as Dylan had committed to supplying a song for the soundtrack to the film *Band of the Hand*.

Dylan's handwritten draft lyrics—one of the few surviving lyric sheets from the period in the Bob Dylan Archive—are astonishing. Written on Wellington Park Royal hotel notepaper, the words Dylan sketched out before the session amount to almost a Reagan-era rewrite of "Masters of War."

> *Close the book*
> *Write the final report*
> *This is a direct order*

"I remember that I thought it was just a really great song," recalls Tench of the session. "And the lyric is pretty fabulous."

> *Gotta think to survive*
> *Gotta stand together to stay*
> *alive*

"I don't remember being able to focus on the lyrics at the session, because we were just learning the track," says Campbell. "I was just going with the vibe as he cut it. So it wasn't until after I listened to it back that I could really hear the words clearly, but I remember thinking they'd changed a lot."

> *I'd beat some sense with*
> *your head, but that's very*
> *past the point*
> *Gonna blow up your house*
> *of voodoo*

"He sang the shit out of it," says Tench. "And The Queens of Rhythm just sang their asses off. But my most vivid memory is of Don Smith, who engineered it, and who tore the carpet out of the studio, because he hated the sound he was getting."

> *The Man he rips off people*
> *Then sleeps in a soft bed*

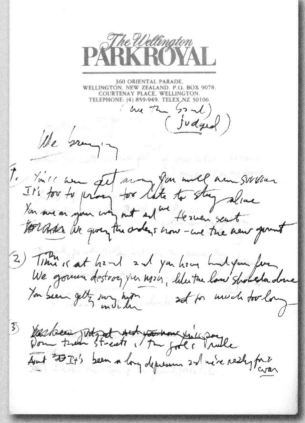

"Band of the Hand (It's Hell Time Man!)" draft manuscript

"Tom's not here, but I can speak for him on some level, because we wrote together for the Heartbreakers," says Campbell. "When we wrote a song, if there were three verses, we'd write three verses and we'd be done. 'We got it,' you know? But Bob said, 'Don't ever stop. If it's a three-verse song, write twenty-five verses. And then go back and pick the best ones. Because down the line, you might come up with better versions than what you're settling for.' So that's what he did on that song. He had written a ton of verses and then just picked the ones for the record that he liked. So that's something Tom and I learned from working with Bob."

> *Out in the streets, the fools rule*
> *Five separate fingers, five separate ways*
> *Choose to live*

"When I'm tracking, I'm usually not focusing on the words, I'm focusing more on changes in the melody," says Tench. "And on 'Band of the Hand,' we were focusing on the groove, because that's one thing that Bob particularly is, he's a sublime groove player. If you listen to 'Breakdown,' we could swing. But what he did for the Heartbreakers—because we were playing with a guy who has the swing that Hank had, that Robert Johnson had, that Elvis and The Beatles and Carl Perkins and Johnny Cash and Little Richard and Lead Belly had—was to really bring out that swing."

> *They'd like us to kill each other*
> *When the enemy they've created for you might be an honest man*

Nothing from Dylan's early draft survived to the final version of "Band of the Hand," but if you sing the words in your head to the rhythm of the track, a completely different, and remarkable, song emerges. But the song remains a forgotten curio in Dylan's vast catalog, and remains long out of print. In fact, Dylan, Petty and the Heartbreakers played the finished version of the song the night I saw them at the Garden. If it weren't for bootlegs, I wouldn't even remember that.

After the session, the collaboration evolved. Every night on stage, Campbell and Tench recall, was like a master class. And Campbell would eventually go on to collaborate with Dylan on one of the Heartbreakers' most enduring songs, "Jammin' Me."

"I had the music, which I'd cut in my studio, and I'd given it to Tom," Campbell recalls. "So he took that to the hotel room where Bob was, to write a song. According to Tom, they put on the TV, and got out the newspaper, and were pulling stuff out and then throwing it on the page. I was not there when that went down, but I'm assuming, because of that method, that there's probably a lot of loose bits that were thrown around that didn't get used. But I was certainly thrilled when Tom called me up and said, 'Hey, you've written a song with Bob!' And I wasn't even there!"

Tench confirms that unused lyrics for the 1987 song, which remained in the Heartbreakers' live set until the very end, existed.

"Somebody sent me a screenshot of some alternate lyrics that were in Tom's handwriting, and there was some great shit in there," he says. "So that gave me a deeper appreciation for Dylan. 'Why didn't I see *that* way back then?' We're walking the earth and Walt Whitman is alive. We're in Shakespeare's lifetime. We're walking the earth when Mary Shelley is thinking up the *Modern Prometheus*. We're in the world with somebody like that. That's crazy."

Back onstage at the Garden, Dylan launches into "To Ramona," before tearing the roof off with "One Too Many Mornings" and "A Hard Rain's A-Gonna Fall." It's epic, breathtaking and masterful. When he pauses, you can hear a pin drop in the huge arena.

But it was a difficult path to my first Dylan show. I was in the midst of my freshman year finals when tickets went on sale. By the time I realized I *needed* to be at the show, a *Rolling Stone* cover story had made tickets all but impossible to obtain.

I finally found a pair—for the then-astronomical amount of $50 each, more than twice the face value—in the back of the *Village Voice*. Thrilled when I picked them up, I was soon crushed when I couldn't get anyone to accompany me.

"Dylan? Petty? Nah."

That was the refrain from my friends. Sure, the show was going to take place during summer break, but also Dylan wasn't the all-capital-letters legend he is to us now. Nor, for that matter, was Petty.

So I scalped my extra ticket out in front of the Garden before the show and sat next to a stranger for my first Bob Dylan performance. I don't remember much about the guy, but he was a Vietnam vet and already a veteran Dylan concertgoer. He'd seen Dylan with The Band in 1974, as well as on tour during his "gospel" period. Both, he said, were bands that had complemented and lifted Dylan's performance far beyond those of his contemporaries. But he whooped and hollered for the Heartbreakers, even during both sets of Petty's numbers, which he said he wasn't all that familiar with.

Whatever my friends had said in passing up the chance to see the show—that Dylan was over the hill, that his voice was shot, that his best days were behind him—I was certain they had missed the opportunity of a lifetime.

"One thing we learned from Bob Dylan was to be brave enough to not be perfect all the time, even in front of people," Campbell recalls. "He'd change the rhythm, or change the key, at the spur of the moment, simply to make something happen. He was brave that way. That seat-of-the-pants thing was something that took a little getting used to, because our band always had this 'professional ethic,' that when we got out

"Band of the Hand (It's Hell Time Man!)" 45 rpm single (back), 1987

onstage, we were going to make sure that we built a set with a certain arc to it. Dylan saw a different arc. His arc would go up and down. He didn't care if there was a lull in the energy if he wanted to do something different. And most of the time, real magic would happen."

"What I got from working with Bob Dylan was the joy and thrill of playing those songs with a guy who did them better than anyone else, because they were his songs," adds Tench. "And I became a better musician—and we became a better band—in the process. From the first moment, it was life changing for me in a lot of ways."

By all accounts, it was a beneficial collaboration for Dylan as well. He went on to co-found The Traveling Wilburys with Petty, and his "never ending tour," which kicked off on the heels of his trek with the Heartbreakers, marked a career renaissance for Dylan that truly has no equal in modern popular culture.

"Bob said to us one day, 'I like playing with you guys, because when I turn around and say something, it's like talking to one guy,'" Campbell recalls with a chuckle. "I think what he meant was that we were such a unit that, even if he had a bunch of great players, he'd have to explain to each one what he wanted, but that, because we were so tuned into each other, he didn't have to do that.

"When I might ponder the future, and how music will be remembered, I think it will be Beethoven, Mozart, Bob Dylan, The Beatles, and maybe a few other people who will be remembered as historically essential artists," he adds. "Because it's everything about him. Nobody writes better songs. Plus, his charisma, his intelligence, his sense of humor, and his musicality is head and shoulders above everybody else."

Tench agrees, and counts himself lucky for his brief time working with Dylan.

"I quickly realized that everything I thought I knew about him was a misconception," he says, emphatically. "That's actually true with almost everybody in the world—any preconception is a misconception—but with Bob Dylan I realized that I really had no idea. I think he's a blessing, and we should all be so grateful that he's around. We have been able to avail ourselves in real-time of somebody who's thinking more clearly

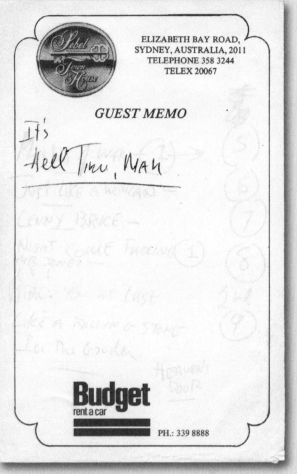

"Band of the Hand (It's Hell Time Man!)" draft manuscript

than the rest of us, and expressing it in a way that we wouldn't express it. You can say it's poetic, but actually it's just plain black and white. Whether I'd played with him or not, I've realized there is always more to learn from Bob Dylan. And his career has lasted so long, and he has continued to surprise us when we've thought he was down and out, because you can always go back to Bob and there's more there. And you don't need to be some scholar, because if you're living in a world with such beauty—like if you were present at the eruption of Vesuvius—just look up. You know? Look up. So everybody should just be grateful. And never, ever try to second-guess Bob Dylan."

DYLAN & THE DEAD

Dylan and the Grateful Dead had been admirers of each other's music since the late 1960s, though they wouldn't collaborate until two decades later. In early June 1987, Dylan traveled to San Rafael, California, to rehearse with the Grateful Dead for an upcoming series of stadium dates. They jammed informally at the Dead's Le Club Front recording and rehearsal studio, running through a number of songs by The Carter Family, Delmore Brothers, Ian & Sylvia, Freddie King, Chuck Willis, and Hank Williams. The Dead also suggested a number of songs from across Dylan's career, many of which he hadn't performed in decades, if at all. Dylan described what it was like to reconnect with these songs in *Chronicles*:

> *I had no feelings for any of these songs and didn't know how I could sing them with any intent. A lot of them might have only been sung once anyway, the time they'd been recorded. . . . I needed sets of lyrics to understand what they were talking about, and when I saw the lyrics, especially to the older, more obscure songs, I couldn't see how I could get this stuff off emotionally.*

In grappling with this older material, Dylan had to dig deep and identify new techniques, as well as reconnect with older ones, that would allow him to go beyond what he refers to in *Chronicles* as "the world of words." Though Dylan may have thought this approach "so simple, so elemental," the breakthrough reinvigorated Dylan's relationship to these songs, and to live performance in general, propelling him into the next chapter of his life on the road.

Dylan and the Dead performed a half-dozen stadium gigs throughout the month of July on the East and West Coasts. Several of the shows were recorded, and highlights were compiled on the 1989 album, *Dylan & the Dead*.

Dylan and the Dead tour song list, circa 1987

© 1988 CBS Records Inc. Permission to reproduce this photography is limited to editorial uses in regular issues of newspapers and other regularly published periodicals and television news programming.

Columbia
8812

FRONT ROW, L–R: Jerry Garcia, Bob Dylan, Bob Weir
BACK ROW, L–R: Brent Mydland, Mickey Hart, Phil Lesh, Bill Kreutzmann, *Dylan & the Dead* album publicity photo, 1988. Photograph by Herb Greene

Each concert would begin with a long set by the Dead, after which Dylan would join them to perform a dozen or so of his own songs. The first show of the tour—on the Fourth of July at Sullivan Stadium in Foxboro, Massachusetts—featured "John Brown" and "Chimes of Freedom," two songs that Dylan hadn't attempted since the early 1960s, as well as the first-ever live performance of "Queen Jane Approximately." "Joey," from *Desire* (1976), also made its live debut, at the urging of Jerry Garcia; Dylan would play the song live more than eighty times over the course of the next fifteen years.

PAGES 422-423: Bob Dylan, George Gershwin Celebration Concert, Brooklyn Academy of Music, NYC, March 11, 1987. Photograph by Larry Busacca

As Natural as Breathing

1988–2000

A lot of people don't like the road, but it's as natural to me as breathing. I do it because I'm driven to do it, and I either hate it or love it. I'm mortified to be on the stage, but then again, it's the only place where I'm happy. It's the only place you can be who you want to be.

—September 1997, Jon Pareles interview,
The New York Times

Bob Dylan, 1993. Photograph by Randee St. Nicholas

Bob Dylan, Los Angeles, May 18, 1993.
Photograph by Merlyn Rosenberg

HITTING RESET

Live performance had gotten stale for Dylan, and he'd strongly considered retiring altogether while on an eighteen-month tour with Tom Petty and the Heartbreakers. "My own songs had become strangers to me, I didn't have the skill to touch their raw nerves, couldn't penetrate the surfaces," Dylan recalled in *Chronicles*. "There was a hollow singing in my heart and I couldn't wait to retire and fold the tent."

Dylan's malaise came to a head on October 5, 1987. As Dylan recalled in *Chronicles*, "it all fell apart" during an outdoor concert at the Piazza Grande Locarno in Locarno, Switzerland.

> *For an instant I fell into a black hole. . . . I opened my mouth to sing and the air tightened up—vocal presence was extinguished and nothing came out. The techniques weren't working.*
>
> *Figuring I had nothing to lose and not needing to take any precautions, I conjured up some different type of mechanism to jump-start the other techniques that weren't working. . . . Instantly, it was like a thoroughbred had charged through the gates. Everything came back, and it came back in multidimension. Even I was surprised. . . . Now the energy was coming from a hundred different angles, completely unpredictable ones. I had a new faculty and it seemed to surpass all the other human requirements. . . . It was like I'd become a new performer, an unknown one in the true sense of the word. In more than thirty years of performing, I had never seen this place before, never been here.*

Rejuvenated, Dylan assembled a new band with G. E. Smith on guitar, Kenny Aaronson on bass, and Christopher Parker on drums for his Interstate 88 Tour. On June 7, 1988. they kicked off the tour in Concord, California. With the exception of 2020, the start of the global COVID-19 pandemic, Dylan has toured annually to the present day.

Although fans have referred to Dylan's schedule since 1988 as the Never Ending Tour, Dylan himself has rejected the sobriquet. Not only have some of his tours been individually named, they've involved a revolving cast of musicians throughout the years. As Dylan wrote in the liner notes for his 1993 album, *World Gone Wrong*:

> *by the way, don't be bewildered by the Never Ending Tour chatter. there was a Never Ending Tour but it ended in '91 with the departure of guitarist G. E. Smith. that one's long gone but there have been many others since then. The Money Never Runs Out Tour (fall of '91) Southern Sympathizer Tour (early '92) Why Do You Look At Me So Strangley [sic] Tour (European '92) The One Sad Cry of Pity Tour (Australia & West Coast America '92) Principles Of Action Tour (Mexico—South American '92) Outburst Of Consciousness Tour ('92) Don't Let Your Deal Go Down Tour ('93) & others too many to mention each with their own character & design. to know which was which consult the playlists.*

428

Concert posters, 1990–1994

Bob Dylan, Roseland Ballroom, NYC, October 1994. Photograph by Larry Busacca

A VISION SHARED

Dylan has always been a keen interpreter of others' songs, and cover songs feature heavily not only in live performances, but also in rehearsals. The mix of original and cover songs on this Parker Méridien notepad seems to match a recording of a tour rehearsal held at the Power Station in New York City in May 1989. Dylan would also integrate some of these cover songs into his sets throughout the following years. Dylan only performed Chuck Berry's "Nadine (Is It You?)" once, on June 17, 1988, whereas the 1956 Sonny Knight hit "Confidential" appeared about a dozen times between 1989 and 1991. (Dylan also sang it in 1956 on an acetate, which many believe is his first recording.)

"The Buffalo Skinners" or "Trail of the Buffalo" is a traditional song that Dylan had been performing since early in his career. One can hear it as part of the so-called East Orange Tape, an informal recording made in February or March 1961 at the home of Bob and Sid Gleason, whom Dylan had befriended in his quest to meet Woody Guthrie upon arriving in New York City. Guthrie's influence is obvious in Dylan's 1961 recording. In 1967, Dylan again recorded the song as "The Hills of Mexico" during *The Basement Tapes* sessions. Two decades later, Dylan returned to the song during the 1987 rehearsals with the Grateful Dead, and he later performed it on numerous occasions between 1988 and 1992.

Song list, late 1980s

In 1988, Dylan recorded "Pretty Boy Floyd," a Guthrie protest ballad romanticizing the famous bank robber as a modern-day Robin Hood, for the compilation *Folkways: A Vision Shared—A Tribute to Woody Guthrie & Leadbelly*. Produced by folk impresario Harold Leventhal—Guthrie's former manager and promoter for Dylan's 1963 Town Hall concert and the 1968 tribute concert to Woody Guthrie—the album featured other figures inspired by the legacies of Guthrie, Lead Belly, and Folkways Records, including Emmylou Harris, Taj Mahal, John Mellencamp, Bruce Springsteen, and U2. That same year, it won the GRAMMY Award for Best Traditional Folk Album.

In a circa 1988 notepad that is part of the Bob Dylan Archive, Dylan wrote out the lyrics for not just "Pretty Boy Floyd," but another of Guthrie's *Dust Bowl Ballads*, "Vigilante Man." Dylan later recorded "Vigilante Man" and Guthrie's "Do Re Mi" along with guitarist Ry Cooder and pianist Van Dyke Parks during a filmed performance for the 2008 film *The People Speak*, a tribute to the *People's History of the United States*, written by Howard Zinn.

```
        BUFFALO SKINNERS

IN THE TOWN OF JACKSBORO IN  THE  YEAR OF SEVENTY  THREE
A MAN BY THE NAME OF CREGO CAME  STEPPING UP TO ME
SAID HOWJADO YOUNG FELLA & HOW'D YOU LIKE  TO GO
& SPEND THE SUMMER  PLEASENT ON THE RANGE OF THE BUFFALO

WELL ME BEING OUT OF  EMPLOYMENT TO OLD  CREGO I DID SAY
GOING OUT ON THE BUFFALO  RANGE DEPENDS UPON THE PAY
BUT IF YOU PAY GOOD  WAGES TRANSPORTATION  TO & FRO
WELL I GUESS SUR  I MIGHT GO WITH   YOU TO THE RANGE OF THE BUFFALO


WELL OUR OUTFIT  WAS SOON COMPLETED  SEVEN ABLE BODIED MEN
WITH NAVY SIX &  NEEDLE GUNS OUR TRIP IT DID BEGIN
OUR TRIP IT WAS   A PLEASANT ONE THE WAY WE HAD TO GO
UNTIL WE CROSSED PEEZE  RIVER IN THE RANGE  OF THE BUFFALO

WHEN WE CROSSED PEEZE  RIVER OUR TROUBLES  SOON BEGUN
FIRST DAMN  TAIL I WENT TO RIP WELL HOW I CUT MY THUMB
SKINNING   THE DAMNED OLD STICKERS OUR LIVES THEY HAD NO SHOW
OUTLSAWS WAITING  TO  PICK US OFF FROM THE HILLS MEXICO

OUR HEARTS WERE CASED  WITH BUFFALO HAWKS & OUR SOULS WERE CASED WITH STEEL
&XHURXTHIX T E HARDSHIPS OF THE SUMMER IT MADE THE STRONGEST KNEEL
WATER SALTY AS HELL FIRE & THE BEEF WE COULD NOT  GO
INDIANS WAITING TO PICK  US OFF  IN THE HILLS OF THE BUFFALO

OUR SUMMER BEING ABOUT OVER,  OLD CREGO HE DDD SAY
YOU BOYS HAVE BEEN  EXTRVEGANT YOURE ALL IN DEBT TO ME
WE BEGGED & WE  PLEADED  BUT STILL IT WAS NO GO
SO WE LEFT  THAT DROVERS BONES TO BLEACH  ON THE HILLS OF THE BUFFALO


AGAIN WE CROSSED PEEZE  RIVER HOMEWARD WE ARE BOUND
NO MORE OF THAT HELL FIRE  CONNTRY  WILL EVER WE BE FOUND
GO HOME TO WIVES & SWEETHEARTS  TELL OTHERS NOT TO GO
GOD HAS FORSAKEN THE BUFFALO RANGE & THE DAMNED OLD BUFFALO
```

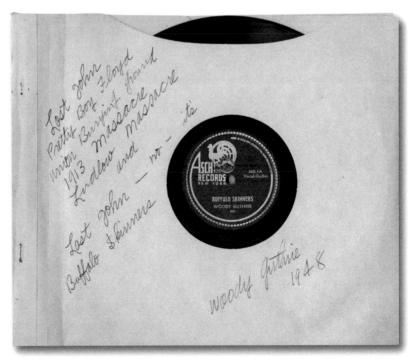

Woody Guthrie's annotated copy of *Struggle: Documentary #1*, 1946, 78 rpm album

THE TRAVELING WILBURYS

The Traveling Wilburys, L–R: Bob Dylan, Jeff Lynne, Tom Petty, George Harrison, Roy Orbison, 1988. Photograph by Neal Preston

THE WILBURYS ARE COMING

In the spring of 1988, while George Harrison was promoting his latest album, *Cloud 9*, Warner Bros. asked him to record a new song for a B-side to the single for "This Is Love." Jeff Lynne, the producer of *Cloud 9*, suggested Harrison work on a new song at Dylan's garage studio in Malibu. Roy Orbison, who had been spending time in Los Angeles and working with Lynne, came along, and Tom Petty entered the picture after Harrison asked to borrow one of Petty's guitars.

"Handle with Care" was the result of this April 3, 1988, session. Mo Ostin, the chief executive at Warner Bros., later recalled that after hearing the track,

> Our reaction was immediate. This was a song we knew could not be wasted on some B-side. . . .
> The guys had really nailed it. Lenny [Waronker] and I stumbled over each other's words asking,
> "Can't we somehow turn this into an album?"

George Harrison is responsible for the name the band landed upon: The Traveling Wilburys. While he and Lynne were working on *Cloud 9*, they'd often say, "We'll bury it in the mix," if a mistake happened during recording. "We'll bury" was shortened to "Wilbury." Adding to the lightheartedness of the collaboration, each member assumed a pseudonym: Nelson Wilbury (George Harrison), Otis Wilbury (Jeff Lynne), Lefty Wilbury (Roy Orbison), Charlie T. Wilbury Jr. (Tom Petty), and Lucky Wilbury (Bob Dylan).

Recorded at Eurythmics member Dave Stewart's studio in Los Angeles in May 1988, *Traveling Wilburys Vol. 1* was released on October 18 to overwhelming critical and commercial success. A series of postcards announcing "The Wilburys Are Coming" were used to announce the album's arrival, which Harrison used to write a note to Dylan. Released as a single, "Handle with Care" won the 1990 GRAMMY Award for Best Rock Performance by a Duo or Group.

Promotional postcard, 1988

On December 6, 1988, less than two months after the release of *Traveling Wilburys Vol. 1*, Roy Orbison died of a heart attack. In the video for their next single, "End of the Line," the group paid tribute to their bandmate with a guitar on an empty rocking chair and a photograph of a young Orbison.

Oct. 30th. 88.

Dear Bob,
I hope you are O.K
after the last 6 months, maybe you
can have a rest. I personally am a
nervous wreck but would like to think
I can recover myself again eventually!
Anyway I want you to know that it
was great being in the band with you—and
you were very generous in being a Wilbury!
thanks for doing the record and video
and I hope it was not too embarassing
for you; who knows — maybe we will
meet again someday on the avenue.
All the best and don't lose Joannie's
phone number — love from
George. 卐

Friar Park Studio, Henley-on-Thames, Oxfordshire, RG9 4NR, England

Letter from George Harrison to Bob Dylan, October 30, 1988

The remaining members reunited to record a second album in the spring of 1990, produced again by Harrison and Lynne. The name of the album—*Traveling Wilburys Vol. 3*—came at Harrison's suggestion as another playful ruse on the part of the band. Released on October 29, 1990, the album went platinum in the United States.

The Traveling Wilburys reissue campaign promotional sticker, 2007

DOWN IN THE GROOVE

Down in the Groove alternate album cover mockup. Photograph by Peter J. Carni

Like Dylan's previous two albums, *Down in the Groove* emerged from a set of recording sessions held across a period of six months that featured a large cast of musicians, including Eric Clapton, guitarist Steve Jones of The Sex Pistols, and bassist Paul Simonon of The Clash. The album featured numerous cover songs, including "Shenandoah," Wilbert Harrison's "Let's Stick Together," and Albert E. Brumley's bluegrass classic "Rank Strangers to Me," which became a highlight of Dylan's live sets in 1989.

Down in the Groove also contained originals, including "Silvio" and "Ugliest Girl in the World," which Dylan co-wrote with Grateful Dead lyricist Robert Hunter. "Silvio," which featured Jerry Garcia, Bob Weir, and Brent Mydland from the Dead on backing vocals, became a fan favorite, earning a place on *Bob Dylan's Greatest Hits Vol. 3* in 1994. "Death Is Not the End" was an outtake from *Infidels*, on which Dylan brought in the notable hip-hop and R&B group Full Force to overdub a vocal chorus. (This was not Dylan's first foray into the world of hip-hop, however; he'd previously rapped a verse for Kurtis Blow's 1986 song "Street Rock.") "Had a Dream About You, Baby" was a garage rocker featuring Ronnie Wood of The Rolling Stones on guitar.

AS NATURAL AS BREATHING

ONE NIGHT AT THE PALOMINO

Down in the Groove was eventually compiled from the highlights of five recording sessions held between March and June 1987. For each session, Dylan assembled a new band, largely running them through different sets of blues, country, and R&B cover songs.

The first of these sessions on March 5 featured members of the group that accompanied John Trudell on *aka Graffiti Man*, which Dylan had told *Rolling Stone* was the best record of 1986. That band was led by Jesse Ed Davis, the Oklahoma-born Native American guitarist whose searing slide work had been a crucial component of Dylan's 1971 single "Watching the River Flow." (Trudell, a noted author, poet, and Native American activist, was featured in Dylan's 2022 book *The Philosophy of Modern Song*, which has Dylan's analysis of "Doesn't Hurt Anymore.")

The wheels for this reunion may have been set in motion just a few weeks before the session, when Dylan, George Harrison, and John Fogerty attended a February 19, 1987, concert of Taj Mahal and the Graffiti Band featuring Trudell at the Palomino Club in Los Angeles. As the evening wore on, the concert turned into a jam session, with the three guests taking the stage to run through a full set of covers and originals from across their careers, including "Watching the River Flow."

L–R: John Trudell, Bob Dylan (top), George Harrison (bottom), Jesse Ed Davis, Palomino Club, Los Angeles, February 19, 1987. Photograph by Abe Perlstein

Hendrix and Dylan

GREG TATE

In Jimi Hendrix's telling, he and Bob Dylan only met once in the flesh, at a club on MacDougal Street, and they were both drunk. A hangout buddy of Hendrix apocryphally recalls another crossroads, however—in her version, the two crossed paths while Hendrix was cruising in a limo and Dylan was on a bicycle, and a whole lotta awkwardness then ensued.

Hendrix's love affair with Dylan's songwriting began before either entered the pop Valhalla of household names. Before Hendrix shipped off to the UK in 1966 to pursue rock superstardom, he lived in Harlem with BFF Fayne (a.k.a. Lithofayne) Pridgon. By Pridgon's account, she couldn't go to the bathroom without Hendrix waylaying her, insisting that she not miss any of the lyrical nuances erupting from their turntable. A device whose decibel count, Pridgon says, was so ear-splitting when Dylan was playing that it could be heard as far from uptown as the East Village. "We almost got put out of our apartment behind Bob Dylan." Fascinating to think of Dylan as Hendrix's personal headbanger's ball.

At the 1967 Monterey Pop festival that broke Hendrix in America, he also debuted his ardor for Dylan with a cocky and mackadocious rendition of "Like a Rolling Stone," Dylan's only chart-busting radio hit. Produced by the rocksteady Tom Wilson, it hung out at the number two spot on radio for weeks, as The Beatles' "Help!" refused to be dislodged from number one. The success of "Rolling Stone," pushing six and a half minutes of proto-rap wordiness, presaged the breakthrough fourteen years later of The Sugar Hill Gang's "Rapper's Delight" performing its miracle work of planting fifteen minutes of vernacular versifying on radio when three minutes was the vinyl ceiling for broadcasters back then.

Hendrix croons "Rolling Stone" in an admixture of his own hipster drawl and a devotional impersonation of Dylan's sing-songy twang. At Monterey, Hendrix and his Experience devoted half their set to revved-up cover versions of tunes by B. B. King, Howlin' Wolf, The Troggs, Billy Roberts, and Dylan, culminating in the gig's famous guitar-splintering, feedback-bantering, and butane-aided paroxysm of a finale—so well captured by documentarian D. A. Pennebaker, who'd already gifted the world with *Dont Look Back*'s historic footage of Dylan on tour in England, and in an alley playing hand jive with a sequence of sheets containing lines from his jaunty pre-rap jam, "Subterranean Homesick Blues."

Among the four originals the Experience premiered at Monterey was "The Wind Cried Mary," which Dylan would later declare was one of his two favorite Hendrix-penned tunes (the other being "Dolly Dagger," a tribute to another of Hendrix's BFFs, Devon Wilson).

"Mary" is one of several where you can hear Hendrix's personal best attempt to write something as symbolist and ingenious as an early Dylan song. With its wan fairy tale imagery of dreary, anthropomorphized brooms and doleful royalty, the tune also boldly provides a reification of happiness, identified as a thing audibly staggering down the street.

The posthumously released *Cry of Love* contains a personal favorite of Hendrix's unabashed oblations into Dylan's metaphoric influence: "My Friend," a barroom-set fable whose fantastical elements abet the story of a narrator who has come to only trust his shadow:

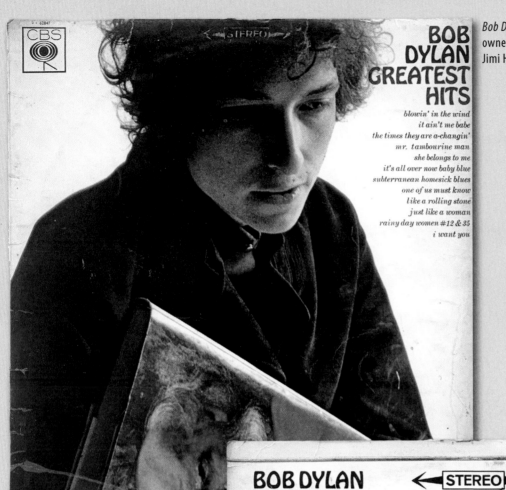

BOB
DYLAN
GREATEST
HITS

blowin' in the wind
it ain't me babe
the times they are a-changin'
mr. tambourine man
she belongs to me
it's all over now baby blue
subterranean homesick blues
one of us must know
like a rolling stone
just like a woman
rainy day women #12 & 35
i want you

Bob Dylan Greatest Hits,
owned and annotated by
Jimi Hendrix, circa 1967

BOB DYLAN GREATEST HITS

← STEREO →

Side 1
BLOWIN' IN THE WIND* (2.46)
IT AIN'T ME BABE† (3.50)
THE TIMES THEY ARE A-CHANGIN'† (3.12)
MR. TAMBOURINE MAN† (5.25)
SHE BELONGS TO ME‡ (2.48)
IT'S ALL OVER NOW BABY BLUE† (4.13)

Production: JOHN HAMMOND* TOM WILSON† BOB JOHNSON‡

Side 2
SUBTERRANEAN HOMESICK BLUES† (2.1)
ONE OF US MUST KNOW‡ (4.59)
LIKE A ROLLING STONE‡ (5.59)
JUST LIKE A WOMAN‡ (4.57)
RAINY DAY WOMEN NOS. 12 & 35‡ (2.06)
I WANT YOU‡ (2.57)

(S) 62022

(S) 62193

(S) 62251

(S) 62515

(S) DDP 66012

(S) 62572

CBS is a Trademark of the Columbia Broadcasting System, Inc., U.S.A.
Recorded in the U.S.A. by CBS Records, a Division of Columbia Broadcasting System, Inc.

Printed and made by Garrod & Lofthouse Ltd. Patents pending

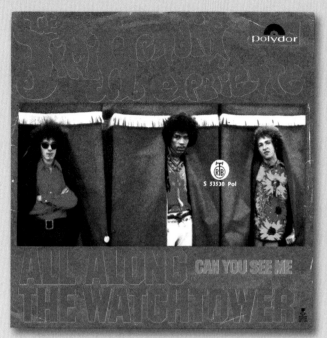

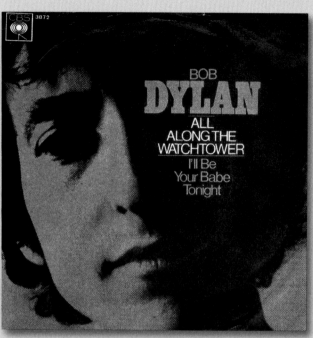

Jimi Hendrix, "All Along the Watchtower" 45 rpm single, Europe, 1968   Bob Dylan, "All Along the Watchtower" 45 rpm single, Germany, 1968

A stagecoach full of feathers and footprints
Pulls up to my soap-box door
Now a lady with a pearl-handled necktie
Tied to the driver's fence
Breathes in my face
Bourbon and coke possessed words
Haven't I seen you somewhere in hell
Or was it just an accident?

Hendrix engineer/co-producer Eddie Kramer long ago revealed Jimi was so self-conscious about his voice that he demanded protective screens go up in the studio every time he had to cut vocals on the mic. But Hendrix admitted that it was Dylan's utterly shameless and fearless bark that gave him the courage to sing at all. Hendrix, having spent the first half of his career as a sideman on tours featuring the church-trained legends of '60s soul, likely measured his instrument besides theirs and found it wanting. So had Hendrix not been emboldened by Dylan to sing the folk balladry of "Hey Joe" when his first manager Chas Chandler was lurking within earshot, there's a fair chance the world may have never heard Hendrix the angelic balladeer of "Castles Made of Sand," "Little Wing," "Have You Ever Been? (To Electric Ladyland)," and "Angel," or the neo-hoodoo blues belter of "Red House," "Hear My Train A Comin'," and "Voodoo Child (Slight Return)."

For his part, Dylan, years after Hendrix's death, let the world know how much respect he had for Jimi as a transformational, guitar-slinging artist, and most especially as an interpreter of Dylan's own material—"All Along the Watchtower" not least such.

When Hendrix claims "All Along the Watchtower" as his own on his well-painted masterpiece, *Electric Ladyland,* there's nothing timorous about his designs on the original. Hendrix treats Dylan's version in a manner akin to that with which Michelangelo went at that mythical block of fungible and metamorphic stone, from which the sculptor carved his epic and divine David.

Dylan's lyrics gift vocal agency to a pair of jumpy Renaissance-fair stragglers beset by apocalyptic forces in the wilderness. Hendrix sonically raises the stakes, staging the ditty with production values straight outta CinemaScope. Dressing the prophetic scene with percussive acoustics, martial drumming, and ionized blues licks, Hendrix delivers a spirited and fiery vocal charged with an evangelical and desperate alarm well met by the battleground year of 1968.

Dylan says he became so enamored of Hendrix's version that he now considers his ongoing concert performances of the song a "tribute" to Jimi:

> It overwhelmed me, really. He had such talent; he could find things inside a song and vigorously develop them. He found things that other people wouldn't think of finding in there. He probably improved upon it by the spaces he was using. I took license with the song from his version, actually, and continue to do it to this day.

Dylan goes further with praise of Hendrix, though, effusively offering, "It's not a wonder to me that he recorded my songs, but rather that he recorded so few of them because they were all his."

"Sometimes I do a Dylan song and it seems to fit me so right that I figure maybe I wrote it," Hendrix mused. "I felt like 'Watchtower' was something I'd written but could never get together. I often feel like that about Dylan."

During a 2015 acceptance speech for the MusiCares Person of the Year, Dylan implored, "We can't forget Jimi Hendrix. . . . He took some small songs of mine that nobody paid any attention to and brought them up into the outer limits of the stratosphere—turned them all into classics."

The public perception of Hendrix and Dylan early in their careers is tinged with a bit of racial irony. Dylan became adopted by the civil rights movement for his many early songs that anthemically took up the banner. He was also frequently interpreted in the era by a bevy of artists who formed the movement's vocal frontline: Odetta, Nina Simone, Richie Havens, Stevie Wonder. Because of his for-whites-only rock-star marketing Hendrix got outrageously mistaken for a race-traitor by certain Black Power individuals. All those pale blonde groupie photo-ops and Anglo bandmates riling their tender knee-jerk militant micro sensitivities.

This writer's good buddy, trumpeter Lewis "Flip" Barnes, was one of them in 1969. Flip grew up in a tense and volatile desegregating Virginia Beach in the late '60s. He recollects being shocked when his card-carrying Black Panther Party cousin "Stevie" damn near demanded he go see Hendrix at a local arena. Flip was taken aback given how *not* down with the cause he'd assumed Hendrix to be. After the show, he reported back to Stevie that as exhilarated as he was after standing next to Hendrix's fire, he was more reeled by "seeing all these white boys who called me 'nigger' all day long in high school acting like they were dying to hand their girlfriends over to Hendrix." (The Black Panther citing in this story is further noteworthy because of the twenty hours BPP founders Huey Newton and Bobby Seale spent replaying Dylan's "Ballad of a Thin Man" for inspiration while composing the Panthers' ten-point platform and manifesto.)

Hendrix took his own sweet time becoming an artist who openly exposed any overt political messaging. His evolution into a more street-fighting Hendrix nearly coincides with Dylan's timely withdrawal from the polemic-lyric frontlines as the integrationist civil rights commune morphed into Black Power's community members only anti-all-things-whitey stance. Such racialized camp-following was not to be Hendrix's fate, however.

His devotion to his great white bard undimmed, Hendrix turns Dylan's panegyric into a chart-racing (#8 with a bullet) jeremiad. Jimi's crescendoing guitar and voice providing demonstrations

it's always nice when another performer takes one of your songs
& does it. usually someone has his own point of view on things
& the lyrics correspond to what he's thinking in some kind of
way & the two meet up. my songs were not written with the idea
in mind that anybody else would sing them. they were written for
me to play live & that is sort of the end of it. i knew jimi
slightly before he became a big star, never saw him much after
that. naturally there was a strong connection because we came
from the same time, similar environments & had more or less the
same likes & dislikes, attitudes & experiences. when i first heard
jimi, he was basically a blues player but unlike everybody else
outside of the old authentic guys, he was young & he was the real
thing. getting back to the songwriting part, it cant be expected
that a performer get under the song, inside & blow it out. it's
like getting inside of another person's soul. most people have
enough trouble getting inside of their own souls & to take on
another one, really most of the time cant be worth the ride. of
course there are different degrees. like for instance, there's not
too much to getting into a chuck berry song. it's all pretty much
there on the surface. you just kind of learn the riffs, mouth the
words & they sing themselves. xxxxxxxxxxxing you dont have to go
far. anybody with half an ear can do it. same thing with the beatles.
you learn the chords & sing the words & youre a beatle. there's
no pain xxxxxx involved here. youre just doing songs that fly along,
dont step on anybody's toes & ▬▬ having a good time doing it. my
songs are different & i dont expect others to make attempts to sing
them because you have to get somewhat inside & behind them & it's
hard enough for me to do it sometimes & then obviously you have
to be in the right frame of mind. but even then there would be a
vague value to it because nobody breathes like me so they couldnt
be expected to portray the meaning of a certain phrase in the correct
way without bumping into other phrases & altering the mood, changing
the understanding & just giving up so that they then become only
verses strung together for no apparent reason, patter for a performer
to kill time, take up space, giving heartless renditions of what
was it to begin with. jimi knew my songs were not like that. he
sang them exactly the way they were intended to be sung & he played
them the same way. he did them the way i wouldve done them if i
was him. never thought too much about it at the time but now that
years have gone by, i xxxx see that the message must have been
his message thru & thru. not that i ever could articulate the message
that well myself, but in hearing jimi cover it, i realize he mustve
felt it pretty deeply inside & out & that somewhere xxxx back there,
his soul & my soul were on the same desert. i cant speak as a
musician but as a songwriter, it's always a humbling feeling to
know that other musicians like your stuff especially if you really
respect them. audiences & xxixx critics give important feedback
but there's nothing like another performer doing what youre doing
to let you know if youre doing it well or not, if youre cutting
thru, that xxxxxx maybe it really ixxxxxxxxxxx is worth all the
time & trouble. in all my years of being on stage, it still means
more to me what other musicians & singers think & feel about my
stuff than anybody else. jimi was a great artist. i wished he
wouldve lived but he got sucked under & that's been the downfall of
alot of us. i feel he had his time & his place & he paid a price
he didnt have to pay. it's not a wonder to me that he recorded my songs
but rather that he recorded so few of them because they were all his.

                              bob dylan

"Jimi" essay, draft typescript, circa December 1988, included in *The Jimi Hendrix Exhibition* at Govinda Gallery, Washington, DC, 1993

Jimi Hendrix with Lenny Bruce, Bob Dylan, and Muddy Waters LPs, circa 1967. Photograph by Petra Niemeier

of exactly how the wind has begun to howl in the same year that dozens of American cities got set ablaze in a fury of Black empowering retaliation for the assassination of Martin Luther King.

Let's speculate a heated baton got passed through Dylan's "Watchtower," one that moved Hendrix to become a more consciously unbridled, societally attentive artist. The same cat who just a few months later will scorch heavens and earth with his electrifying epochal paeans to America's unholy war on Vietnam, "Star Spangled Banner" at Woodstock, and "Machine Gun," unleashed New Year's Eve '69 at the Fillmore East.

The circle of love and inspiration formed between Dylan and Hendrix in the moment not only reveals them vigorously completing each other, but also finds them consecrating their mutual, hip-joined legacy as the most incandescent and timeless troubadours of that bygone but still-zeitgeist-crackling age.

441   GREG TATE

In 1988, Dylan suffered a hand injury that sidelined him from live performances and songwriting. Dylan reflected on the moment in *Chronicles*, "The one thing that I had no strong desire to do was to compose songs." However, during his recovery, inspiration suddenly hit:

> *All that changed. I wrote about twenty verses for a song called "Political World" and this was about the first of twenty songs I would write in the next month or so. They came from out of the blue.*

Dylan showed some of the new lyrics to Bono, the lead singer of U2, who suggested that Dylan consider working with Daniel Lanois, the producer of U2's recent GRAMMY Award–winning album, *The Joshua Tree*. That September, Dylan met with Lanois in New Orleans, and the two decided to work together on some new material.

In the spring of 1989, Lanois, along with engineer Mark Howard, set up an ad hoc recording studio at a house they'd rented on Soniat Street in New Orleans' Uptown District. From these sessions came Dylan's *Oh Mercy*, released on September 12, 1989, an album that was widely hailed as a return to form.

The songs didn't necessarily fall into place easily in the studio, however. In the case of "Most of the Time," Dylan had lyrics, but no melody, and the song evolved slowly over the March 12 sessions. Dylan later recalled,

> *I never did come up with any definite melody, only generic chords, but Dan [Lanois] thought he heard something. Something that turned into a slow, melancholy song. On this, Danny was contributing as much as any musician. He added layers of parts and soon the song seemed to have some kind of attitude and purpose.*

The version of "Most of the Time" from *Oh Mercy* has been featured on many critics' "top Dylan songs" lists. However, Dylan continued to work on the track after its release. He recorded additional versions of the song during the sessions for his next album, *Under the Red Sky*. Dylan would go on to perform the song live three dozen times between October 1989 and May 1992.

"Political World" 45 rpm single, Netherlands, 1990

1. we livin in a political world...where love dont have any place
we livin in times/ when men commit crimes...& crime dont have any face

2. we livin in a political world...where science rules over the mind
whats been invented/ could've been prevented...by any half-hearted attempt to be kind

3. we livin in a political world...where wisdom is thrown into jail
it rots in a cell/ missguided as hell...leavin' no one to pick up the trail

4. we livin in a potical world...where truth is the outlaw of live
it's hunted & slain/ in the snow & the rain...or put under a doctor's knife

5. we livin in a political world...where the word is a broken down lie
the peddling of dreams/ nothin's what it seems...nothin more'n hello & goodbye

6. we livin in a potitical world...where mercy walks the plank
life is in mirrors/ death disappears/...up the steps into the nearest bank

7. we livin in a politcal world/ where conscience dont have any clue
you climb into bed ? & talk outa yer head...& youre not even sure that it's you

8. we livin in a political world...where courage is a thing of the past
the houses are haunted/ children are unwanted...& your next day could be your last

9. we livin i a political world...the one we can see & can feel
but there's no one to check/ it's all a stacked deck...but we all know for sure that it's real

10. we livin in a political world...under the evil star
you dont have to do much/ to get thru it untouched...but you got to find out who you are

11. we livin in a politicl world...in the ~~furnace of~~ hers & his
you'd climb ~~into~~ crawl the flame & shout G-d's name...but youre not even sure what it is

"Political World" draft typescript

Most of the time she ain't even in my mind
I wouldn't know her if I saw her, she's that far behind
Most of The Time I can't even be sure
If she was even with me or if I was even with her

$$ Most - Time I'm halfway content
Most of Time I know exactly where it all went
I don't cheat on myself I don't run & hide
Hide from my feelings That are buried inside
Don't compromise & I don't pretend
Don't care if I ever see her again
Most y - Time

New Orleans
March 10/89

"Most of the Time" draft manuscript

"Dignity" draft manuscripts

"DIGNITY"

With more than forty-five pages devoted to the song (not including entries in various notebooks), no other song in the Archive has more lyric drafts than "Dignity." Dylan first began working on the song during the 1989 *Oh Mercy* sessions, but after trying the song out in numerous arrangements—solo and with a band, on guitar and at the piano—he ultimately shelved it.

In 1994, Columbia Records brought in producer Brendan O'Brien to rework one of the "Dignity" outtakes from the *Oh Mercy* sessions, for release on *Bob Dylan's Greatest Hits Volume 3*. Dylan performed this new version at the November 18, 1994, taping of *MTV Unplugged*, with O'Brien at the organ. The song was featured on the television broadcast and accompanying live album, and was released as a single.

AS NATURAL AS BREATHING

Bob Dylan and Stevie Wonder, GRAMMY Awards, Los Angeles, February 24, 1984. Photographer unknown

STEVIE WONDER

Stevie Wonder was inducted into the Rock & Roll Hall of Fame on January 1, 1989, and Dylan, who had been inducted as part of the inaugural class of 1988, penned an essay for *Rolling Stone* in honor of Wonder's talent and influence. Dylan and Wonder had been longtime admirers of one another's music, dating back to Wonder's 1966 cover of "Blowin' in the Wind," which went to #9 on the *Billboard* Hot 100 and #1 on the R&B chart.

Dylan and Wonder shared the same stage on a number of occasions in the 1980s, co-presenting at the 1984 GRAMMY Awards, and singing together at the "We Are the World" sessions. On January 20, 1986, Dylan and Wonder appeared together at the Kennedy Center for the Performing Arts in Washington, DC, as part of *An All-Star Celebration Honoring Martin Luther King Jr.*, where they performed Wonder's "The Bells of Freedom" and "Happy Birthday" and Dylan's "I Shall Be Released" and "Blowin' in the Wind" (with Peter, Paul and Mary). In 1992, as part of Dylan's *30th Anniversary Concert Celebration*, Wonder took the stage to perform "Blowin' in the Wind," which he introduced as a song that "will always be relevant to something that is going on in this world of ours."

```
stevie wonder can do it all. he is a great performer, great singer,
                        writer
great musician, great xxxxxx. xxxxxxxxxxxxxxxxxxxxxxxxxxxxxxxxxxxxx
xxxxxxxxxxxxxxxxxxxxxx if anybody can be called a genius, he can be.
```

Bob Dylan's *Rolling Stone* tribute to Stevie Wonder, draft typescript, circa 1989

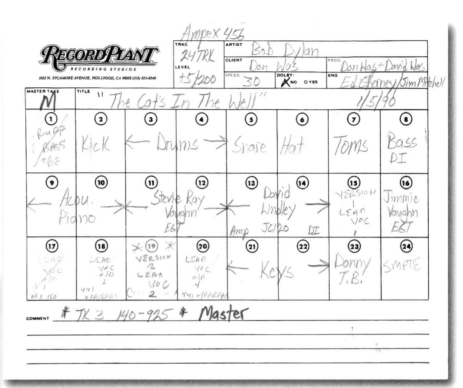

"The Cat's in the Well" track sheet

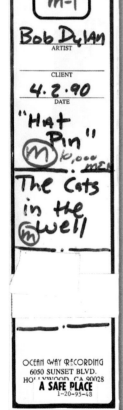

Under the Red Sky audiotape box

Released on September 10, 1990, *Under the Red Sky* was the first album including a producer credit for "Jack Frost," alongside brothers Don and David Was. ("Jack Frost" shows up numerous times on subsequent Dylan albums, and many assume that it's a pseudonym for Bob Dylan.) Three of the songs—"Born in Time," "God Knows," and "TV Talkin' Song"—were songs he'd attempted during the *Oh Mercy* sessions, whereas others were newly composed for the album. Despite the seeming simplicity of the lyrical themes on the album, drafts of the lyric manuscripts in the Archive reinforce Dylan's never-ceasing attention to detail.

Under the Red Sky included a number of high-profile guest musicians, among them David Crosby, Bruce Hornsby, Randy Jackson (who later hosted the *American Idol* TV show), Elton John, Al Kooper, and Jimmie Vaughan, with featured guitar solos by Slash ("Wiggle Wiggle"), Stevie Ray Vaughan ("10,000 Men"), and George Harrison ("Under the Red Sky"). Although the album did not receive the same praise as his previous record, *Oh Mercy*, the album's first single, "Unbelievable," reached #20 on the *Billboard* Mainstream Rock chart, with a music video featuring Dylan alongside actors Molly Ringwald and Sally Kirkland.

AS NATURAL AS BREATHING

Original photograph used for cover of *Under the Red Sky*, Mojave Desert, California, circa 1990. Photograph by Camouflage Photo

Is "Handy Dandy" Another Bob Dylan Alias?

LARRY SLOMAN

After a series of undistinguished albums in the '80s, 1989's *Oh Mercy* was seen by most rock critics as a triumph for Dylan, a true return to form. But when *Under the Red Sky* was released a year later, the critics got their knives out again. "One of the worst albums of his career," "sloppily written songs, lazily performed," "most of the lyrics seem like first drafts," "lyrics were mostly like nursery rhymes, sung with no apparent attention." The album's opening song, "Wiggle Wiggle," came in for the harshest criticism, making many Top Ten Worst Bob Dylan songs lists. One critic wrote, "'Wiggle Wiggle' sounds like the theme song to one of those tripped-out television shows beloved by toddlers and drug users."

So was *Under the Red Sky really* one of Bob's worst albums? I beg to differ.

* * *

There are quite a few songs that deserve rigorous inquiry on the *Under the Red Sky* album. But I think "Handy Dandy" is the one song from that album that stands out, as the music and the lyrics work together seamlessly to paint a portrait of the artist as a middle-aged man. For me, it's one of the most personal and autobiographical songs in Bob's canon.

"Handy Dandy" came out of a long jam. Right before they began recording the song, Bob told the producer Don Was about the time he had been to a Miles Davis mixing session. The band had improvised for about an hour and then the producer, Teo Macero, cut the song down to a coherent five minutes. So they decided to do the same thing with "Handy Dandy." The take went for thirty-four minutes, with Bob calling out the chords through the headphones and then saying "go to the bridge" at the right time. Both Jimmie and Stevie Ray Vaughan laid down some amazing solos. Then Bob and Don began to craft the jam into a song.

Dylan didn't show Don the lyrics to "Handy Dandy" until he came into the studio a few weeks later and overdubbed them. So let's take a look at the final version and then see how the critics received them.

"Handy Dandy" seemed to be "contaminated" by the visceral reaction to some of the other songs on *Under the Red Sky*. In his *Rolling Stone* review, Paul Evans writes, "The drag is that Dylan doesn't have much to say—or a really memorable way to say it."

Of course, I beg to differ.

Oliver Trager, who wrote *Keys to the Rain: The Definitive Bob Dylan Encyclopedia*, seems to inch closer to our pal, Handy.

> What a fabulous character this Handy Dandy is—a charming rogue who could have walked off the pages of a Damon Runyon story or be found sipping absinthe in an after-hours Storyville bucket-of-blood a century ago . . . "Handy Dandy" portrays a guy

PAGE 450: Bob Dylan, 1993. Photograph by Randee St. Nicholas

451

LARRY SLOMAN

not to be messed with. He visits the wrong women, hangs with the wrong friends, plays with guns, drinks too much, and leaves an ever-ballooning bar tab. Love him or hate him, he demands to be dealt with.

All right, I think the picture is coming a bit more into focus here. This isn't a frivolous song with throwaway lyrics. Handy Dandy "demands to be dealt with."

Which brings us finally to the dueling Dylan academics—Michael Gray and Christopher Ricks. Both men believe "Handy Dandy" is a brilliant piece of work, drawing on nursery rhymes, Shakespeare, the Bible, T. S. Eliot, and a hip vernacular to paint a portrait of our hero, Handy. Except that one of them (Gray) thinks it's a "warm, humorous—often black humorous—hymn of celebration to human quirkiness and flexibility," while the other (Ricks) sees it as a scary cautionary tale of a "scoundrel," a "shady character," a drug dealer or a gangster or a denizen of a "polymorphous perverse world."

For Ricks, the song is "a sequence of filmy moments, or photo opportunities, about the life-and-death styles of the rich and famous. Or infamous." I concur that this is a song about the lifestyles of the rich and famous, especially one that famously lives in a mansion, albeit with windows, in Malibu. But I don't see Handy Dandy as a gangster or a sexual deviate or a drug dealer. What I see when I look at the entire song is a poignant portrayal of a rich and famous entertainer who despite all the crazed adulation ("the voice of the promise of the '60s counterculture") finds, like Kinky Friedman says, that "money can buy you a fine dog, but only love can make him wag his tail." Is Handy Dandy really the poet laureate of rock 'n' roll in disguise?

* * *

Thanks to the Bob Dylan Archive, we can chart the evolution of the lyrics of "Handy Dandy." There's a folder with about eight pages of either typewritten text, handwritten scribbling, or both on the same page, where Dylan has painstakingly worked on the words to this song, despite what some of the critics viewed as "first draft" lyrics.

I've had to guess at the chronology of the pages, since none of them are dated. But what seems to be the oldest page contains eight numbered verses with edits done on the same page. Here we have the first verse as "handy dandy controversy always surrounds him," but then a change from the final draft, "wherever he goes too bad for him something bad there always hounds him." The second verse goes, "handy dandy he's in a room pacing the floor that supports him / in better times anything he desired would have just kept walking on pushing toward him." The third stanza adds detail to our main character—"handy dandy tower of strength and stability / he does it with mirrors but he don't really do actually / he don't need to lie cause he's so full of humility / accessible." Then the fourth—"handy dandy compulsive and healthy, plausible obsessive automatic / blowing his horn for the girls & bringing them up to the attic." The fifth verse starts with a handwritten line, "Does he wear dark sunglasses, well yeah. Does he know he's so stupid, ignorant & blind well maybe."

The sixth verse is unedited and reads, "He's in a room full of people & suddenly there's nobody cheering / He says c'mon baby let's both take the wheel to this car it don't matter who is steering." In the next verse, he returns to the room: "He's in a strange room & suddenly there's nobody looking" "He slips into a shadow he slips until no one is aware of him." The last numbered verse, 8, reads, "handy dandy pissing on the (rug) floor of a penthouse / quiet as a churchmouse." Then

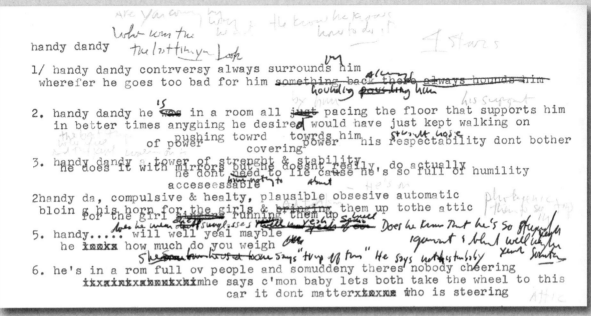

there's a number of striking disparate images—"He's standing in front of a used car dealership." "Singing the song of redemption he says hey the 2nd verse is worse just stick around." "He don't find it a surprise to see the pumpkin on his table slowly rising." "You got it all going on girl stealing, lickin', kickin', where you're sleeping . . . bloodbath suckers beatin', cheatin'—there's new ways to sell out everyday." "He calls life a prison and he tells it to anybody who will listen / he invites you to the bloodbath he says you don't know what you're missin'." "There's a woman named giabella & another rondella / estrella returning you see him & he returning from munich—dead as a doorknob he's either so damn fake or just plain sick." Then there are handwritten phrases that include "Boys I'll see you tomorrow," "he been photographed one time too many," "bag full of sorrow."

Quite a page. Well, these words suggest that Ricks's view is more correct than Gray's. There are drug references and obvious references to fame (who else could get away with pissing on the rug of a penthouse?). But there are many references to songwriting and music making. The next page is a page of handwritten notes. A few lines stand out: "He's all things to everybody and nothing to those that don't know him." "One time he pawned everything he owned." "Get within a hundred yards of him and you feel something vibrate (quiver)." "Wearing a velvet coat he says boys I'll see you tomorrow." "Fierce looking eyes / people either turn away or else they don't look." "He finishes his drink he says I'll meet you outside in ten minutes / He presses the buzzer a voice says Who is it? He says me then the voice says again is anybody with you?"

Wildly disparate images, but all consistent with a rock 'n' roll lifestyle. The next page shows that Bob is beginning to edit the ideas and put the best ones in some semblance of order. Now the verses are numbered again. Verse 1 starts out with the "controversy surrounds him" image, but then he writes, "When it's all downhill" after crossing out "When it's too bad for him" and continues, "you never know an old memory still hounds him." And now we have the first mention of Handy Dandy, sugar and candy. The second verse has the "all-girl orchestra" image, but now when he says strike up the band, they *better* hit it. In this second verse he adds, "If every bone in his body was broken he would never admit it" and "He's been around the world and back again he'd sell it all for a penny." The third verse has the "fierce looking eyes" image, and now he tells the boys "there's new ways to sell out every day c'mon I'm gonna teach you another one." And in the fourth and final verse he's back up in his room "in case they start spraying the street with machine guns" before he comes back and tells the woman she has to be able to be trusted before pressing on the buzzer and being interrogated by the person in the building to make sure no one is with him.

We're getting closer. The next iteration is close to the final draft, but now when Handy finishes his drink, he "leaves his cards on the table" before saying goodbye to the boys. What this file in the Archive shows us is the fascinating twists and turns and false starts and detours that Dylan embraces until he hones the final lyrics of the song. He may have written "Lenny Bruce" in fifteen minutes in the back of a cab, but "Handy Dandy" shows he expended a lot of perspiration along with the inspiration. But finally, who is this Handy Dandy character?

* * *

"When Bob first sang those lyrics in the studio, I wasn't necessarily picturing a musician," Don Was told me. "I pictured Ben Gazzara in the [John] Cassavetes movie *Death of a Chinese Bookie*. We never talked about any of this stuff ever so I don't know what Bob had in mind. But the more I thought about it, the more I realized that 'Handy Dandy' is a song about a guy who seems to have had all the trappings of success. He's been around the world and back. He has a fortress on a hill, he's got the pocket full of money and all the sycophants and all the girls that go along with it. Despite all of that he's still not satisfied. And something in the moonlight still hounds him. Even with the basket of flowers he's still got a bag full of sorrow and nobody really knows him. He reveals nothing. And he's about as isolated as the fortress itself that he built. Everyone who is successful is driven by the quest for that cure. Of course you find out when you obtain that material success that you aspired to that it doesn't make any fucking difference at all. That to me is what the song is about. Now we both know someone who fits that exactly."

For me, the first line is a tell as to the meaning of the song. Controversy surrounds him. Getting booed at Newport. Following *Blonde on Blonde* with *John Wesley Harding*, *Nashville Skyline*, and *Self Portrait*. Having absurd stories about him planted in the press. Being crucified for putting out albums with a born-again theme. But he keeps moving, goes around the world and back again because he's hounded by something in the moonlight. Maybe he's compelled. When I interviewed Dylan at the end of the Rolling Thunder tour, he told me that he realized that touring was in his blood when he was in Corsica in the spring of 1975. "I was just sitting in a field overlooking some vineyards, the sky was pink, the sun was going down and the moon was sapphire," Bob told me. "I recall getting a ride into town with a man with a donkey cart and I was sitting on this donkey cart, bouncing around on the road there, and that's when it flashed on me that I was gonna go back to America and get serious and do what it is that I do, because by that time people didn't know what it was that I did. All kinds of people, most people don't know what I do, only the people that see our show know what it is that I do, the rest of the people just have to imagine it."

In Scorsese's brilliant documentary about the Rolling Thunder Revue, the boxer Rubin Carter talks about Bob's addiction to the road as a spiritual quest. "Have you found it yet, Bob?" he'd ask him every time they talked. Obviously he hadn't. So Dylan marches on, around the world and back again, dispensing his unique form of sugar and candy for those lucky enough to experience it.

He does it with incredible dedication and willfulness too. You know that if every bone in his body was broken he would never admit it. Dylan once told me how he tried to manage his fame. I asked him if "Idiot Wind" was a means for him to exorcize the demons of fame.

I don't want to answer them kinds of direct questions. I mean what can I say? [Being] a public figure can be like something that walks on you. I just decided it ain't gonna walk on me. It can be the horse riding on you, sooner or later, but you just got to realize that you can ride it and drive it into the ground, if necessary.

Who can ever forget those press conferences in 1966 where Dylan took control of that horse and broke it?

You say, "What are ya made of?"
He says, "Can you repeat what you said?"
You'll say, "What are you afraid of?"
He'll say, "Nothin'! Neither 'live or dead."

And he'll say that even if every bone in his body was broken.

But there are some advantages to fame and acclaim. You get to walk around with a nice walking stick, a top hat, and a pocket full of money. Just watch Dylan's video for "Blood in My Eyes" shot on the streets of London. Bob is like a pied piper, and people of every description, age, and ethnicity follow him, asking for autographs and more. You just know that every darling there would give him all the time in the world, honey.

Even with his basket of flowers (are they the flowers of evil?) he's still lugging around a bag full of sorrow. But that doesn't deter him. He finishes his brandy, gets up from the table. and gets through the night to do it all again tomorrow.

"The thing that tipped me off that the song might be autobiographical was the line about getting up from the table and saying goodbye," Was told me. "That was how every session we did ended. Bob would get up and say, 'OK boys, see you tomorrow.' That's what he did every day."

Don also told me that when they had to do some additional vocal recordings in New York, Allen Ginsberg was at the sessions. Ginsberg told Don one thing that stuck with him to this day.

"Handy Dandy" draft manuscript

"Allen said, 'Everything that Bob writes is autobiographical. All these songs are about himself. He's talking to himself about himself.'" So was Handy Dandy just one more layer of skin that Bob would shed on his trips around the world and back again? Hey, who am I to argue with Allen Ginsberg?

THE BOOTLEG SERIES VOLUMES 1–3 (RARE & UNRELEASED) 1961–1991

In 1969, *Great White Wonder* was released, the unofficial double-LP collection of Dylan songs that is widely regarded as the first significant rock bootleg. Shortly after its release, Columbia Records gave the following comments to *Rolling Stone*:

> We consider the release of this record as an abuse of the integrity of a great artist. By releasing material without the knowledge or approval of Bob Dylan or Columbia Records, the sellers of this record are crassly depriving a great artist of the opportunity to perfect his performances to the point where he believes in their integrity and validity. They are at one time defaming the artist and defrauding his admirers.

Despite the direct and terse language in Columbia's statement, bootleggers were not deterred. Dylan has become, according to the Recording Industry Association of America, the most bootlegged artist of all time. (Columbia Records managed to suppress their outrage regarding artistic integrity after Dylan briefly left the label and they released a series of outtakes themselves on the album *Dylan* in 1973, a move many thought Columbia did in spite.)

In 1991, Dylan and Columbia Records issued *The Bootleg Series Volumes 1–3 (Rare & Unreleased) 1961–1991*, an authorized career-spanning retrospective that merely scratched the surface of the immense trove of unissued music that Dylan had amassed in his thirty years as a recording artist. The three-volume set, released on vinyl, cassette, and compact disc, featured fifty-eight tracks, many of which had never been officially released, including numerous studio outtakes, demos, and live performances.

The Bootleg Series has continued to date, delighting fans and winning critical acclaim with sets devoted to pivotal moments in Dylan's career, including individual albums, tours, and musical periods.

The Bootleg Series Volumes 1–3 (Rare & Unreleased) 1961–1991 unused album longbox mockups

ACME RECORDING SESSIONS, 1992

After the uneven reception that greeted *Under the Red Sky*, Dylan stepped back to recalibrate by immersing himself in the wellsprings of the music that has sustained him throughout his career: traditional blues, R&B, country, and folksongs.

In June 1992, while on a break from touring, Dylan went to Chicago to record at Acme Studios with producer David Bromberg, who had played guitar on Dylan's 1970 albums *Self Portrait* and *New Morning*. Over the course of three days, from June 3 to 5, Dylan and Bromberg's band ran through numerous songs by artists such as Tim Hardin, Blind Willie Johnson, Jimmie Rodgers, and Bromberg himself.

Dylan may have planned to release these sessions in one form or another, but they were shelved indefinitely. Two of the Bromberg Acme recordings found their way onto *The Bootleg Series Vol. 8: Tell Tale Signs: Rare and Unreleased 1989–2006*: "Miss the Mississippi and You," recorded by Jimmie Rodgers in 1932, and "Duncan and Brady," the traditional murder/crime ballad recorded by Wilmer Watts and His Lonely Eagles, Lead Belly, Dave Van Ronk, and many others.

Bob Dylan, Los Angeles, May 18, 1993.
Photograph by Merlyn Rosenberg

GOOD AS I BEEN TO YOU

After a brief European tour, Dylan returned home to Malibu in late July 1992 to record a collection of folksongs, blues numbers, and ballads at his home studio. Of the approximately forty songs Dylan recorded, he selected thirteen for *Good as I Been to You*, his first solo acoustic record since *Another Side of Bob Dylan* in 1964.

Among the songs included is the ballad "Tomorrow Night," a 1948 crossover hit by Lonnie Johnson, a bluesman who Dylan met in his early days in New York City and whose guitar technique would come to exert a great deal of influence on Dylan's later guitar style. Dylan also released his versions of bluegrass standards like "Little Maggie" as well as the Mississippi Sheiks standard, "Sittin' on Top of the World."

During these sessions, Dylan also recorded songs by Johnny Cash, The Delmore Brothers, The Carter Family, Muddy Waters, and Charlie Poole, as well as the ballad "You Belong to Me," which had been recorded by the likes of The Duprees, Jo Stafford, Patsy Cline, and Dean Martin. Dylan had been intrigued with the song since at least the late 1960s, when he jotted the opening lines down in a pocket notebook. Although the song was not selected for *Good as I Been to You*, it later appeared in the 1994 film *Natural Born Killers*.

Good as I Been to You was received warmly, with many critics noting Dylan's phrasing and his unique approach to interpreting the songs. *Rolling Stone* called it a "fascinating exploration of musical roots [that] is more than a diversion for musicologists" as well as "a passionate, at times almost ragged piece of work that seems to have been recorded rather than produced in any conventional sense," while comparing the feel of the album to Dylan's intimate acoustic sets he'd been doing during his recent tours. David Bowie was a fan, as was Irish folksinger Paul Brady, whom Dylan had met in 1962 during his first visit to the UK. Brady wrote to express his admiration for Dylan's version of "Arthur McBride," an old broadside ballad that was his signature song.

Dear Bob,

I just wanted to let you know how much I like your version of Arthur M' Bride. The whole album is great. I used to sing a version of Frankie & Albert way back in the sixties which I learnt from an old Folkways recording by Mike Seeger & it was great to hear you singing it. Hearing this record is making me feel like doing an acoustic album again!

Letter from Paul Brady to Bob Dylan, January 18, 1993

Kindest regards

Paul Brady

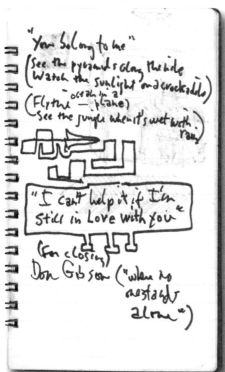

"You Belong to Me" draft manuscript, circa late 1960s

AS NATURAL AS BREATHING

Bob Dylan, Los Angeles, May 18, 1993.
Photograph by Merlyn Rosenberg

Pay-per-view broadcast promotional poster, 1992

On October 16, 1992, Madison Square Garden hosted *The 30th Anniversary Concert Celebration*, a massive live concert—which Neil Young playfully dubbed Bobfest—honoring Dylan's first thirty years as a recording artist. The musicians who gathered to pay tribute included The Band, June Carter and Johnny Cash, Rosanne Cash, Tracy Chapman, The Clancy Brothers, Richie Havens, Chrissie Hynde, John Mellencamp, Willie Nelson, Sinéad O'Connor, Pearl Jam, Lou Reed, and Stevie Wonder. G. E. Smith and Booker T. served as the musical directors for the evening, leading the band that included members of the legendary Stax Records house band, Booker T. and the MG's.

Dylan himself finished the concert with a selection of tunes including his first original song to be released officially, "Song to Woody," followed by "It's Alright, Ma (I'm Only Bleeding)." Eric Clapton, George Harrison, Roger McGuinn, Tom Petty, and Neil Young joined him for "My Back Pages," and all of the performers came onstage for a rendition of "Knockin' on Heaven's Door." Dylan ended the concert with a solo performance of "Girl from the North Country."

The entire proceedings were recorded and filmed, including backstage and pre-performance footage, as part of a pay-per-view telecast and have subsequently been released on two occasions: on home video in 1993, in conjunction with the album release, and again in 2014 in a deluxe edition format.

L–R: Roger McGuinn, G. E. Smith, Ronnie Wood, George Harrison, Bob Dylan, Donald "Duck" Dunn, Tom Petty, Anton Fig, Neil Young, Steve Cropper, Madison Square Garden, NYC, October 16, 1992. Photograph by Ken Regan

WORLD GONE WRONG

ABOUT THE SONGS (what they're about)

BROKE DOWN ENGINE is a Blind Willie McTell masterpiece. it's about trains, mystery on the rails-the train of love, the train that carried my girl from town-The Southern Pacific, Baltimore & Ohio whatever- it's about variations of human longing-the low hum in meters & syllables. it is about dupes of commerce & politics colliding on tracks, not being pushed around by ordinary standards. It's about revival, getting a new lease on life, not just posing there-paint chipped & flaked, mattress bare, single bulb swinging above the bed. it's about Ambiguity, the fortunes of the privileged elite, flood control-watching the red dawn not bothering to dress.

"About the Songs (what they're about)," *World Gone Wrong* liner notes, draft typescript, circa 1993

Dylan spent the beginning of 1993 doing one-off sessions and concerts, including performing "Heartland" with Willie Nelson and friends at the Grand Ole Opry, and returning to the steps of the Lincoln Memorial to offer a rendition of "Chimes of Freedom" for Bill Clinton's presidential inauguration. After touring Europe and the United States, Dylan repaired to his home studio to cut another set of traditional tunes. Out of the approximately forty recorded, Dylan selected ten for his next album, *World Gone Wrong*. In addition to the Scottish ballad "Love Henry" (a.k.a. "Young Hunting"), Willie Brown's "Ragged and Dirty," and Blind Willie McTell's "Delia," Dylan covered both sides of a 78-rpm disc released in 1932 by the Mississippi Sheiks: "The World Is Going Wrong," which became the album's title track, and "I've Got Blood in My Eyes for You," which Dylan released as a music video, directed by longtime friend Dave Stewart of Eurythmics. Among the outtakes from the sessions were the Gershwin brothers' standard "Someone to Watch over Me," the Webb Pierce country hit "There Stands the Glass," and Robert Johnson's "Traveling Riverside Blues."

For *World Gone Wrong*, Dylan returned to providing his own liner notes, much as he had done for his albums in the mid-1960s. The album was both commercially and critically successful, winning the GRAMMY Award for Best Traditional Folk Album in 1995.

Dave Stewart of Eurythmics and Bob Dylan on the set of "Blood in My Eyes" music video, Fluke's Cradle, London, 1993. Photograph by Ana María Vélez Wood

THE SUPPER CLUB

In 1989, MTV introduced *MTV Unplugged*, a new television series that featured performers from across genres and generations performing acoustic versions of their songs. The show quickly became a cultural phenomenon. In addition to performances by popular grunge and alternative groups like 10,000 Maniacs, Midnight Oil, Nirvana, and Pearl Jam, the show featured hip-hop artists LL Cool J, MC Lyte, De La Soul, and A Tribe Called Quest. However, among the most successful *MTV Unplugged* episodes were those by Eric Clapton, The Eagles, Paul McCartney, Rod Stewart, and Stevie Ray Vaughan.

Inspired in part by *MTV Unplugged*, Dylan decided to record and film an acoustic concert for release, but on his own terms. Dylan chose the Supper Club in midtown Manhattan as the venue and on November 16 and 17, 1993, he performed his first club shows in over twenty years. Tickets were only available at the Tower Records downtown. Lines formed around the block, as fans slept out overnight hoping to secure a ticket.

Four sets over two nights were filmed of Dylan backed by his touring band, which then included John Jackson (guitar and banjo), Bucky Baxter (pedal steel guitar and electric slide guitar), Tony Garnier (bass), and Winston Watson (drums and percussion). Dylan created a unique set list for each of the four shows, emphasizing songs from his recent albums, with highlights including "Ring Them Bells" and his arrangements of "Delia" and "Weeping Willow." Yet Dylan also reached into his back catalog to perform classics like "I Want You," "I'll Be Your Baby Tonight," and "Queen Jane Approximately," which prompted the crowd to give a standing ovation. He ended his Supper Club residency with the only encore of the entire set of shows: a stunning rendition of "I Shall Be Released."

Bob Dylan with John Jackson (obscured), Supper Club, NYC, November 16–17, 1994.
Photograph by Ken Regan

AS NATURAL AS BREATHING

MTV UNPLUGGED

L–R: John Jackson, Bob Dylan, Winston Watson, Tony Garnier, Bucky Baxter, *MTV Unplugged*, Sony Music Studios, NYC, November 18, 1994. Photograph by Frank Micelotta

Ultimately, Dylan decided to shelve the Supper Club project, and he agreed to an official appearance on *MTV Unplugged*. Gathering at Sony Music Studios on November 17 and 18, 1994, Dylan and his band rehearsed and taped more than a dozen songs for the show. Producer Brendan O'Brien, who'd been working with Dylan to complete the song "Dignity" for *Dylan's Greatest Hits Vol. 3*, was brought on to add Hammond organ and additional guitar. Not all of the songs they rehearsed were aired, including "Hazel" and "Everything Is Broken." However, four outtakes from the show itself—"Tombstone Blues," "John Brown," "Desolation Row," and "Love Minus Zero/No Limit"—were included on the album version of *MTV Unplugged*, released May 2, 1995.

Bob Dylan, 1995. Photograph by Mark Seliger

AS NATURAL AS BREATHING

468

TIME OUT OF MIND

"Love Sick" draft manuscript

Released on September 30, 1997, *Time Out of Mind*, Dylan's thirtieth studio album, was an album that changed the trajectory of his long career. The critical and popular reappraisal of Dylan's music underscored Dylan's vitality as an artist, especially at a time when few of his contemporaries were making albums that could stand alongside their past triumphs. The album won Dylan his first-ever GRAMMY Award for Album of the Year, and presaged a mid-career resurgence that continues to this day. Yet the success of the album hadn't come from out of the blue; rather, Dylan's touring regimen, the solidification of his backing band, and his re-immersion in his musical roots all set the stage for the work contained on *Time Out of Mind*.

With production by Daniel Lanois, who had produced *Oh Mercy*, *Time Out of Mind* offered a stark soundscape of blues and ballads that provided the perfect setting for Dylan's lyrical ruminations on love, loss, and mortality. Album opener "Love Sick" set the tone with its dead streets, ticking clocks, and silence sounding like thunder, all delivered by a vocal that Dylan described as a "harmonica when you over-drive it through a small guitar amplifier." The handwritten manuscript shown here is close to the version Dylan sang on record, the subtle differences revealing Dylan refining his imagery.

The *Time Out of Mind* sessions began in the fall of 1996 at Lanois's Teatro Studios in Oxnard, California, with Dylan, Lanois, longtime bassist Tony Garnier, and drummer and percussionist Tony Mangurian. In January 1997, Dylan moved the sessions to Criteria Studios in Miami, Florida, and invited multi-instrumentalist Bucky Baxter, bassist Tony Garnier, and drummers David Kemper and Winston Watson of his touring band, as well as guitarists Duke Robillard and Robert Britt, keyboardists Jim Dickinson and Augie Meyers, and drummer Jim Keltner, to contribute to the album. Lanois invited slide guitarist Cindy Cashdollar and drummer Brian Blade, and brought along Tony Mangurian as well. In the end, a dozen musicians contributed to the sessions to create what Dickinson later called "an orchestral concept." As Dylan noted when he collected his GRAMMY award for Album of the Year in 1998, "We got a particular type of sound on this record that you don't get every day."

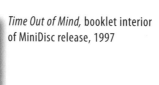

Time Out of Mind, booklet interior of MiniDisc release, 1997

On July 29, 1996, Dylan visited Rolling Stones guitarist Ronnie Wood at his home in Kildare, Ireland, called Sandymount House. There in Wood's home studio, the pair jammed on largely instrumental versions of Dylan's new songs, including "Love Sick," "Dirt Road Blues," and "Can't Wait." Wood sent Dylan home with a cassette of the session, into which he inserted this decorated newspaper clipping.

Newspaper clipping annotated by Ronnie Wood, 1996

AS NATURAL AS BREATHING

470

Bob Dylan, Hotel Ambassador, Los Angeles, 1999. Photograph by Danny Clinch

Bob Dylan, 1995. Photograph by Mark Seliger

Promotional pocket watch, 1997

Song list from *Time Out of Mind* era, 1997

"MAKE YOU FEEL MY LOVE"

One track on the album, "Make You Feel My Love," took on a life of its own in the hands of other artists. Billy Joel released his version of the song in August 1997, a month before the release of *Time Out of Mind*, as the lead single for his *Greatest Hits Volume III*, which reached #50 on *Billboard*'s Hot 100. The following year, Garth Brooks followed suit, releasing his version on the *Hope Floats* soundtrack; the single version reached #1 on the *Billboard* country charts and won a GRAMMY award for Best Male Country Vocal Performance (Dylan was nominated for Best Country Song).

A decade later, in 2008, "Make You Feel My Love" ended up reaching millions, through an unlikely source. Adele, a then little-known Londoner, released the song as a single and a music video from her debut album *19* (named after the age she was when she recorded it). The song did well, but it was the British reality TV show *The X Factor* that brought Adele's version back to the top of the charts. In 2010, a number of fledgling hopefuls performed Adele's version of the song on the show, which created a sensation. Since that time, hundreds of cover versions have been recorded and posted online, many of which mistakenly credit Adele as the song's author.

L–R: "Make You Feel My Love," Billy Joel sheet music (1997); Garth Brooks CD single (1998); Adele CD single (2008); Bob Dylan 7" Japanese EP (2019)

Reflections on "Not Dark Yet" ALLISON MOORER

Discomfort inside, discomfort outside.
No relief around.
Another shift in shape, imminent.

Rabble rousing lover/bard turned romantic, rock 'n' roll explorer senses specter of wise gentleman laureate—timepiece in his breast pocket and open book of life in his gnarled hand—standing in the corner of the room.
The peripheral wraith closes in to sniff at the wounds.
The incessant ticking grows heavier with the suspense of what waits on the next page. No matter the jolt that comes with the realization that the newly noticed ghost-of-yet-to-come emanates from his own collected loss, it is a realization nonetheless.

The surprise of lost love turned into the surprise of dwindling time.
Suspicion of beauty, indifference to kindness, listlessness and dispassion—a new and other sort of hardening begins.
The pain of lost love turned into the pain of the aging body.
There is a shock, then a drilling down into a legs-kicking-under-the-blanket style temper tantrum brought on by an unavoidable awareness, then burgeoning acceptance.

Surroundings are suddenly unfamiliar.
Eyes that just a little while ago felt jabbed cry no more.
They look for nothing in those that protrude from other faces, and only peer down a rusty double barrel to find loneliness and mortality.
They are clearly seen, like the river, like the sea.
Experience and memory feel too heavy.
The iron fist of unwelcome consciousness delivers a right cross.
The big idea of love turned into the big idea of life.
There is no hand to hold, is there?

Resignation and gravitas, detached yet still reported with the depth and cool of one who suddenly discovers there is
                              simply no way out of this.
What?
Huh. Ain't that something.
Again we wonder, "How did he do that? He never stopped moving before."
Now a pause, all the more effective.
And both reassuring and disturbing.
What? He is not impenetrable?
Not now, not this time, for this visitor comes to every door, and takes every one of us on a one-way trip.

It's as if there sprung a scrawled-on wall in the path and the words had to be read to us before it could be scaled.
Before the other side could be seen.
And wrestled to the ground.

Still and forever a shape-shifter.
Again we wonder, "How did we not know we needed it said that way?"

We didn't know we needed it until it was given, until it was received.
Inelegant stabs taken by those who would deny the truth of time and would instead fake vigor and youthful energy appear nostalgic, even ridiculously immature next to what the words on this sheet of yellow legal pad paper would become: A brutal but graceful guide to navigating the encroaching black of the last third.

Discomfort inside, discomfort outside.
No relief to be found anywhere.
One more shift.
We bow our heads in recognition and respect, as if we can now acknowledge the funeral procession approaching us too.

NOT DARK YET

1. Shadows falling, I been here all day
It's too hot to sleep, time's running away
I feel like my soul has been turned into steel
There's a gentle wind (morning?) blowing but it doesn't seem real
There's not even room enough to be anywhere
It's not dark yet but it's getting there

2. My sense of humanity's gone down the drain
Behind every beautiful thing there's been some kind of pain
Just being in the same country as her is making me blue
I got nothing left even from the love that we knew
A love that I know I never can share
It's not dark yet but it's getting there

Bridge 1
Feel like I'm going crazy, I feel so numb
Can't remember what it was that I come here to get away from

3. My room looks like it ain't been lived in for years
I'm waiting for the dust to settle on my tears
It's like somebody jabbed their finger in my eye
And left me dangling on the other end of the sky
There must be something funny going on somewhere (Sometime my burden seems more than I can bear)
It's not dark yet but it's getting there

Bridge 2
There was no doubt in my mind that our love was strong
That nothing could crush it. Obviously I was wrong (Cynicism)

4. Somewhere I can smell the wood burning fire
I'm thinking of her but I hide my desire
Her eyes were so lovely, her skin was so soft
I can see the whole thing from a long ways off
All I do is sit here and stare
It's not dark yet but it's getting there (in the hot sticky air)

Alternate (I'm thinking I'm heart —) (Feeln sick and I can't get well)
Over the bare trees I heard a swan go by (Maybe I'm just too vulnerable)
I'm not good enough for heaven I'm not bad enough for hell (But I don't think... I don't know I can't tell)
The air is so heavy it's pulling me down
All I can do is sit here and stare

"Not Dark Yet" draft manuscript

Fax letter from John Lee Hooker to Bob Dylan, May 29, 1997

Concert advertisement, *The Village Voice*, April 20, 1961

SUDDEN ILLNESS

On May 28, 1997, Dylan entered the hospital suffering from what turned out to be a serious heart ailment, histoplasmosis pericarditis. This near-fatal illness colored the release of *Time Out of Mind,* an album whose lyrics dealt extensively with the theme of mortality. Though Dylan was discharged the following week, his illness and recuperation forced the cancellation of a European tour that had been slated to start on June 1. Dylan said at the time, "I'm just glad to be feeling better. I really thought I'd be seeing Elvis soon."

As soon as the news of Dylan's condition broke, well wishes poured in from around the world. Frank Sinatra and his wife Barbara not only called, but also sent along a fax that read, "Give 'em hell in there. . . . We're betting on you."

John Lee Hooker also sent a fax to Dylan offering a speedy recovery. Dylan had known Hooker since receiving his first big break opening for the blues legend at Gerdes Folk City in April 1961. As Hooker later recalled,

> Every night he'd be right there with me. We'd stay there, we'd party there, drink gin. He'd sit around and watch me play; he'd be right there every night, and we'd be playing guitars in the hotel. I don't know what he got from me, but he must've got something.

Dylan later namechecked Hooker in the 2020 epic "Murder Most Foul," imploring the radio DJ Wolfman Jack to

> *Play John Lee Hooker play Scratch My Back*
> *Play it for that strip club owner named Jack*

Bob Dylan, 1999.
Photograph by Danny Clinch

L–R: Larry Campbell, David Kemper, Bob Dylan, Tony Garnier, Bucky Baxter in rehearsal, January 1999. Photograph by Gilles Peress

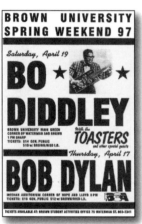

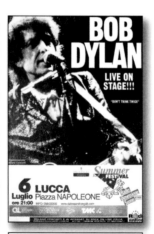

Concert posters, 1997–2000

L–R: Larry Campbell, Bob Dylan, Tony Garnier in rehearsal, January 1999. Photograph by Gilles Peress

ON THE ROAD

Even as Dylan worked on one of his mid-career masterworks and celebrated its worldwide success, he did not slow his touring pace. As Dylan's musical vision evolved, so did his band, with multi-instrumentalist Larry Campbell and drummer David Kemper joining in 1997 followed by guitarist Charlie Sexton in 1998. The following year, steel guitarist Bucky Baxter departed, leaving the group a five-piece, which it would remain until the arrival of multi-instrumentalist Donnie Herron in 2005.

Although North America and Europe were frequent destinations, Dylan toured Japan in 1997 and Australia and New Zealand in 1998. That same year, Dylan performed in South America with "them British bad boys The Rolling Stones," as he'd call them in the 2021 song "I Contain Multitudes." During these years, Dylan also toured alongside Joni Mitchell, Van Morrison, Paul Simon, and Grateful Dead bassist Phil Lesh.

1988–2000

Bob Dylan and Tony Garnier in rehearsal,
January 1999. Photograph by Gilles Peress

GRAMMY AWARDS, 1998

On February 25, 1998, Dylan beat out Paul McCartney, Babyface, Paula Cole, and Radiohead to win Album of the Year at the 40th Annual GRAMMY Awards. Taking the stage alongside producer Daniel Lanois, Dylan joked that "everybody worked extra-special hard, even the musicians," before closing with a line from "the immortal Robert Johnson, 'the stuff we got'll bust your brains out,' and we tried to get that across."

Dylan not only won Album of the Year, but also Best Contemporary Folk Album and Best Male Rock Vocal Performance for the song "Cold Irons Bound." Notes of congratulations came pouring in. Jim Dickinson, who'd played on the record and whom Dylan had called his "brother from Mississippi" in his acceptance speech, wrote to thank Dylan again for the experience of playing on the record. Willie Nelson sent a telegram of congratulations, as did Billy Joel, whose version of "Make You Feel My Love" from *Time Out of Mind* made the song a breakout hit.

President Bill Clinton also wrote to congratulate Dylan on his GRAMMY win. Less than three months earlier, Clinton had presented Dylan with the Kennedy Center Honors for lifetime contributions to American culture through the performing arts. During the December 7, 1997, ceremony, Bruce Springsteen performed "The Times They Are A-Changin'," and gospel queen Shirley Caesar delivered a passionate rendition of "Gotta Serve Somebody." Actor Gregory Peck spoke as the voice of the nation when he offered an extended tribute:

> When I was a little kid in La Jolla, California, which is a very small town, we had a parade on the Fourth of July and I remember clearly the sight of Civil War veterans marching down the main street, kicking up the dust. The first time I heard Bob Dylan, it brought back that memory. And I thought of him as something of a Civil War type. A kind of nineteenth-century troubadour. A maverick American spirit. The reediness of his voice and the spareness of his words go straight to the heart of America.
>
> Some time ago I bought a new Dylan album and I was listening to a song called "Brownsville Girl" and I heard these lines:

> *There was a movie I seen one time*
> *I think I saw it through twice*
> *It starred Gregory Peck*
> *He wore a gun and was shot in the back*
> *I just can't get it out of my head*

> Dylan was singing about a picture that I made called *The Gunfighter* about the lone man in town with people comin' in to kill him and everybody wants him out of town before the shooting starts.
>
> When I met Bob, years later, I told him that meant a lot to me and the best way I could sum *him* up is to say—Bob Dylan has never been *about* to get out of town before the shootin' starts. Thank you, Mr. Dylan, for rocking the country . . . and the ages.

GRAMMY Awards seating arrangement, 1998

PAGE 483: *Time Out of Mind* GRAMMY Awards promotional poster, 1998

AS NATURAL AS BREATHING

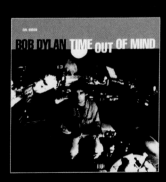

Bob Dylan, Hotel Ambassador, Los Angeles, 1999.
Photographs by Danny Clinch

HOTEL AMBASSADOR, 1999

In 1999, Danny Clinch photographed Dylan wandering the grounds at the defunct Hotel Ambassador in Los Angeles. In its heyday, the hotel played host to every president from Hoover to Nixon and was home to the glamorous Cocoanut Grove nightclub. A staple of Hollywood culture for nearly seventy years, the nightclub hosted celebrities and entertainers such as Charlie Chaplin, Nat King Cole, Clark Gable, Judy Garland, Katharine Hepburn, Carole Lombard, Frank Sinatra, Rudolph Valentino, and many, many others. In 1968, Senator Robert F. Kennedy was assassinated in the hotel's kitchen after addressing supporters in the Embassy Ballroom following his victory in the state's Democratic presidential primary.

Bob Dylan with Oscar statuette on amplifier, Bournemouth, UK, May 5, 2002. Photograph by Harry Scott

"THINGS HAVE CHANGED"

In 2000, Dylan wrote "Things Have Changed" for the film *Wonder Boys*. Recorded on July 25, 1999, at Clinton Recording Studios in New York City during a day off from touring, the song came together quickly. As drummer David Kemper later recalled, "In about five hours we learned it, recorded it, mixed it."

Dylan wrote an early draft of "Things Have Changed" on the back of a January 13, 1999, fax from Leonard Cohen containing a draft of Cohen's song, "A Thousand Kisses Deep." Although Dylan had worked out the song's meter at that point, only a few of the recorded lyrics are present, including the line, "Any minute now I'm expecting all hell to break loose." "Things Have Changed" won both the Golden Globe and Academy Awards for Best Original Song. Although Dylan was on tour in Australia at the time of the March 21, 2001, Academy Awards presentation, a satellite link allowed him to participate in the ceremony. Dylan performed the song and made an acceptance speech where he noted, "I want to thank the members of the Academy who were bold enough to give me this award for this song, which obviously is a song that doesn't pussyfoot around nor turn a blind eye to human nature."

A lifelong fan of cinema, Dylan acknowledged the win by giving his Oscar statuette a place of pride onstage each night on the tour.

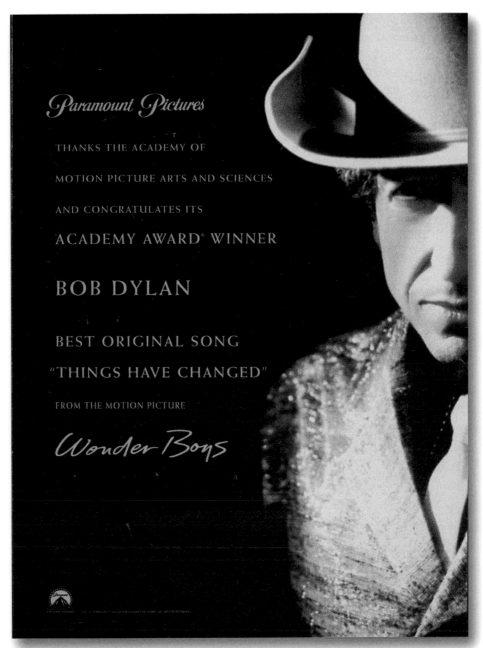

Paramount Pictures Academy Award accolades page, *Variety*, 2001

"Things Have Changed" draft manuscript

Bob Dylan, Hotel Ambassador, Los Angeles, 1999. Photograph by Danny Clinch.

Themes, Dreams, and Schemes

2001–2013

The difference between me now and then is that back then, I could see visions. The me now can dream dreams.

—October 2004, David Gates interview, *Newsweek*

Bob Dylan, 2006. Photograph by William Claxton

"LOVE AND THEFT"

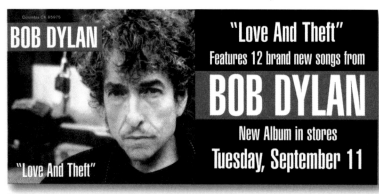

"Love and Theft" promotional poster, 2001

Dylan followed up his award-winning *Time Out of Mind* with *"Love and Theft,"* a further exploration of America's musical roots, from Tin Pan Alley and Western swing to stomping blues and rockabilly. According to Dylan the album explored "business, politics and war, and maybe love interest on the side." Lyrically, he drew upon work as varied as the classical Roman poet Virgil, Japanese Yakuza gangster stories, and the Delta bluesman Charley Patton.

With Dylan's touring band in tow, augmented by organist Augie Meyers, Dylan cut more than a dozen tracks over the course of twelve days in May 2001 at Clinton Recording Studios in New York City. Jack Frost, which many assume is Dylan's *nom du disque*, is listed as producer, and Chris Shaw, who'd worked on Dylan's "Things Have Changed," engineered. Shaw subsequently engineered several of Dylan's records, including *Modern Times* and *Rough and Rowdy Ways*.

Although the album was released on September 11, 2001, the day of the largest terrorist attack on US soil, it went on to enormous critical and commercial success. The album was nominated for the GRAMMY for Album of the Year and Best Male Rock Performance, and Dylan ended up winning the GRAMMY for Best Contemporary Folk Album. Johnny Cash declared the album his favorite of Dylan's catalog.

Bob Dylan in center behind mixing desk, *"Love and Theft"* sessions, Clinton Recording Studios, NYC, May 2001. Photograph by Kevin Mazur

Bob Dylan, *"Love and Theft"* sessions,
Clinton Recording Studios, NYC, May 2001.
Photograph by Kevin Mazur

L–R: Augie Meyers, Tony Garnier, David Kemper, Charlie Sexton, Larry Campbell, Bob Dylan, *"Love and Theft"* sessions, Clinton Recording Studios, NYC, May 2001. Photograph by Kevin Mazur

"High Water (for Charley Patton)" draft manuscript

THEMES, DREAMS, AND SCHEMES 496

"HIGH WATER (FOR CHARLEY PATTON)"

Named in honor of the influential early Delta bluesman Charley Patton and his account of the Great Mississippi Flood of 1927, "High Water Everywhere," Dylan's "High Water (For Charley Patton)" uses the refrain from Patton's song as a jumping-off point. Much like Dylan's early work, "High Water (For Charley Patton)" namechecks a wide range of characters, from *Jane Eyre*'s Bertha Mason to nineteenth-century English naturalist Charles Darwin to blues shouter Big Joe Turner. Drafts of the song show that at one time Dylan's mythic South was also home to Dr. Frankenstein, English modernist James Joyce, and Way Out Willie.

L–R: Charlie Sexton, David Kemper, Larry Campbell, Bob Dylan, Augie Meyers, Tony Garnier, *"Love and Theft"* sessions, Clinton Recording Studios, NYC, May 2001.
Photograph by Kevin Mazur

497

Bob Dylan, Coney Island, NYC, June 2001. Photograph by David Gahr

THEMES, DREAMS, AND SCHEMES

"Mississippi" draft manuscript

"MISSISSIPPI"

"Mississippi," an epic ballad built around the refrain of the traditional folk song "Rosie," was first recorded during the sessions for *Time Out of Mind*. Starting at the 1996 Teatro sessions as an acoustic number, with Dylan accompanied by Lanois on electric guitar, in Miami, "Mississippi" was tried in a number of different musical configurations and arrangements, from a walking-the-floor shuffle to greased-up rocker. In the end, Dylan was ultimately unsatisfied with any of the versions caught on tape and left the song off the record. He subsequently gave the song to singer-songwriter Sheryl Crow for her 1998 album *The Globe Sessions*, where "Mississippi" appeared in a substantially revised arrangement.

At the end of the sessions for *"Love and Theft,"* Dylan reintroduced the song. After just four takes, the song was finished. During a press conference in Rome for the album's release, Dylan spoke to the song's resurrection:

> *I've been asked: "So how come you're such a bad judge of your material?" I've been criticized for not putting my best songs on certain albums but it is because I consider that the song isn't ready yet. It's not been recorded right.*
>
> *With all of my records, there's an abundance of material left off—stuff that, for a variety of reasons, doesn't make the final cut.*
>
> *Once it gets out, or is recorded by someone else, I'm not keen on going in and re-recording it. It's already been contaminated for me. I turn my back and move on to something else. Except on this album, for which we re-cut the song "Mississippi." We had that on the* Time Out Of Mind *album. It wasn't recorded very well but thank God, it never got out, so we recorded it again. But something like that would never have happened ten years ago. You'd have probably all heard the lousy version of it and I'd have never re-recorded it. I'm glad for once to have had the opportunity to do so.*

PAGES 500–501: Video stills from *"Love and Theft"* commercial featuring magician Ricky Jay (in blue shirt), 2001. Directed by Kinka Usher

Postcard from Tulsa

PETER CAREY

I n another lifetime I met the Russian poet Yevgeny Yevtushenko. We drove to the wide cow-
town streets of Tulsa in his three-thousand-dollar Cadillac. Then, this century, I rode the same
streets in an Uber pickup truck. The backseat was filled with poets. The driver was a "character"
from Dallas.

Where you folk from.

New York, replied the poets.

The driver wore a cowboy hat. Get a rope, he cried.

It was the old weird violence of America. Dang me, I thought. They ought to find a rope and
hang me.

Get a rope, the driver insisted. You must a seen it? The Pace Salsa commercial? There was a
cook, he said, and some cowboys out on the range and the boys were real unhappy with the Cookie's
new Picante Sauce. It weren't right. Real Salsa is made in San Antonio by folks who know how
picante sauces should taste.

Where was the Salsa made, the TV cowboys asked the TV cookie, a poor physical specimen with
a bad case of rhinophyma. Cookie peered at the label before he finally replied, "New York."

NEW YORK, the cowboys cry in unison. "Get a rope."

Was it hysterical to think of lynching? I didn't say a word.

What color was the Cookie? asked Eileen Miles.

How do you mean.

What was the color of his skin?

It has been sometimes said that Tulsa is an unlikely place to house the Bob Dylan Archive, but
Dylan is the encyclopedia of American music, which must include not only freight trains and moon
and spoon, but also racial injustice and bloody murder, Hurricane, Joey, the Jack of Hearts, and
Desolation Row.

And when I stepped down out of the Uber I walked into the Archive, where they offer postcards
of the hanging in Box 55, Folder 09.

I could have looked or listened to "Desolation Row" or almost anything relating to Dylan's
massive catalog. Instead I chose "Tweedle Dee & Tweedle Dum," a song I had already heard a
hundred times, never once being able to stabilize or isolate the source of my own fierce and bitter
joy. "Tweedle-dee Dum says to Tweedle-dee Dee / 'Your presence is obnoxious to me.'"

There are twelve verses of four lines. They seemed so spontaneous, flickering, unstable, weirdly at
odds with each other. The surviving manuscript pages were delivered encased in mylar, six crammed
pages, the signs of a long and painful labor. As I picked up the first sheet I felt myself become that
awful character in "Ballad of a Thin Man," Mister Jones, of whom Dylan wrote: "You walk into the
room / With your pencil in your hand / You see somebody naked / And you say, 'Who is that man?'"

What a creep, I had thought, fifty years ago, never imagining that one day I would be in Tulsa,
called to play the part of Mister Jones. I had brought three pencils with me, but I had never expected
to understand a genius by examining his droppings. What I intended was to show respect. I would

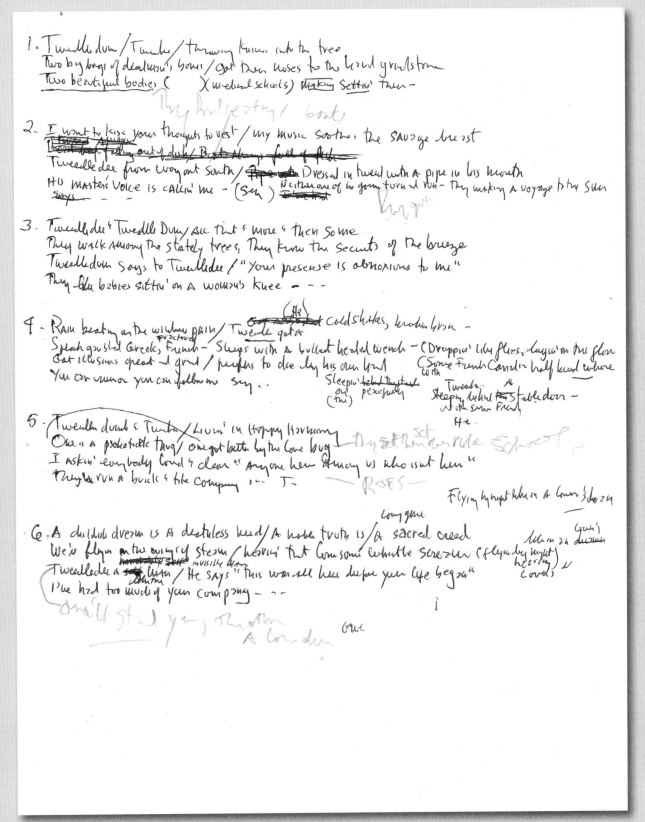

"Tweedle Dee & Tweedle Dum" draft manuscript

PETER CAREY

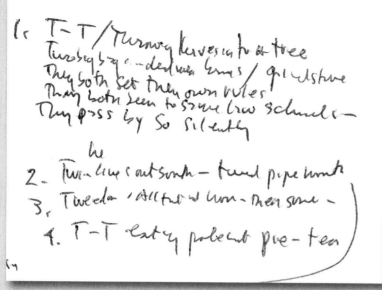

"Tweedle Dee & Tweedle Dum" draft manuscript

do this by transcribing Dylan's words, my hand following his as he excavates the mud of memory, throws dice, loots history, dredging the bottom of the river, trusting the hidden truth of rhyme, succeeding sometimes, crashing often, until having stood so naked before the future, he erases half the evidence and jumps off the cliff edge of the page.

In this way I was witness to the birth of Tweedle Dum and Tweedle Dee. It should have been enough.

But then I got to looking for something I already knew would not be there. I mean, a *key* that might reveal the song "about" something. Lord forgive me. I mean, was it *about* Palestine and Israel? Al Gore and George Bush?

Well, each man kills the thing he loves. I discovered, in the author's hand, that Tweedle Dum and Tweedle Dee were *"both sons of the same mother but they don't recognize each other."* I found *Venus* next to *Adonis* and *Protestantism* next to *Dr. Faustus.*

Opposing pairs? There was no key and there is no lock.

Just the same, I found, squeezed between some verses, *evil violence righteous violence, not always enough to tell which is which between the two.*

And of course this is not the key to the song, although it might well be its DNA, evidence of which is scattered all throughout the pages. Corruption and violence is everywhere. This is America after all.

So my mind wandered back to 1920, to postcards of a hanging that had once been sold in Duluth, Minnesota, and from there to the deep roots of racial violence in Tulsa, Oklahoma. This Bob Dylan Archive would eventually live on Tulsa's Reconciliation Way, which had been previously named Brady Street, after W. Tate Brady, a founder of the city and member of the Ku Klux Klan. Here, in Tulsa's Greenwood District, known colloquially as Black Wall Street, in the year of 1921, whites launched war on the well-off residents. Here they murdered Black men and women in their homes, machine gunned churches, dropped turpentine bombs from Curtiss JN-4 Jenny biplanes conveniently made available by Army Surplus for $1,500 each.

One could presumptuously imagine this as a Dylan narrative, the tale of "Diamond Dick" that triggers the most obscene racial massacre in the history of the United States. A Black teenager was said to have "ripped the clothes" from a white girl. This was "reported" in the *Tulsa Tribune,* which never even hinted that she may well have been his girlfriend. His real name was Dick Rowland, but the *Tulsa Tribune* named him as "Diamond Dick," and put him forward as a candidate for lynching, made him into a fantastic sexualized shoeshine boy clad in gold and diamonds. One guesses Dick Rowland stood for everything threatening about all those prosperous Black people in those thirty-five city blocks, containing twenty-one churches and twenty grocery stores, a hospital, a post office, six hundred businesses that the white citizens now burned to ash. Three hundred people died. No one got to lynch that frightened boy.

One might think I'm playing Mister Jones again, unreasonably connecting Tulsa history with the concerns of Tweedle Dum and Tweedle Dee. But look at the manuscript. See what was on Bob Dylan's mind as he assembled those cubist scenes.

"monstrous citizen, sacking cities" he wrote as an aside amongst the verses.

*"tyrannical conqueror preform horrible cruelties
die peacefully in your bed."*

But it seemed OK for me, if only me, to encounter the ghosts of Greenwood's dead between the archived lines of Tweedle Dee and Tweedle Dum.

*Tweedle-dee Dum and Tweedle-dee Dee
They're throwing knives into the tree*

I don't know how the lyric carries such a savage freight, but it is not an effect that has been easily or accidentally achieved. *Dylan's* lyrics are like Hindu gods with twenty arms. They deal a different hand each time you throw the dice. The Jack of Hearts, the Kings, and Queens are all scrapped down and over-painted. The cards have become tarnished mirrors with no single explanation. You can sit in the Archive until it is time to snap your pencil's neck. By then the girls are playing five-card stud and Mister Jones is bored and no one speaks except that neighbor boy who mutters, *Nothing is revealed.*

* * *

DR. SOLOMON BURKE

"Stepchild" was among the numerous songs Dylan wrote during his 1978 tour; he performed it live as "Am I Your Stepchild?" fifty-three times before he set it aside. Under US copyright law, a songwriter has the right to release the first recording of a song unless they give permission to somebody else. In 2002, Dylan gave "Stepchild" to Dr. Solomon Burke, one of the foundational figures in the development of soul music (Burke had also covered Dylan's "Maggie's Farm" in 1965). Released on *Don't Give Up on Me*, Burke's version also featured Dylan collaborator Daniel Lanois on guitar. Pioneering rock 'n' roll pianist Jerry Lee Lewis (for whom Dylan had originally written *Nashville Skyline*'s "To Be Alone with You") released his own version of "Stepchild" on the 2014 album *Rock & Roll Time*.

From the office of

Dr. Solomon Burke

April 25, 2002

Bob Dylan

315 S. Beverly Drive
Suite 216
Beverly Hills, CA 90212

Dear Mr. Dylan:

What a thrill for me to record *Stepchild*! It was my privilege and honor that you would choose a song for me to sing, and as a fan of yours, recording this song was a personal high point in my singing career.

And then, to have Daniel Lanois on guitar… who ever would have envisioned my recording of a rock blues?! I loved the experience. I hope you are as pleased with the result as I was with the song.

May God bless and keep you.

Sincerest regards,

Dr. Solomon Burke

SVB:

Post Office Box 2044 ⋊ Beverly Hills, California 90213
310 285-3295 (Tel.) ⋊ 310 281-3347 (Fax)

Letter from Dr. Solomon Burke to Bob Dylan, April 25, 2002

MASKED AND ANONYMOUS

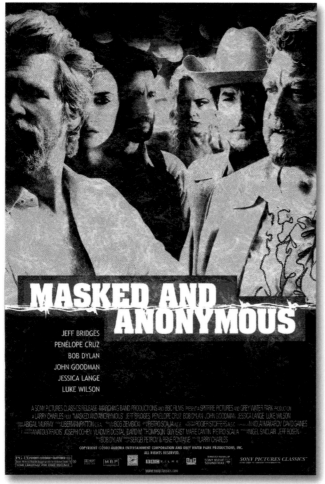

Masked and Anonymous theatrical poster, 2003

Luke Wilson and Bob Dylan on set of *Masked and Anonymous,* 2002. Photograph by Lorey Sebastian

In 2003, Dylan returned to the silver screen in the role of mysterious musician Jack Fate in *Masked and Anonymous*, a film he also co-wrote with writer, director, and producer Larry Charles, of *Seinfeld* and *Borat* fame.

The plot of *Masked and Anonymous* is perhaps best summarized by its distributor Sony Pictures Classics: "In a fictional America caught up in a civil war that is tearing the nation apart, a benefit concert is being organized. A traveling troubadour named Jack Fate [Bob Dylan] is sprung from jail by his scheming former manager, Uncle Sweetheart [John Goodman], to headline a concert with the expectations to bring peace to a country that is entrenched by chaos, lawlessness and pandemonium."

Dylan and Charles had originally pitched HBO on a comedy show in the vein of Jerry Lewis, but after their initial meeting with the network, Dylan and Charles shifted gears and began working on the script that would become *Masked and Anonymous*. According to Charles, Dylan initially came in with a box full of scraps of paper torn from hotel stationery, on which he'd written various ideas, plot points, and character names. The two worked together to assemble the ideas into a unified story, what Charles referred to as "basically a William Burroughs cut-up version of the script," while keeping the overall arc of Dylan's ideas intact. Charles recalled, "Most of those great monologues—the John Goodman monologues, the Luke Wilson monologues, the Jessica Lange monologues—in some form or another came from Dylan."

Suit worn by Bob Dylan in
Masked and Anonymous

Bob Dylan and Jeff Bridges on set of *Masked and Anonymous,* 2002. Photograph by Lorey Sebastian

Shot over the course of nearly three weeks at a warehouse that had been converted into a soundstage, *Masked and Anonymous* featured an all-star cast that included Angela Bassett, Jeff Bridges, Penélope Cruz, Bruce Dern, John Goodman, Ed Harris, Val Kilmer, Jessica Lange, Cheech Marin, Chris Penn, Mickey Rourke, Christian Slater, Fred Ward, and Luke Wilson. According to director Charles, Dylan was the magnet for the film: "We did have kind of a dream cast and those people had all expressed interest. . . . As soon as the word went out that Bob Dylan was gonna make a movie, you couldn't stop people from wanting to get involved."

In a 2022 interview with the Bob Dylan Center, Jeff Bridges, who played the role of Tom Friend while also managing to take photographs on set, described what it was like to work with Dylan on his acting during the film shoot:

One of the high points of my life was working with Bob, playing with him in that movie *Masked and Anonymous*. Larry said, "You know, you're kind of the senior 'thespo' on the show, why don't you go out and jam with Bob and do some acting exercises or something?" I said, "You're kidding." He said, "No, do it." Bob was totally up for it, and we spent a half a day acting. I remember how much fun it was and how *good* he was at it. I think he's such a wonderful actor.

Luke Wilson, who played the role of Bobby Cupid in the film, also sat for an interview with the Bob Dylan Center, and recalled a similar experience of working with Dylan:

Masked and Anonymous set photos, 2002. Photographs by Jeff Bridges

Masked and Anonymous set photos, 2002. Photographs by Lorey Sebastian

I remember doing a scene where it was me and John Goodman and Jeff Bridges and Bob. Larry Charles is directing it, saying, "Jeff, when Bob finishes his dialogue you walk out the door." And Jeff was like, "Okay, all right. So why do I go out the door?" And Dylan was like, "Cause it's a door." And I was like, "*Come on Jeff. Cause it's a door.*"

There were so many moments like that where he can make these little things seem kind of poetic and so much larger than life. And then it gets you thinking about him. My God, all this guy has done is just keep going through the next door. And after that he goes through another door and this one, there's success, and this one's failure, but he just keeps going.

Among the highlights of *Masked and Anonymous* are the blistering live performances given by Dylan and his band (Charlie Sexton and Larry Campbell, guitars; Tony Garnier, bass; and George Receli, drums). They performed two Dylan tunes, "Down in the Flood" (*The Basement Tapes*) and "Cold Irons Bound" (*Time Out of Mind*), and two traditional tunes, "Dixie" and "Diamond Joe," as well as fragments of numerous other songs, including "Standing in the Doorway" and "I'll Remember You."

The official soundtrack for the film featured four of the film's performances, as well as other covers of Dylan songs by well-known artists such as Shirley Caesar, Jerry Garcia, the Grateful Dead, and Los Lobos. However, the most forward-thinking and surprising interpretations of Dylan songs on the soundtrack belong to the international artists, including Articolo 31, Sertab Erener, Francesco De Gregori, and Sophie Zelmani.

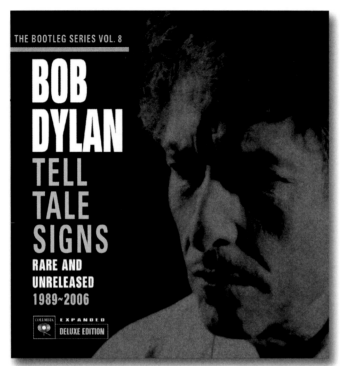

The Bootleg Series: Vol. 8: Tell Tale Signs: Rare and Unreleased 1989–2006

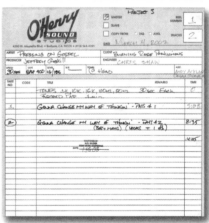

"Waitin' for You," "Keep on the Firing Line," and "Gonna Change My Way of Thinking" audiotape boxes, O'Henry Sound Studios, Burbank, CA, March 2002

"WAITIN' FOR YOU"

Throughout the 1990s and beyond, Dylan participated in a number of special recording projects. Most notably, he wrote an original song, "Things Have Changed," for the soundtrack of the 2000 film *Wonder Boys*. He also recorded a cover version of "Red Cadillac and a Black Mustache" for the tribute record *Good Rockin' Tonight: The Legacy of Sun Records* (2001). In a handful of instances, Dylan made guest appearances on albums by other artists, as in his collaboration with Mike Seeger on "Ballad of Hollis Brown" from *Third Annual Farewell Reunion* (1994). Some of these songs, including "'Cross the Green Mountain" (from the film *Gods and Generals*), "The Lonesome River" (with Ralph Stanley), and "Tell Ol' Bill" (from the film *North Country*), were eventually compiled on the 2008 release, *The Bootleg Series Vol. 8: Tell Tale Signs: Rare and Unreleased 1989–2006*.

During one session in March 2002, Dylan worked on a handful of songs for special releases at O'Henry Sound Studios in Burbank, California. On March 1 and 2, he recorded the waltz "Waitin' for You" for the film *Divine Secrets of the Ya-Ya Sisterhood,* a song Dylan has performed live more than 150 times between 2005 and 2015. On the 3rd, he recorded a version of The Carter Family's "Keep on the Firing Line" for a tribute album that never materialized. The next day, he joined Mavis Staples for a new version of "Gonna Change My Way of Thinking," for the 2003 compilation, *Gotta Serve Somebody: The Gospel Songs of Bob Dylan.*

"THE LONESOME RIVER"

One of Dylan's earliest country music influences was The Stanley Brothers. In 1985, Dylan told journalist Bill Flanagan:

> *If you go back and listen to The Stanley Brothers or The Country Gentlemen or Jim and Jesse, any of the bluegrass groups, there's quite a few songs where they put themselves into the first person. I've done that myself. I've written songs from the first person. I haven't recorded too many of them, but I have done it.*

He included "Stone Walls and Steel Bars," a first-person song by The Stanley Brothers, in his live performances between 1997 and 2002.

Dylan had the opportunity to record with Dr. Ralph Stanley on November 30, 1997, when they recorded The Stanley Brothers classic "The Lonesome River" for Stanley's *Clinch Mountain Country* album. A few weeks later, after Dylan was honored at the Kennedy Center, Stanley sent along a telegram to congratulate him and to thank him for recording together.

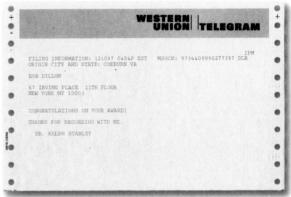

Telegram from Dr. Ralph Stanley to Bob Dylan, December 10, 1997

"TELL OL' BILL"

For the 2005 film *North Country*, starring Charlize Theron, Frances McDormand, and Woody Harrelson, Dylan contributed the song "Tell Ol' Bill." A version of the ballad appeared in Carl Sandburg's influential 1927 folksong collection *The American Songbag*, and the song was later popularized by Bob Gibson and Dave Van Ronk.

Dylan had attempted the song before, under the title "This Evening So Soon," during the sessions for *Self Portrait*, though the song went unreleased until *The Bootleg Series Vol. 10: Another Self Portrait (1969–1971)* from 2013. Dylan namechecks Gibson at the beginning of the recording.

Dylan's 2005 "Tell Ol' Bill" resembles the earlier recordings in name only. Of the more than two dozen takes attempted at Studio 4 in Conshohocken, Pennsylvania, on June 17, 2005, the version that was released was an upbeat number in the style of traditional Western swing. Dylan defers the original song's refrain until the penultimate verse (the final verse in the manuscript), when it becomes the culminating point for the verses that precede it. Along the way, Dylan weaves a tale of a mysterious, lovelorn traveler, with potential nods to The Carter Family and Edgar Allan Poe, among others.

"Tell Ol' Bill" draft manuscript

Bob Dylan with *Movin' On: Luke the Drifter—Songs of Hank Williams* LP, 1978. Photograph by Morgan Renard

THE LOST NOTEBOOKS OF HANK WILLIAMS

As Dylan noted in *Chronicles*, "The songs of Woody Guthrie ruled my universe, but before that, Hank Williams had been my favorite songwriter." Dylan recalled the first time he heard Williams in a handwritten note on a transcription of his interview included in the 1985 retrospective *Biograph*: "I listened to Hank Williams for the 1st time singing 'Hey Good Lookin'" on an old 78 record and it triggered something. I stared out the window and began the dream." In a typescript from around 1992, Dylan said that his music "elevated the soul from a material human life to some celestial communion. . . . it was almost like he invented music."

Dylan was able to pay musical tribute to Williams on more than one occasion. In 2001, he recorded "I Can't Get You Off My Mind" for the album *Timeless: Hank Williams Tribute*. Then an unlikely opportunity presented itself. In 2008, Sony Music invited Dylan to put music to a set of unfinished Hank Williams lyrics that a janitor had found in a dumpster at the Nashville offices of Sony/ATV Music Publishing two years earlier. Dylan completed "The Love That Faded," then turned to other artists to help, including Sheryl Crow, Merle Haggard, Alan Jackson, Norah Jones, and Lucinda Williams. Dylan released the resulting record, titled *The Lost Notebooks of Hank Williams*, on his imprint Egyptian Records in 2011.

One of the "Lost Notebooks of Hank Williams," circa 1951

515

Searching in vain

I

I walk the lonely streets of life day after day
hopeing and praying that you will pass my way
Longing for just a glimpse of your face again
walking the road of life and searching in vain

II

Searching for a treasure that I know is forever gone
still I walk this lonely road from twilite tile dawn
Like a dove up in the blue that has lost his mate
I know I'll never find you but still I search and wate

III

The flowers she planted when love was true have wilthdrow & died
The home we planed is dark and cold without her love inside
All the joy's of life are gone there's nothing left but pain
as I walk the lonely road of life and search but all in vain

IV

Sometimes I stop and tell my self there's no use to pretend
no matter how long the road somewere there's an end
Then I'll here the whistle blow of a lonesome train
and my journey starts anew searching but in vain

Jan 17, 1951
Hank Williams

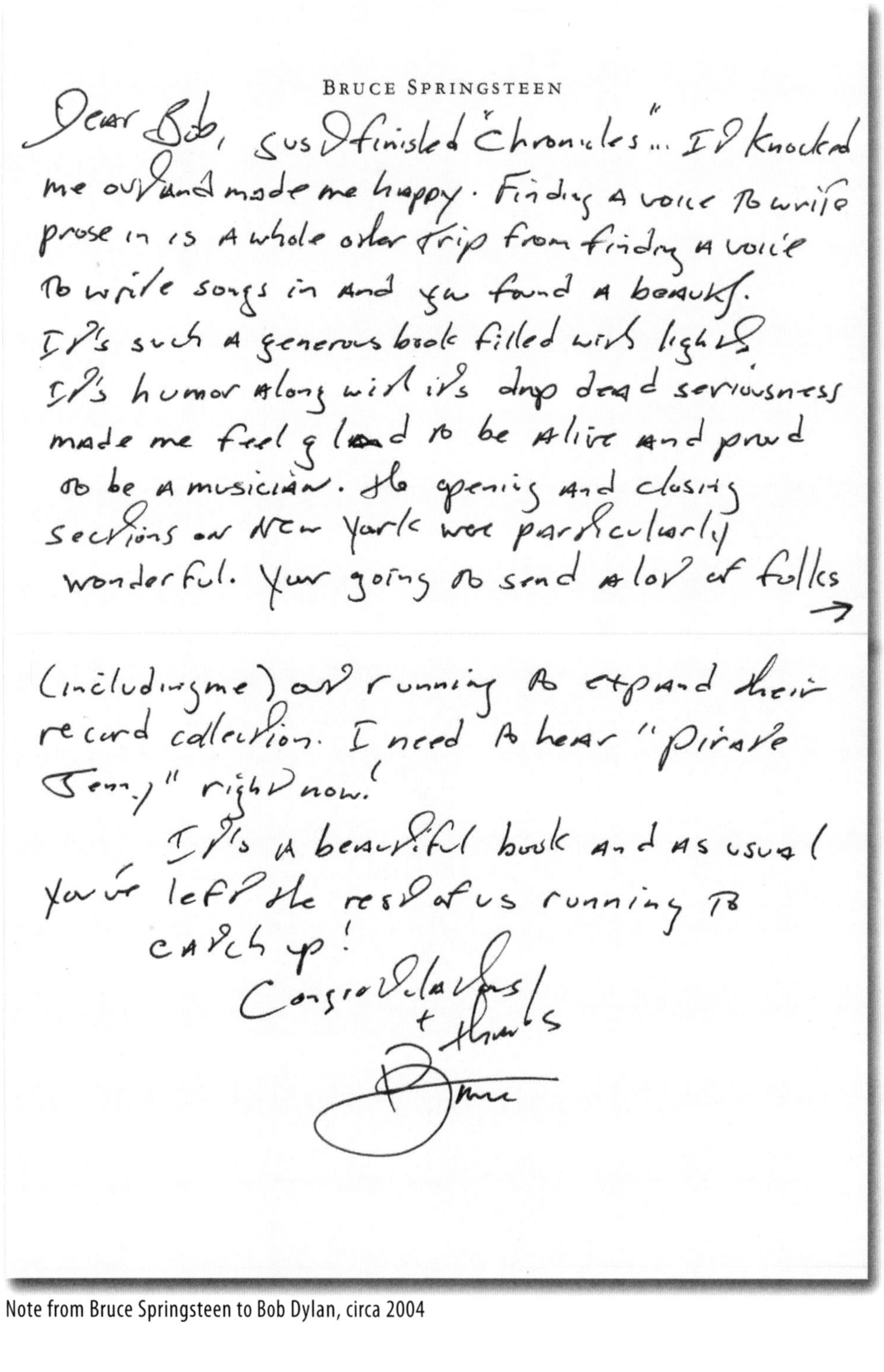

BRUCE SPRINGSTEEN

Dear Bob, just finished "Chronicles"... It knocked me out and made me happy. Finding a voice to write prose in is a whole other trip from finding a voice to write songs in and you found a beauty. It's such a generous book filled with light & it's humor along with it's drop dead seriousness made me feel glad to be alive and proud to be a musician. The opening and closing sections on New York were particularly wonderful. Your going to send a lot of folks →

(including me) out running to expand their record collection. I need to hear "Pirate Jenny" right now!

It's a beautiful book and as usual you've left the rest of us running to catch up!

Congratulations!
+ thanks

Bruce

Note from Bruce Springsteen to Bob Dylan, circa 2004

Dylan's first long-form literary work since the 1971 publication of *Tarantula* was his memoir, *Chronicles: Volume One*. Although it began as a series of liner notes for reissues of his older albums, Dylan told Mikal Gilmore of *Rolling Stone* in 2001,

> *I got completely carried away in the process of . . . I guess call it novelistic writing. So what started out as just maybe notes for a record turned out to be something much more than that, where I got a handle on how to write something which could deal with the present, the past and the future, because I was writing from the future.*

Hebrew edition of *Chronicles*, 2007

Bob Dylan, 1963 photograph used on cover of *Chronicles: Volume One*.
Photograph by Ralph Baxter

US edition of *Chronicles*, 2017

Over the course of five chapters and more than three hundred pages, Dylan focuses on three major episodes: his earliest years in New York City leading up to the recording of his debut album; his aborted collaboration with Archibald MacLeish and the development of *New Morning*; and the circumstances around the writing and recording of *Oh Mercy*. Released on October 5, 2004, *Chronicles: Volume One* spent nineteen weeks on *The New York Times* Best Seller list and was a finalist for the National Book Critics Circle Award in the category of Biography/Autobiography.

Chinese edition of *Chronicles*, 2006

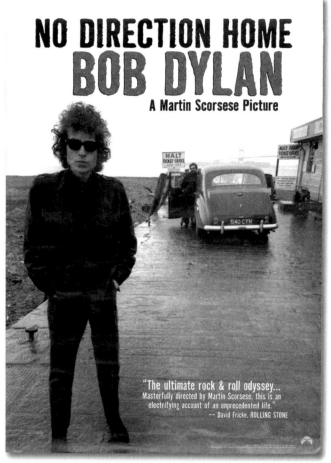

No Direction Home: Bob Dylan
theatrical poster, 2005

Martin Scorsese's landmark documentary *No Direction Home: Bob Dylan* was the first authorized documentary about the life and early career of a musician who had been famously reluctant to delve into the past. The film centers mainly on the story of Dylan's meteoric rise to fame between his 1961 arrival in New York City and his motorcycle accident on July 29, 1966; it also evocatively captures Dylan's early years in Minnesota.

Begun a decade earlier, the film melded archival footage and photography with dozens of hours of interview footage with more than thirty of Dylan's contemporaries, including Joan Baez, Allen Ginsberg, Bob Johnston, Al Kooper, Roy Silver, and Izzy Young. Dylan himself sat for an unprecedented ten-hour interview for the project, in which he provided rare, honest insight into those early years.

Broadcast in two parts on PBS's *American Masters* series and BBC Two's *Arena* on September 26 and 27, 2005, *No Direction Home* garnered rave reviews and won a Peabody Award in April 2006. An accompanying album of material from the film was compiled on *The Bootleg Series Vol. 7: No Direction Home: The Soundtrack*, released alongside the film. In 2019, Scorsese would once again turn his attention to Dylan in the Netflix documentary *Rolling Thunder Revue: A Bob Dylan Story by Martin Scorsese*.

MODERN TIMES

In February 2006, Dylan brought his touring band—guitarists Denny Freeman and Stu Kimball, multi-instrumentalist Donnie Herron, bassist Tony Garnier, and drummer George Receli—into New York City's Clinton Recording Studios to record his thirty-second studio album.

> *This is the best band I've ever been in, I've ever had, man for man. When you play with guys a hundred times a year, you know what you can and can't do, what they're good at, whether you want 'em there. It takes a long time to find a band of individual players.*

Released on August 29, 2006, *Modern Times* continued the success of *Time Out of Mind* and "*Love and Theft*." It was Dylan's first album to reach #1 since *Desire* in 1976. Debuting in the top spot of the *Billboard* 200, the album also went to the top of the charts in Canada, Australia, New Zealand, Ireland, Denmark, Norway, and Switzerland. *Modern Times* has since sold more than four million copies worldwide. Dylan himself noted the trajectory and continuity of his recent work in a 2006 interview with Jonathan Lethem:

> Time Out of Mind *was me getting back in and fighting my way out of the corner. But by the time I made "Love and Theft," I was out of the corner. On this record, I ain't nowhere, you can't find me anywhere, because I'm way gone from the corner.*

Modern Times advertisement

Bob Dylan, 2001 photograph used for promotion of *Modern Times*.
Photograph by David Gahr

"THUNDER ON THE MOUNTAIN"

The lead-off track on *Modern Times*, "Thunder on the Mountain," notably namechecks the contemporary R&B singer-songwriter Alicia Keys in a set of lines that seem to echo Memphis Minnie's 1940 tribute "Ma Rainey." When asked about the reference at the time the song was released, Dylan himself replied,

> *I remember seeing her on the* GRAMMYS *[in 2002]. I think I was on the show with her, I didn't meet her or anything. But I said to myself, "There's nothing about that girl I don't like."*

A draft of the song shows that Dylan was indeed familiar with Keys's 2001 breakthrough album *Songs in A Minor*, and several variations of the lines reference her track "Butterflyz":

"Thunder on the Mountain" CD single, Europe, 2006

I'm thinkin' 'bout Alicia Keys
"Butterflies" in my mind
When she was born in Hell's Kitchen
I was livin' down the line

I was thinkin' 'bout Alicia Keys
Couldn't keep from cryin'
When she made that record "Butterflies"
I was livin' down the line

"Thunder on the Mountain" draft manuscript

"SPIRIT ON THE WATER"

Although this manuscript version of "Spirit on the Water" resembles a finished song with everything just so, upon closer inspection, only the first verse would make the released version of the song without significant revision—the rest was subject to rearrangement, if it made the cut at all.

Dylan offered glimpses of his writing process for the album in an interview with Edna Gundersen in 2006:

> *I tend to overwrite stuff, and in the past*
> *I probably would have left it all in. On this,*
> *I tried my best to edit myself, and let the facts*
> *speak. You can easily get a song convoluted.*

Modern Times has been an album that critics, fans, and trainspotters have taken pains to pick apart in order to identify musical and lyrical influences. These conversations led to larger discussions about folk and blues traditions and the transformation of source material.

One such song was the track "Rollin' and Tumblin'." First recorded by Hambone Willie Newbern as "Roll and Tumble Blues" in 1928, this early version shared similarities with Gus Cannon's Jug Stompers' "Minglewood Blues" recorded the previous year, evidence of the folk process already at work. Robert Johnson later adapted the musical setting for "If I Had Possession Over Judgment Day" and "Traveling Riverside Blues," both of which Dylan heard on the 1961 compilation *King of the Delta Blues Singers*, which had been given to him by John Hammond Sr. In 1950, Muddy Waters electrified the arrangement, recording it in two versions: one on Aristocrat under his own name, and the other as part of the Baby Face Leroy Trio with Little Walter on vocals. Back in the mid-1960s, Dylan had scribbled the lyrics from the Aristocrat release in a notebook. Whatever the antecedents, Dylan's new take on "Rollin' and Tumblin'" adds yet another version to this distinguished song lineage.

Bob Dylan, photograph used on back cover of *Modern Times*, 2006. Photograph by Kevin Mazur

"Spirit on the Water" draft manuscript

Notebook with lyrics from Muddy Waters's 1950 recording of "Rollin' and Tumblin'," circa 1966

Dylan himself even weighed in on how his songwriting continued to engage the folk process in a 2004 interview with Robert Hilburn of the *Los Angeles Times*:

Well, you have to understand that I'm not a melodist.... My songs are either based on old Protestant hymns or Carter Family songs or variations of the blues form. What happens is, I'll take a song I know and simply start playing it in my head. That's the way I meditate. A lot of people will look at a crack on the wall and meditate, or count sheep or angels or money or something, and it's a proven fact that it'll help them relax. I don't meditate on any of that stuff. I meditate on a song. I'll be playing Bob Nolan's "Tumbling Tumbleweeds," for instance, in my head constantly— while I'm driving a car or talking to a person or sitting around or whatever. People will think they are talking to me and I'm talking back, but I'm not. I'm listening to a song in my head. At a certain point, some words will change and I'll start writing a song.

Bob Dylan, 2001 photograph used for promotion of *Modern Times*. Photograph by David Gahr

Theme Time Radio Hour logo, circa 2007

THEME TIME RADIO HOUR

In *Theme Time Radio Hour*, Bob Dylan seemed to relish his newfound role of disc jockey. During the course of an initial run of one hundred episodes originally broadcast on Sirius/XM digital radio between May 2006 and April 2009, Dylan took listeners on weekly one-hour journeys that covered thematic ground from "Baseball" and "Cats" to "Death & Taxes" and "Thanksgiving Leftovers." Across the episodes, the music reflects Dylan's eclectic and expansive musical sensibility, easily taking in the blues of Tampa Red, the rocksteady of The Melodians, the punk of Buzzcocks, the hip-hop of LL Cool J, the honky-tonk of George Jones, and everything in between. Deftly weaving the songs together, Dylan's charming banter was the show's glue, full of jokes, musical insights, esoteric facts, and even the occasional poetry recitation. There were also segments devoted to fan mail and guest appearances from the likes of Cat Power, Elvis Costello, Keb Mo, Amy Sedaris, and Tom Waits. Fun, informative, and always full of great music, *Theme Time Radio Hour* was as unique as its host.

Illustrated by Jaime Hernandez, co-creator of the comic book *Love & Rockets*, this promotional art print pays homage to some of "themes, dreams, and schemes" of the show's creator. Look closely for a glimpse of the fictional Abernathy Building and, of course, Samson's Diner.

In the years since, there have been two additional episodes of the show. The first, titled "Kiss," was a lost episode from the series' original run, whereas the special two-hour "Whiskey" episode from 2020 was made to promote Heaven's Door, Dylan's whiskey company.

Musician Jack White wrote to Dylan with admiration for *Theme Time Radio Hour*, and provided a music recommendation of his own: The Shaggs, the group of sisters from New Hampshire who developed a rabid cult following in the decades after their 1969 album *Philosophy of the World* was released. White later made several cameos in the second season of the show.

White had long been a fan of Dylan, and his band The White Stripes had included Dylan covers in their sets from very early on. "One More Cup of Coffee (Valley Below)" found a home on The White Stripes' 1999 eponymous debut album, and the group often performed a fiery live version of "Isis" between 2001 and 2006. In spring 2004, during a series of Detroit shows in which The White Stripes opened for Dylan, he repaid the compliment, inviting White to join for an encore version of the group's "Ball and Biscuit." Dylan and White have since shared the stage on a number of occasions, resulting in the first live performances of Dylan's "Meet Me in the Morning" and "Outlaw Blues."

BOB DYLAN THEME TIME RADIO HOUR

Paul (McCartney)

6th May 2009

Dear Bob,

Just had the pleasure of listening to your Theme Time radio show, "Friends and Neighbours", and enjoyed it so much that I had to write and tell you. The music you played was fabulous and the chat in between was both edifying and amusing. Thanks for an hour of listening pleasure.

Hope all is well with you.

All the best you lovely boy,

Cheers,

Paul

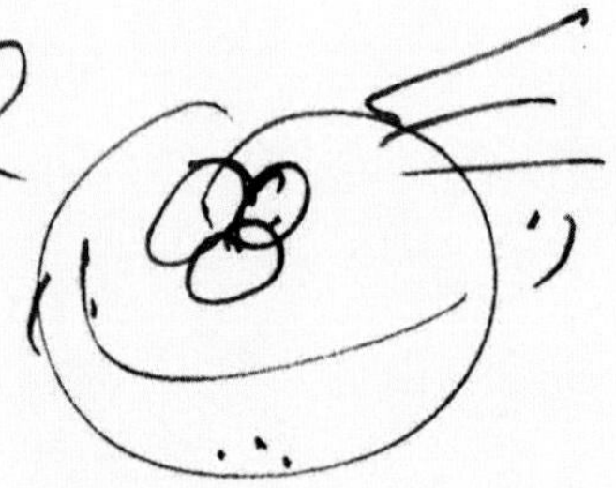

Letter from Paul McCartney to Bob Dylan, May 6, 2009

LETS SHAKE HANDS
JIMMY THE EXPLODER
WASTING MY TIME
ASTRO
CANNON
I JUST DON'T KNOW
LOVE SICK
DEAD LEAVES
ST. JAMES
SUZY LEE
STOP BREAKING DOWN
LAFAYETTE BLUES
SAME BOY
BROKEN BRICKS

JULY
30th
MAGIC
BAG

The White Stripes early set list with Dylan's
"Love Sick," The Magic Bag, Ferndale, MI,
July 30, 1998

Theme Time Radio Hour compilation
promotional poster, 2010

HOPE YOU ARE WELL. LOVING YOUR
DJING/HISTORY LESSON ON THAT THERE RADIO.
HERE IS THAT RECORD BY "THE SHAGGS" I TOLD
YOU ABOUT. PRETTY HEAVY SHIT. FRANK ZAPPA
SAID "BETTER THAN THE BEATLES... ANYDAY" ABOUT
THESE GIRLS. DOES THAT MAKE 'EM BETTER THAN JESUS?
WAIT A MINUTE...
CHECK OUT THE DRUMS ON "MY PAL FOOT FOOT"!

GOING DOWN SLOW
JACK WHITE
III

Letter from Jack White to Bob Dylan, late 2000s

Get Jailed, Jump Bail

ED RUSCHA

The music of Bob Dylan, Joan Baez, and the folksingers was an abrupt change to everything I had always listened to. In order for me to understand this rather new music, I had to view it in context with the music sounds that were in my history. Below I list this history with a tally of musicians and groups that were my choice of sounds from the late '40s to the early '60s:

Clyde McPhatter
All R&B Race Music
All Leiber & Stoller
Webb Pierce
Jenks Carman
Faron Young
Hank Williams
Marty Robbins
Charlie Feathers
Collins Kids
Gene Vincent
Rockabilly including Elvis
Lefty Frizzell
Sleepy LaBeef
Count Basie
Spike Jones
Billy Eckstine
Stan Kenton
West Coast Jazz
Wardell Gray
Eric Dolphy
Louis Jordan
Slim Gaillard
Jesse Belvin
Jimmy Liggins
Thelonious Monk
Little Walter
Rosco Gordon
I'd better stop here

Folksinging of the late '50s and early '60s seemed to introduce sensitive and poetic messages that the above didn't exhibit. Social protest was also absent from the music on this list.

I had imagined that Bob Dylan had no knowledge or interest in this music or musicians. How wrong I was, as I found out much later, when Dylan hosted a radio program called *Theme Time Radio Hour* featuring himself as deejay. This amounted to one of the finest compilations of American music across its history and was narrated with great intensity and originality by Dylan himself.

GET JAILED, JUMP BAIL 2001–2013

528

On the subject of musical inspiration affecting my art, for titles of my pieces I have borrowed phrases from Captain Beefheart: "A Squid Eating Dough in a Polyethylene Bag / Is Fast and Bulbous . . . Got Me?"(1982), and Frank Zappa: "Slobberin Drunk at the Palomino" (1975).

I have a particular attachment to Dylan's "Subterranean Homesick Blues." There is one line that I recall: "Get jailed, jump bail" and have wondered if that line could have cosmically (through the back door?) triggered the painting of mine titled *Bail Jumper* (1990).

Bail Jumper, Ed Ruscha, acrylic on canvas, 1990

Together Through Life, Dylan's thirty-third album, released on April 28, 2009, had its origins in another film soundtrack project. French director Olivier Dahan had approached Dylan about coming up with some new songs for his film *My Own Love Song*, in particular a ballad that could serve as the film's centerpiece. But once Dylan got writing, he ended up with an album's worth of material, including that ballad, titled "Life Is Hard" (sung by actress Renée Zellweger in the film).

Dylan turned to Grateful Dead lyricist Robert Hunter, with whom he'd co-written lyrics for two songs on his 1989 album *Down in the Groove*. Together they wrote the lyrics for nine of the ten tracks on the album. Their last collaboration was for "Duquesne Whistle," released on *Tempest* in 2012.

Dylan's band included Donnie Herron, Tony Garnier, and George Receli from his touring band, as well as Heartbreakers guitarist Mike Campbell and Los Lobos' multi-instrumentalist David Hidalgo, whose accordion added a new Tex-Mex sound to Dylan's musical landscape. On songs where it's featured, like the ballad "I Feel a Change Comin' On," the instrument is used almost like a lead guitar, responding to each of Dylan's lines. Over the course of just nine days, the band cut an entire album's worth of material.

In an interview with the Bob Dylan Center, Campbell recalled his experiences working on the album:

> *Together Through Life* was so much fun. The first thing Bob said to me [in the studio] was "Have you ever made a record in mono?" And I said, "No, we've never done an entire record, but we've done recordings in mono before." And he said, "Well, I wanna do this record in mono with one microphone on the whole band." His idea was just like a Bing Crosby record or whatever, put this really nice microphone in the middle of the room. It was really exciting, but we'd listen back to it and Bob would say, "Well turn up the guitar," and the engineer would say, "Well, we can't turn it up. It's all on one microphone." So he'd look at me, he said, "Next time play a little louder." So we made it work and it was a real challenge, but it was really inspiring.

My Own Love Song French theatrical poster, 2010

CHRISTMAS IN THE HEART

Not long after the release of *Together Through Life*, Dylan returned to the studio to record a collection of Christmas songs for release that fall. In addition to his touring band members Donnie Herron, Tony Garnier, and George Receli, Dylan brought guitarist Phil Upchurch, keyboardist Patrick Warren, and David Hidalgo, who'd provided accordion and guitar on his previous album. Over the course of the sessions, the band ran through popular Christmas songs ranging from "Here Comes Santa Claus" to "Little Drummer Boy," but it was the more obscure "Must Be Santa" that quickly became a holiday classic. Released as the album's sole single, "Must Be Santa" was also turned into a music video with Dylan appearing in a blond wig alongside Santa Claus at a holiday house party run amok.

"Must Be Santa" 45 rpm single, US, 2009

Released on October 13, 2009, *Christmas in the Heart* debuted at #1 on the holiday charts, #5 on the folk album charts, and #10 on the rock album charts. Critics were initially unsure about Dylan's decision to record such an album, but for Dylan the songs were part of a larger American musical tradition, which included the folksongs from earlier in his career, and the Great American Songbook tunes he'd record a few years later. As he said in an interview around the release of the album, "These songs are part of my life, just like folk songs." All of Dylan's royalties in perpetuity from *Christmas in the Heart* went to organizations fighting food insecurity around the world.

Bob Dylan, 2006.
Photograph by William Claxton

2001–2013

Letter from President Bill Clinton to Bob Dylan, May 9, 2000

Fax letter from President Jimmy Carter to Bob Dylan, April 11, 2006

Bob Dylan's music has been appreciated by several presidents of the United States. In addition to performing at the inauguration of Bill Clinton in January 1993, Dylan enjoyed a warm relationship with Jimmy Carter, whom he first met when Carter was governor of Georgia in 1974.

Dylan's only performance at the White House occurred during President Barack Obama's time in office. The February 9, 2010, concert, "In Performance at the White House: Songs of the Civil Rights Movement," featured musical performances and speeches by Yolanda Adams, Joan Baez, Natalie Cole, Morgan Freeman, Jennifer Hudson, John Mellencamp, Dr. Bernice Johnson Reagon, Smokey Robinson, The Blind Boys of Alabama, and the Howard University Choir. For his part of the program, Dylan offered a stately acoustic version of "The Times They Are A-Changin'," accompanied by his longtime bassist Tony Garnier and pianist Patrick Warren.

On May 29, 2012, President Obama awarded Bob Dylan the Presidential Medal of Freedom in the East Room of the White House. The ceremony, which started in 1963 under John F. Kennedy, bestowed upon the recipient the nation's highest civilian honor for "for especially meritorious contribution to (1) the security or national interests of the United States, or (2) world peace, or (3) cultural or other significant public or private endeavors." Dylan was honored alongside twelve other recipients, including former Secretary of State Madeleine Albright, astronaut John Glenn, labor leader Dolores Huerta, and novelist Toni Morrison. President Obama personally introduced each recipient, and said the following about Dylan:

Bob Dylan with President Barack Obama, Presidential Medal of Freedom ceremony, 2012. Photograph by Mandel Ngan

Bob Dylan started out singing other people's songs. But, as he says, "There came a point where I had to write what I wanted to say, because what I wanted to say, nobody else was writing." So, born in Hibbing, Minnesota, a town, he says, "where you couldn't be a rebel—it was too cold"— Bob moved to New York at age 19. By the time he was 23, Bob's voice, with its weight, its unique, gravelly power, was redefining not just what music sounded like, but the message it carried and how it made people feel. Today, everybody from Bruce Springsteen to U2 owes Bob a debt of gratitude. There is not a bigger giant in the history of American music. All these years later, he's still chasing that sound, still searching for a little bit of truth. And I have to say that I'm a really big fan.

TEMPEST

For *Tempest*, Dylan returned to the studio with his touring band—Charlie Sexton, Stu Kimball, Donnie Herron, Tony Garnier, and George Receli—as well as David Hidalgo. Produced by "Jack Frost," *Tempest* was engineered by Scott Litt, who'd worked with alternative rock bands like R.E.M., Nirvana, and The Replacements. In an interview with Mikal Gilmore shortly after the release of the record, Dylan demurred on the album he'd just created:

> *Tempest was like all the rest of them: The songs just fall together. It's not the album I wanted to make, though. I had another one in mind. I wanted to make something more religious. That takes a lot more concentration—to pull that off 10 times with the same thread—than it does with a record like I ended up with, where anything goes and you just gotta believe it will make sense.*

Regardless, the result was one of Dylan's most uncompromising and austere albums, one that seamlessly interweaves classical literature, religious texts, blues idioms, and tales of the French Quarter. Widely hailed by critics and fans, songs like "Pay in Blood," "Soon After Midnight," and "Long and Wasted Years" became standouts in the tours that followed.

Tempest promotional poker chips

L–R: Donnie Herron, Tony Garnier, Bob Dylan, George Receli, Stu Kimball, Charlie Sexton, 2012. Photograph by John Shearer

PAGE 535: *Tempest* pop-up store poster, 2012

THEMES, DREAMS, AND SCHEMES

BOB DYLAN
TEMPEST

SEPT. 10
- SEPT. 16

THE NEW YORK STORE

"TEMPEST"

At fourteen minutes in length, "Tempest" was Dylan's longest song to date. As evidenced by this draft manuscript written on hotel stationery from a June 4 concert in Skopje, Macedonia, Dylan had been working on the epic disaster ballad about the 1912 sinking of the RMS *Titanic* during his 2012 summer tour. (Another notepad from the era shows Dylan sketching out nautical terms for use in the song.)

Using as a point of departure the melody of the 1956 Carter Family recording, "The Titanic," Dylan wove together over the course of forty-five stanzas a dense narrative melding real and fictional characters. John Jacob Astor IV, the richest passenger aboard the ship, appears as "Mr. Astor," whereas Leo is most likely a reference to Leonardo DiCaprio, who portrayed the fictional Jack Dawson in the 1997 blockbuster film *Titanic*. As Dylan told Mikal Gilmore during a 2012 interview in *Rolling Stone*:

> *People are going to say, "Well, it's not very truthful." But a songwriter doesn't care about what's truthful. What he cares about is what should've happened, what could've happened. That's its own kind of truth.*

Holiday Inn Skopje

Moša Pijade Str. 2
1000 Skopje
Macedonia

Tel: +389 02 329 29 29
Fax: +389 02 311 55 03
E-mail: hiskopje@holiday-inn.com.mk
www.holiday-inn.com/skopje

Guest Stationery

"Tempest" draft manuscript

THEMES, DREAMS, AND SCHEMES

L–R: George Receli, Donnie Herron, Charlie Sexton, Bob Dylan, Tony Garnier, Stu Kimball, 2012. Photograph by John Shearer

"LONG AND WASTED YEARS"

As intense as "Long and Wasted Years" sounds on *Tempest*, that version paled in comparison to the vicious showstopper that Dylan used in 2014 to conclude his concerts. The weight of the lyrics, the incessantly descending chord progression, the absence of a chorus, and especially Dylan's grit-filled vocal gave the song an emotional center of gravity that was impossible to escape. A mainstay of Dylan's sets through 2018, "Long and Wasted Years" has become one of Dylan's essential songs.

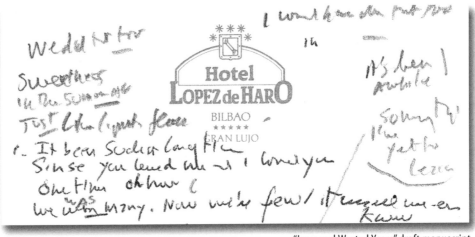

"Long and Wasted Years" draft manuscript

ON THE ROAD AGAIN

From 2001 to 2012, Dylan kept up his touring schedule, playing nearly one hundred concerts a year around the world. As Dylan pointedly told Jonathan Lethem in 2006,

> *I see that I could stop touring*
> *at any time, but then,*
> *I don't really feel like it right now.*
> *I think I'm in my middle years now.*
> *I've got no retirement plans.*

L–R: David Kemper, Tony Garnier, Bob Dylan, Larry Campbell, Charlie Sexton on the tour bus, Telluride, CO, August 2001. Photograph by Ken Regan

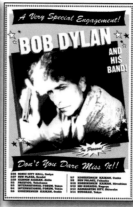

Concert posters, advertisements, and tickets, 2000–2012

Beijing Workers' Stadium, China, April 2011. Photographer unknown

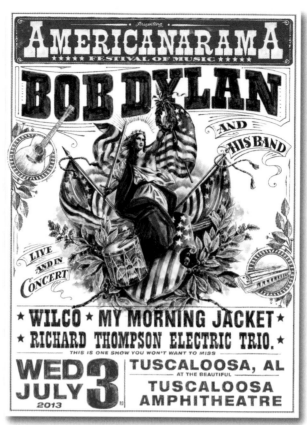

Americanarama: Festival of Music tour poster, 2013

Despite being in his fifth decade of touring, Dylan found myriad ways to keep his routine fresh and to keep moving forward. In 2001, Dylan returned to Japan for the first time in four years. The year 2003 brought brief reunions on the road with The Dead (the survivors of the Grateful Dead), as well as Tom Petty and the Heartbreakers. In 2004, Dylan embarked on a US summer tour of minor league baseball stadiums with Willie Nelson. The following year Dylan toured with Merle Haggard. In the summer of 2009, Dylan and Willie Nelson set out on a US tour with John Mellencamp, and the following year Dylan and Mellencamp co-headlined a tour of their own. In April 2011, Dylan traveled to the Far East for his first-ever shows in Vietnam and China. That fall he toured Europe with Mark Knopfler, and they toured the US the following year. A show on May 5, 2012, in Heredia, Costa Rica, was not only Dylan's first in the country, but also his first in Central America. In 2013, Dylan staged a twenty-six-date summer tour across the United States called Americanarama: Festival of Music, with Wilco and My Morning Jacket in support.

Over the course of this dozen-year stretch, the members of Dylan's band also shifted. Drummer George Receli joined the group at the beginning of 2002 and remained until the fall of 2019. Stu Kimball became the group's second guitarist in 2004, a role he held until his departure in 2018. Guitarist Charlie Sexton left the group in 2002, only to return in 2009. In his absence, guitarist Denny Freeman came aboard in 2005, as did multi-instrumentalist Donnie Herron. Dylan even went through his own musical shift by reconnecting with his original instrument of his youth, the piano, which took on an increasingly larger role in his playing and the band's arrangements. Through it all, bassist Tony Garnier remained a constant.

PAGE 543: Bob Dylan, 2006. Photograph by William Claxton

The Here and Now

2014–2023

What made my songs different, and still does, is I can create several orbits that travel and intersect each other and are set up in a metaphysical way. They all came out of the folk music pantheon, and those songs have lasted. So if my songs were written correctly and eloquently, there's no reason they wouldn't last.

—Bob Dylan, October 2004, Edna Gundersen interview, *USA Today*

Video still from *Shadow Kingdom*, 2021. Directed by Alma Har'el

SHADOWS IN THE NIGHT

Shadows in the Night back cover photograph, 2014. Photograph by John Shearer

Throughout 2014, Dylan seemed to have something new in the works. On May 13, he issued a studio recording of the popular standard, "Full Moon and Empty Arms," on his website. Months later, at a show in Los Angeles on October 26, he debuted the hymn-like "Stay with Me," by Jerome Moross and Carolyn Leigh. ("Stay with Me" was the theme from the 1963 film *The Cardinal*, directed by Otto Preminger. The following year, Dylan visited Preminger on the set of his next film, *In Harm's Way*.)

On December 9, Dylan announced *Shadows in the Night*, his thirty-sixth studio album. *Shadows*—along with his next two studio efforts—comprised popular standards from what is often called the Great American Songbook and the repertoire of one of its finest interpreters, Frank Sinatra.

With songs by Irving Berlin, Rodgers and Hammerstein, and Johnny Mercer, Dylan's new direction might have seemed like a radical departure for those familiar with the trajectory of his career. Yet Dylan had been steeped in the history of American music his entire life, and the Great American Songbook was part of his musical DNA, even if the connections may not have always been so obvious. Dylan's interpretations stripped the songs down to their essentials. In doing so, he was able to find new meaning in songs that had been done countless times, from the classic movies of Hollywood to the records of Barbra Streisand and more recently Rod Stewart.

As Dylan explained in the press release announcing *Shadows in the Night*,

> *I don't see myself as covering these songs in any way. They've been covered enough. Buried, as a matter of fact. What me and my band are basically doing is uncovering them. Lifting them out of the grave and bringing them into the light of day.*

Released on February 3, 2015, *Shadows in the Night* was unmistakably a Bob Dylan record. Moody and provocative, the album explored dimensions of his music that, although long present, had never been configured in such stark relief. "The Night We Called It a Day" was so expressively vivid that Dylan teamed up with director Nash Edgerton for a film noir–inspired music video that nodded to Dylan's love of the genre.

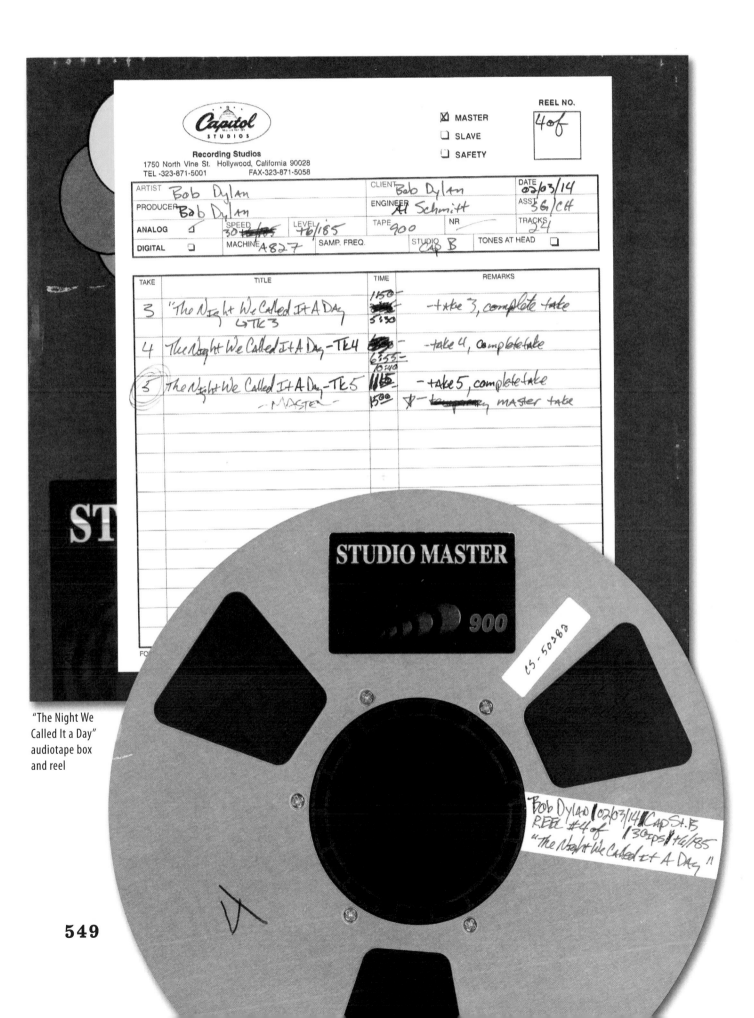

"The Night We
Called It a Day"
audiotape box
and reel

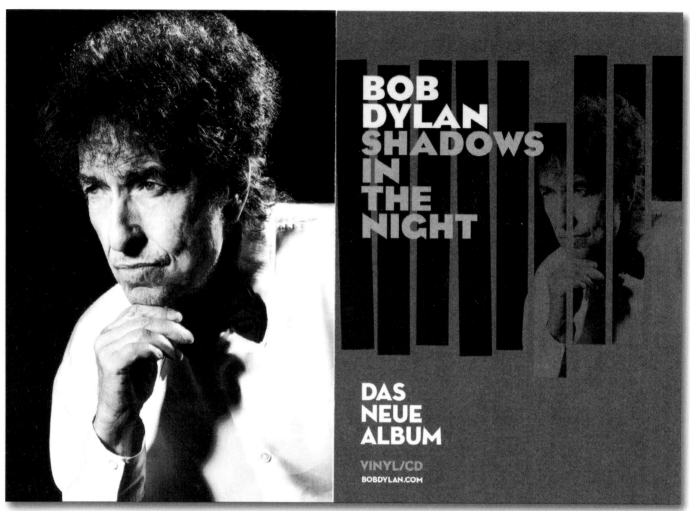

Shadows in the Night advertisement, Germany, 2014

Dylan's primary interview to promote the album's release was with *AARP: The Magazine*, which has one of the largest circulations in the United States. As a bonus, AARP gave out fifty thousand copies of the album to randomly selected readers. Speaking with editor in chief Robert Love, Dylan discussed many topics, including the importance of family, his career, and the influence of Frank Sinatra on his new music:

> *When you start doing these songs, Frank's got to be on your mind. Because he is the mountain. That's the mountain you have to climb, even if you only get part of the way there.*

Dylan had long admired Sinatra, and the feeling was mutual: Sinatra made a special request for Dylan to perform "Restless Farewell" at his 80th birthday celebration in 1995, which was notable, as Dylan was the only performer who didn't cover a Sinatra song.

"THAT LUCKY OLD SUN"

Shadows in the Night was not quite as radical a departure as it may have seemed; Dylan had been singing these songs throughout his career. "That Lucky Old Sun," the album's final, stirring track, was a song that he had played live more than two dozen times prior to recording it. Dylan first publicly performed the song at Farm Aid, September 22, 1985, accompanied by Tom Petty and the Heartbreakers and Willie Nelson, and in 1971, he recorded a version with Leon Russell on piano.

Shadows in the Night established a template for Dylan's next couple of albums. As Dylan's previous explorations of country, gospel, and other genres had informed his own music, so too would these albums influence his music to come, whether in the live transformation of "Like a Rolling Stone" with an extended rubato section in 2019, or in the meditative "Mother of Muses" on the 2020 album *Rough and Rowdy Ways*.

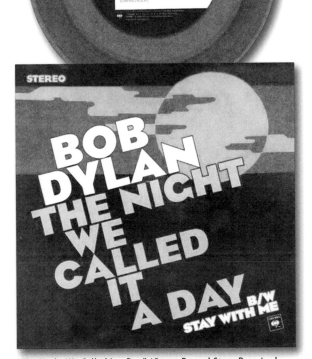

"The Night We Called It a Day" 45 rpm Record Store Day single, 2015

"That Lucky Old Sun" track sheet, 2014

FOLLOWING PAGES (552–553):
Video stills from "The Night We Called It a Day" music video, 2015. Directed by Nash Edgerton

ALL RIGHTS RESERVED.
COPYRIGHT MADE BY COLUMBIA RECORDS.
A DIVISION OF SONY MUSIC ENTERTAINMENT

The Night
WE CALLED IT
a Day

The End

L–R: Bob Dylan; Jimmy Carter; Neil Portnow, CEO, MusiCares; MusiCares, 2015. Photograph by Michael Kovac

Sheryl Crow and Don Was, MusiCares, 2015. Photograph by Kevork Djansezian

MUSICARES

On February 6, 2015, on the occasion of his acceptance of the MusiCares Person of the Year Award in Los Angeles, Dylan delivered a thirty-minute reflection on his influences, songwriting, and career. After generous remarks from former US president and Dylan fan Jimmy Carter, Dylan took the stage and spoke candidly about his songwriting process.

I'm glad for my songs to be honored like this. But you know, they didn't get here by themselves. It's been a long road and it's taken a lot of doing. These songs of mine, they're like mystery plays, the kind that Shakespeare saw when he was growing up. I think you could trace what I do back that far. They were on the fringes then, and I think they're on the fringes now. And they sound like they've been on the hard ground.

Willie Nelson, MusiCares, 2015. Photograph by Larry Busacca

THE HERE AND NOW

Bob Dylan delivers his MusiCares Person of the Year Award acceptance speech, 2015. Photograph by Kevin Mazur

Billy Lee Riley promotional photograph, inscribed to Bob Dylan

Throughout his speech, Dylan offered thanks to the many people who had helped him along the way, ranging from music publisher Lou Levy ("He told me outright, there was no precedent for what I was doing, that I was either before my time or behind it"), to Joan Baez ("I learned a lot of things from her. A woman with devastating honesty. And for her kind of love and devotion, I could never pay that back").

As Dylan closed his speech, he explained what had moved him to speak so publicly:

> I'm proud to be here tonight for MusiCares. I think a lot of this organization. They've helped many people. Many musicians who have contributed a lot to our culture. I'd like to personally thank them for what they did for a friend of mine, Billy Lee Riley. A friend of mine who they helped for six years when he was down and couldn't work. Billy was a son of rock 'n' roll, obviously.
>
> He was a true original. He did it all: He played, he sang, he wrote. He would have been a bigger star but Jerry Lee [Lewis] came along. And you know what happens when someone like that comes along. You just don't stand a chance.
>
> So Billy became what is known in the industry—a condescending term, by the way—as a one-hit wonder. But sometimes, just sometimes, once in a while, a one-hit wonder can make a more powerful impact than a recording star who's got twenty or thirty hits behind him. And Billy's hit song was called "Red Hot," and it was red hot. It could blast you out of your skull and make you feel happy about it. Change your life.

FALLEN ANGELS

"Melancholy Mood" EP, Japan, 2016

Fallen Angels was Dylan's second album exploring popular standards. To help him realize his vision for those sessions, Dylan enlisted legendary recording engineer Al Schmitt. After getting his start as an engineer at age 19 recording Duke Ellington and his Orchestra in 1949, Schmitt spent the next seven decades amassing two thousand album credits and twenty-three GRAMMYS for his work with the likes of Tony Bennett, Ray Charles, Rosemary Clooney, Miles Davis, Lady Gaga, Michael Jackson, Jefferson Airplane, Diana Krall, Madonna, Willie Nelson, Elvis Presley, and Frank Sinatra.

For the sessions at Capitol Records Studios' historic Studio B in Hollywood, Dylan assembled a band that included Charlie Sexton, Stu Kimball, Donnie Herron, Tony Garnier, and George Receli from his touring band, and rounded out the group with guitarist Dean Parks and a small horn ensemble. Schmitt's magic came in a simple but difficult-to-get-right method: he relied mainly on the sound of the room, mic placement, and strong performances, rather than a lot of equalization, effects, or mixing. The resulting recording was lush and immediate. Dylan described the recording process in a 2015 interview:

> *There are only two guitars in there, and one is just playing the pulse. Stand-up bass is playing orchestrated moving lines. It's almost like folk music in a way. I mean, there are no drums in a Bill Monroe band. Hank Williams didn't use them either. Sometimes the beat takes the mystery out of the rhythm. Maybe all the time. I could only record these songs one way, and that was live on the floor with a very small number of mics. No headphones, no overdubs, no vocal booth, no separate tracking. I know it's the old-fashioned way, but to me it's the only way that would have worked for songs like this. Vocally, I think I sang about six inches away from the mic. It's a board mix, for the most part, mixed as it was recorded. We played the song a few times for the engineer. He put a few microphones around. I told him we would play it as many times as he wanted. That's the way each song was done.*

Although this focus continued to confuse some, fans and critics largely responded enthusiastically to this second helping of Dylan's vision of the Great American Song-book. Unlike in past years, when he had been nominated in the GRAMMY folk or rock categories, this time Dylan was nominated for the Best Traditional Pop Vocal Album award for *Fallen Angels*.

TRIPLICATE

In February 2016, Dylan once again teamed up with engineer Al Schmitt at Capitol Studios in Hollywood to work through another set of popular standards. This time the collaboration produced thirty songs, released as *Triplicate*, which was divided into three thematically arranged ten-song volumes: *'Til the Sun Goes Down*, *Devil Dolls*, and *Comin' Home Late*. Recorded live, without any overdubs, *Triplicate* once again showed Dylan's mastery at animating these melodramas in miniature. Dylan discussed the album with music writer Bill Flanagan, in an interview that was posted to Dylan's website:

> These songs are some of the most heartbreaking stuff ever put on record and I wanted to do them justice. Now that I have lived them and lived through them I understand them better. They take you out of that mainstream grind where you're trapped between differences which might seem different but are essentially the same. Modern music and songs are so institutionalized that you don't realize it. These songs are cold and clear-sighted, there is a direct realism in them, faith in ordinary life just like in early rock and roll.

Frank Sinatra with Bob Dylan, *Tribute to Frank Sinatra: 80 Years My Way*, Los Angeles, November 19, 1995. Photographer unknown

Although the repertoire again consisted of tunes popularized by Frank Sinatra, songs like "The Best Is Yet to Come" and "I Guess I'll Have to Change My Plans" were also associated with Tony Bennett. Prior to the album's release on March 31, 2017, Dylan paid tribute to the master in a pre-taped segment for the NBC television special, *Tony Bennett Celebrates 90: The Best Is Yet to Come*, broadcast on December 20, 2016. Standing front and center, wielding a microphone on a stand, Dylan sang and looked the part of a crooner as he performed "Once Upon a Time" in the arrangement that appeared on *Triplicate*.

Video still from *Tony Bennett Celebrates 90: The Best Is Yet to Come*, 2016. Directed by Jennifer Lebeau

BOB DYLAN
Triplicate

Nobel Prize in Literature poster featuring award winners, 1901–2016

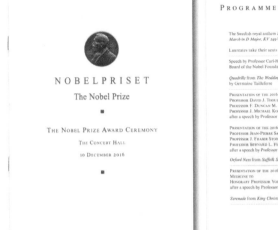
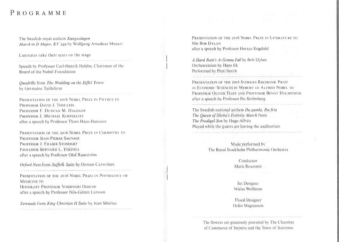

Nobel Prize in Literature Award Ceremony program, 2016

On October 13, 2016, news broke that the Swedish Academy had awarded Bob Dylan the Nobel Prize in Literature "for having created new poetic expressions within the great American song tradition." Dylan was only the twelfth American to win the Prize, joining Saul Bellow, Joseph Brodsky, Pearl Buck, T. S. Eliot, William Faulkner, Ernest Hemingway, Sinclair Lewis, Isaac Bashevis Singer, John Steinbeck, Toni Morrison, and Eugene O'Neill. More importantly, however, he was the first-ever songwriter to win the prestigious award, which had to that point been given only to "traditional authors."

The Swedish Academy's decision proved controversial. In the best cases, the episode provoked thoughtful conversation on the literary merits of songwriting. Distinguished author Salman Rushdie dubbed Dylan "the brilliant inheritor of the bardic tradition." Similar validation came from Dylan's peers in music, with Leonard Cohen, himself a poet and author of note, remarking, "To me, [the Nobel] is like pinning a medal on Mount Everest for being the highest mountain."

Having just embarked upon another tour, Dylan didn't respond to the news for a few days. He later explained that the "news about the Nobel Prize left me speechless." Although he was unable to attend the Nobel Banquet in Stockholm that December, the US Ambassador to Sweden Azita Raji spoke in his absence, and Patti Smith performed "A Hard Rain's A-Gonna Fall" with orchestral accompaniment. The following April, when Dylan's tour passed through Sweden, Dylan met with the Academy for a private ceremony to accept his medal and diploma. In a statement from Academy secretary Sara Danius, she noted, "Quite a bit of time was spent looking closely at the gold medal, in particular the beautifully crafted back, an image of a young man sitting under a laurel tree who listens to the Muse."

One of the requirements of a Nobel Laureate is to deliver a lecture. Dylan decided to record his speech with an improvised piano accompaniment by Alan Pasqua, Dylan's sideman in 1978. Opening with a discussion of the vernacular he learned from folk music, Dylan turned to the way his songs reflected the "principles and sensibilities and an informed view of the world" that he'd absorbed from three formative books from his adolescence: *The Odyssey* by Homer, *Moby-Dick* by Herman Melville, and *All Quiet on the Western Front* by Erich Maria Remarque. "If a song moves you, that's all that's important," Dylan asserted, while contemplating the relationship of music and literature:

> *Our songs are alive in the land of the living. . . . The words in Shakespeare's plays were meant to be acted on the stage. Just as lyrics in songs are meant to be sung, not read on a page. And I hope some of you get the chance to listen to these lyrics the way they were intended to be heard: in concert or on record or however people are listening to songs these days.*

HONORS AND AWARDS

Over the course of his career, Bob Dylan has received numerous prestigious awards and honors in recognition of his "profound impact on popular music and American culture marked by lyrical compositions of extraordinary poetic power," as the Pulitzer Prize Committee described it when he was awarded a special citation in 2008. These accolades go beyond the field of music, reflecting Dylan's immense and enduring impact on culture and society. He is the recipient of the Médaille Légion d'Honneur Ordonnance Chevalier and the Presidential Medal of Freedom, the highest civilian awards in France and the United States, respectively.

1963:	Tom Paine Award, Emergency Civil Liberties Committee
1970:	Princeton University Honorary Doctorate of Music
1979:	Mississippi Colonel
1982:	Songwriters Hall of Fame
1986:	American Society of Composers, Authors, and Publishers (ASCAP) Founders Award
1988:	Rock & Roll Hall of Fame
1990:	Commandeur des Arts et des Lettres (France)
1991:	GRAMMY Lifetime Achievement Award
1995:	Arkansas Traveler
1997:	Dorothy and Lillian Gish Prize
1997:	Kennedy Center Lifetime Achievement Award
1998:	GRAMMY Awards, Album of the Year, *Time Out of Mind*
2000:	Polar Music Prize (Sweden)
2001:	Golden Globe, Best Original Song for a Motion Picture, "Things Have Changed"
2001:	Academy Award, Best Original Song in a Motion Picture, "Things Have Changed"
2002:	Nashville Songwriters Hall of Fame
2004:	University of St. Andrews (Scotland) Honorary Doctorate of Music
2007:	Prince of Asturias Prize for the Arts (Spain)
2008:	Pulitzer Prize Special Citation
2010:	National Medal of the Arts in Washington, DC
2012:	Presidential Medal of Freedom
2013:	American Academy of Arts and Letters
2013:	Akademie der Künste (Germany)
2013:	Chevalier de la médaille Légion d'Honneur (France)
2016:	Nobel Prize in Literature (Sweden)

Nobel Prize diploma given by the Swedish Academy, 2016

PAGE 561: Bob Dylan, 2017. Photograph by John Shearer

ROLLING THUNDER REVUE:
A BOB DYLAN STORY BY MARTIN SCORSESE

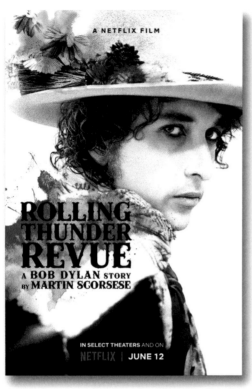

Rolling Thunder Revue: A Bob Dylan Story by Martin Scorsese was the second film the director made about Dylan. Released on June 12, 2019, the Netflix film blurs the line between fact and fiction to tell a story of Dylan's famed 1975 tour.

Interspersing restored outtakes from Dylan's 1978 film *Renaldo and Clara* with talking head interviews from a handful of invented characters both revealed and imagined, Scorsese created a playful alternate history of the Rolling Thunder Revue, which captured its mischievous spirit better than any straight documentary. In conjunction with the documentary, 148 rehearsal and live tracks, including some rarities, were released on the box set *The Rolling Thunder Revue: The 1975 Live Recordings*.

Rolling Thunder Revue: A Bob Dylan Story by Martin Scorsese promotional poster, 2019

RETROSPECTRUM

Opening on September 29, 2019, at the Modern Art Museum in Shanghai, China, *Retrospectrum* collected more than 250 pieces of artwork spanning the full breadth of Dylan's work as a visual artist. Oil, acrylic, and watercolor paintings were displayed alongside ink, pastel, and charcoal drawings, which were in turn set off by Dylan's ironwork sculptures. From the original works making up his earliest published drawings (from the 1973 book *Writings and Drawings*), to his *Mondo Scripto* (at that time his most recent work), the retrospective also featured some of Dylan's most iconic artworks, including the *Train Tracks* of the *Drawn Blank* series and a monumental new version of *Endless Highway* from *The Beaten Path* series.

> *Seeing many of my works years after I completed them is a fascinating experience. I don't really associate them with any particular time or place or state of mind, but view them as part of a long arc; a continuum that begins with the way I go forth in the world and changes direction as my perception is shaped and altered by life.*

Retrospectrum has since toured the world, with stops at the Patricia and Phillip Frost Art Museum in Miami (2021) and the MAXXI Museum in Rome (2022–23).

PAGE 563: *Retrospectrum* catalog cover, featuring Bob Dylan's painting *Sunset, Monument Valley*, from Modern Art Museum exhibition (Shanghai, China), 2019

光/谱 鲍勃·迪伦艺术大展 **Retrospectrum**
Bob Dylan

ROUGH AND ROWDY WAYS

"Murder Most Foul" single, 2020

On March 15, 2020, the world went into lockdown to prevent the spread of COVID-19. Less than two weeks later, on March 26, Dylan surprised everyone by releasing his first new composition in nearly eight years: the epic ballad "Murder Most Foul." At sixteen minutes and fifty-six seconds in length, Dylan's longest song to date focused on the December 1963 assassination of President John F. Kennedy and its reverberations throughout American history.

Sprawling in structure and unfurling kaleidoscopically, the song evokes the fugue state that can accompany a trauma—in this case the trauma of Kennedy's assassination. Keyboards, strings, and drums ebb and flow underneath Dylan's elegiac recitation. Around the actual details of Kennedy's murder, Dylan develops a set of lyrics where history is moving in both directions at once. After crashing through time, space, and even celestial planes, the song concludes with Dylan imploring legendary radio DJ Wolfman Jack to play a litany of songs that conjures nothing less than the soul of America.

In a real-life moment where time already seemed to stand still, "Murder Most Foul" caused a true cultural moment, and it became Dylan's first-ever song to top a *Billboard* chart. Musicians Elvis Costello and Margo Price claimed the song moved them to tears. All the while, fans and critics alike pored over the lyrics in an attempt to pinpoint each reference, and, like Kennedy conspiracy theorists, tried to connect the dots to arrive at the truth of the song. But for Dylan, it was all relatively simple.

> *It's the combination of them that adds up to something more than their singular parts. To go too much into detail is irrelevant. The song is like a painting, you can't see it all at once if you're standing too close. The individual pieces are just part of a whole.*

To accompany the release of "Murder Most Foul," Dylan provided a statement via his website and social media channels:

> *Greetings to my fans and followers with gratitude for all your support and loyalty across the years. This is an unreleased song we recorded a while back that you might find interesting. Stay safe, stay observant and may God be with you. Bob Dylan*

Dylan's note prompted intense debate as to exactly when it was recorded and with whom. A second single, "I Contain Multitudes," was released less than a month later, on April 17, stoking the speculation. However, it wasn't until the release of "False Prophet" on May 8 that the release of *Rough and Rowdy Ways*, Dylan's thirty-ninth album, was announced.

Recorded in January and February 2020 in Los Angeles, the album featured Dylan's touring band including Bob Britt, Matt Chamberlain, Tony Garnier, Donnie Herron, and Charlie Sexton, with additional contributions from Fiona Apple, Blake Mills, Alan Pasqua, Tommy Rhodes, and Benmont Tench. From the tender "I've Made Up My Mind to Give Myself to You" and rough-and-tumble blues of "Crossing the Rubicon," to the poem-song of "Black Rider" and the dreamlike "Key West (Philosopher Pirate)," *Rough and Rowdy Ways* built upon his original work through *Tempest*, while incorporating the atmosphere and spontaneity of his excursions into the Great American Songbook.

In an interview shortly after the album's release, Dylan acknowledged that the writing of the songs took place in sort of a "trance state," noting that:

The lyrics are the real thing, tangible, they're not metaphors. The songs seem to know themselves and they know that I can sing them, vocally and rhythmically. They kind of write themselves and count on me to sing them.

Following the seismic stir of the album's rollout, *Rough and Rowdy Ways* debuted at #1 on *Billboard*'s charts for Top Rock and Americana/Folk Albums. On the *Billboard* 200 chart—which encompasses all popular music regardless of genre—*Rough and Rowdy Ways* debuted at #2, making Dylan the first artist to have an album chart in the Top 40 in every decade since the 1960s.

Rough and Rowdy Ways advertisement, 2020

Tangled Up in Improv

ALAN LICHT

Back in the late '90s I went to see Jerry Lee Lewis at Tramps in NYC. Lewis had a large backing band, with the musicians stationed laterally along the wide stage, and he opened the show with "Slippin' and Slidin'." For the instrumental break he would call out someone's name, and the band member would take a solo; then he'd call out another person's name, and they too would play a solo. Lewis went back into a verse, and then just kept noodling on the piano for a spell, only to start singing a different song, unannounced, without taking a break. He repeated the pattern of singing a verse or two, calling out soloists, and jumping into another tune; this make-it-up-as-we-go-along medley went on for fifteen or twenty minutes, with each band member vamping distractedly and craning their neck to look at Lewis, hoping for a clue as to which song was coming up, or who would next be anointed to take a solo. Lewis finally brought it to a crashing end with an abrupt head nod, and shot a withering look—one worthy of his nickname, "The Killer"—at a guitarist who had not fully complied with the signal to stop; The Killer really had the band on their toes.

I was reminded of this show while watching an outtake from Bob Dylan's 1976 *Hard Rain* TV special, filmed at Hughes Stadium, Fort Collins, Colorado. Facing the band, his back to the audience, Dylan toggles between two barre chords, a B and an A, strumming rather brashly. His guitar sound is distorted and bruising; the rhythm suggests a faster, punchier "Yea! Heavy and a Bottle of Bread." Bassist Rob Stoner locks in with Dylan immediately and the rest of the band soon follows, drummer Howie Wyeth striking up a rollicking beat similar to the ones he's used earlier in the set on "Maggie's Farm" and "Stuck Inside of Mobile with the Memphis Blues Again." Dylan moves down the neck to an E chord; Stoner joins him but then moves to F#, mistakenly, instead of back to B. That's the first hint that they're playing "Tangled Up in Blue," albeit in a different key than either the *Blood on the Tracks* album track (which is in A), or the '75/'76 Rolling Thunder solo acoustic version (in G) the band may have heard before.

The song's true identity is confirmed once Dylan starts singing. At the end of each verse the band grinds to a halt after the title phrase, waiting until Dylan brings them back in with the B chord. As the third verse enters, confusion

Set list for first show of US tour, September 15, 1978, Civic Center, Augusta, ME

reigns; Dylan hits a B chord but just lets it ring, and he begins singing the verse without restarting the rhythm part. He plays the chords freely as the band tries to shadow him rather than back him up. There are occasional clumsy interjections from the other guitarists; midway through, Wyeth flirts with a half-time beat but quickly abandons it. As the verse concludes, Dylan picks up the rhythm, and the band comes roaring back in at full force. When the sixth verse starts, they shift gears to a slow blues shuffle feel, but it's only for that verse; they kick into a steady backbeat for the final verse. At the close of this tumultuous nine-minute rendition—almost double the length of the *Blood on the Tracks* cut—there is no visible reaction from Dylan; he's already thinking about the next song.

"Tangled" is a prime example of Dylan songs that weather numerous metamorphoses both in the studio and live. By the time of the Fort Collins concert, it had already seen an evolution from the reasonably gentle acoustic guitar/bass run-through at the initial *Blood on the Tracks* New York recording session (with Dylan's jacket audibly rattling against his guitar's soundboard) to the loping full band arrangement that wound up opening the album. It would later undergo a stately yet somehow cheesy MOR/Vegas ballad conversion on the 1978 tour and be heavily reworked lyrically (and slightly modified musically) in several 1984 live solo acoustic versions, not to mention a weird, funky band run-through in Marseilles, 1993, where Dylan's rapid-fire vocal is uncannily reminiscent of Steven Tyler's delivery in Aerosmith's "Walk This Way" (and in turn reveals how much Tyler's cadence owes to "Like a Rolling Stone"). Fort Collins is a unique case, because it seems to be approached from another angle in almost every verse (coincidentally mirroring the lyrics' device of shifting first- and third-person perspectives). Each verse seems to ask the question, what could the song be here? What would happen if the band dropped out? Or if we made it a blues shuffle? These decisions all appear to be made in the moment, with little if any advance directive from Dylan. It's hard to tell if the song was originally in the set list, or had even been attempted by this band before (looking at previous set lists from the tour, it appears that it was only done solo acoustic at a couple of shows; perhaps they tried it at sound check).[1] As Paul Williams has written of the version of "Lay Lady Lay" on the *Hard Rain* album, recorded in Fort Worth a week before Fort Collins, "This kind of music . . . can't be written out beforehand. Instead, the musicians have to rely on the sound of Dylan's voice and the movement of his hands and their accumulated experience of working with him and with each other, so that finally it's 80% intuition. . . ."[2]

To a great extent, these extensive reworkings come out of the folk tradition. Folk musicians are, ideally, expected to interpret a song in a unique way to distinguish themselves from other folksingers, so there are theoretically as many different readings of a Child ballad, say, as there are performers of it. Dylan went beyond the folk template in treating his own material that way, as if the 1976, 1984, or 1993 versions of "Tangled Up in Blue" amount to one song covered by three separate artists in three varying ways. But a fashion-conscious pop sensibility is also a factor here. The Rolling Thunder Dylan who is doing reggae, funk, "waltzy," and "fast metal" versions of "Isis," according to Stoner,[3] is also reckoning with the musical trends of the day. By the time he gets to the crude guitar sound and ragged attack of *Hard Rain*, he's taking cues from (or at least in sync with) the latest rage looming on the horizon, punk rock. One of Dylan's true innovations is fusing the adaptive mentality of folk music with the sound-of-the-moment attitude and variegated nature of pop music in the way he engages with his own catalog.

Dylan sometimes pushes this fluidity into the realm of improvisation, as is evident in the riotous Fort Collins "Tangled" but even more radically in a privately made black-and-white video of the 1970 *New Morning* recording sessions, where Dylan conjures a blues instrumental on the spot in the middle of tracking another song,[4] or in a four-chord ditty called "Rock Me Mama" that materialized out of nowhere during the *Pat Garrett & Billy the Kid* recording sessions. Dylan's love of and commitment to spontaneity is obvious in these instances, and while we cannot consider him to be a free improviser, it is clear that improvisation is meaningful to him. He never abandons song structure, to be sure, but the changeability he imparts to his material is reminiscent of free improvisers' ability to alter the course of a group improvisation on a dime, at will, just by inserting a certain sound or technique. His long streams of lyric writing—the original twenty-page draft of "Like a Rolling Stone," for instance—also recall long free improvised music pieces that are eventually edited down for a track on an album; the difference is that the material is revised before being performed or recorded, not just edited out or re-ordered as recorded instrumental free improvised music would be.[5] The way free improvisers just keep playing continually, ostensibly waiting for something to click, is also like Dylan's constant writing and rewriting (but again, a free improviser is not going to go back and rework something they've already played before presenting it to the public).

Dylan's unscripted four-hour film *Renaldo and Clara*, shot during the 1975 Rolling Thunder Revue tour, contains many improvised scenes acted out by the musicians on the tour. Dylan has cited the Italian form of *commedia dell'arte* (street theater in which masked actors improvise their lines) as an influence on the film's working process and the tour itself (Dylan's own onstage white face makeup was inspired by the masks of *commedia dell'arte*). In an interview he did with Dylan about *Renaldo and Clara*, poet Allen Ginsberg comments, "You chose to do it as an improvisation." Dylan's response is worth quoting in full:

> How else? Life itself is improvised. We don't live life as a scripted thing. Two boxers go into the ring and they improvise. You go make love with someone and you improvise. Go to sports car races, total improvisation. It's obvious everyone was acting in the movie for dear life. Nobody was thinking of time. People were told this, this, this—the rest of it is up to you, what you say in this scene is your business, but at the same time beyond that, the only directions you have are: you're going to die in a year, or see your mother for the first time in twenty years. So far as instructions to actors go, less is more. And I made it clear to the cameraman, Paul [Goldsmith], that it wasn't a documentary, and I told him not to shoot it like that.[6]

It's clear that Dylan was hoping that the musicians/actors would come up with their own dialogue spontaneously in the dramatic scenarios he devised on the spot during filming, similar to the way that his band was expected to respond to his laconic directions while performing his songs in the studio or onstage.[7] This was largely unsuccessful, and interestingly, when Dylan teamed with the Grateful Dead, a group renowned for their capacity for extemporization, the combination failed to ignite. The ability to improvise does not seem to be much of a factor for Dylan in choosing musicians to work with, despite his proclivity for making unexpected variations in the songs. The key line in Dylan's answer to Ginsberg is "Life itself is improvised." That insight informs the unpredictability of his own performances, and the shape-shifting quality of his songs from their inception through every iteration in recording and in concert, where they seldom if ever stay faithful to their recorded incarnations. Dylan has chosen to work with predetermined music—songs—but with an understanding, seemingly girded to his entire concept of bringing a song into existence, that in the greater scheme of things, all is subject to chance and change in the heat of the moment.

Or at least he did for a time. Clinton Heylin has noted that after 1984, onstage lyrical reinvention was largely a thing of the past, although songs were still often heavily overhauled in the studio.[8] Seeing Dylan at the Beacon Theatre during a ten-show run in December 2019, there was precious little evidence of any improvisation outside of the musicians' solos and likely some nuances of Dylan's phrasing, and a search online confirmed that the set list was identical night after night, indeed month after month. Dylan admitted as much in a *New York Times* interview in 2020; when asked what role improvisation played in his music, he replied:

> *None at all. There's no way you can change the nature of a song once you've invented it. You can set different guitar or piano patterns upon the structural lines and go from there, but that's not improvisation. Improvisation leaves you open to good or bad performances and the idea is to stay consistent. You basically play the same thing time after time in the most perfect way you can.*[9]

And yet . . . at the Beacon "Not Dark Yet" was hardly recognizable from the studio take on *Time Out of Mind*. What's more, back in 2017, "Tangled Up in Blue" was pulled out in Washington, DC, and given the full blues shuffle treatment that had only lasted one verse in Fort Collins forty years earlier, in the same key of B no less, and with some different lyrics to boot. And the first leg of the 2021–22 tour saw some adjustments to *Rough and Rowdy Ways'* "Key West" reminiscent of the Dylan nightly variations of yore, culminating in an entirely new chord structure, as documented by one audio upload on YouTube of six live recordings from November to March.[10] As Dylan's tour rolls on and on, Dylan may feel the same about every show, but, every now and then, he can still see his songs from a different point of view.

Beacon Theatre ten-night run
concert poster, 2019

HEAVEN'S DOOR

In April 2018, Dylan announced the creation of Heaven's Door Spirits, saying "I wanted to create a collection of American Whiskeys that, in their own way, tell a story." Alongside its three signature offerings of Straight Bourbon, Straight Rye, and Double Barrel Whiskey, the company also offered special editions, such as its lavish annual Bootleg Series releases. Dylan's visual art adorned every bottle of Heaven's Door.

Fittingly, on September 21, 2020, Dylan brought back his radio show *Theme Time Radio Hour* for a special episode built around the theme "Whiskey." Dylan displayed a deep knowledge of the history and production of whiskey in his commentary as he played whiskey-themed songs such as Julie London's "Coming Through the Rye," Thin Lizzy's "Whiskey in a Jar," and "Corn Whiskey" by Jimmy Witherspoon.

Dylan also included the Clancy Brothers performing "The Parting Glass," a tune that Dylan learned from The Clancy Brothers and Tommy Makem during their nights at Greenwich Village's White Horse Tavern back in the early 1960s. Eventually Dylan developed the melody into his own song, "Restless Farewell," which closed his 1964 album, *The Times They Are A-Changin'*.

Theme Time Radio Hour "Whiskey" episode advertisement, 2020

Bob Dylan, Heaven's Door promotional shoot at Dylan's Black Buffalo Ironworks, 2017. Photograph by John Shearer

GIRL FROM THE NORTH COUNTRY

In crafting the musical *Girl from the North Country*, Irish playwright Conor McPherson was given carte blanche to use whatever Dylan songs he wanted. Opening at the storied Old Vic in London on July 8, 2017, the production moved to the Noël Coward Theatre in the West End, before moving Stateside for an off-Broadway run at the Public Theater. *Girl from the North Country* made its Broadway debut on March 5, 2020, at the Belasco Theatre.

Set in a boarding house in Duluth, Minnesota, during the height of the Great Depression, the production draws on twenty of Dylan's songs from across his career, delivered by a cast backed by musicians playing circa 1930s instruments. "I Want You" is reimagined as a back-and-forth dialogue between a star-crossed couple. "Tight Connection to My Heart (Has Anybody Seen My Love)" becomes an act of faith sung to a universe that won't give any relief. The songs are deconstructed, abstracted, and melded in ways that emphasize the musical's themes. Singling out the collaboration between McPherson and orchestrator, arranger, and music supervisor Simon Hale, Richard Williams's review in *The Guardian* lauded the pair's ability "to find shades of meaning within some of the songs that would surely surprise even Dylan himself, a famously protean interpreter of his own creations."

Even Dylan was a fan of the show, telling Douglas Brinkley in 2020,

> *I saw it as an anonymous spectator,*
> *not as someone who had anything to do*
> *with it. I just let it happen. The play had*
> *me crying at the end. I can't even say*
> *why. When the curtain came down,*
> *I was stunned.*

Despite the COVID-19 pandemic shutting down Broadway on March 12, 2020, *Girl from the North Country* survived; it re-opened on October 13, 2021, and ran through June 19, 2022. The musical received nominations for seven Tony Awards, including Best Musical, as well as a GRAMMY Award for Best Musical Theater Album. Since then, the musical has played to rave reviews with touring productions staged around the world. In February 2023, *Variety* broke the news that Chlöe Bailey, Tosin Cole, Olivia Colman, and Woody Harrelson would star in the film adaptation of the musical, also to be written and directed by McPherson.

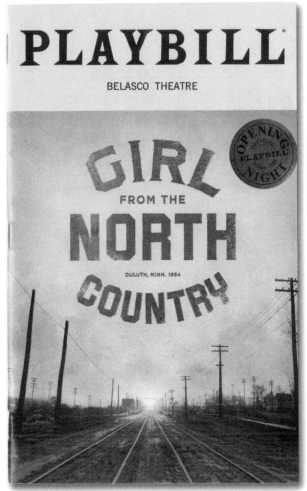

Girl from the North Country opening night
Broadway Playbill, 2020

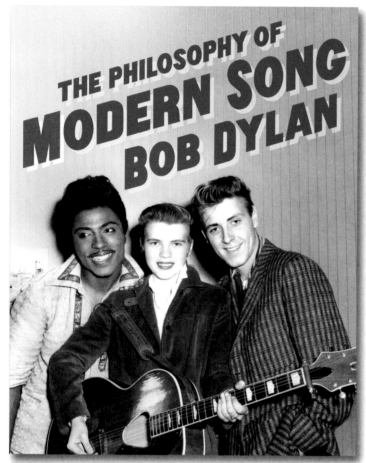

The Philosophy of Modern Song book cover, 2022

Notebook with notes about Perry Como's version of "Without a Song," late 1960s

Notes on Jimmy Reed's "Big Boss Man," early 1990s

The Philosophy of Modern Song, released on November 1, 2022, to widespread acclaim, found Dylan examining sixty-six songs, getting inside of each one to figure out what makes them tick. In a series of essays, riffs and accompanying images, he provides insights into songwriting and performance that could only be communicated by a master of the form.

Although *The Philosophy of Modern Song* had precursors in Dylan's role as DJ for *Theme Time Radio Hour* and his liner notes accompanying the 1993 album *World Gone Wrong*, the book continued to develop the writing style that Dylan adopted in the Nobel Lecture and in the songs of *Rough and Rowdy Ways*. Yet the book also showcased Dylan's wry sense of humor, as evidenced in the iconic photo of Jack Ruby shooting Lee Harvey Oswald to illustrate "Ruby, Are You Mad at Your Man?"

Although Dylan began writing *The Philosophy of Modern Song* in 2010, he'd clearly been thinking about many of the songs for years. In the Archive, there are traces of his relationship not only to those songs and performers, but also to the particular versions Dylan selected to explore.

In *The Philosophy of Modern Song*, Dylan reflects upon Rosemary Clooney and her song "Come On-a My House": "Clooney was a good pop singer with a jazz sensibility. She knew how to sell a song, even a little trifle like this"; in writing about Perry Como's "Without a Song," Dylan proclaims, "Perry Como was the anti–Rat Pack, like the anti-Frank; wouldn't be caught dead with a drink in his hand, and could out-sing anybody. His performance is just downright incredible. There is nothing small you can say about it." In Dylan's notebooks from the mid-to-late 1960s, he mentions both Clooney and Como, demonstrating once again that his listening is shaped not by popular taste but by his own discerning ear.

Having written "Goodbye Jimmy Reed" for *Rough and Rowdy Ways*, Dylan turned his attention to Reed's hit performance "Big Boss Man," a song he'd listed on a notepad from the 1980s and covered while sitting in with the Dead in 2003. Speaking about Reed, Dylan noted, "You can play twelve-bar blues in hundreds of variations and Jimmy Reed must have known them all. None of his songs ever touch the ground. They don't stop moving."

Dylan dedicated *The Philosophy of Modern Song* to another musical icon he'd admired for years: Doc Pomus. As Dylan once remarked, "'This Magic Moment.' 'Lonely Avenue.' 'Save the Last Dance for Me.' Those songs broke my heart." However, it was not the first time he'd paid tribute to Pomus. In 1995, he contributed "Boogie Woogie Country Girl" to the compilation *Till The Night Is Gone: A Tribute to Doc Pomus*. (Big Joe Turner had included this Pomus song as the B-side to his 1956 single "Corrina, Corrina," which Dylan himself had recorded on his 1962 album, *The Freewheelin' Bob Dylan*.)

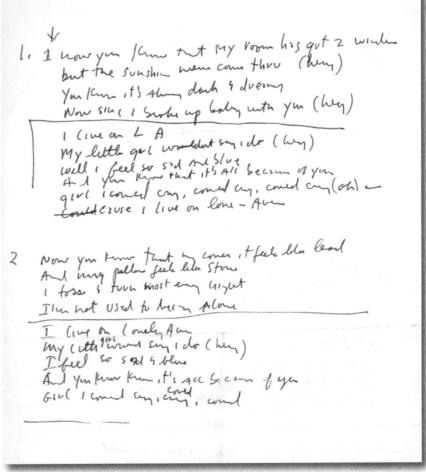

Notes on Rosemary Clooney's cover of "Come On-a My House," late 1960s

Bob Dylan's handwritten lyrics for "Lonely Avenue" by Doc Pomus, late 1980s

Bob Dylan, 2023. Photograph by Hedi Slimane

PORTRAIT SESSION, 2023

In 2023, Dylan sat for portraits by distinguished photographer Hedi Slimane. As an artist and curator, Slimane has often explored the intersections of music, fashion, and the visual arts across the world. His photographs of Dylan were taken as part of the "Portrait of a Performer" campaign for Celine, the French luxury brand, where Slimane acts as artistic, creative, and image director.

Bob Dylan, 2023. Photograph by Hedi Slimane

THE HERE AND NOW

On July 18, 2021, *Shadow Kingdom: The Early Songs of Bob Dylan* premiered on the live-streaming platform Veeps. Dylan used the opportunity to stage thirteen of his songs as vignettes at the surreal smoke-filled Bon Bon Club in Marseilles, France. Shot in alluring black and white, the Alma Har'el–directed neo-noir concert film found Dylan re-engaging with work from the first half of his career, ranging from the early 1965 release of "It's All Over Now, Baby Blue" to "What Was It You Wanted?" from the 1989 album *Oh Mercy*. All of the songs had been rearranged, and, in the cases of "When I Paint My Masterpiece" and "To Be Alone with You," had been rewritten as well.

The public reaction was effusive, with critics and fans captivated by Dylan's latest musical offering. Columbia Records officially released the film and an accompanying album on June 2, 2023.

Shadow Kingdom video stills, 2021. Directed by Alma Har'el

ROUGH AND ROWDY WAYS WORLD WIDE TOUR

The global pandemic halted Dylan's annual touring schedule for the first time since the mid-1980s. On December 8, 2019, Dylan performed his final pre-pandemic show, and did not return to the stage again until the launch of his Rough and Rowdy Ways World Wide Tour on November 2, 2021. Scheduled to run for three years, the tour began with a new working band: guitarists Bob Britt and Doug Lancio, multi-instrumentalist Donnie Herron, bassist Tony Garnier, and drummer Charley Drayton. In April 2023, Jerry Pentecost replaced Drayton behind the drums for Dylan's Japanese tour.

True to the name of the tour, the group introduced audiences to live versions of many of the songs from *Rough and Rowdy Ways*, with "Key West (Philosopher Pirate)" quickly developing into a showstopper. The revamped songs from *Shadow Kingdom* also became a critical part of Dylan's sets in 2021 and 2022. He provided a few surprises during the tour as well, as in the case of his October 28, 2022, concert in Nottingham, England, where he paid tribute to rock 'n' roll icon Jerry Lee Lewis on the day of his passing with a performance of Lewis's "I Can't Seem to Say Goodbye."

During his April 2023 tour in Japan, Dylan introduced a number of Grateful Dead–related cover songs to his set lists. He performed the Dead's "Brokedown Palace" and "Truckin'"—which he'd just written about in *The Philosophy of Modern Song*—as well as Bob Weir's "Only a River." Dylan also returned to his earliest rock 'n' roll roots with a cover of Buddy Holly and the Crickets' "Not Fade Away," which the Dead had also frequently featured in their concerts dating back to the late 1960s.

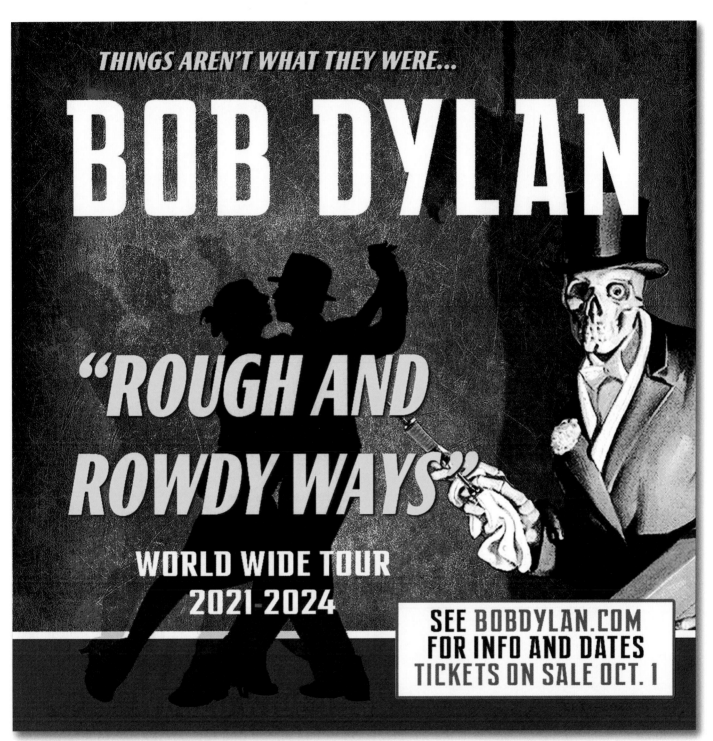

Rough and Rowdy Ways Tour advertisement, 2021

ED BRADLEY:

Why do you still do it? Why are you still out here?

BOB DYLAN:

Well, it goes back to that destiny thing.
I made a bargain with it a long time ago.
And I'm holding up my end.

—60 Minutes interview, November 19, 2004

EPILOGUE **Our Wells Are Deep** DOUGLAS BRINKLEY

Ever since *Rolling Stone* commissioned me to write a 2009 cover story on Bob Dylan based on interviews conducted in Paris and Amsterdam, I've stayed in regular touch with America's premier music and poetry artist. There is a country-boy sweetness about Bob that belies the coiled legend. Yet it's also true that Dylan doesn't suffer fools lightly. The takeaway from any conversation with him is that he is a learned world-beat man with piercing blue eyes that could burn through disingenuous people like a blowtorch. No detail or nuance slips past his notice. When relaxed, however, Bob enjoys chatting about Valley Forge and the Mexican–American War, the Homestead Acts and the Dakota War of 1862, Theodore Roosevelt and Helen Keller, Louis Armstrong and Frank Zappa. He is extremely well read; his knowledge about the Civil War and Native American culture is beyond impressive. An Americanist at heart, his cultural curiosity goes back to Thomas Paine's *Common Sense* and "Yankee Doodle" during the Revolutionary War. Over time, we've discussed the country-and-western star Hank Williams and gospel singer Shirley Caesar, comedian Lord Buckley and Beat poet Gregory Corso. There is no ceiling on his muse. Simply put, Dylan is a storehouse of Americana garnered from art, books, road travel, wanderlust, and gutsy intuition. And he is equally well versed in European and Russian schools of thought.

Whether Dylan is songwriting, sketching, painting, welding, or engaging with religious texts, his creativity is often fermented by the English poet William Blake. "Blake was an evangelizing poet," Dylan told me. "You can see it in his paintings and drawings as well. A Blake poem is writing on the wall. It's the moving finger. He had the dread of life simplified and down pat. So, yeah, his work is inspiring in a way that tells you that whatever strange and out-of-the-way thoughts you have are not so strange after all, and that he put it all down before you."

Dylan, the evangelist poet of our modern times, has been the moving finger of my own life ever since I bought his album *Nashville Skyline* in 1969, a purchase I made originally because Johnny Cash was involved with the record, joining in for the duet, "Girl from the North Country." From that listening experience forward, I was hooked on all things Dylan. There has barely been a day that I haven't listened to Dylan masterpieces such as "Visions of Johanna," "Don't Think Twice, It's All Right," "I Dreamed I Saw St. Augustine," "Not Dark Yet," and "The Times They Are A-Changin'" for rank pleasure and divine brightness. Listening to Dylan energizes me to write and think in fresh new and mysterious ways. Just hearing "My Back Pages" jars my social justice conscience more viscerally than reading Dorothy Day or Cesar Chavez. His art elevates me in both profound and mundane ways.

In the fall of 2012, right after Dylan released *Tempest*, his thirty-fifth studio album, he and I were talking about Johnny Cash when the conversation turned to Chuck Berry, the rock 'n' roll performer for whom, Dylan said, he felt the greatest respect. "There is Chuck," he told me, "and

PAGE 582: Bob Dylan, 1965. Photograph by Rowland Scherman

then all the rest." When I asked Bob which lyricist he considered a kindred spirit, thinking he'd name Woody Guthrie or possibly Johnny Mercer, he said William Shakespeare. I chuckled, but he was perhaps serious. Certainly, the vibrant wordplay of Shakespeare emerges in the very best of his most recent songs. "Just like there are hundreds of books written about Shakespeare," he said, waving his hands, "the same thing is happening to me. Our wells are deep."

In the twenty-first century, Dylan has to date released five albums of original songs: *"Love and Theft"* (2001), *Modern Times* (2006), *Together Through Life* (2009), *Tempest* (2012), and *Rough and Rowdy Ways* (2020). My favorite of these is *Tempest*, which is unabashedly mythical, starting with the album cover that features an Austrian statue personifying the river Moldau in the guise of the face of a young woman. Within the album's tracks, Dylan alludes to Bottom's visitation from Titania in Shakespeare's *A Midsummer Night's Dream* with the line "It's soon after midnight / And I've got a date with the fairy queen"; he paraphrases *Julius Caesar* in "Pay in Blood" with the line "I came to bury not to praise"; and the album's title ballad goes meta-mythic, evoking the sinking of the actual *Titanic* and including as a character Leonardo DiCaprio from the movie version. Meanwhile, the mesmerizing "Scarlet Town" takes the listener on a hypnotic stroll through a cursed cityscape. The lyrics are otherworldly, with one verse referring to ancient Rome on the day described by the Gospel of Luke 8:43–48, when an ailing woman touched the hem of Jesus' garment as he passed by. She thought she was healed by the mere contact, but Jesus assured her it was her faith that cured her. "I touched the garment," Dylan wrote of the desolation of Scarlet Town, "but the hem was torn."

Because of memorable lines like those, and the stubborn defiance and raw contempt with which Dylan takes down corporate hustlers, smug literati, crafty politicians, and culture critics, I'll say it clear: There is no artist, in any medium, who's brought me more unalloyed joy than Bob Dylan. The fact that, as of this writing, he's still touring and still writing new masterpieces like "Early Roman Kings," "Po' Boy," and "Key West (Philosopher Pirate)" in the twenty-first century is cause for celebration.

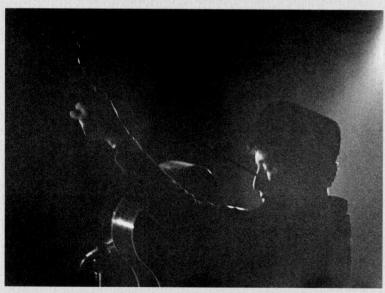

Bob Dylan, 1962. Photograph by Joe Alper

Once I got to know Bob personally, his creative genius became more evident. Talking with him was like getting to know Henry David Thoreau, Frank Sinatra, Stephen Crane, Duke Ellington, or Langston Hughes. Like these American icons—and as this elegant book demonstrates—Dylan is *sui generis,* a one-of-a-kind artist of his own making and of his own mythos. As Beat poet Allen Ginsberg put it, "It's Dylan against the world." In Rimbaudian language, he is our "wild vagabond" wandering far and wide to sing truths. There isn't a throwaway line or unnecessary syllable when Dylan sings new showpieces such as "Nettie Moore," "Ain't Talkin'," "Workingman's Blues #2," and "Mississippi." All four are alive with characteristic Dylan traits: kinetic audacity, memorable melody, raven tricksterism, stark historical awareness, seer profundity, wild-eyed zest, sad laments, ancient wisdom, blues sensibility, and even comedic asides.

The works of great painters are locked in frames and preserved in a fixed and unchanging state. An artist like Dylan, on the other hand, gets to constantly reinvent his past works. "None of my songs are set in stone," Dylan has told me. "They all bend and fall, rise and sink, in different ways at different times. I *never* listen to my albums. Those are logged. What I *do* do is live performance, which is for me to rethink my songs in fresh ways."

I once asked Dylan which covers of his songs he most admired. At first he shrugged off the question—just nodded off that line of thought. But then, in "I guess" fashion, he reluctantly offered Jimi Hendrix's "All Along the Watchtower," The Jerry Garcia Band's "Señor (Tales of Yankee Power)," Johnny Winter's "Highway 61 Revisited," and Nina Simone's "Just Like a Woman." Then he turned slightly annoyed when I ventured down that highway of inquiry. When I cited my admiration for Gregg Allman's 2017 rendition of "Going, Going, Gone" from his *Southern Blood* CD, he was surprised.

Bob Dylan, 1969. Photograph by Al Clayton

Seemingly, he was unaware of the remake (but complemented the musicians in the old Allman Brothers Band like guitarist Dickey Betts). "You know," he said, "a song like 'Ramblin' Man' or the Grateful Dead's 'Friend of the Devil' were built to last."

In Saratoga Springs, New York, I got into a discussion with Bob about the songs "Heart of Mine," "Watered-Down Love," and "Lenny Bruce" from his 1980 album *Shot of Love*, compositions he was still refining three decades after they were recorded. When I mentioned how much I'd enjoyed his rendition of "Lenny Bruce" at a show at the Beacon Theatre in New York City, he lit up. Beguiling and brave, Bruce was a controversial stand-up comedian, largely forgotten today, who died of a drug overdose in 1966. In that era, some addicts sought help from Synanon, a drug-rehabilitation group that metamorphized into a cult.

"Yeah," Dylan told me. "I left that song alone for a long time, but then I heard somebody doing it in a club in Amsterdam, and I loved it. I couldn't get past the 'Synanon' line, though I was wondering what that meant. And then I realized, oh yeah, it was a drug clinic when Lenny was around. I couldn't relate to it, and if I couldn't relate to it, I couldn't expect anyone else to. But I wanted to do the song, so I changed the line. Now the song is what it is. What it was supposed to be. Just a little thing like that could bring something out of obscurity and into the light. Funny, isn't it?" So it was that the original lines about Bruce—"Never did get any Golden Globe Award / Never made it to Synanon" became "Never did make it to the Promised Land / Never made it out of Babylon." With that, Dylan gladly included the song in his live performances.

Something of the irreverent spirit of Lenny Bruce can be seen in Dylan's delightful, if at times acerbic, personality. With a baked-in satirical bent combined with an inbred Dada sagacity for reading the motives of others, he conducts conversations with the precocious nod-and-wink of Adam Sandler or Dave Chappelle. For most of the twenty-first century, Dylan has produced his own

DOUGLAS BRINKLEY

albums, playfully using the pseudonym Jack Frost. It was after being overproduced by Don Was (*Under Red Sky*) and Arthur Baker (*Empire Burlesque*) that Dylan decided to be his own producer. Why not? Dylan is the consummate iconoclast, the last troubadour strumming alone in a technology-obsessed world of groupthink and computer synthesizers.

I asked Dylan what feeling he sought in his role as pseudonymous producer Jack Frost. "Just a plain sound with depth, a lot of room ambiance," he said. "Everybody close in, hardly any headphones or separation. Each song has its own mood though, so the sound quality would vary. And no one sound quality would apply to everything. The lyrics won't marry themselves to just any old thing, so the sound has to be forthcoming. But it's not the sound as much as the style in which the lyrics are sung that give them meaning."

People close to Dylan intuited that after Dylan won a Nobel Prize for Literature in 2016, a new wave of over-intellectualized critical writing would emerge (for better or worse). That's fine. I'm guilty as charged in this regard. But first and foremost, I *do* recognize that Dylan is a creative *performing* artist, committed to the American songbag, jazz ethics, and old-time sweatbox blues, as well as rock 'n' roll theater. Over-analyzing him does his art a disservice. Dylan is an *experience* more like a meteorite

Bob Dylan, 1975. Photograph by Ken Regan

than a mummified artifact of scholarly pursuit. At concerts, he reliably presses forward even when he is mining the poetry of nineteenth-century writers like Emily Dickinson, Herman Melville, and Henry Timrod. Admirers of Dylan should always remember how he responded to the Nobel honor: "I consider myself a poet first and a musician second. I live like a poet and I die like a poet." Although Dylan's Nobel Prize elevated his stature (he was dubbed the Ovid and Homer of American letters), most of his longtime admirers considered the award an unnecessary reaffirmation of his inherent genius. As Leonard Cohen said, it was "like pinning a medal on Mount Everest for being the highest mountain."

In 2020, Dylan sold his entire song catalog, numbering more than six hundred compositions. Two years later, he sold the rights to his recorded music. People who didn't understand Dylan assumed that these moves were a sign of retirement: a record-breaking cashout with a Nobel Prize raised high over his head. There was no retirement in the offing, however. That interpretation ignores a simple fact: live performance isn't a task for Dylan, but a merry pursuit. Just like a carpenter builds homes and a pilot flies planes, Dylan embraces songwriting and performing as his vocation in an old-fashioned way. Even as an octogenarian, his artistic drive is as alive as it was in 1962 when he was twenty-one, playing "Blowin' in the Wind" in public for the first time at Gerdes Folk City in Greenwich Village.

Dylan's unceasing popular appeal was demonstrated in 2020, when he released *Rough and Rowdy Ways,* his first album of original songs since 2012's *Tempest.* The centerpiece, "Murder Most Foul," is a poetic explication of John F. Kennedy's assassination and the loss of American innocence. At nearly seventeen minutes, it's the longest song Dylan has ever released. When he and I discussed the song, I asked where he was when he heard the grim news on November 22, 1963. "I was somewhere in midtown Manhattan," he recalled. "I watched it later on TV like everybody else."

Once, when performing in Dallas, Dylan visited the scene of the shooting, seeing the Texas Book Depository from which Lee Harvey Oswald supposedly fired his shots, and the grassy knoll that some believe harbored a second gunman. I never learned whether Dylan thinks Oswald acted alone, but I was struck by his observations about time moving on. "There's nothing really there that indicates anything," he offered. "The events of that day have faded out long ago. If you go to Dealey Plaza now, it's hard to imagine anything important ever happening there."

Walt Whitman wrote a poem, "When Lilacs Last in the Dooryard Bloom'd," about Lincoln's death. I wondered whether it was an influence on Dylan when he was writing his song about the JFK assassination and if he'd ever thought of writing verses about Lincoln's assassination. "Not so much," he responded, "because I can't imagine what a typical day was like for them when they were alive. The casualties back then had their own peculiarity, and I think you would have had to live back then to feel the full force of it. Whitman's poem is a poem of mourning. Mourning is just a small part of 'Murder Most Foul.' I just don't think those times and our times correlate at all. Maybe in a metaphysical way but not in real terms. . . . The quest for Booth and the elimination of Lincoln would be two different stories and would have to be two different songs. It's interesting though."

"Murder Most Foul" is about both the crime in Dallas and an entire era in America. It's replete with references to artists and songs Americans turned to for comfort and identity. Dylan and I had a lively talk about the various artists he mentions in "Murder Most Foul," like Charlie Parker, Patsy Cline, Oscar Peterson, and Buster Keaton. When I asked him if he had ever met Wolfman Jack—the pioneering rock 'n' roll DJ repeatedly cited in the song—he expressed admiration for Jack's unique ability to make listeners sit up and take notice. "His voice was very caustic," Dylan explained. "Unusual in a unique way. Raw and grating. But every disc jockey back then had their own personality, and that was his. His whole being was wrapped up in the songs that he played on the radio. I think he had the perfect voice for the Industrial Age. But no. I never met him."

Dylan expressed genial surprise that "Murder Most Foul" was his first #1 hit, topping *Billboard*'s Rock Digital Song Sales chart after its March 2020 release. "Strange, isn't it?" he said. "A song that long, touching people. That was because of the pandemic and people having free time to listen to something that wasn't just entertainment. That turned out right by accident, really."

The following year, Dylan released a black-and-white film called *Shadow Kingdom*. The pandemic had made touring impossible, so he taped a private concert at a Santa Monica soundstage and then streamed it on the Internet. With clear enunciation of lyrics,

Bob Dylan, 1984. Photograph by Ken Regan

DOUGLAS BRINKLEY

Dylan performed ethereal versions of "When I Paint My Masterpiece" and "Just Like Tom Thumb's Blues." The standout of the remarkable event was a slow-tempo, deeply felt version of "What Was It You Wanted?" (originally from 1989's *Oh Mercy* album and covered exquisitely by Willie Nelson four years later). If you want to pull one post-Nobel video of Dylan to watch, I'd go with "What Was It You Wanted?"—perhaps one of the most underrated songs in Dylan's songwriting cabinet.

On November 1, 2022, Dylan's book *The Philosophy of Modern Song* was released to critical acclaim. Starting with Uncle Dave Macon's 1924 recording of "Keep My Skillet Good and Greasy," and ending with Alvin Youngblood Hart's 2004 recording of Stephen Foster's "Nelly Was a Lady," Dylan writes sixty-six essays on popular songs, weaving historical facts, dreamlike riffs, and brilliant musicological insights into a seamless meditation on the durability of certain mid-twentieth-century unforgettable songs. I particularly reveled in Dylan's take on Townes Van Zandt's "Pancho and Lefty" and The Fugs' "CIA Man."

During that same year, 2022, a giant sequoia tree about three thousand years old, named the Grizzly Giant, almost burned in a wildfire that encircled Yosemite National Park. As danger loomed, a park ranger reassured me in a memorable way, saying that even if the fire destroyed the part of the tree we can see, its root system would live on forever. It's that way with Dylan. Epic songs like "With God on Our Side," "Masters of War," "Mr. Tambourine Man," "Jokerman," "Desolation Row," "Slow Train," and "Dark Eyes" are eternal. As assuredly as Dylan himself has been reimagining his compositions since he recorded the original "Song to Woody" in 1962, future musicians will forever be reinterpreting his timeless standards. Dylan changed the landscape of American popular music by melding his literary vision with folk tradition, blues, gospel, and rock idioms. Wherever Dylan performs live or records in the studio, mysterious music falls from the starry sky. Rankings would be futile, but I concur with President Barack Obama, who said in 2012 when offering my friend the prestigious Presidential Medal of Freedom: "There is not a bigger giant in the history of American music than Bob Dylan."

Bob Dylan, 2023. Photograph by Hedi Slimane

NOTES

"HIGHWAY TO THE SEA: DYLAN, CONRAD, AND THE 'TOMBSTONE BLUES,'"
Griffin Ondaatje, 166–70

1. James Wright, "As I Step over a Puddle at the End of Winter, I Think of an Ancient Chinese Governor," *The Branch Will Not Break* (Middletown, CT: Wesleyan University Press, 1963), 11.

2. Joseph Conrad, 1921, letter to Richard Curle, quoted in Leo Robson, "Joseph Conrad's Journey," *New Yorker*, November 20, 2017.

3. Sam Shepard, *The Rolling Thunder Logbook* (Cambridge: Da Capo Press, 2004), 78.

4. Joseph Conrad, *Victory: An Island Tale* (New York: Penguin Random House, 2015), 199.

5. Conrad, *Victory*, 409.

6. Bob Dylan, interview with Paul Zollo, *SongTalk*, 1991.

7. Conrad, *Victory*, 204.

8. Conrad, *Victory*, 408.

9. Bob Dylan, interview with Nora Ephron and Susan Edmiston, August 1965, in *Positively Tie Dream (and Other Assorted Interviews and Tall Tales)*, comp. John Bauldie (Forban, England: Ashes and Sand, 1979).

10. Bob Dylan, blurb for *Last Train to Memphis* by Peter Guralnick (Little, Brown and Company, 1994).

11. "Bob Dylan Turns Up at Neil Young's Childhood Home," CBC News, November 10, 2008.

12. Bob Dylan, interview with Jonathan Cott, *Rolling Stone*, January 26, 1978.

13. Larry Sloman, *On the Road with Bob Dylan* (New York: Three Rivers Press, 2002), 61.

14. Conrad, *Victory*, 91.

15. Bob Dylan, interview with Allen Ginsberg, December 1977.

16. Joseph Conrad, *Youth, Selected Short Stories: Joseph Conrad* (Hertfordshire: Wordsworth Editions, 1997), 94.

17. Conrad, *Youth*, 69.

18. Bob Dylan, press release (*Mood Swings*), Halcyon Gallery, London, October 1, 2013.

19. Conrad, *Youth*, 91.

20. Joan Didion, interview with Hilton Als in the *Paris Review*, Spring 2006.

21. Bob Dylan, *Chronicles: Volume One* (New York: Simon & Schuster, 2004), 92.

22. G. Jean-Aubry, *Joseph Conrad: Life and Letters*, vol. 2 (London: Heinemann, 1927), 103.

"I'M LEARNING IT THESE DAYS,"
Richard Hell, 294–97

1. "In a little hilltop village, they gambled for my clothes
I bargained for salvation an' they gave me a lethal dose
I offered up my innocence and got repaid with scorn
'Come in,' she said, 'I'll give you shelter from the storm.'"
—Bob Dylan, "Shelter from the Storm"
from *Blood on the Tracks*

"And they crucified him, and parted his garments, casting lots: that it might be fulfilled which was spoken by the prophet. They parted my garments among them, and upon my vesture did they cast lots."
—Matthew 27:35, King James Version

2. Bob Dylan Archive, Box 99, Folder 5, "Blood Notebook 1," 8–9.

3. Bob Dylan Archive, Box 99, Folder 6, "Blood Notebook 2," 14–15.

4. Bob Dylan Archive, Box 99, Folder 5, "Blood Notebook 1," 19.

5. Second "from what we used" inserted later. Bob Dylan Archive, Box 99, Folder 5, "Blood Notebook 1," 14–15.

6. Bob Dylan Archive, Box 99, Folder 6, "Blood Notebook 2," 37.

"*THE GUNFIGHTER*'S NEVER ENDING TOUR,"
Robert M. Rubin, 406–9

1. Robert Warshow, "Movie Chronicle: The Westerner," *Partisan Review* (March–April 1954), reprinted in *The Western Reader*, edited by Gregg Kitses and Jim Rickman (New York: Limelight Editions, 1998), 35–48; Richard Slotkin, *Gunfighter Nation: The Myth of the Frontier in Twentieth-Century America* (New York: Atheneum, 1992), 383.

2. Slotkin, *Gunfighter Nation*, 385.

3. Slotkin, *Gunfighter Nation*, 385.

"TANGLED UP IN IMPROV,"
Alan Licht, 566–69

1. Further research via a bootlegged audiotape shows that the song was rehearsed fairly extensively with the band the day before, at the Colorado Hotel. They had worked up a comparable but far more cohesive arrangement in B, with the first two verses rocked out (though much less aggressively), the fourth and sixth

verses done with the decelerated blues shuffle, and the final verse reverting to the rock beat. However, Dylan omits the third (and most of the fifth) verse at the rehearsal but sang them at the concert, which may have added to the band's discombobulation (no pun intended) onstage the next day.

2. Paul Williams, *Bob Dylan: Performing Artist, The Middle Years, 1974–1986* (London: Omnibus Press, 1994), 86.

3. Rob Stoner, quoted in Clinton Heylin, *Bob Dylan: Behind the Shades: A Biography* (New York: Summit Books, 1991), 268.

4. Dylan is playing piano, and during the take he shouts out for players to take solos—another, even more specific reminder of the Jerry Lee Lewis Tramps show. A different section of the *New Morning* sessions video (shot two days earlier, at the June 3 session) shows Dylan working on a cover of Lefty Frizzell's "Long Black Veil" and demonstrating a lick to play on the piano to Al Kooper—virtually the same riff that will form the basis of the blues instrumental two days later. Kooper plays it once, and then it's lost as they keep playing the song. But it had obviously stuck in Dylan's mind as something to be developed, albeit in an impromptu fashion with the same musicians gathered rather than honed in private.

5. Perhaps a closer analogy might be to Western European classical composers like Bach, who often improvised pieces at the organ that were later transcribed and turned into compositions, rather than composed on paper first, although I'm not aware of any evidence that Bach revised his work as continually as Dylan does.

6. Allen Ginsberg, "Bob Dylan & *Renaldo & Clara*," in *Wanted Man: In Search of Bob Dylan*, ed. John Bauldie (New York: Citadel Underground Press, 1990), 124.

7. Drummer Kenny Buttrey recalled that at the recording session for "Sad-Eyed Lady of the Lowlands," Dylan told musicians it would be verse, chorus, harmonica, verse, chorus, harmonica, "and then we'll see." It turned out to be over ten minutes long, the first (and only) take. The musicians just kept playing along, not knowing when the song would end or how long it would go for. Clinton Heylin, *Bob Dylan: The Recording Sessions 1962–1994* (New York: St. Martin's Press, 1995), 51. Robbie Robertson said of the 1966 tour with The Hawks, in a 1975 conversation with Larry Sloman, "We were playing so out of this world, we didn't even know what the fuck we were doing, because he didn't want to learn any of the songs. It was just play them." Williams, *Bob Dylan: Performing Artist*, 214.

8. Clinton Heylin, *Still on the Road: The Songs of Bob Dylan, 1974–2006* (Chicago: Chicago Review Press, 2010), 4–5.

9. Douglas Brinkley, "Bob Dylan Has a Lot on His Mind," *The New York Times*, June 12, 2020. The stark contrast between Dylan's attitude towards improvisation here and in the Ginsberg interview from a quarter-century before underscores his mercurial nature, musically and otherwise.

10. "Bob Dylan—Key West Evolution So Far (November 2021–March 2022)," YouTube Video. 01. Milwaukee, November 2, 2021; 02. Chicago, November 3, 2021; 03. Washington, December 2, 2021; 04. Phoenix, March 3, 2022; 05. Albuquerque, March 6, 2022; 06. Irving, March 10, 20.

WRITERS

DOUGLAS BRINKLEY is the Katherine Tsanoff Brown Chair in Humanities and Professor of History at Rice University. He is author of *Silent Spring Revolution: John F. Kennedy, Rachel Carson, Lyndon Johnson, Richard Nixon, and the Great Environmental Awakening* (HarperCollins, 2023), and he wrote the liner notes to Bob Dylan's *The Bootleg Series Vol. 17: Fragments—Time Out of Mind Sessions (1996–1997)*.

PETER CAREY was born in Bacchus Marsh, Australia, and now lives in New York. He has been short-listed for the Booker Prize four times and has won it twice (for *Oscar and Lucinda* and *True History of the Kelly Gang*). His most recent novel is *A Long Way from Home* (Knopf, 2018).

ANNE MARGARET DANIEL teaches at the New School in New York City. Her essays on literature, music, books, and culture have appeared for the past twenty-five years in books, critical editions, magazines, and journals including *The New York Times*, *Hot Press*, *The Spectator*, and *The Times Literary Supplement*. She is the editor of F. Scott Fitzgerald's last unpublished short stories, *I'd Die for You and Other Lost Stories* (2017), and the Norton Library Edition of *The Great Gatsby*. She has published extensively on American Modernism and Modern Irish literature, and in spring 2017 she taught the first course at a New York university on Dylan's combined arts and letters.

JOHN DOE, a founding member of the legendary punk rock band X, released *ALPHABETLAND* in April 2020. In addition, Doe has released eleven solo records, including *Fables in a Foreign Land* (Fat Possum Records, 2022). Doe has also appeared in over sixty film and television productions, including a lead role as Frank Bigelow in a period correct remake of the 1949 film noir *D.O.A.* (2022). He lives with his wife, artist Krissy Teegerstrom, in Austin, Texas.

RAYMOND FOYE (b. 1957, Lowell, Mass.) studied film with Stan Brakhage at the Art Institute of Chicago and worked as a literary editor at City Lights Books, where he edited *The Unknown Poe* (1980) and other titles.

While living in San Francisco he edited two issues of *Beatitude* magazine and was a contributor to the punk zine *Search and Destroy*. His close friendship with the poet Bob Kaufman resulted in his editing Kaufman's final book of poems, *The Ancient Rain* (1981), for New Directions. In 2019, he co-edited Kaufman's *Collected Poems* for City Lights, for which he received the American Book Award. In 1985, he traveled with Francesco Clemente to India, where they founded Hanuman Books and published fifty books over the next ten years, including original titles by Cookie Mueller, Patti Smith, Robert Frank, and William Burroughs. From 1990 to 1995, he worked as director of exhibitions and publications at Gagosian Gallery in New York. Since 1995 he has worked as an independent curator, editor, and writer. Most recently he co-edited (with George Scrivani) *Gregory Corso: The Golden Dot, Last Poems 1980–2000*, for the Lithic Press. He is a contributing editor to the *Brooklyn Rail* and is a regular contributor to *Gagosian Quarterly*.

TERRY GANS has worked as a journalist, grocer, advertising executive, songwriter, corporate controller, and an elected official and mayor of Longboat Key, Florida. Among other things, He began listening to and learning about Bob Dylan in 1962. Since the 1980s he has contributed to Dylan-centric publications such as the *Telegraph*, *Look Back*, the *Bridge*, and *ISIS Magazine*. His 1970 master's thesis at Miami University (the real one in Ohio) was published in 1983 as *What's Real and What Is Not*. In 2020, his second book, *Surviving in a Ruthless World: Bob Dylan's Voyage to Infidels*, was the first published book to make use of the Bob Dylan Archive in Tulsa.

JEFF GOLD is a GRAMMY Award–winning music historian, author, and former record label executive, profiled by *Rolling Stone* as one of the five "top collectors of high-end music memorabilia." As a top executive at Warner Bros. Records and A&M Records, Gold worked with artists including Prince, R.E.M., Red Hot Chili Peppers, Iggy Pop, The Police, and Cat Stevens. A four-time GRAMMY-nominated Art Director, Gold won the 1990 Best Album Package GRAMMY for Suzanne Vega's *Days of Open Hand*. Gold has consulted for the Rock & Roll Hall of Fame and the Experience Music Project, and appeared as an expert on PBS's *History Detectives*. He and colleague Laura Woolley appraised the Bob Dylan Archive for Dylan's management, and his discovery of previously undocumented tapes has led to major label releases, including *Bob Dylan in Concert at Brandeis University 1963*. Gold's books include *101 Essential Rock Records: The Golden Age of Vinyl*; *Total Chaos: The Story of the Stooges, As Told by Iggy Pop*; and *Sittin' In: Jazz Clubs of the 1940s and 1950s*. Gold owns music collectibles website *Recordmecca* and writes about topics of interest to collectors on its blog.

JOY HARJO is an internationally renowned performer and writer of the Muscogee (Creek) Nation. She served three terms as the 23rd Poet Laureate of the United States from 2019 to 2022. The author of nine books of poetry, including the highly acclaimed *An American Sunrise*, several plays and children's books, and two memoirs, *Crazy Brave* and *Poet Warrior*, she is the recipient of honors including the Ruth Lily Prize for Lifetime Achievement from the Poetry Foundation, the Academy of American Poets Wallace Stevens Award, two NEA fellowships, and a Guggenheim Fellowship. As a musician and performer, Harjo has produced seven award-winning music albums, including her newest, *I Pray for My Enemies* (2021). She is executive editor of the anthology *When the Light of the World Was Subdued, Our Songs Came Through: A Norton Anthology of Native Nations Poetry*, and the editor of *Living Nations, Living Words: An Anthology of First Peoples Poetry*, the companion anthology to her signature Poet Laureate project. She is a chancellor of the Academy of American Poets, board of directors chair of the Native Arts & Cultures Foundation, and the first Artist-in-Residence for Tulsa's Bob Dylan Center. She lives in Tulsa, Oklahoma.

RICHARD HELL is the author of several books of fiction, poetry, essays, notebooks, autobiography, and collaborations, including *The Voidoid, Go Now, Godlike, Across the Years, Artifact, Hot and Cold, I Dreamed I Was a Very Clean Tramp, Massive Pissed Love, Wanna Go Out?* by Theresa Stern (with Tom Verlaine), and *Psychopts* (with Christopher Wool). His book of poems, an essay, and eighty-eight notebook entries, entitled *What Just Happened,* was published in June 2023. He lives in New York.

CLINTON HEYLIN, who has been described by *The New York Times* as "the only Dylanologist worth reading," is the author of the acclaimed *Bob Dylan: Behind the Shades* and more than two dozen other books on music and popular culture. These include biographies of Sandy Denny, Van Morrison, and Orson Welles, and two classic studies of punk's origins, *From the Velvets to the Voidoids* and *Anarchy in the Year Zero*. An ex-pupil of Manchester Grammar School who went on to earn two history degrees, he has been a full-time historian and critic for more than three decades. Heylin lives in Somerset, England.

MARVIN KARLINS received his PhD from Princeton University in social psychology. He is currently senior full professor of management at the University of South Florida's Muma College of Business. Dr. Karlins consults worldwide and, for twenty years, trained all operational staff at Singapore Airlines. He has published thirty books and more than 150 articles in professional, academic, and popular journals. Several of his co-authored books have become international bestsellers, including *What Every BODY Is Saying: An Ex-FBI Agent's Guide to Speed-Reading People* and *The Like Switch: An Ex-FBI Agent's Guide to Influencing, Attracting, and Winning People Over*. His book *Paying It Backward: How a Childhood of Poverty and Abuse Fueled a Life of Gratitude and Philanthropy*, co-authored with Tony March, was published in 2020. Dr. Karlins is a member of the Authors Guild and the International Federation of Journalists.

ALAN LICHT is a musician, writer, and curator based in New York City. Appearing on nearly one hundred recordings, he is known for his guitar work in the underground rock bands Run On and Love Child and with such legendary figures as Yoko Ono, Arthur Lee, and Tom Verlaine. A frequent contributor to *Artforum*, *The Wire*, and other publications, Licht is the author of *Common Tones: Selected Interviews with Artists and Musicians 1995–2020* (Blank Forms, 2021) and *Sound Art Revisited* (Bloomsbury Academic, 2019), the revised edition of *Sound Art: Beyond Music, Between Categories* (Rizzoli, 2007), the first full-length study of sound installations and sound sculpture to appear in English, and he edited *Will Oldham on Bonnie "Prince" Billy* (Faber & Faber/W. W. Norton, 2012).

GREIL MARCUS is the author of numerous books about music and culture, including *The Old Weird America: The World of Bob Dylan's Basement Tapes* (1997), which was originally titled *Invisible Republic* (now the author doesn't know what to call it), and *Folk Music: A Bob Dylan Biography in Seven Songs* (2022). He was born in San Francisco, lives in Oakland with his wife, Jenny, and can just see a bit of the bridge that was turned purple when Prince died from their apartment in Minneapolis.

ALLISON MOORER is a singer/songwriter, producer, and author who has released ten critically acclaimed albums. Her first memoir, *Blood*, was released in October 2019 to high praise and received starred reviews in *Publishers Weekly*, *Kirkus*, and *Booklist*. Her second, *I Dream He Talks to Me*, was published in October 2021 and received starred reviews in *Publishers Weekly* and elsewhere. Allison has been nominated for an Academy Award (in 1999 for Best Original Song) and also GRAMMY, Americana Music Association, and Academy of Country Music Awards. Allison holds an MFA in Creative Writing from the New School; her work has been published in *The New York Times*, *The Wall Street Journal*, *American Songwriter*, *Guernica*, *No Depression*, *Literary Hub*, and *The Bitter Southerner*. She received the Hall-Waters Prize for Excellence in Southern Writing in 2020 and the Alabama Library Association's Authors Award in 2022. She lives in Nashville.

BARRY OLLMAN is a lifelong singer/songwriter and a longtime collector of rare letters and manuscript material of famous people, particularly in the fields of music, literature, science, and social movements, with a special focus on Woody Guthrie and his circle, including Lead Belly, Pete Seeger and the Weavers, Bob Dylan, and '50s-and '60s-era rock 'n' roll. Ollman has gathered the largest private collection of Guthrie's letters and artworks over the past thirty-five years and was closely involved with the initial formation of Tulsa's Woody Guthrie Center beginning in 2007.

GRIFFIN ONDAATJE is a writer and documentary filmmaker born in Kingston, Canada. His documentary film about Bob Dylan, *Complete Unknown,* premiered at festivals in North America and the UK in 2003. His books include *The Mosquito Brothers, Muddy,* and *The Camel in the Sun*, which was selected for the Austria Children's Book Prize and the Middle East Book Award. He also edited *The Monkey King and Other Stories*, a collection of South Asian folktales and legends, and worked for many years as a researcher for documentary films. His books have been translated into German, Korean, Arabic, Swedish, Italian, and Turkish. Currently he is writing *Half Wild*, a book of essays and interviews based on the music of Bob Dylan. He lives near Toronto with his family.

MICHAEL ONDAATJE is a poet and novelist. His novels include *Coming through Slaughter*, *In the Skin of a Lion*, *The English Patient*, *The Cat's Table*, *Warlight*, and *Anil's Ghost*. His poetry books include *The Cinnamon Peeler* and *Handwriting*. He has also done a book of interviews called *The Conversations: Walter Murch and the Art of Editing Film*. His next book, *A Year of Last Things*, appears early in 2024 with Knopf USA.

GREGORY PARDLO is the author of *Digest*, winner of the 2015 Pulitzer Prize for Poetry. His first poetry collection, *Totem*, won the 2007 *American Poetry Review* Honickman Prize. He is the author of a memoir in essays titled *Air Traffic* (2018). Other

honors include fellowships from the New York Public Library's Cullman Center, the New York Foundation for the Arts, the National Endowment for the Arts, and the Guggenheim Foundation. He is co-director of the Institute for the Study of Global Racial Justice at Rutgers University–Camden. He and his family currently live in the UAE, where he serves as a visiting professor of creative writing at NYU Abu Dhabi. His forthcoming poetry collection is *Spectral Evidence*.

AMANDA PETRUSICH is a staff writer at *The New Yorker* and the author of three books. She is the recipient of a Guggenheim Fellowship in nonfiction and has been nominated for a GRAMMY Award. Her criticism and features have appeared in *The New York Times*, *Oxford American*, *Spin*, *Pitchfork*, *GQ*, *Esquire*, *The Atlantic*, and the *Virginia Quarterly Review*. Her most recent book, *Do Not Sell at Any Price*, explored the obsessive world of 78-rpm record collectors. She is the writer-in-residence at New York University's Gallatin School.

TOM PIAZZA is celebrated both as a novelist and as a writer on American music. His books include the novels *The Auburn Conference*, *A Free State*, and *City of Refuge*, the post-Katrina manifesto *Why New Orleans Matters*,

and *Devil Sent the Rain*, a collection of his essays and journalism. Of Piazza's short-story collection *Blues and Trouble*, Bob Dylan wrote, "Tom's stories are like the silence in a queer room—they pulsate with nervous electrical tension, reveal the emotions that we can't define." He was a principal writer for the innovative HBO drama series *TREME*, and the winner of a GRAMMY Award for his album notes to *Martin Scorsese Presents the Blues: A Musical Journey*. His writing has appeared in *The New York Times*, *The Atlantic*, *Bookforum*, *Oxford American*, and many other periodicals. He lives in New Orleans.

LEE RANALDO, musician, visual artist, and writer, co-founded Sonic Youth (1981–2011), played in Glenn Branca's early ensembles and symphonies (1980–84), and has been active both in New York and internationally for forty years as a composer, performer, collaborator, and producer. He has also exhibited visual art and has published several books of journals, poetry, and writings on music. Ranaldo's thirty-year performance partnership with Leah Singer, currently Contre Jour performances, have been large-scale, multi-projection sound+light events with suspended electric guitar phenomena that challenge the usual performer/audience relationship. He lives and works in New York City.

ALEX ROSS has been the music critic of *The New Yorker* since 1996. His first book, *The Rest Is Noise: Listening to the Twentieth Century*, published in 2007, was a finalist for the Pulitzer Prize. An essay collection, *Listen to This*, appeared in 2010; his third book, *Wagnerism: Art and Politics in the Shadow of Music*, was published in 2020. In 2008, Ross received a MacArthur Fellowship.

ROBERT M. RUBIN has written about Richard Avedon, Reyner Banham, Alexander Calder, Pierre Chareau, Buckminster Fuller, Allen Ginsberg, Glenn O'Brien, Jean Prouvé, and Richard Prince. He has contributed to *Bookforum, Art in America, Cahiers d'Art, Le Monde*, and *Libération,* as well as museum and gallery publications. His most recent book is *Richard Prince Cowboy* (2020). He also curated the exhibition *Richard Prince: American Prayer* at the Bibliothèque Nationale de France in 2011. His next project is a book about the 1971 film *Vanishing Point*.

ED RUSCHA oscillates between sign and substance, locating the sublime in landscapes both natural and artificial. Working in diverse media with humor and wit, he has brought words—as form, symbol, and material—to the forefront of painting. Born in Omaha, Nebraska, in 1937, Ruscha spent his formative years in Oklahoma City. In 1956, he moved to Los Angeles, to attend the Chouinard Art Institute. After graduation, he began to work for ad agencies, honing his skills in schematic design and considering questions of scale, abstraction, and viewpoint, which became integral to his painting and photography. He has created more than a dozen artists' books, including the twenty-five-foot-long, accordion-folded *Every Building on the Sunset Strip* (1966). His paintings of the 1960s explore the noise and the fluidity of language. Since his first exhibition with Gagosian in 1993, Ruscha has had twenty-one solo exhibitions with the gallery. The first retrospective of his drawings was held in 2004 at the Whitney Museum of American Art. Ruscha represented the United States at the 51st Venice Biennale (2005). Ruscha continues to influence contemporary artists worldwide, his formal experimentations and clever use of the American vernacular evolving in form and meaning as technology and internet platforms alter the essence of human communication.

LUCY SANTE is the author of numerous books including *Low Life*, *Evidence*, *The Factory of Facts*, *Kill All Your Darlings*, *The Other Paris*, *Maybe the People Would Be the Times*, and *Nineteen Reservoirs*. Her awards include a Whiting Writers Award, an Award in Literature from the American Academy of Arts and Letters, a GRAMMY (for album notes), an Infinity Award from the International Center of Photography, and Guggenheim and Cullman fellowships. She teaches writing and the history of photography at Bard.

JEFF SLATE is a New York City–based songwriter and music journalist. His writing can be found in *The New Yorker*, *Esquire*, *The Wall Street Journal*, and *Rolling Stone*, among others. Jeff has appeared on stage and worked with music legends like Pete Townshend, Roger McGuinn, Jeff Tweedy, Sheryl Crow, and others, and his music has appeared in advertising and films and on television, including in the show *Gossip Girl*. Jeff is also a regular guest host on SiriusXM's Volume channel, is the co-author of the 2017 book *The Authorized Roy Orbison* with the late legend's sons, and has written liner notes for albums by Orbison, The Beatles, The Rolling Stones, and Jimi Hendrix, among many others, including Bob Dylan's *The Bootleg Series Vol. 14: More Blood, More Tracks.*

LARRY "RATSO" SLOMAN is a Renaissance Jew. He is best known for his work with Howard Stern on Stern's two groundbreaking books *Private Parts* (Simon & Schuster, 1993) and *Miss America* (HarperCollins, 1995). Ratso has had seven *New York Times* bestsellers, including two books with Mike Tyson. Bob Dylan has publicly acclaimed him as "our favorite reporter," and Ratso's first book, *On the Road with Bob Dylan* (Bantam, 1978), an account of Dylan's 1975 Rolling Thunder Revue, prompted Bob to blurb "the *War and Peace* of rock and roll." In 2020, Sloman released his first album, *Stubborn Heart*, at the ripe age of 70. Sloman also has a budding career as a thespian, appearing in several movies, including a memorable cameo with Adam Sandler in Josh and Benny Safdie's *Uncut Gems* (2019), along with

a featured role in Martin Scorsese's Dylan documentary about the aforementioned *Rolling Thunder Revue: A Bob Dylan Story* (2019). Ratso also has a major role in the 2022 award-winning documentary about Leonard Cohen and his worldwide hit song "Hallelujah" called *Hallelujah: Leonard Cohen, a Journey, a Song.*

GREG TATE was a writer, cultural producer, and musician who had lived in Harlem since 1984. He was a staff writer at *The Village Voice* from 1987 to 2004. His books include *Flyboy in the Buttermilk* (2015, Touchstone), *Everything but the Burden—What White People Are Taking from Black Culture* (2003, Crown), *Midnight Lightning: Jimi Hendrix and the Black Experience* (2003, Chicago Review Press), and *Flyboy 2: The Greg Tate Reader* (2013, Duke University Press). In 1985, he helped co-found the Black Rock Coalition with guitarist Vernon Reid. Beginning in 1999, he led the improv ensemble Burnt Sugar the Arkestra Chamber, who released 16 albums on their own Avant Groidd imprint. Tate passed away on December 7, 2021, at the age of 64.

SEAN WILENTZ is the George Henry Davis 1886 Professor of American History at Princeton University and the author of, among many books, *Bob Dylan in America* (2010).

EDITORS

MARK DAVIDSON is the Curator of the Bob Dylan Archive and the Senior Director of Archives and Exhibitions for the Bob Dylan and Woody Guthrie Centers in Tulsa, Oklahoma. He holds a PhD in musicology from the University of California, Santa Cruz, with an emphasis on folk music collecting, and an MSIS in archiving and library science from the University of Texas at Austin. He has written widely on music and archives, including his dissertation, "Recording the Nation: Folk Music and the Government in Roosevelt's New Deal, 1936–1941," and the essay "Blood in the Stacks: On the Nature of Archives in the Twenty-First Century," published in *The World of Bob Dylan* (2021).

PARKER FISHEL is an archivist who served as co-curator of the inaugural exhibitions at the Bob Dylan Center. His company, Americana Music Productions, provides consulting, research, and production work for artists and estates, record labels, and other entities looking to preserve archives and share the important stories found in them. His selected credits include *Ann Arbor Blues Festival 1969* (Third Man Records), the Chelsea Hotel–inspired *Chelsea Doors* box set (Vinyl Me, Please), and several volumes of Bob Dylan's GRAMMY Award–winning Bootleg Series (Sony/Legacy). Fishel is also a board member of the Hot Club Foundation and a co-founder of the nonprofit improvised music archive Crossing Tones.

ACKNOWLEDGMENTS

GEORGE KAISER FAMILY FOUNDATION/ TULSA COMMUNITY FOUNDATION

George Kaiser, Ken Levit, Jeff Stava

SONY MUSIC ENTERTAINMENT

Rob Stringer, Richard Story, Jeroen van der Meer, Greg Linn, Jeffrey Schulberg, Rob Santos, Matt Kelly, Thomas Tierney, Toby Silver

UNIVERSAL MUSIC PUBLISHING GROUP

Marc Cimino, Joy Murphy

AMERICAN SONG ARCHIVES—BOB DYLAN CENTER/WOODY GUTHRIE CENTER

Steve Higgins, Steve Jenkins, Jessica McKenzie, Cady Shaw, Jourdan Srouji, Sydney Buchheister, Sam Flowers, chloë fourte, Zac Fowler, Mallory Geary, Quinn Carver Johnson, Avery Marshall, Jaye McCaghren, Ryan McGovern, Corie Montgomery, Meagan Mulgrew, Gregg Pagano, Melissa Payne, Rebecca Roseberry, Stephanie Stewart, Ethan Voelkers, Nathan Adrian, Grace Asher, Zoë Bridgwater, Sophia Crumback-Tarrien, Leah Daniel, Alex De Hart, Ryan Gleason, Paul Hicks, Colette Huff, Holly Minter, Grace Stroud, Felicia Sutton, Dylan Tuttle

BOB DYLAN CENTER FOUNDING PARTNERS

Douglas and Anne Brinkley; Joseph W. Craft III Foundation; the Darby Family; Teresa Knox, Ivan Acosta, and The Church Studio; Earl Minnis; Jody and Lee Parker; Bob Ramsey and Jenny Lee Norton; Leigh and John Reaves; Great Neck Richman and the Richman Family Foundation; WPX Energy Legacy

SPECIAL THANKS

Peter Agelasto and Richard Averitt, Starchive; Joe Andoe; John and Laura Avedon; Joan Baez; Ann Becker; Andrew Bailey; Olof Björner; Ben Blackwell; Mitch Blank; Aileen Boyle; Jon Bream; Erin Brenner, Right Touch Editing, Wendy Scavuzzo, and Susan Kokura; Jeff Bridges; Jason Brown; Marc Bushala; Issey, Nicholas, Nikeyu and Reeves Callaway; Mike Campbell; Rosanne Cash; Michael Chaiken; Larry Charles; Sam Chase; CITIC: Hannah Zhang; Rufus Cohen; Elvis Costello; Amy Cuthbertson; Claudia and Matt Davidson, and Renee Park; Mary Dean; Arie de Reus; Mandy, Linda, and Oak Durham; Fred Dorwart, Marcia Scott, and Susan Bynum; Stanton Doyle; David Eckstrom; Editions Seghers: Antoine Caro and Anne Dieusaert; Editorial Planeta: Maria Salvador Manzana and David Figueras Pérez; Jane B. Farnol, Astor Indexers; Peter Fetterman; Jim Fishel, Barbara Micale, and Gwen Fishel; Janice Fisher; Jeff Friedman; Geoff Gans; Jeff Gold; Gorgeous George; Michael Gray; Mark Grimmer, Ben Pearcy, and 59 Productions; Steve Gunn; Nora Guthrie, Anna Canoni, and Woody Guthrie Publications, Inc.; Hachette Book Group: Billy Clark, Todd McGarrity, and Vanessa Vazquez; Joy Harjo; Olivia Harrison; Jeff Hochberg; Howard and Sandra Hoffen; Kate Hofland; J. J. Holiday; Garth Hudson; Lewis Hyde; Larry Jenkins; Hannibal Johnson; Jessica Jonap; Magne Karlstad; Jerry Kelly; Jim Keltner; Margit Ketterle; Danny Kortchmar; Jeremy Lamberton; Sean Latham and the University of Tulsa; Jennifer Lebeau; Elizabeth Lovero and Otis Fishel; Tony Marsico; James Martin; Alan Maskin, Marlene Chen, and Olson Kundig; Toshiya Masuda; Daryl Matthews; Peter May; Roger McGuinn; Toni Mendell; Mark Mingelgreen; The Morgan Library; Chris Murray and Govinda Gallery; Ian Nagoski; Susan Neal and Gilcrease Museum; Tony Norton; Alice Notley; Kevin Odegard; Barry and Judy Ollman; Bill Pagel; Thomas Palmer; Jody Parker; Bennett Parnes; Nelson Peltz; Frazer Pennebaker; Miguel Perez; Robert Polito; Hall Powell; Richard Prince; James Pullen; Suzanne Regan; Krystal Reyes; Charlene Ripley; Elvis Ripley; Ben Rollins; Manuela Roosevelt; Robert M. Rubin; Robert Russell; Oddbjørn Saltnes; Jessica Savran; Jerry Schatzberg; Udi Schregel; Denise Schweida; Coco Shinomiya; Austin Short; Michael Shulman; Hedi Slimane; Thames & Hudson: Georgia Gray Andrews, Christian Friederking, and Mark Garland; True Sims; Nigel Sinclair and Spitfire Pictures/White Horse Pictures; Marcia Stehr; Stephen Sullens and the Sullens Family; Denise Sullivan; Fred Tackett; Mary Herr Tally; Brian Tate, Geri Augusto, and Chinara Tate; Cosett Torres; Happy Traum; Peter Utz; Sherri Whalen and Shelby Zempel; Jack White; Edith and Glenn Wilson; Luke Wilson; Ivan Wong; Andrew Wylie

PERMISSIONS

All songs, text, and quotations by Bob Dylan, copyright ©
Bob Dylan, unless otherwise noted.

Excerpts from *Tarantula*, *Chronicles*, *The Nobel Lecture*,
and *The Philosophy of Modern Song*, copyright © Bob Dylan.

Artwork by Bob Dylan, copyright © Bob Dylan: *Endless
Highway*, p. 23; "As I Went Out One Morning," p. 210;
Guitar Player, p. 214; *Music from Big Pink*, p. 215; *Self
Portrait*, p. 235; drawing from the "Morris Zollar Wants
to Know" series, p. 261; "Guitar," pp. 261, 608.

Songs by Bob Dylan, copyright © Universal Tunes:
"Subterranean Homesick Blues," front endpapers, pp. 133,
529, back endpapers; "Song to Woody," pp. 14, 77; "Love
Sick," pp. 19, 469; "Highlands," p. 20; "Summer Days,"
p. 20; "Last Thoughts on Woody Guthrie," p. 96; "Chimes
of Freedom," pp. 110–11; "Mama, You Been on My Mind,"
pp. 124, 125; "It Ain't Me, Babe," p. 125; "My Back Pages,"
p. 125; "Jet Pilot," p. 126; "Tombstone Blues," pp. 126–27,
166, 167, 169, 170; "Maggie's Farm," p. 137; "Bob Dylan's
115th Dream," pp. 143–44; "Like a Rolling Stone," p. 163;
"Ballad of a Thin Man," pp. 164, 165, 240, 502; "Highway 61
Revisited," p. 165; "Romance in Durango," p. 168; "Shelter
from the Storm," pp. 168, 297, 590; "Never Say Goodbye,"
p. 169; "Mississippi," pp. 170, 499; "One of Us Must Know
(Sooner or Later)," p. 182; "Visions of Johanna," p. 183;
"Dear Landlord," p. 203; "Wanted Man," p. 203; "Santa
Fe," p. 206; "I Threw It All Away," p. 218; "Minstrel Boy,"
p. 223; "Desolation Row," pp. 236, 241; "The Man in Me,"
pp. 242, 381; "When I Paint My Masterpiece," pp. 247, 255;
"Knockin' on Heaven's Door," p. 267; "It's Alright, Ma (I'm
Only Bleeding)," p. 278; "On a Night Like This," p. 282;
"Dirge," pp. 286, 287, 289; "Positively 4th Street," p. 286;
"You're a Big Girl Now," pp. 295, 296, 297; "Tangled Up
in Blue," pp. 300–301; "Isis," p. 322; "Abandoned Love,"
p. 324; "Hurricane," p. 326; "If You See Her, Say Hello,"
p. 331; "Where Are You Tonight? (Journey Through
Dark Heat)," p. 342; "Changing of the Guards," p. 343;
"Do Right to Me Baby (Do Unto Others)," p. 354; "Slow
Train Coming," p. 354; "Gotta Serve Somebody," p. 355;
"Pressing On," p. 360; "Saved," p. 361; "Caribbean Wind,"
p. 365; "The Groom's Still Waiting at the Altar," pp. 366,
367, 368, 369; "Every Grain of Sand," p. 370; "Lenny
Bruce," pp. 371, 585; "Tight Connection to My Heart (Has
Anybody Seen My Love)," pp. 380, 396; "Jokerman,"
p. 382; "Blind Willie McTell," pp. 383, 393; "Brownsville
Girl," pp. 393, 406, 407, 408, 482; "Dark Eyes," p. 395;
"Band of the Hand (It's Hell Time Man!)," pp. 416, 417,
419; "Political World," p. 443; "Most of the Time," p. 445;
"Dignity," p. 446; "Handy Dandy," pp. 452, 453, 454, 455;
"Not Dark Yet," p. 475; "Murder Most Foul," p. 476; "I
Contain Multitudes," p. 479; "Things Have Changed,"

p. 487; "High Water (For Charley Patton)," p. 496;
"Tweedle Dee & Tweedle Dum," pp. 502, 503, 504, 505;
"Tell Ol' Bill," p. 513; "Thunder on the Mountain," p. 520;
"Spirit on the Water," p. 521; "Long and Wasted Years,"
p. 537; "Tempest," p. 536; "Soon After Midnight," p. 584;
"Pay in Blood," p. 584; "Scarlet Town," p. 584.

Bob Dylan and George Harrison, "I'd Have You Anytime,"
copyright © Universal Tunes/Harrisongs Ltd., p. 227.

"Epilogue: Our Wells Are Deep" copyright © Douglas
Brinkley, 2023; "Postcard from Tulsa" copyright © Peter
Carey, 2023; " 'Hi Bob, It's Tony': The Dylan/Glover
Interviews" copyright © Anne Margaret Daniel, 2023;
"Preface: The Perpetual Motion of Illusion" copyright ©
Mark Davidson and Parker Fishel, 2023; "Reflections on
'As I Went Out One Morning' "copyright © John Doe,
2023; "Reflections on 'Dirge' "copyright © Raymond Foye,
2023; "Widescreen" copyright © Terry Gans, 2023; "On
Mojo" copyright © Jeff Gold, 2023; "Tangled" copyright ©
Joy Harjo, 2023; "I'm Learning It These Days" copyright
© Richard Hell, 2023; "Dear Paul" copyright © Clinton
Heylin, 2023; "Every Wednesday at 2 P.M." copyright ©
Marvin Karlins, 2023; "Tangled Up in Improv" copyright
© Alan Licht, 2023; "Madison, WI / Fall–Winter 1960 /
Bob Dylan, Danny Kalb, Jeff Chase" copyright © Greil
Marcus, 2023; "Reflections on 'Not Dark Yet' " copyright
© Allison Moorer, 2023; "Collecting and Connecting
Woody and Bob" copyright © Barry Ollman, 2023;
"Highway to the Sea: Dylan, Conrad, and the 'Tombstone
Blues' "copyright © Griffin Ondaatje, 2023; "Two Possible
Lies and the Truth" copyright © Michael Ondaatje,
2023; "Huey Digs Dylan" copyright © Gregory Pardlo,
2023; "Reflections on *Tarantula*" copyright © Amanda
Petrusich, 2023; "American Dream #115" copyright ©
Tom Piazza, 2023; "I Just Wanna See It" copyright ©
Lee Ranaldo, 2023; "If You See Her on Fannin Street"
copyright © Alex Ross, 2023; "*The Gunfighter*'s Never
Ending Tour" copyright © Robert M. Rubin, 2023; "Get
Jailed, Jump Bail" copyright © Ed Ruscha, 2023; "A
Daily Reminder of Important Matters" copyright © Lucy

CREDITS

All items from the Bob Dylan Archive unless otherwise noted.

FRONT COVER by Jerry Schatzberg.
BACK COVER by Randee St. Nicholas.

FRONT MATTER

p. 6, Photographer unknown; pp. 8–9, courtesy of Sony Music Entertainment.

PREFACE

p. 11, Ralph Baxter; p. 12, Ken Regan.

INTRODUCTION

pp. 15, 16, Don Hunstein © Sony Music Entertainment; p. 17, Barry Feinstein; p. 19, Ken Regan; p. 20, John Shearer; p. 22, Robert Frank, *U.S. 285, New Mexico*, 1955, © The June Leaf and Robert Frank Foundation, from *The Americans*; p. 23 (top), painting by Bob Dylan; p. 23 (bottom), PictureLux/The Hollywood Archive/Alamy Stock Photo.

1941–1960: AN ACCIDENT OF GEOGRAPHY

p. 24, ARCHIVIO GBB/Alamy Stock Photo; pp. 26 (top), 27, 28–29 (all), 32–33, 34 (top left and right), 35–37 (all), 45 (all), 47 (left), 51 (right), from the Bill Pagel Collection; p. 30, John Vachon, Farm Security Administration, Library of Congress Office of War Information Photograph Collection; p. 31, John Shearer; p. 34 (bottom left), photographer unknown, courtesy of Minnesota Historical Society Manuscript Collection; p. 38, painting by Duncan Hannah, © Duncan Hannah; p. 41, photographer unknown, from the Bill Pagel Collection, courtesy of Lance Williams; p. 44 (left), Sharon Johnson, courtesy of Armory Arts and Music Center, © Armory Arts and Music Center; p. 47 (right), video still by Elvis Ripley/Jeremy Lamberton; p. 49, photographer unknown, courtesy of Marvin Karlins; p. 50, photographer unknown, courtesy of Hennepin County Library; p. 51 (left), Bill Savran; p. 56, photographer unknown, courtesy of Woody Guthrie Publications, Inc.; p. 57, Deanna Harris Hoffman, from the Bill Pagel Collection; pp. 26 (bottom), 34 (bottom right), photographer unknown.

1961–1964: A WAY OF LIFE

p. 58, Hank Parker, courtesy of Sony Music Archives; pp. 60–61, 65, John Cohen via Getty Images; p. 62 (top), Ben Martin via Getty Images; p. 62 (bottom), John Orris/New York Times Co. via Getty Images;

pp. 63, 64, photographer unknown, © NLA/reportdigital.co.uk; pp. 66 (left), 89 (all), 91 (all), 92, 105, courtesy of Jeff Gold/Recordmecca; p. 66 (right), from the Cynthia Gooding Archive; p. 67, Ted Russell, © Ted Russell/Govinda Gallery; p. 69 (all), Marcia Stehr, courtesy of Barry and Judy Ollman; pp. 70 (left), 71 (top), David Gahr via Getty Images; p. 70 (right), David Gahr/Gahrchive Inc.; pp. 71 (bottom right), 77, 78 (all), 95, courtesy of Barry and Judy Ollman; pp. 72 (all), 73, 97, Don Hunstein © Sony Music Entertainment; pp. 75, 99, 116–17, 117 (right), from the Bill Pagel Collection; pp. 80–81, Brian Shuel/Redferns via Getty Images; pp. 82, 83, courtesy of Andrew Bailey; pp. 86, 87, Ralph Baxter; p. 98, CBS Photo Archive via Getty Images; pp. 100 (top), 119, David Gahr/Newport Festivals Foundation via Getty Images; pp. 100 (middle), 101 (bottom), Daryl Matthews; pp. 100 (bottom), 101 (top), Rowland Scherman via Getty Images; pp. 102–3, Fred W. McDarrah/MUUS Collection via Getty Images; pp. 106, 107, Richard Avedon, © The Richard Avedon Foundation; pp. 112 (right), 120 (left), film stills from 1966 European Tour footage, by D. A. Pennebaker; p. 113, Barry Feinstein, © Barry Feinstein Photography Inc.; p. 116 (left), Edward Grazda; p. 121 (top), Al Clayton, courtesy of Sony Music Archives; p. 74, photographer unknown; pp. 114–15, filmmaker unknown.

1965–1966: THE SOUND OF THE STREETS

pp. 128, 132, 134–35, 136, 140–41, 148–49 (all), 172–73, Daniel Kramer; pp. 130–31, 188–89, Barry Feinstein, © Barry Feinstein Photography Inc.; pp. 138, 139, 161 (jacket), Kenneth Ruggiano/Gilcrease Museum; p. 146 (left), © Dick Waterman/Govinda Gallery; p. 146 (right), painting by Eric von Schmidt, from the Mitch Blank Collection; p. 150, Richard Avedon, © The Richard Avedon Foundation; p. 151 (tickets and advertisement), courtesy of Oddbjørn Saltnes; pp. 152–53, film stills by D. A. Pennebaker, courtesy of Pennebaker Hegedus Films and Sony Music Entertainment; pp. 154–55, photographer unknown, from Bridgeman Images; p. 156 (left), W. Eugene Smith, © The Heirs of W. Eugene Smith; pp. 156–57, photographer

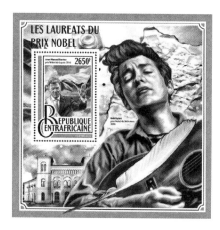

unknown, Michael Ochs Archives via Getty Images; pp. 158 (top), 159 (top left, top right, bottom left), 160 (middle left), 168, film stills from 1965 Newport Folk Festival footage, by Murray Lerner; pp. 158 (middle left and right), 159 (bottom right), 160 (top, middle right, bottom), David Gahr/Gahrchive Inc.; pp. 158 (bottom), 161 (right), David Gahr/Newport Festival Foundation via Getty Images; p. 162, Don Hunstein © Sony Music Entertainment; p. 171 (all), Gloria Stavers; p. 174, Dale Smith; p. 175, Fred W. McDarrah/MUUS Collection via Getty Images; p. 176, Ken Regan; p. 177, Ettore Sottsass, © 2023 Artists Rights Society (ARS), New York/ADAGP, Paris; pp. 182 (left), 183 (bottom), photographs by Jerry Schatzberg, courtesy of Sony Music Entertainment; pp. 182 (right), 196–97, Jerry Schatzberg; pp. 185, 187, 188 (top), film stills from 1966 European Tour footage, by D. A. Pennebaker; pp. 186, 190–91, Björn H. Larsson Ask; p. 194 (top left), Jeremy Lamberton; p. 195 (right), from the Bill Pagel Collection.

1967–1973: EVERYBODY'S SONG

p. 198, Frank Dandridge, ZUMA Press Inc./Alamy Stock Photo; pp. 200–201, 243, Len Siegler; p. 205 (left), courtesy of Garth Hudson; pp. 207 (right), 216–17, 219, Elliott Landy/Magnum Images; p. 208 (top), Don Hunstein © Sony Music Entertainment; p. 208 (bottom left), artwork by Marcel Duchamp, courtesy of Hauser & Wirth Publishers; p. 209, artwork by Milton Glaser, courtesy of Ryder Road Foundation; p. 210 (left), drawing by Bob Dylan; p. 210 (right), courtesy of Sony Music Entertainment; p. 212, David Gahr/Gahrchive Inc.; p. 213 (all), courtesy of Barry and Judy Ollman; p. 214 (top), painting by Bob Dylan; p. 215, painting by Bob Dylan, courtesy of Universal Music Group; pp. 221 (photo), 232–33 (all), Al Clayton, courtesy of Sony Music Archives; p. 222, courtesy of Oddbjørn Saltnes; p. 225 (photo), Michael Ochs Archives via Getty Images; pp. 228 (top), 229 (bottom), Stephen Goldblatt; pp. 230–31, Barry Feinstein; p. 234 (middle), 268–69, John Cohen; p. 235, painting by Bob Dylan, courtesy of Sony Music Entertainment; p. 237, Stephen Shames; pp. 238, 240, 241, Ted Russell © Ted Russell/Govinda Gallery; p. 244, William E. Sauro/New York Times Co. via Getty Images; pp. 248 (top), 250 (right), from the Mitch Blank Collection; p. 249, Henry Diltz/Corbis via Getty Images; p. 250 (top left),

courtesy of Michael Chaiken; p. 251, Jerry Schatzberg; p. 253, John Byrne Cooke, John Byrne Cooke Estate via Getty Images; p. 257 (right), film stills from *Eat the Document*, directed by Bob Dylan, from 1966 European Tour footage, by D. A. Pennebaker; p. 261 (bottom left and right), drawings by Bob Dylan; pp. 262, 264–65, courtesy of Oddbjørn Saltnes; p. 204 (left), filmmaker unknown; pp. 245, 260, photographer unknown.

1974–1978: THE CONSTANT STATE OF BECOMING

pp. 270, 274 (bottom), 275 (bottom), 276–77, 278–79, 280 (top), 281, 284–85, 303, Barry Feinstein; pp. 272–73, 310–11, 312 (left), 314–15, 316, 317, 318–19 (all), 323 (bottom), 325 (top right), 326–27 (photos), 328–29 (all), 330, Ken Regan; pp. 274–75 (tickets), 292 (ticket), 308–9 (all), 336 (bottom), courtesy of Oddbjørn Saltnes; pp. 282 (bottom left and right), 283 (all), courtesy of Warner Music Group; pp. 305 (all), 326 (top left), 332 (bottom), courtesy of Sony Music Entertainment; pp. 292 (top), 293, Marcelo Montealegre; pp. 298, 299, Paul Till; pp. 306–7, Reid Miles, courtesy of Sony Music Entertainment; pp. 320–21 (all), 324 (top), Ruth Bernal; p. 332 (top), from the Bill Pagel Collection; p. 333, video stills by TVTV; p. 334 (all), from the Mitch Blank Collection; pp. 338–39, Joel Bernstein; pp. 340 (bottom), 341 (all), Hirosuke Katsuyama; pp. 342 (top), 343 (bottom), 344–47 (all), Morgan Renard; p. 349, Annie Leibovitz/Trunk Archive; p. 280 (bottom), filmmaker unknown.

1979–1987: SURVIVING IN A RUTHLESS WORLD

pp. 350, 390–91, Ken Regan, courtesy of Camera 5/Regan Pictures, Inc.; pp. 352–53, 358–59, Arthur Rosato; p. 360 (top), 362 (all), 363, Tony Wright; pp. 354 (bottom right), 355 (bottom all), 384 (top left), 398 (top), courtesy of Sony Music Entertainment; pp. 355 (top left), 360 (bottom), Dick Cooper; p. 356 (bottom right), design by William Stetz, drawing by Catherine Kanner; pp. 357 (tickets), 390 (top right and bottom), courtesy of Oddbjørn Saltnes; p. 361 (top left), artwork by Tony Wright, courtesy of David Eckstrom; p. 361 (bottom left), artwork by Tony Wright, courtesy of Sony Music Entertainment; p. 365 (top), Richard McCaffrey/Michael Ochs Archive via Getty Images; p. 368, film still by Bill Pagel, from the Bill Pagel Collection; pp. 371 (top), 372–73, 374, 375, 376–77 (all), Howard Alk; p. 383 (top right and bottom), photographer unknown, courtesy of Arie de Reus; p. 384 (right), Ken Regan; pp. 386–87 (all), film stills from 1983 promotional footage, directed by Albert and David Maysles;

p. 394, courtesy of The Morgan Library & Museum; p. 397, Deborah Feingold/Corbis via Getty Images; p. 398 (bottom), Peter J. Carni, courtesy of Sony Music Archives; p. 399 (bottom right), videographer unknown, courtesy of Jeff Friedman; p. 400 (top), Deborah Feingold via Getty Images; p. 401 (top), Steve Kagan via Getty Images; p. 401 (bottom), Ebet Roberts via Getty Images; p. 402, Vinnie Zuffante/Michael Ochs Archive via Getty Images; p. 403, courtesy of Sony Music Entertainment; pp. 404–5, David Michael Kennedy; p. 409, Everett Collection Inc./Alamy Stock Photo; p. 410 (top), photographer unknown, Michael Ochs Archive via Getty Images; p. 411 (right all), film stills from *Hard to Handle*, directed by Gillian Armstrong; pp. 413, 415, 418, courtesy of Universal Music Group; p. 421, Herb Greene, courtesy of Sony Music Archives; pp. 422–23, Larry Busacca/WireImage via Getty Images; pp. 385, 388–89 (all), photographer unknown; p. 399 (top right and left), filmmaker unknown.

1988–2000: As Natural as Breathing

pp. 424, 450, Randee St. Nicholas; pp. 426–27, 458–59, 460–61, Merlyn Rosenberg; p. 429, Larry Busacca; p. 431 (bottom), from the Woody Guthrie Archive, courtesy of Woody Guthrie Publications, Inc.; p. 432, Neal Preston; p. 434, photograph by Peter J. Carni, courtesy of Sony Music Entertainment; p. 435, Abe Perlstein; p. 437 (all), courtesy of Jeff Gold/Recordmecca; p. 438 (left), courtesy of Universal Music Group; pp. 438 (right), 442, 456–57, 462 (left), 470 (top left), 473 (bottom right), 483, courtesy of Sony Music Entertainment; p. 441, Petra Niemeier; p. 444, Suzie Q; p. 446, Ethan Voelkers; p. 447 (top), CBS Photo Archive via Getty Images; p. 449, Camouflage Photo; pp. 462–63, 466, Ken Regan, courtesy of Camera 5/Regan Pictures, Inc.; pp. 464–65, Ana María Vélez Wood; p. 467, Frank Micelotta via Getty Images; pp. 468, 472, Mark Seliger; pp. 470–71, 477, 484, 485 (all), 488–89, Danny Clinch; p. 473 (top left), 487 (top), courtesy of Oddbjørn Saltnes; p. 473 (bottom second from left), courtesy of Universal Music Group; p. 473 (bottom second from right), courtesy of XL Recordings; pp. 478 (top), 479 (top), 480–81, Gilles Peress; p. 482, from the Mitch Blank Collection; p. 486, Harry Scott/Redferns via Getty Images.

2001–2013: Themes, Dreams, and Schemes

pp. 490, 531 (bottom), 543, William Claxton; pp. 492–93, 498, 519 (right), 523, David Gahr; pp. 494 (bottom), 495, 496 (top), 497, 521 (top), Kevin Mazur; pp. 500–501, video stills from *"Love and Theft"* commercial, directed by Kinka Usher, courtesy of Sony Music Entertainment; p. 506 (left), courtesy of Sony Pictures Classics; p. 506 (right), 507 (right), 508 (left), 510, 511 (all), Lorey Sebastian, courtesy of Grey Water Park Productions/Spitfire Pictures/White Horse Pictures; p. 507 (left), Kenneth

Ruggiano/Gilcrease Museum; pp. 508–9 (top and bottom), Jeff Bridges; p. 512 (top left), 519 (left), 520 (top), 531 (top), courtesy of Sony Music Entertainment; p. 514, Morgan Renard; p. 515 (all), AP Photo/Mark Humphrey; p. 517 (left), Ralph Baxter; p. 517 (top right), courtesy of Modan Publishing House Ltd; p. 517 (middle right), courtesy of Simon & Schuster; p. 517 (bottom right), courtesy of Tiang Su People's Publishing House; p. 518, courtesy of Paramount Pictures; pp. 534 (top), 540 (ticket), courtesy of Oddbjørn Saltnes; p. 525, art print by Jaime Hernandez; p. 527 (top right), courtesy of Ben Blackwell; p. 529, painting by Ed Ruscha, © Ed Ruscha; p. 530, from Alamy Stock Photo; p. 533, Mandel Ngan/AFP via Getty Images; pp. 534 (bottom), 537 (top), John Shearer; pp. 538–39, Ken Regan, courtesy of Camera 5/Regan Pictures, Inc.; p. 540 (advertisements), from the Bill Pagel Collection; p. 541, UPI/Alamy Stock Photo.

2014–Present: The Here and Now

pp. 544, 548, 561, 570 (bottom), John Shearer; pp. 546–47, 576–77 (all), video stills from *Shadow Kingdom*, directed by Alma Har'el; pp. 550, 558, 560, courtesy of Oddbjørn Saltnes; pp. 551 (left), 556, 564, 565, courtesy of Sony Music Entertainment; pp. 552–53, video stills from "The Night We Called It a Day" music video, directed by Nash Edgerton, courtesy of Sony Music Entertainment; p. 554 (left), Michael Kovac/WireImage via Getty Images; p. 554 (top right), Kevork Djansezian/WireImage via Getty Images; p. 554 (bottom right), Larry Busacca via Getty Images for NARAS; p. 555 (left), Kevin Mazur/WireImage via Getty Images; p. 557 (top), Bei/Shutterstock; p. 557 (bottom), video still from *Tony Bennett Celebrates 90: The Best Is Yet to Come*, directed by Jennifer Lebeau; p. 559 (all), 566, from the Bill Pagel Collection; p. 562, courtesy of Netflix; p. 563, painting by Bob Dylan, book cover courtesy of Modern Art Museum, Shanghai; p. 571, courtesy of Parker Fishel; p. 572 (left), courtesy of Simon & Schuster; pp. 574, 575, Hedi Slimane; p. 580, Carol Friedman.

Epilogue

p. 582, Rowland Scherman; p. 584, Joe Alper, courtesy of Joe Alper Photo Collection LLC; p. 585, Al Clayton, courtesy of Sony Music Archives; p. 586, Ken Regan; p. 587, Ken Regan, courtesy of Camera 5/Regan Pictures, Inc.; p. 589, Hedi Slimane.

Bob Dylan: Mixing Up the Medicine was first published on October 24, 2023, by Callaway Arts & Entertainment. The creative director was Nicholas Callaway. The book was researched, written, and edited by Mark Davidson and Parker Fishel under the direction of Manuela Roosevelt. Additional editorial assistance and rights clearances were provided by Austin Short. Design and layout were by Nicholas Callaway, Jerry Kelly, and Toshiya Masuda. Copyediting and proofreading were by Janice Fisher. Digital imaging, pre-press, and file preparation were by Thomas Palmer and Jason Brown. True Sims was the production director, and Ivan Wong was the production manager and on-press supervisor. The project was produced under the direction of Steve Higgins for the Bob Dylan Center, Tulsa. The English-language edition was printed and bound in Canada.

CALLAWAY

CALLAWAY ARTS & ENTERTAINMENT
76 Georgica Road, East Hampton, New York 11937

Please visit callaway.com/dylan

Distributed by Hachette Book Group in the US and Canada
and by Thames & Hudson outside of North America

1 3 5 7 9 10 8 6 4 2

Library of Congress Cataloging-in-Publication Data available.

ISBN 978-1-7345377-9-6

Colophon drawing by Bob Dylan

Printed in Canada

FIRST EDITION

man in a coonskin cap in the pigpen

i stumble downtown

               man wants a

a voice come sounding like a passer
look out kid, it's something you di
god knows when but you're doing it
better duck down the doorway/ looki
man in a coonskin cap xxxxx does a back
here comes maggie/ strutting donw t
maggie comes fleetfoot/ face full o
talking that the heat put/plants in
the phone's tapped anyway/maggie sa
they must bust in early May/ orders
look out kid/ it dont matter what y
kabe careful what they sell yuh/ or
they only try t tail you if they wa
xpexxxxpxkkxxkxxkxdxxxx   dont be
mailman coming down the chimney lik

dont be bashful if you see they war

careful if they tail you/they only